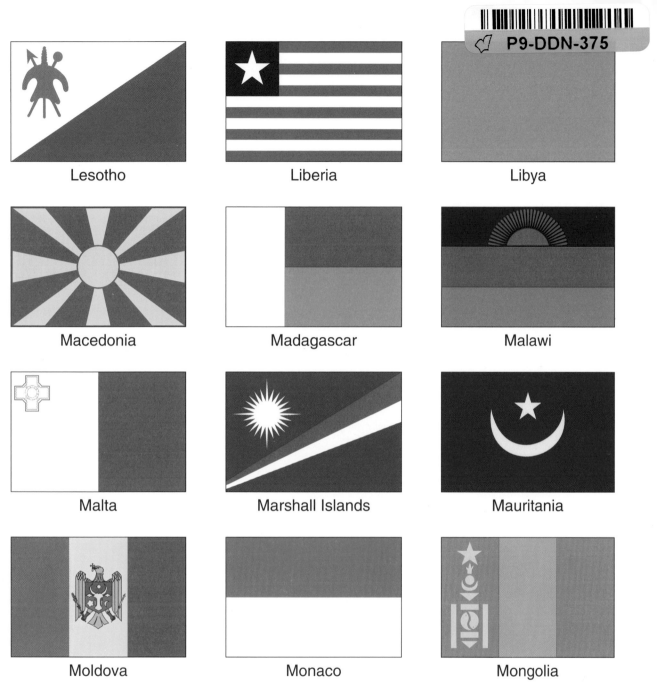

Lesotho

Liberia

Libya

Macedonia

Madagascar

Malawi

Malta

Marshall Islands

Mauritania

Moldova

Monaco

Mongolia

Junior Worldmark Encyclopedia of the Nations

Junior Worldmark Encyclopedia of the Nations

Junior Worldmark Encyclopedia of the Nations

Second Edition

VOLUME **5**

Laos to Myanmar

AN IMPRINT OF GALE

JUNIOR WORLDMARK ENCYCLOPEDIA OF THE NATIONS, SECOND EDITION

Timothy L. Gall and Susan Bevan Gall, *Editors*
Daniel M. Lucas and Rosalie Wieder, *Senior Editors*
Deborah Baron, *Associate Editor*
Brian Rajewski, *Graphics and Layout*
Cordelia R. Heaney, *Editorial Assistant*
Dianne K. Daeg de Mott, Janet Fenn, Matthew Markovich,
    Ariana Ranson, and Craig Strasshofer, *Copy Editors*
Janet Fenn and Matthew Markovich, *Proofreaders*
Maryland Cartographics, Inc., *Cartographers*

U•X•L Staff

Jane Hoehner, *U•X•L Senior Editor*
Allison McNeill, *U•X•L Contributing Senior Editor*
Carol DeKane Nagel, *U•X•L Managing Editor*
Thomas L. Romig, *U•X•L Publisher*
Mary Beth Trimper, *Production Director*
Evi Seoud, *Assistant Production Manager*
Cindy Range, *Production Assistant*
Cynthia Baldwin, *Product Design Manager*
Barbara J. Yarrow, *Graphic Services Supervisor*
Mary Krzewinski, *Cover Designer*
Margaret Chamberlain, *Permissions Specialist (Pictures)*

Library of Congress Cataloging-in-Publication Data

Junior Worldmark Encyclopedia of the nations / [Timothy L. Gall and
    Susan Bevan Gall, editors]. -- 2nd ed.
        p. cm.
    Includes bibliographical references and index.
    Contents: v. 1. Afghanistan to Brunei Darussalam -- v. 2. Bulgaria
to Czech Republic -- v. 3. Denmark to Guyana -- v. 4. Haiti to
Kyrgyzstan -- v. 5. Laos to Myanmar -- v. 6. Namibia to Portugal --
v. 7. Qatar to South Africa -- v. 8. Spain to Tuvalu -- v. 9. Uganda
to Zimbabwe.
    ISBN 0-7876-3801-3 (set). -- ISBN 0-7876-3802-1 (v. 1). -- ISBN
0-7876-3803-X (v. 2)
    1. Geography--Encyclopedias, Juvenile. 2. History--Encyclopedias,
Juvenile. 3. Economics--Juvenile literature. 4. Political science-
-Encyclopedias, Juvenile. 5. United Nations--Encyclopedias,
Juvenile. [1. Geography--Encyclopedias.)   I. Gall, Timothy L.
II. Gall, Susan B.
G63.J86   1998   98-32238
910'.3--dc21   CIP
                                                            AC

ISBN 0-7876-3801-3 (set)
ISBN 0-7876-3802-1 (vol. 1)   ISBN 0-7876-3803-X (vol. 2)   ISBN 0-7876-3804-8 (vol. 3)
ISBN 0-7876-3805-6 (vol. 4)   ISBN 0-7876-3806-4 (vol. 5)   ISBN 0-7876-3807-2 (vol. 6)
ISBN 0-7876-3808-0 (vol. 7)   ISBN 0-7876-3809-9 (vol. 8)   ISBN 0-7876-3810-2 (vol. 9)

CONTENTS

Guide to Country Articles

Every country profile in this encyclopedia includes the same 35 headings. Also included in every profile is a map (showing the country and its location in the world), the country's flag and seal, and a table of data on the country. The country articles are organized alphabetically in nine volumes. A glossary of terms is included in each of the nine volumes. This glossary defines many of the specialized terms used throughout the encyclopedia. A keyword index to all nine volumes appears at the end of Volume 9.

Flag color symbols

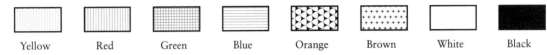

| Yellow | Red | Green | Blue | Orange | Brown | White | Black |

Alphabetical listing of sections

Agriculture	21	Income	18
Armed Forces	16	Industry	19
Bibliography	35	Judicial System	15
Climate	3	Labor	20
Domesticated Animals	22	Languages	9
Economy	17	Location and Size	1
Education	31	Media	32
Energy and Power	27	Migration	7
Environment	5	Mining	25
Ethnic Groups	8	Plants and Animals	4
Famous People	34	Political Parties	14
Fishing	23	Population	6
Foreign Trade	26	Religions	10
Forestry	24	Social Development	28
Government	13	Topography	2
Health	29	Tourism/Recreation	33
History	12	Transportation	11
Housing	30		

Sections listed numerically

1	Location and Size	19	Industry
2	Topography	20	Labor
3	Climate	21	Agriculture
4	Plants and Animals	22	Domesticated Animals
5	Environment	23	Fishing
6	Population	24	Forestry
7	Migration	25	Mining
8	Ethnic Groups	26	Foreign Trade
9	Languages	27	Energy and Power
10	Religions	28	Social Development
11	Transportation	29	Health
12	History	30	Housing
13	Government	31	Education
14	Political Parties	32	Media
15	Judicial System	33	Tourism/Recreation
16	Armed Forces	34	Famous People
17	Economy	35	Bibliography
18	Income		

Abbreviations and acronyms to know

GMT= Greenwich mean time. The prime, or Greenwich, meridian passes through Greenwich, England (near London), and marks the center of the initial time zone for the world. The standard time of all 24 time zones relate to Greenwich mean time. Every profile contains a map showing the country and its location in the world.

These abbreviations are used in references to famous people:
b.=born
d.=died
fl.=flourished (lived and worked)
r.=reigned (for kings, queens, and similar monarchs)

A dollar sign ($) stands for US$ unless otherwise indicated.

LAOS

Lao People's Democratic Republic
Sathalanalat Paxathipatai Paxaxon Lao

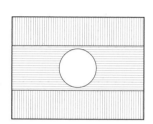

CAPITAL: Vientiane (Viangchan).

FLAG: The national flag, officially adopted in 1975, is the former flag of the Pathet Lao, consisting of three horizontal stripes of red, dark blue, and red, with a white disk, representing the full moon, at the center.

ANTHEM: *Pheng Sat Lao (Hymn of the Lao People).*

MONETARY UNIT: The new kip (κ) is a paper currency of 100 at (cents). There are notes of 10, 20, 50, 200, and 500 new kip. κ1 = $0.0011 (or $1 = κ920).

WEIGHTS AND MEASURES: The metric system is the legal standard, but older local units are also used.

HOLIDAYS: Anniversary of the Founding of the Lao People's Democratic Republic, 2 December. To maintain production, the government generally reschedules on weekends such traditional festivals as the Lao New Year (April); Boun Bang-fai (Rocket Festival), the celebration of the birth, enlightenment, and death of the Buddha (May); Boun Khao Watsa, the beginning of a period of fasting and meditation lasting through the rainy season (July); Boun Ok Watsa (Water Holiday), a celebration of the end of the period of fasting and meditation (October); and That Luang, a pagoda pilgrimage holiday (November).

TIME: 7 PM = noon GMT.

1 LOCATION AND SIZE

Laos is a landlocked Southeast Asian country on the Indochinese peninsula. The Indochinese peninsula includes Vietnam, Cambodia, and Thailand. It occupies an area of 236,800 square kilometers (91,429 square miles), slightly larger than the state of Utah. It has a total boundary length of 4,513 kilometers (2,804 miles).

The capital of Laos, Vientiane, is located along the country's western boundary.

2 TOPOGRAPHY

The land is rugged and mountainous, especially in the north and in the Annam Cordillera (mountain range) along the border with Vietnam. The mountains reach heights of more than 2,700 meters (8,860 feet), with Mount Bia, the highest point in Laos, rising to 2,820 meters (9,252 feet). Three passes cross the mountains to link Laos with Vietnam. There are two prominent high plateaus, one in the northeast and the fertile Bolovens Plateau in the south. Broad plains, where much of

Geographic Profile

Geographic Features

Size ranking: 80 of 192
Highest elevation: 2,820 meters (9,252 feet) at Mount Bia
Lowest elevation: 70 meters (230 feet) at the Mekong River

Land Use†

Arable land:	3%
Permanent pastures:	3%
Forests:	54%
Other:	40%

Weather††

Average annual precipitation: 168.3 centimeters (66.3 inches)
Average temperature in January: 21.5°C (70.7°F)
Average temperature in July: 27.7°C (81.9°F)

†*Arable land:* Land used for temporary crops, like meadows for mowing or pasture, gardens, and greenhouses. *Permanent crops:* Land cultivated with crops that occupy its use for long periods, such as cocoa, coffee, rubber, fruit and nut orchards, and vineyards. *Permanent pastures:* Land used permanently for forage crops. *Forests:* Land containing stands of trees. *Other:* Any land not specified, including built-on areas, roads, and barren land.

††The measurements for precipitation and average temperature were taken at weather stations closest to the country's largest city. Precipitation and average temperature can vary significantly within a country, due to factors such as latitude, altitude, coastal proximity, and wind patterns.

inches) a month, but from November through March the monthly average is only about 1.3 centimeters (0.5 inches). Humidity is high throughout the year, even during the season of drought. Average daily temperatures in Vientiane range from 14° to 28°C (57–82°F) in January, the coolest month, and from 23° to 34°C (73–93°F) in April, the hottest.

4 PLANTS AND ANIMALS

Nearly two-thirds of Laos is covered by forest or thick jungle. The forests of southernmost Laos are an extension of the Kampuchean type of vegetation, while the highland forests of the north resemble central Vietnam. Bamboo, lianas, rattan, and palms are found throughout Laos.

Roaming the forests are panthers and a dwindling number of tigers, elephants, and leopards. Native reptiles include cobras, geckos, kraits, and Siamese crocodiles.

5 ENVIRONMENT

Soil erosion, loss of forest land, and flood control are the principal environmental concerns in Laos, there being only minimal industrial development. During 1983–93, Laos had an 11.3% decline in its forest and woodland area.

In 1994, 23 of Laos's mammal species and nearly one-fifth of its bird species were threatened. Three of the nation's plant species were endangered.

the rice crop is grown, are found in the south and west along the Mekong River. Of these, the Vientiane plain is the most extensive.

Laos is drained by the Mekong River and its tributaries. Floods are common in the rainy season.

3 CLIMATE

From May through September, rainfall averages 28 to 30 centimeters (11–12

6 POPULATION

The population was estimated at nearly 5.3 million in 1998. A population of 6.3 million is projected for the year 2005.

The overall density in 1998 was only about 21 persons per square kilometer (54 per square mile), but the population is unevenly spread, with the greatest concentration in the Mekong Valley. The capital, Vientiane, had a metropolitan population of about 534,000 in 1995.

7 MIGRATION

Since May 1975, thousands of Laotian refugees have fled to Thailand or elsewhere. Between 1975 and 1990, over 360,000 Laotians—including Hmong, Yao, and other mountain tribesmen—crossed into Thailand and China. Most eventually resettled in Western nations. As of 1996, some 6,000 remained in refugee camps.

8 ETHNIC GROUPS

There are officially 68 ethnic groups in Laos. About 50–60% of all Laotians are Lao-lum, or lowland Lao, a people related to the people of Thailand. Other groups include the Lao-theung, or slope dwellers, who form about one-third of the population; and the Lao-soung, or mountain dwellers, who constitute about one-tenth of the population. Important among the Lao-soung are the Hmong (Meo), a people of Tibeto-Burman origin who, after 1975, became the targets of harassment by government and Vietnamese troops.

LOCATION: 100° to 107°E; 13°40′ to 22°40′N. BOUNDARY LENGTHS: China, 425 kilometers (264 miles); Vietnam, 1,555 kilometers (966 miles); Cambodia, 541 kilometers (336 miles); Thailand, 1,754 kilometers (1,090 miles); Myanmar, 238 kilometers (148 miles).

9 LANGUAGES

Lao, the official language and the language of the ethnic Lao, is closely related to the language of Thailand. It consists of one-syllable words that are differentiated mainly by the speaker's tone of voice. Lao contains words borrowed from Sanskrit, Pali, and Farsi. Pali, a Sanskritic language, is used among the Buddhist priesthood.

Other groups speak the Tibeto–Burman, Non–Khmer, or Miao–Yao languages.

10 RELIGIONS

Almost two-thirds of all Laotians, including nearly all the Lao-lum, are followers of Hinayana Buddhism. Buddhist temples, found in every village, town, and city, serve as intellectual as well as religious centers. Despite the major role that Buddhism plays in Laotian life, the average lowland Lao also practices animism, believing that certain spirits (phi) have great power over human destiny.

About one-third of Laotians, including the upland tribes, are mostly spirit worshippers, although influenced somewhat by Buddhism.

11 TRANSPORTATION

Of the approximately 14,130 kilometers (8,780 miles) of roads, only 14% are surfaced; many are impassable in the rainy season. Only a single major road connects the northern and southern regions. As of 1992, there were only 17,000 motor vehicles registered, including 8,500 passenger cars. There are no railroads in Laos.

Major cities in Laos are connected by air services operated by state-run Lao Aviation. There are a number of airfields, but Vientiane has the only international airport. Landlocked Laos's only water-transport link with the outside world is via the Mekong River, which is navigable by small transport craft.

12 HISTORY

Archaeological evidence indicates that settlers along the Mekong had learned agriculture, metallurgy, and pottery making by 3000 BC; however, little is known about the early history of the land that today bears the name of Laos. The lowland Lao are believed to be the descendants of Thai tribes that were pushed southward in the eighth century AD.

According to tradition, the kingdom called Lan Xang ("a million elephants") was established in 756 by King Thao Khoun Lo. In 1353, it was reunified by Fa-Ngoum, who is believed to have introduced Hinayana Buddhism into Laos. Lan Xang waged periodic wars with the Khmers, Burmese, Vietnamese, and Thai and developed an effective administrative system, an elaborate military organization, and an active commerce with neighboring countries.

In 1707, internal conflicts brought about a split of Lan Xang into two kingdoms, Louangphrabang in the north (present-day upper Laos) and Vientiane in the south (lower Laos). Strong neighboring states took advantage of this division to invade the region. Vientiane was overrun and annexed by Siam (Thailand) in 1828, while Louangphrabang came under the control of both the Chinese and the Vietnamese. In 1893, France, which had already established a protectorate over what is now central and northern Viet Nam, extended its control to both Vientiane and Louangphrabang, and Laos was ruled by France as part of French Indochina.

During World War II (1939–45), Laos was occupied by Japan. After the war, French forces reoccupied Laos and established Sisavang Vong, the king of Louang-phrabang, as king of Laos under French domination. In May 1947, the king established a constitution providing for a democratic government, and by 1953 Laos had achieved full sovereignty.

Communist Invasion

In the meantime, Vietnamese communist (Viet-Minh) forces had invaded Laos in the spring of 1953. A Laotian communist movement, the Pathet Lao (Lao State), collaborated with the Viet-Minh during its Laotian offensive. Under the terms of a 1954 cease-fire, the Pathet Lao pulled back to two northern provinces, but the group was to continue fighting for control of Laos until it finally prevailed some 20 years later.

In the 1960s, Laos was steadily drawn into the role of a main theater in the escalating Vietnam war. The Laotian segment of the so-called Ho Chi Minh trail was the target for heavy United States bombing raids. While the Vientiane government was heavily bolstered by United States military and economic support, the Pathet Lao received key support from the Democratic Republic of Vietnam in the north.

By the end of the war, the Pathet Lao controlled over three-fourths of Laos. Following the fall of the US-backed regimes in Vietnam and Cambodia in April 1975, the Laotian communists embarked on a campaign to achieve complete military

Photo credit: AP/Wide World Photos.

Business is good in the markets of Vientiane, the capital. Lifting of many controls on the economy in 1979 created a mini-boom partly fueled by money sent home by refugees abroad to relatives in Laos.

and political supremacy in Laos. On 23 August, Vientiane was declared "liberated," and on 2 December 1975, the Lao People's Democratic Republic (LPDR) was established, with Prince Souphanouvong as president. King Savang Vatthana abdicated his throne, ending the monarchy that had survived in Laos for 622 years.

During the late 1970s, the communists moved to consolidate their control and socialize the economy. Private trade was banned, factories were nationalized, and forcible collectivization of agriculture was initiated. "Reeducation" camps for an estimated 40,000 former royalists and military leaders were established in remote areas.

Government Changes Direction

However, with the economy near collapse in 1979, in part because of severe drought followed by flooding, the Laotian government slowed the process of socialization and announced a return to private enterprise and a readiness to accept aid from the non-communist world.

In April 1994 the first international bridge, the Mittaphap (Friendship) Bridge, linking Laos and Thailand across the Mekong River, was opened. The 1,174-meter (3,852-foot) bridge, built and paid for by Australia, is part of a plan for an Asian super-highway to facilitate travel from Singapore to Shanghai. The most immediate benefits are anticipated by the tourism industry and as a spur to real estate investment.

The US Department of State notes that despite constitutional guarantees, freedom of speech, assembly, and religion are restricted, and political killings have accompanied continued rebellion, primarily among Hmong tribesmen.

13 GOVERNMENT

Under a new constitution adopted in 1991, the executive branch consists of the president, prime minister and two deputy prime ministers, and the Council of Ministers (cabinet) who are appointed by the president with the approval of the National Assembly. The legislative branch is the National Assembly, which is elected by universal suffrage for a period of five years. The judicial branch is the Supreme People's Court Leaders. The constitution calls for a strong legislature elected by secret ballot, but most political power continues to rest with the party-dominated council of ministers.

Laos consists of 16 provinces (*khoueng*), each subdivided into districts (*muong*), townships (*tasseng*), and villages (*ban*).

14 POLITICAL PARTIES

The only legal political party was the communist Lao People's Revolutionary Party (LPRP) which includes the Lao Front for National Construction (LFNC).

15 JUDICIAL SYSTEM

The government is now in the process of developing a codified body of laws. The constitution contains provisions designed to guarantee the independence of judges and prosecutors, but in practice the courts appear to be subject to influence of other government agencies. There is a Central Supreme Court in Vientiane. In 1993 the government began publishing an official gazette in which all laws and regulations are disseminated.

16 ARMED FORCES

In 1995 the armed forces in Laos numbered 37,000, with 18 months of military service compulsory for all males. A total of 33,000 Laotians served in the army. The navy, equipped with 84 patrol craft and boats, enlisted 500. The air force, with 3,500 men, was equipped with anti-aircraft missiles and 31 combat aircraft. The village self-defense force numbers 100,000. There are also about 2,000 rebels in Laos ready to confront the armed forces.

17 ECONOMY

One of the world's poorest and least-developed nations, Laos is overwhelmingly agricultural, with about 80% of the population engaged in farming, which accounts for about 56% of the gross domestic product (GDP). Because industrialization is minimal, Laos imports nearly all the manufactured products it requires.

The hostilities of the 1960s and 1970s badly disrupted the economy, forcing the country to depend on imports from Thailand to supplement its daily rice requirements. The third five-year plan (1991–95) emphasized improvement of communications and transportation networks, export growth, and development of domestic industry to decrease reliance on imports.

By 1997, there was more than $5 billion in foreign investment, as Laos had opened up its economy. However, inflations and problems with tax collection have contributed to increasing budget deficits.

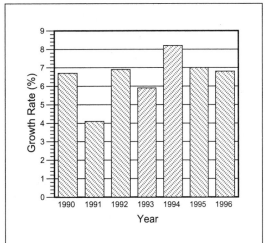

Yearly growth rate of the economy. This economic indicator tells by what percent the economy has increased or decreased when compared with the previous year.

18 INCOME

In 1995, Laos's gross national product (GNP) was $1.7 billion, or about $400 per person.

19 INDUSTRY

Manufacturing is largely confined to the processing of agricultural and forestry products. There are some small mining operations, charcoal ovens, a cement plant, a few brick works, carpenter shops, a tobacco factory, rice mills, some furniture factories, and more than two dozen sawmills.

Handicrafts account for an important part of the income of many Laotians. Some villages or areas specialize in certain types of products: silk fabrics, baskets, lacquerware, and gold and silver jewelry and ornaments. Bricks, pottery, iron products, and distilled beverages are made in individual villages.

20 LABOR

The estimated labor force is about 1.5 million. It is estimated that 85% are farmers, with most of the remainder government employees. In November 1990, the government permitted the formation of labor unions in private enterprises. The employment of children is not uncommon, particularly on family farms and in urban shops.

21 AGRICULTURE

Agriculture covers 4% of the country's total area and accounts for over half of its economy. The main crop is rice; production was 1.4 million tons in 1995. Other crops include corn, manioc, peanuts, and soybeans.

The main commercial crops, emphasized by the government as part of its export drive, are coffee, cotton, and tobacco. Also grown are cardamom, tea, ramie, hemp, sugar, bananas, and pineapples. The mountain peoples have been known to grow large quantities of opium poppies, sold to dealers in the plains.

22 DOMESTICATED ANIMALS

As of 1995, livestock included an estimated 1.3 million buffalo, 1.2 million head of cattle, 1.7 million hogs, and 9 million chickens. Livestock products in 1995 included 25,000 tons of pork, 26,000 tons

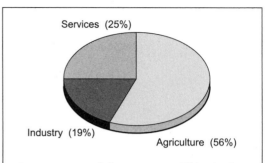

Components of the economy. This pie chart shows how much of the country's economy is devoted to agriculture (includes forestry, hunting, and fishing), industry, or services.

of buffalo meat, 7,000 tons of beef and veal, and 35,000 tons of eggs.

23 FISHING

Edible fish, found in the Mekong and other rivers, constitute the main source of protein in the Laotian diet. The prize catch is the pa beuk, weighing 205 kilograms (450 pounds) or more. The total catch in 1994 was 35,000 tons.

24 FORESTRY

About 54% of Laos's total area is forested, and about half the forested area is commercially exploitable. Aside from timber, firewood, and charcoal, forestry products include bamboo, copra, kapok, palm oil, rattan, and various resins. Production of roundwood totaled an estimated 5.5 million cubic meters (7.2 million cubic yards) in 1995; over 80% of the annual output goes for fuel. Sawnwood output in 1995 was about 546,000 cubic meters (715,000 cubic yards).

25 MINING

Tin production totaled 200 tons of tin concentrate in 1995. Important iron deposits, with reserves of 68% ore estimated at 11 billion tons, have been discovered, as well as a substantial deposit of low-grade anthracite coal. Other mineral resources known to exist in Laos are magnesium, rock salt, antimony, copper, gold, gypsum, lead, manganese, pyrites, sulfur, and precious stones. Sapphire production went from 8,000 carats in 1987 to 40,000 carats in 1995.

26 FOREIGN TRADE

In 1994, major exports included garments and textiles, electricity, timber, plywood, and coffee. Major imports included vehicles, cement, iron, and fabrics. In 1995, the value of exports was estimated at $347.8 million, and the value of imports was $540.2 million. In 1995, the major trade partners included Viet Nam, Thailand, the European Union nations, and Japan.

27 ENERGY AND POWER

The potential for electricity generation based on its water resources has led to Laos being called the "battery" of Southeast Asia. Production of electricity in 1994 totaled 893 million kilowatts per hour, of which 96% was hydroelectric and 4% came from conventional thermal sources. That year, Laos exported 71% of its electrical production.

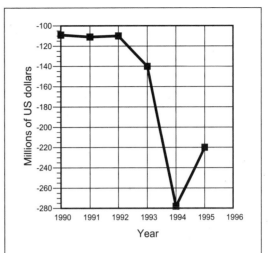

Yearly balance of trade measured in millions of US dollars. The balance of trade is the difference between what a country sells to other countries (its exports) and what it buys (its imports). If a country imports more than it exports, it has a negative balance of trade (a trade deficit). If exports exceed imports, there is a positive balance of trade (a trade surplus).

28 SOCIAL DEVELOPMENT

Laos is one of the world's most impoverished nations. Food intake does not meet basic requirements, and contamination of drinking water is widespread. In 1980, the government indicated that it regarded the nation's population as too low. Family planning programs were disbanded and the use of contraceptives banned. The Laotian population increased by 2.4% per year during 1980–90.

Almost no families own cars, and bicycles and radios are considered luxuries. In general, the lowland Lao have the highest

Selected Social Indicators

These statistics are estimates for the period 1993 to 1996. For comparison purposes, data for the United States and averages for low-income countries and high-income countries are also given.

Indicator	Laos	Low-income countries	High-income countries	United States
Per capita gross national product†	$400	$490	$25,870	$28,020
Population growth rate	2.6%	1.7%	0.6%	0.9%
Population growth rate in urban areas	5.3%	3.8%	0.9%	1.2%
Population per square kilometer of land	21	82	30	29
Life expectancy in years	53	63	77	77
Number of physicians per 1,000 people	2.5	1.0	2.5	2.5
Number of pupils per teacher (primary school)	30	41	17	14
Illiteracy rate (15 years and older)	43%	34%	<5%	3%
Energy consumed per capita (kg of oil equivalent)	40	393	5,123	7,905

† The gross national product (GNP) is the total dollar value of all goods and services produced by a country in a year. The per capita GNP is calculated by dividing a country's GNP by its population. The World Bank defines low-income countries as those with a per capita GNP of $785 or less. High-income countries have a per capita GNP of $9,636 or more. About 16% of the world's 5.7 billion people live in high-income countries, while almost 56% live in low-income countries.   n.a. = data not available   > = greater than   < = less than

Sources: World Bank, World Development Indicators on CD-ROM, Washington, D.C.: The World Bank, 1998. Central Intelligence Agency, The World Fact Book, Washington, D.C.: Government Printing Office, 1998.

living standards, with lower standards prevailing among the upland tribes.

Women in Laos have traditionally been subservient to men and have generally been discouraged from obtaining an education.

29 HEALTH

In 1990–95, only 45% of the population had access to safe water, and only 27% had adequate sanitation. In parts of Laos, malaria—the most serious health threat—is known to affect the majority of children. Other health problems are acute upper respiratory infections (including pneumonia and influenza), diarrhea and dysentery, parasites, yaws, skin ailments, various childhood diseases, hepatitis, venereal disease, and tuberculosis.

30 HOUSING

The traditional Laotian dwelling is rectangular, built entirely of wooden planks and bamboo, with a thatched roof, and raised off the ground on wooden pilings 1–2 meters (3–6 feet) high. There is a critical housing shortage in the towns, and many dwellings are substandard. As of 1990, 47% of urban and 25% of rural dwellers had access to a public water supply, while

30% of urban and 8% of rural dwellers had access to sanitation services.

31 EDUCATION

Education in Laos is compulsory for eight years. In 1993, there were 8,361 primary schools with 22,649 teachers and 681,044 students. In all secondary schools, there were 12,713 teachers and 155,366 students. Sisavongvong University is located in Vientiane. In 1993 there were 998 teaching faculty and 6,179 students enrolled at all higher-level institutions. The illiteracy rate is 43%.

32 MEDIA

All communications, including the radio network, are operated by the government. Most broadcasts are in Lao, but government news broadcasts are also in English, French, and other languages. Domestic television service from Lao National TV began in 1983. In 1995 there were over 8,600 telephones, about 560,000 radios, and about 28,000 television sets in use.

The press is government-controlled. The sole news agency is run by the Ministry of Information. The principal Vientiane newspapers are *Paxaxon* (*The People*), with a 1995 circulation of 11,500; *Viangchan May* (*New Vientiane*), with a circulation of 4,200; and *Khao San Pathet Lao* (*Laos Newsletter*), with a circulation of 1,700.

33 TOURISM AND RECREATION

The Pathet Lao government has had little interest in tourism, and foreigners are

Photo credit: Cory Langley.
Tourist attractions in Laos include cultural treasures like the statues pictured here.

rarely granted permits to travel outside Vientiane. However, the government tourist organization, Inter-Lao Tourisme, has been issuing growing numbers of visas to tour groups. The main tourist destinations are Vientiane, with its Buddhist pagodas, and the city of Louangphrabang on the Mekong River in the north.

34 FAMOUS LAOTIANS

One of the most cherished figures in Laotian history is Fa-Ngoum, who unified Lan

Xang in the fourteenth century. Another dynastic personage still revered is the monarch Sethathirat, in whose reign (1534–71) the famous That Luang shrine was built.

Important twentieth-century figures include Souvanna Phouma (1901–84), former prime minister and Prince Soupha-nouvong (1902–95), a half-brother of Souvanna Phouma, leader of the Pathet Lao and president of Laos from 1975 to 1986.

35 BIBLIOGRAPHY

Castle, Timothy N. *At War in the Shadow of Vietnam: U.S. Military Aid to the Royal Lao Government, 1955–1975.* New York: Columbia University Press, 1993.

Cordell, Helen. *Laos.* Santa Barbara, Calif.: Clio, 1991.

Diamond, J. *Laos.* Chicago: Children's Press, 1989.

Stuart-Fox, Martin. *Buddhist Kingdom, Marxist State: The Making of Modern Laos.* Bangkok, Thailand: White Lotus, 1996.

White, Peter T. "Laos Today." *National Geographic,* June 1987, 772–795.

LATVIA

Republic of Latvia
Latvijas Republika

CAPITAL: Riga

FLAG: The flag consists of a single white horizontal stripe on a maroon field.

ANTHEM: *Dievs, svēti Latviju! (God bless Latvia!)*

MONETARY UNIT: The lat was introduced as the official currency in May 1993; $1 = Ls0.55.

WEIGHTS AND MEASURES: The metric system is in force.

HOLIDAYS: New Year's Day, 1 January; Good Friday (movable); Midsummer Festival, 23–24 June; National Day, Proclamation of the Republic, 18 November; Christmas, 25–26 December; New Year's Eve, 31 December.

TIME: 2 PM = noon GMT.

1 LOCATION AND SIZE

Latvia is located in northeastern Europe, bordering the Baltic Sea, between Sweden and Russia. Comparatively, Latvia is slightly larger than the state of West Virginia, with a total area of 64,100 square kilometers (24,749 square miles). Latvia's boundary length totals 1,150 kilometers (715 miles). Latvia's capital city, Riga, is located in the northern part of the country along the Baltic Sea coast.

2 TOPOGRAPHY

The topography of Latvia consists mainly of a lowland plain.

3 CLIMATE

The mean temperature is between 16.8° and 17.6°C (62–64°F) in July and between –6.6° and 2.6°C (20–27°F) in January. Mean annual rainfall is between 60–65 centimeters (24–26 inches).

4 PLANTS AND ANIMALS

Woodlands make up 41% of the country's territory, with about half the forests consisting of pines, birch, and firs. The woodlands and plant life support 14,000 different animal species. Species native to Latvia are the wild boar, Eurasian beaver, and brown bear.

5 ENVIRONMENT

Latvia's air and water pollution are largely related to a lack of waste treatment facilities. Cars and other vehicles account for 70% of Latvia's air pollution. Acid rain has contributed to the destruction of the nation's forests.

Geographic Profile

Geographic Features

Size ranking: 121 of 192
Highest elevation: 311 meters (1,020 feet) at Gaizina (Gaizinkalns)
Lowest elevation: Sea level at the Baltic Sea

Land Use†

Arable land:	27%
Permanent crops:	0%
Permanent pastures:	13%
Forests:	46%
Other:	14%

Weather

Average annual precipitation: 60–65 centimeters (23.6–25.6 inches)
Average temperature range in January (Riga): –10°C to –4°C (14°F to 25°F)
Average temperature range in July (Riga): 11°C to 22°C (52°F to 72°F)

†*Arable land:* Land used for temporary crops, like meadows for mowing or pasture, gardens, and greenhouses. *Permanent crops:* Land cultivated with crops that occupy its use for long periods, such as cocoa, coffee, rubber, fruit and nut orchards, and vineyards. *Permanent pastures:* Land used permanently for forage crops. *Forests:* Land containing stands of trees. *Other:* Any land not specified, including built-on areas, roads, and barren land.

Latvia's water supply is dangerously polluted by agricultural chemicals, industrial waste, and high levels of bacteria. As of 1993, 119 animal species were endangered.

6 POPULATION

The population of Latvia was estimated at 2.4 million in mid-1998. A population of 2.2 million is estimated for 2005 by the US Bureau of the Census. The estimated population density in 1993 was about 40 persons per square kilometer (104 persons per square mile). The population of Riga, the capital, was estimated at 921,000 in 1995.

7 MIGRATION

Immigration from other former Soviet republics totaled 4,590 in 1992. A total of 51,778 persons emigrated from Latvia that year, 48,058 to former Soviet republics. Almost all of them went to Russia, Ukraine, or Belarus.

8 ETHNIC GROUPS

In 1935, the population was 77% Latvian, but by 1994 the percentage of Latvians had dipped to only 54.2%. That year, 33.1% of the population was Russian, 4.1% Belarusan, 3.1% Ukrainian, 2.2% Polish, 1.3% Lithuanian, 0.5% Jewish, and 0.3% Roma (Gypsy).

9 LANGUAGES

Latvian (also called Lettish) is a Baltic language written in the Roman alphabet. Latvian is the language used in schools. In 1995, 85% of Latvia's 700,000 non-citizen residents were Russian-speakers.

10 RELIGIONS

In 1993, Latvia's congregations (and number of members) included the following: Lutheran, 290 (300,000); Roman Catholic, 191 (300,000); Russian Orthodox, 101 (100,000); Old Believer (a breakaway Orthodox sect dating from the seventeenth century), 55 (60,000–70,000); Baptist, 69 (6,000–7,000); Jewish, 5; and others, 43.

LATVIA

LOCATION: 57°0′N; 25°0′E. **BOUNDARY LENGTHS:** Total boundary lengths, 1,150 kilometers (715 miles); Belarus, 141 kilometers (88 miles); Estonia, 339 kilometers (211 miles); Lithuania, 453 kilometers (281 miles); Russia, 217 kilometers (135 miles).

11 TRANSPORTATION

Railroads extend for 2,400 kilometers (1,500 miles), linking port cities with Russia. In 1992 there were 66,718 kilometers (41,456 miles) of highways. Maritime ports include Riga, Ventspils, and Liepāja. Riga has international air links to Helsinki, Stockholm, Copenhagen, and New York, as well as direct flights to Austria, Germany, Israel, Russia, and Belarus.

12 HISTORY

Germans, Poles, Swedes, and Russians competed for influence in what is now Latvia from the Middle Ages until the eighteenth century, when it was incorporated into the Russian Empire. During the 19th century, a Latvian nationalist movement occurred and on 18 November 1918, the independent Republic of Latvia was proclaimed. It was recognized by Moscow ten years later. However, the 1939 Nazi-

Photo credit: Anne Kalosh.

Students in traditional dress in Riga, Latvia.

failed coup against Gorbachev—Latvia once again proclaimed its independence.

In April 1994 the Latvian and Russian governments agreed to a schedule that withdrew all Russian troops from Latvia by 31 August 1994. The agreement did not include 599 soldiers at the Skrunda Radar Station, which Russia may operate until 31 August 1998 and must dismantle by 29 February 2000. In June 1995, Latvia signed an accord with the European Union that may eventually lead to full membership.

13 GOVERNMENT

The new parliament (Saeima) elected in June 1993 consists of a single chamber with 100 deputies. The executive branch of government is made up of the president, prime minister, and the cabinet. Latvia's territory is divided into four historical districts.

14 POLITICAL PARTIES

In the October 1995 elections, nine parties gained representation in the parliament (Saeima). The Democratic Party won the most seats, at 18.

15 JUDICIAL SYSTEM

The courts are being reorganized along democratic lines. Regional courts were added in 1995 to hear appeals of lower court decisions. There is also a Supreme Court and a Constitutional Court.

16 ARMED FORCES

The Latvian armed forces total 8,000, including 1,500 National Guard personnel for border and coastal defense with only

Soviet pact placed Latvia under Soviet influence. Soviet forces invaded Latvia on 17 June 1940 and incorporated it into the Soviet Union. Latvia was seized by the Germans in July 1941, when Hitler launched his attack on the Soviet Union, but was recaptured by Soviet forces in 1944.

In the 1980s, Soviet President Mikhail Gorbachev's liberal policies allowed Latvians to voice their long-suppressed desire for national self-determination. The Latvian Popular Front (LPF) gained a majority in the elections for the Latvian Supreme Council in the spring of 1990. On 21 August 1991—shortly after the

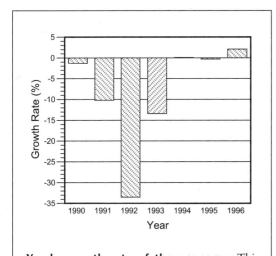

Yearly growth rate of the economy. This economic indicator tells by what percent the economy has increased or decreased when compared with the previous year.

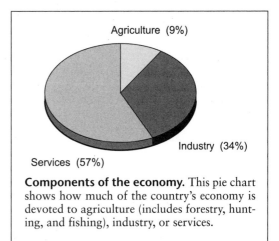

Components of the economy. This pie chart shows how much of the country's economy is devoted to agriculture (includes forestry, hunting, and fishing), industry, or services.

one battalion ready for mobile warfare. The 16,500-man militia serves as a reserve.

17 ECONOMY

Latvia has a relatively well-developed transport and communications network and a variety of industries. Agriculture makes up approximately 20% of national income and centers around the cultivation of potatoes, cereals, fodder (animal feed), and other crops, as well as dairy farming. The growth rate of the gross domestic product (GDP) increased from –33.5% in 1992 to 2.1% in 1996. During that time, the inflation rate declined from 960% to 16%.

18 INCOME

In 1995, the gross national product (GNP) was $5,708 million at current prices, or $2,300 per person. During 1985–95, the average annual decline in the real growth rate of the GNP per person was 6.6%.

19 INDUSTRY

Latvia has mainly heavy industries such as chemicals and petrochemicals, metal working, and machine building. Major manufactured items include railway carriages, buses, mopeds, washing machines, and telephone systems.

20 LABOR

In 1995, 48.8% of the 1.2 million persons employed in Latvia were women. Unemployment in 1995 was officially reported at 6.6%. Approximately 18% of the labor force works in agriculture (which accounts for 9% of the economy), and 23% in industry (which makes up 34% of the economy).

21 AGRICULTURE

In 1994, 27% of Latvia's total land area was devoted to crops and 13% was per-

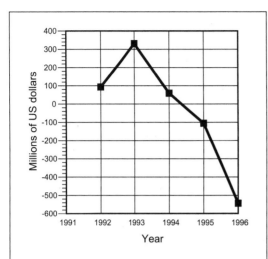

Yearly balance of trade measured in millions of US dollars. The balance of trade is the difference between what a country sells to other countries (its exports) and what it buys (its imports). If a country imports more than it exports, it has a negative balance of trade (a trade deficit). If exports exceed imports, there is a positive balance of trade (a trade surplus).

23 FISHING

The total catch in 1994 was 138,665 tons. Principal species included mackerel, herring, sprat, and redfish.

24 FORESTRY

Latvia's forests and woodlands covered about 46% of the total land area in 1994 (up from 24.7% in 1923). The timber cut in 1995 was 6.9 million cubic meters (9 million cubic yards), with 18% used as fuel wood. Latvia's wood processing industry produces sawn timber, saw logs, particleboard, plywood, pulp for paper, and paper and paperboard.

25 MINING

Coal, limestone for cement, sand, and gravel mines are spread throughout Latvia. Ceramic clays, dolomite, and gypsum are also produced.

26 FOREIGN TRADE

In 1995, total imports were valued at over $1.28 billion, and exports at $1.74 billion. Leading export markets that year were Russia (24.9%), Germany (13.9%), Sweden (9.5%), and the United Kingdom (9.2%). The leading origins for imports that year were Russia (20.4%), Germany (14.6%), Finland (9.9%), and Sweden (7.6%). The main exports are timber, textiles, and dairy products. The leading imports are fuels, cars, and chemicals.

manent pastureland. Farms have rapidly been turned over from government to private ownership since 1991. Production of primary crops in 1995 (in thousands of tons) included wheat, 160; barley, 383; rye, 64; potatoes, 927; sugar beets, 222; vegetables, 232; and fruit, 88.

22 DOMESTICATED ANIMALS

In 1995, there were 551,000 head of cattle, 501,000 pigs, 86,000 sheep, 4 million chickens, and 27,000 horses. In 1995, some 132,000 tons of meat were produced. Milk and egg production in 1995 totaled 937,000 and 22,891 tons, respectively.

27 ENERGY AND POWER

During 1994, Latvia produced about 4.27 billion kilowatt hours of electricity. In 1995, petroleum was consumed at a rate of 39,100 barrels per day and natural gas

Selected Social Indicators

These statistics are estimates for the period 1993 to 1996. For comparison purposes, data for the United States and averages for low-income countries and high-income countries are also given.

Indicator	**Latvia**	Low-income countries	High-income countries	United States
Per capita gross national product†	**$2,300**	$490	$25,870	$28,020
Population growth rate	**–1.0%**	1.7%	0.6%	0.9%
Population growth rate in urban areas	**–0.6%**	3.8%	0.9%	1.2%
Population per square kilometer of land	**40**	82	30	29
Life expectancy in years	**69**	63	77	77
Number of physicians per 1,000 people	**3**	1.0	2.5	2.5
Number of pupils per teacher (primary school)	**13**	41	17	14
Illiteracy rate (15 years and older)	**<1%**	34%	<5%	3%
Energy consumed per capita (kg of oil equivalent)	**1,471**	393	5,123	7,905

† The gross national product (GNP) is the total dollar value of all goods and services produced by a country in a year. The per capita GNP is calculated by dividing a country's GNP by its population. The World Bank defines low-income countries as those with a per capita GNP of $785 or less. High-income countries have a per capita GNP of $9,636 or more. About 16% of the world's 5.7 billion people live in high-income countries, while almost 56% live in low-income countries.   n.a. = data not available   > = greater than   < = less than

Sources: World Bank, *World Development Indicators on CD-ROM,* Washington, D.C.: The World Bank, 1998. Central Intelligence Agency, *The World Fact Book,* Washington, D.C.: Government Printing Office, 1998.

consumption totaled 23 billion cubic meters (800 billion cubic feet).

28 SOCIAL DEVELOPMENT

The 1990 law on social insurance established old age, disability, and survivorship pensions for all wage and salary earners.

Although employment discrimination based on sex is illegal, women are barred from certain occupations considered dangerous. Some employers hesitate to hire women because they are legally required to pay childbirth benefits to female employees.

29 HEALTH

Life expectancy in 1995 was 69 years. In 1993, there was one physician for every 278 people. Heart disease is the cause of death for 40% of all Latvians over age 65.

30 HOUSING

Housing construction lags behind demand. At the beginning of 1990, 165,000 families (one out of five) were registered for new housing.

31 EDUCATION

Compulsory education lasts for nine years beginning at the age of six. Secondary education generally lasts for three years. In the 1996, there were 1,066 public schools with 345,214 students and 24 private schools with 1,655 students. Latvia has two major universities: the University of Latvia and the Riga Technical University. In 1995, there were 45,828 students at 17 state institutions and 3,112 students at 10 private institutions of higher learning.

32 MEDIA

Latvian Radio broadcasts in Latvian, Russian, Swedish, English, and German. In 1995, there were about 694,300 telephones, 1.6 million radios, and 1.2 million television sets in use. Latvia publishes newspapers in both Latvian and Russian.

33 TOURISM AND RECREATION

Riga is the major tourism center of the Baltic states. Its historic architecture has undergone extensive restoration. Horseback riding, sailing, water sports, and winter sports are available to visitors. In 1994, Latvia had 90,000 tourist arrivals, and tourism receipts totaled $18 million.

34 FAMOUS LATVIANS

Guntis Ulmanis and Valdis Birkavs have been president and prime minister, respectively, of Latvia since July 1993. Turis Alumans was an early Latvian poet.

35 BIBLIOGRAPHY

Carson, George B., ed. *Latvia: An Area Study.* New Haven: Yale University Press, 1956.

Estonia, Latvia, and Lithuania: Country Studies. Washington, D.C.: Department of the Army, 1996.

Plakans, Andrejs. *The Latvians: A Short History.* Stanford, Calif.: Hoover Institution Press, 1995.

LEBANON

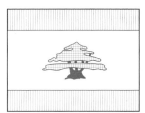

Republic of Lebanon
Al-Jumhuriyah al-Lubnaniyah

CAPITAL: Beirut (Bayrut).

FLAG: The national flag, introduced in 1943, consists of two horizontal red stripes separated by a white stripe which is twice as wide; at the center, in green and brown, is a cedar tree.

ANTHEM: *Kulluna lil watan lil'ula lil'alam (All of Us for the Country, Glory, Flag).*

MONETARY UNIT: The Lebanese pound, or livre libanaise (LL), is a paper currency of 100 piasters. There are coins of 1, 2½, 5, 10, 25, and 50 piasters and 1 Lebanese pound, and notes of 1, 5, 10, 25, 50, 100, 250, 1,000 and 10,000 Lebanese pounds. LL1 = $0.00064 (or $1 = LL1,556.0).

WEIGHTS AND MEASURES: The metric system is the legal standard, but traditional weights and measures are still used.

HOLIDAYS: New Year's Day, 1 January; Arab League Day, 22 March; Independence Day, 22 November; Evacuation Day, 31 December. Christian religious holidays include Feast of St. Maron, 9 February; Good Friday; Easter Monday; Ascension; Assumption, 15 August; All Saints' Day, 1 November; and Christmas, 25 December. Muslim religious holidays include 'Id al-Fitr, 'Id al-'Adha', and Milad an-Nabi.

TIME: 2 PM = noon GMT.

1 LOCATION AND SIZE

Situated on the eastern coast of the Mediterranean Sea, Lebanon has an area of 10,400 square kilometers (4,015 square miles), about three-fourths the size of the state of Connecticut, and a total boundary length of 656 kilometers (407 miles).

Lebanon's capital city, Beirut, is located on the Mediterranean coast.

2 TOPOGRAPHY

The Lebanon Mountains area is rugged. There is a rise from sea level to about 2,000–3,000 meters (6,600–9,800 feet) in less than 40 kilometers (25 miles). East of the Lebanon Mountains is the Bekaa Valley, an extremely fertile flatland. At the eastern flank of the Bekaa stands Mount Hermon, straddling the border with Syria. Lebanon contains few rivers, and its harbors are mostly shallow and small.

3 CLIMATE

Lebanon has an extraordinarily varied climate: within 45 minutes' drive in winter, spring, and fall, both skiing and swimming are possible. Rainfall averages about 90 centimeters (35 inches) yearly along the coast, about 125 centimeters (50 inches) on the western slopes of the mountains, and less than 38 centimeters (15 inches) in the Bekaa Valley. The average annual temperature in Beirut is 21°C (70°F), with a

Geographic Profile

Geographic Features

Size ranking: 159 of 192
Highest elevation: 3,083 meters (10,115 feet) at
  Mount Sawda
Lowest elevation: Sea level at the Mediterranean Sea

Land Use†

Arable land:	21%
Permanent crops:	9%
Permanent pastures:	1%
Forests:	8%
Other:	61%

Weather††

Average annual precipitation: 51.7 centimeters (20.4
  inches)
Average temperature range in January (Beirut): 11–
  17°C (52–63°F)
Average temperature range in July (Beirut): 23–31°C
  (73–88°F)

†*Arable land:* Land used for temporary crops, like
meadows for mowing or pasture, gardens, and greenhouses. *Permanent crops:* Land cultivated with crops
that occupy its use for long periods, such as cocoa,
coffee, rubber, fruit and nut orchards, and vineyards.
Permanent pastures: Land used permanently for forage crops. *Forests:* Land containing stands of trees.
Other: Any land not specified, including built-on
areas, roads, and barren land.

††The measurements for precipitation were taken at
weather stations closest to the country's largest city.
Precipitation and average temperature can vary significantly within a country, due to factors such as latitude, altitude, coastal proximity, and wind patterns.

range from 13°C (55°F) in winter to 28°C
(82°F) in summer.

4 PLANTS AND ANIMALS

Lebanon is rich in plants, with approximately 2,500 species. Olive and fig trees
and grapevines are abundant on lower
ground, while cedar, maple, juniper, fir,
cypress, valonia oak, and Aleppo pine
trees occupy higher altitudes. Although
hunting has killed off most wild mammals,
jackals are still found in the wilder rural
regions, and gazelles and rabbits are
numerous in the south. Many varieties of
rodents and reptiles may be found.
Thrushes, nightingales, and other song-
birds are native to Lebanon; there are also
partridges, pigeons, vultures, and eagles.

5 ENVIRONMENT

Coastal waters show the effects of
untreated sewage disposal, particularly
near Beirut, and of oil tanker discharges
and oil spills. Air pollution is a serious
problem in Beirut because of vehicle
exhaust and the burning of industrial
wastes.

The effects of war and the growth of
the nation's cities have combined to
threaten animal and plant life in Lebanon.
Four of the nation's mammal species and
14 of its bird species are endangered. Five
of its plant species are also threatened
with extinction.

6 POPULATION

In 1998, the Lebanese population was estimated by the US Census Bureau at 3.5 million and by the United Nations at 3.2
million. The US Bureau of the Census projected a population of 3.9 million in the
year 2005. Population density is estimated
at 399 persons per square kilometer
(1,033 per square mile). Beirut, the capital, had an estimated population of 1.8
million in 1995.

7 MIGRATION

In 1986, the Lebanese World Cultural
Union estimated that some 13.3 million
persons of Lebanese extraction were living

abroad, the largest numbers in Brazil, the United States, and Argentina. In 1993, the number of refugees in various parts of Lebanon was estimated at over 600,000. As of mid-1997, there were still 350,000 Palestinians who had asylum in Lebanon.

8 ETHNIC GROUPS

Ethnic mixtures dating back to various periods of immigration and invasion are represented, as are peoples of almost all Middle Eastern countries. While most Lebanese are Arabs, they are divided into Muslims and Christians, each in turn subdivided into a number of faiths or sects. The Muslims are divided into Sunnis and Shi'ites. The Druzes, whose religion derives from Islam, are a significant minority. Other ethnic groups include Armenians, a small number of Jews, Syrians, and Kurds. The number of Palestinians is estimated at 450,000–500,000.

9 LANGUAGES

Arabic is the official language and is spoken throughout the country. Much of the population is bilingual, with French as the main second language. There are also significant numbers of English, Armenian, and Turkish speakers.

10 RELIGIONS

The imbalance of power between Christians and Muslims, compounded by the presence of large numbers of Palestinians, was a major factor contributing to the bitter civil war. Christians, mostly Maronite, constituted about 30% of the population in the mid-1990s, and Muslims and Druzes about 70%. The Christians are

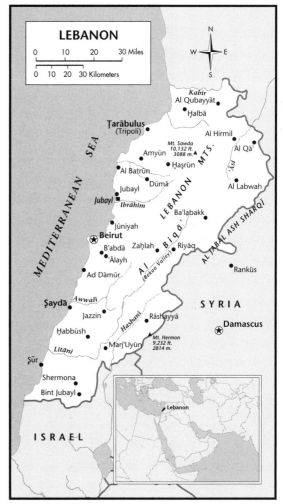

LOCATION: 35°6′ to 36°36′E; 33°4′ to 34°41′N. **BOUNDARY LENGTHS:** Syria, 359 kilometers (223 miles); Israel, 102 kilometers (63 miles); Mediterranean coastline, 195 kilometers (121 miles). **TERRITORIAL SEA LIMIT:** 12 miles.

divided mainly among Maronites, Greek Orthodox, and Greek Catholics. Muslims are divided into Sunni and Shi'ites.

11 TRANSPORTATION

As of 1995, Lebanon had about 7,300 kilometers (4,500 miles) of roads, of which 85% were paved. The 222-kilometer (138-mile) state-owned railway consists of a 1.435-meters-gauge line running parallel to the coastal area.

Beirut, a major Mediterranean port, was closed during the 1975–76 war and intermittently thereafter, reopening by March 1991. In 1995, there were 58 ships in the merchant fleet with a capacity of 192,000 gross registered tons.

Beirut's airport has become more active since the end of the war. Bombing during the Israeli invasion had forced its closure in June–October 1982, and service was limited during the 1980s. In 1995, 770,000 passengers were carried in scheduled flights across Lebanon.

12 HISTORY

Both Lebanon and Syria were historically linked from early times as part of Phoenicia (c.1600–c.800 BC), and both were later swept up into the Roman Empire. In the seventh century AD, the Arabs conquered part of Lebanon, where Maronite Christians had long been established.

Islam gradually spread by conversion and migration, although the country remained mostly Christian. In the eleventh century, the Druzes established themselves in the south of the Lebanon Mountains area as well as in Syria. Parts of Lebanon fell temporarily to the Crusaders; invasions by Mongols and others followed, and trade declined until the reunification of the Middle East under the Ottoman Empire.

Ottoman Control

For the most part, Ottoman officials of the surrounding areas left the Lebanese under the control of their own emirs and sheikhs. The Egyptian occupation of Syria (1832–40) opened the region to large-scale European penetration and tied Lebanese affairs to international politics. The British invasion of 1840–41 delivered Lebanon from Egyptian rule.

Conflicts between Christians, Muslims, and Druze led to the creation of an autonomous province of Mount Lebanon in 1864, with a Christian governor who, though the servant of the Ottoman state, relied upon European backing in disputes with his sovereign.

The entry of the Ottoman Empire into World War I (1914–18) led to the destruction of Lebanese prosperity. In 1920, an Allied conference gave France a mandate (authorization to govern) over Syria, in which Mount Lebanon was included. The mandate years were a time of material growth and little political development.

Lebanon came under control of the French Vichy (Nazi-ruled) government in 1940. However, in 1941, Lebanon and Syria were taken by a combined Anglo–Free French force. After growing conflicts between the Lebanese nationalists and the French, Lebanon gained complete independence in 1946.

The 1950s and 1960s were generally characterized by economic and political stability. Beginning in 1952, Lebanon received increased United States aid. It also benefited from an influx of Western

A Lebanese man takes his two children for a scooter ride through Beirut's war-ravaged Chiyah district. Many streets that were previously barricaded were reopened after the signing of the 1989 Taif Accord, which called for a ceasefire among the many factions fighting for control of the country.

commercial personnel and from growing oil royalties. During this time, Lebanon seemed the calmest part of the Middle East. It took little part in the Arab-Israeli war of 1948, and no action in the wars of 1967 and 1973.

Rise of the PLO

However, in the late 1960s and early 1970s Lebanon's role began to change. This was due to the presence of the Palestinian Liberation Organization (the PLO). The PLO was a terrorist organization fighting for an independent homeland within the borders of Israel. Well-armed members of the PLO had moved into the area of Lebanon that borders with Israel. This led to clashes between the PLO and Lebanon's army. In 1969, Jordan's government, fearing a civil war, signed the so-called Cairo Accord with the PLO. This agreement made the terrorist organization practically a separate state within Lebanon, with the right to establish military bases and launch cross-border raids into Israel.

The PLO presence inflamed tensions between Christians and Muslims and, by 1975, led to a civil war. The war pitted Maronite Christians against Muslims and against other Christian sects. It also pitted rightist militants against Palestinian guerrillas and other leftist Arab forces. At least 100,000 people on all sides were killed. In addition, some 600,000 persons were displaced during the 18 months of fighting. A ceasefire arranged through the mediation of Sa'udi Arabia and other Arab countries enabled a peacekeeping force (including Syrian troops) to separate the combatants and end the war in October 1976.

The conflict devastated Lebanon economically. It also weakened the central government to the point where different parts of the country were under the control of the Syrians, the Palestinians, and the militias of some 30 factions.

The UN Moves In

In March 1978, the Israeli army invaded southern Lebanon, destroying PLO bases. It withdrew, and a United Nations (UN) force was assigned to keep the peace.

However, the PLO continued rocket attacks on northern Israel. In addition, the Syrian military remained in Lebanon. Israel saw the Syrian military presence in Lebanon as a threat to its security. These factors prompted Israel to launch a full-scale invasion of Lebanon in June 1982. Following a two-month Israeli siege of West Beirut, where the Palestinians were encamped, a truce was agreed to by Israel, the PLO, and Syria. A multinational peacekeeping force, composed of British, French, and Italian soldiers and US marines, was stationed in the Beirut area in early September.

Despite the truce, the violence continued. On 14 September 1982, Bashir Gemayel, a Christian Phalangist leader who in August had been elected president by the Lebanese parliament, was assassinated. He was succeeded by his brother Amin Gemayel. The Phalangists blamed the PLO and soon afterwards, Israel allowed Christian Phalangist forces into the refugee camps. In the fighting that followed, at least 600 Palestinians, many of them civilians, were massacred. In 1983, Israeli and Syrian troops still occupied large portions of Lebanon, and they became targets of attack by Muslim and Druze forces.

The American embassy in Beirut was bombed in April 1983, and US marines were harassed by sniper fire. On 23 October, 241 marines were killed by a truck-bomb explosion in the US barracks at Beirut airport. Israel's withdrawal of its troops from most of Lebanon in early 1985 left in its wake renewed fighting for the evacuated territory.

The badly divided factions could not agree on a successor to president Amin Gemayel when his term expired in September 1988. Christian Army Commander Michel Aoun asserted himself as prime minister, giving Lebanon two governments, a Muslim one in West Beirut and a Christian one in East Beirut. Aoun was opposed by the Syrians and Muslims and by rival Christian factions.

In September 1989, a committee appointed by the Arab League arrived at a seven-point ceasefire, called the Taif Accord.

In 1991–92, the government gradually began to reassert its authority. Almost all militias were dissolved, and Palestinian militants were repressed in Sayda (Sidon). Internally, the poor economy aggravated political instability, but the appointment of Prime Minister Rafiq al-Hariri in November 1992 promised a serious effort at reconstruction.

Al-Hariri, who became a self-made billionaire in Sa'udi Arabia, had a long history of making charitable donations to help rebuild Beirut. As prime minister, however, he has been frequently accused of corruption. His efforts to reunite the country have generally won the people's approval, and al-Hariri was reelected in 1996.

Southern Lebanon, occupied by Israeli forces, is still subject to political violence. In 1996, 255 people (including 27 Israeli soldiers) were killed in violence.

13 GOVERNMENT

As defined by the constitution of 1926 and subsequent amendments, Lebanon is an independent republic. Executive power is vested in a president (elected by the legislature for six years) and a prime minister and cabinet, chosen by the president but responsible to the legislature. Legislative power is exercised by a 128-member National Assembly elected for a four-year term by universal adult suffrage. The Taif Accord of 1989 set the Christian-Muslim balance in parliament at 50–50, but the failure of Christians to participate in the elections of 1992 and 1996 gave Muslim groups the largest number of seats in the Chamber.

Lebanon is divided into five provinces (*muhafazat*), which are subdivided into districts *(aqdiya)*, municipalities, and villages.

14 POLITICAL PARTIES

Principal political groups, with mainly Christian membership, are the National Liberal Party and the Phalangist Party. There are various parties of the left, including the Progressive Socialist Party (of mostly Druze membership), the Ba'th Party, and the Lebanese Communist Party.

The various Palestinian groups have played an important role in the political life of Lebanon since the late 1960s. Amal, a conservative grouping, and Hezbollah, more militant, represent the Shi'ite Muslim community.

15 JUDICIAL SYSTEM

Ultimate supervisory power rests with the minister of justice, who appoints the magistrates. Courts of first instance, of which there are 56, give cases their first hearing; they are presided over by a single judge and deal with both civil and criminal cases. Appeals may be taken to 11 courts of appeal, each made up of three judges.

Religious courts—Islamic, Christian, and Jewish—deal with marriages, deaths, inheritances, and other matters of personal status in their respective faiths. In the Palestinian refugee camps, rival factions try opponents without any semblance of due process.

16 ARMED FORCES

In 1995, the regular Lebanese army numbered 47,500 men. There was a small navy

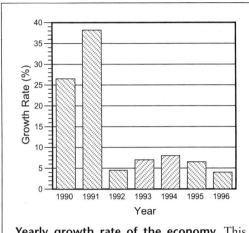

Yearly growth rate of the economy. This economic indicator tells by what percent the economy has increased or decreased when compared with the previous year.

After the 1989 Taif Accord for National Reconciliation ended hostilities, the economy began to recover. Economic activity surged in 1991, and in 1993 the al-Hariri government was able to stabilize the economy and launch a program to reconstruct the country's transportation and communication networks. Since 1992, annual economic growth has averaged about 7%, but a rising budget deficit may threaten further reforms.

18 INCOME

In 1995 the gross national product (GNP) was $10.7 billion, or $2,970 per person.

19 INDUSTRY

The civil war caused tremendous damage to the industrial sector. By 1993, it was estimated that the Lebanese industry suffered losses of $1.5 billion. Inadequate transport and communications networks and a shortage of skilled labor are major obstacles in the process of rehabilitation. In 1995, industry accounted for 28% of the gross domestic product. Major industrial products are clothing, metal, food, marble and sanitary equipment, cement, jewelry, furniture, paper, beverages, and plastic.

of 600 and an air force of 800 personnel, neither well-armed.

Although many of the militias have disbanded, the Muslim Hezbollah (3,000) is the only significant communal army remaining. The South Lebanese Army, mostly Christian, numbers 2,500 and receives Israeli support for its border patrol duties.

17 ECONOMY

Lebanon is traditionally a trading country, with a relatively large agricultural sector and small but well-developed industry. Until the 1975–76 civil war, it had always figured prominently as a center of tourist trade. The war caused an estimated $5 billion in property damage and reduced economic activities to about 50% of the prewar level.

20 LABOR

The labor force in 1996, having been drastically reduced by the results of war—death, injury, and emigration—was estimated at 900,000 people. Many Lebanese work in Persian Gulf area nations. Labor productivity is low compared with the United States and Western Europe, but higher than in many developing countries.

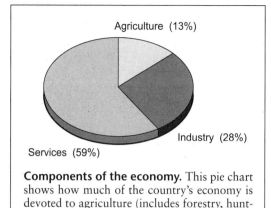

Components of the economy. This pie chart shows how much of the country's economy is devoted to agriculture (includes forestry, hunting, and fishing), industry, or services.

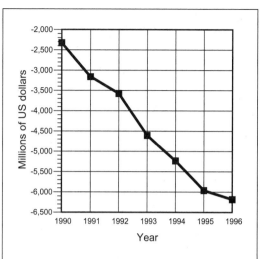

Yearly balance of trade measured in millions of US dollars. The balance of trade is the difference between what a country sells to other countries (its exports) and what it buys (its imports). If a country imports more than it exports, it has a negative balance of trade (a trade deficit). If exports exceed imports, there is a positive balance of trade (a trade surplus).

In 1996, unemployment was about 30%. There are some 160 labor unions and organizations. Agricultural and most trade workers are not organized. Palestinians in Lebanon are free to organize their own unions, but few do so because of their restrictions on the right to work in the country.

21 AGRICULTURE

Less than 30% of Lebanon's total area can support crop production. Expansion of cultivated areas is limited by the arid and rugged nature of the land. Agricultural production was severely disrupted by the 1975–76 war and by Israeli-Syrian fighting during 1982.

Principal crops and estimated 1995 production (in thousand tons) were potatoes, 220; oranges, 280; sugar beets, 215; apples, 165; lemons and limes, 96; bananas, 63; grapefruit, 55; olives, 50; and wheat, 49. Two profitable, although illegal, crops produced are opium poppy and cannabis, or marijuana.

22 DOMESTICATED ANIMALS

In 1995 there were an estimated 480,000 goats, 400,000 sheep, 79,000 head of cattle, and 18 million poultry. Meat and milk production is below consumption needs.

23 FISHING

The catch in 1994 was 2,425 tons.

24 FORESTRY

Forests comprised about 80,000 hectares (197,700 acres), or nearly 8% of the total area, in 1994. Most forests are pine and

Selected Social Indicators

These statistics are estimates for the period 1993 to 1996. For comparison purposes, data for the United States and averages for low-income countries and high-income countries are also given.

Indicator	Lebanon	Low-income countries	High-income countries	United States
Per capita gross national product†	**$2,970**	$490	$25,870	$28,020
Population growth rate	**1.8%**	1.7%	0.6%	0.9%
Population growth rate in urban areas	**2.3%**	3.8%	0.9%	1.2%
Population per square kilometer of land	**399**	82	30	29
Life expectancy in years	**70**	63	77	77
Number of physicians per 1,000 people	**1.9**	1.0	2.5	2.5
Number of pupils per teacher (primary school)	**n.a.**	41	17	14
Illiteracy rate (15 years and older)	**8%**	34%	<5%	3%
Energy consumed per capita (kg of oil equivalent)	**1,120**	393	5,123	7,905

† The gross national product (GNP) is the total dollar value of all goods and services produced by a country in a year. The per capita GNP is calculated by dividing a country's GNP by its population. The World Bank defines low-income countries as those with a per capita GNP of $785 or less. High-income countries have a per capita GNP of $9,636 or more. About 16% of the world's 5.7 billion people live in high-income countries, while almost 56% live in low-income countries.   n.a. = data not available   > = greater than   < = less than

Sources: World Bank, *World Development Indicators on CD-ROM*, Washington, D.C.: The World Bank, 1998. Central Intelligence Agency, *The World Fact Book*, Washington, D.C.: Government Printing Office, 1998.

oak; few of the ancient cedars have survived.

25 MINING

Mining activity is slight. According to 1995 estimates, cement production amounted to 3 million tons; gypsum, 2,000 tons; lime, 30,000 tons; and salt, 3,000 tons.

26 FOREIGN TRADE

Exports officially reached $1.72 billion in 1996, while imports were reported at $9.39 billion. Some 40% of exports are actually reexports of machinery, metal products, foods, wood products, textiles, and chemicals. Lebanon exports its own cement, jewelry, nonmetallic minerals, clothing, and aluminum products. Industrial hardware, motor vehicles, oil, foodstuffs, and electrical equipment are leading imports.

Some 48% of Lebanon's exports went to other Middle Eastern countries in 1995. That year, Lebanon's principal export markets were Sa'udi Arabia, Switzerland, and the United Arab Emirates. Leading import suppliers were Italy, France, and the United States.

27 ENERGY AND POWER

Kuwait is Lebanon's leading source of crude petroleum. The Tripoli refinery only satisfies about 15% of domestic demand. Lebanon's largest hydroelectric plants are on the Litani River. In 1994, electricity production totaled 4.8 billion kilowatt hours.

28 SOCIAL DEVELOPMENT

A government social security plan, not fully implemented, is intended to provide sickness and maternity insurance, accident and disability insurance, and family allowances.

Women must obtain permission from their husbands in order to engage in trade. Many of the religious laws governing family and personal status discriminate against women.

29 HEALTH

In 1991, there were 6,638 physicians. Average life expectancy is 70 years. In 1994, 100% of the population had access to safe water and 95% had access to health care services.

30 HOUSING

A housing shortage in the early 1970s was aggravated by the civil war and subsequent fighting, in which half of the country's real estate was severely damaged or destroyed. According to the latest available information for 1980–88, total housing units numbered 820,000 with 3.3 people per dwelling. Housing needs until 2000 have been estimated at 400,000 units. With the return of stability, a boom in construction is underway in Beirut.

31 EDUCATION

Lebanon's illiteracy rate is relatively low for the Middle East; an estimated 8% (5.3% of adult males and 9.7% of adult females) cannot read and write. In 1994 there were 365,174 primary school pupils and 277,646 general secondary school students. In 1991, the total enrollment for all higher level institutions was 85,495. Leading universities include the American University in Beirut, St. Joseph University, and the Lebanese (State) University.

32 MEDIA

Government-controlled Radio Lebanon broadcasts in Arabic, and Tele-Liban broadcasts on three channels in Arabic, French, and English. An estimated 2.4 million radios and 920,000 television sets were in use in 1995.

Historically, Lebanon has had the freest press in the Arab world. Even during the civil war, newspapers and magazines were published without restriction. The largest Arabic dailies are *An-Nahar* (1995 circulation, 65,000) and *As-Safir* (35,000).

33 TOURISM AND RECREATION

Before the civil war, Lebanon's historic sites combined with a pleasant climate and scenery to attract many tourists (more than 2 million in 1974), especially from other Arab countries. During the war, however, fighting and bombing destroyed or heavily damaged major hotels in Beirut and reduced the number of tourists to practically zero.

34 FAMOUS LEBANESE

Khalil Gibran (Jibran, 1883–1931), a native of Lebanon, achieved international renown through his paintings and literary works. He is best known for his long poem *The Prophet*. Charles Habib Malik (1906–87), for many years Lebanon's leading diplomat, was president of the thirteenth United Nations General Assembly in 1959.

35 BIBLIOGRAPHY

Bleaney, C. H. *Lebanon*. Santa Barbara, Calif.: Clio Press, 1991.

Eshel, Isaac. *Lebanon in Pictures*. Minneapolis: Lerner, 1988.

Foster, L. *Lebanon*. Chicago: Children's Press, 1992.

Hiro, Dilip. *Lebanon: Fire and Embers: A History of the Lebanese Civil War*. New York: St. Martin's, 1993.

Marston, Elsa. *Lebanon: New Light in an Ancient Land*. New York: Dillon Press, 1994.

LESOTHO

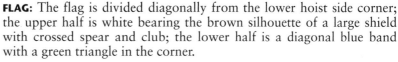

Kingdom of Lesotho
Muso oa Lesotho

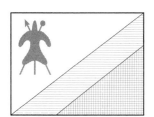

CAPITAL: Maseru.

FLAG: The flag is divided diagonally from the lower hoist side corner; the upper half is white bearing the brown silhouette of a large shield with crossed spear and club; the lower half is a diagonal blue band with a green triangle in the corner.

ANTHEM: *Lesotho Fatse La Bo-nata Rona (Lesotho, the Country of Our Fathers).*

MONETARY UNIT: Lesotho is part of the South African monetary area; the maloti of 100 lisente, introduced in 1980, is on a par with the South African rand (R), which is also legal tender. There are coins of 1, 2, 5, 10, 25, and 50 lisente, and notes of 2, 5, 10, 20, and 50 maloti (M). M1 = $0.21268 (or $1 = M4.702).

WEIGHTS AND MEASURES: British and metric weights and measures are in general use.

HOLIDAYS: New Year's Day, 1 January; Moshoeshoe's Day, 12 March; Family Day, 1st Monday in July; King's Birthday, 17 July; Independence Day, 4 October; National Sports Day, 6 October; Christmas, 25 December; Boxing Day, 26 December. Movable Christian holidays include Good Friday, Easter Monday, and Ascension.

TIME: 2 PM = noon GMT.

1 LOCATION AND SIZE

Lesotho is located entirely within the borders of the Republic of South Africa, with an area of 30,350 square kilometers (11,718 square miles), slightly larger than the state of Maryland. Lesotho's capital city, Maseru, is located on the country's northwest border.

2 TOPOGRAPHY

The western quarter of the country is a plateau averaging 1,500 to 1,850 meters (4,900–6,100 feet) with poor, badly eroded sandstone-derived soil. The remainder of the country is highland. A zone of rolling foothills, ranging from 1,800 to 2,100 meters (5,900–6,900 feet), forms the border between the lowlands and the mountains in the east. The Drakensberg Range of mountains forms the entire eastern and southeastern border. The Caledon River forms the western border. The Orange and Caledon rivers, together with their tributaries, drain more than 90% of the country.

3 CLIMATE

Temperatures vary widely from one geographical zone to another, and frequently within zones, depending on the altitude. In the lowlands, temperatures reach 32°C (90°F) or more in the summer and rarely

Geographic Profile

Geographic Features

Size ranking: 137 of 192
Highest elevation: 3,482 meters (11,425 feet) at
  Mount Thabana Ntlenyana
Lowest elevation: 1400 meters (4593 feet) at junction
  of the Orange and Makhaleng Rivers

Land Use†

Arable land:	11%
Permanent crops:	0%
Permanent pastures:	66%
Forests:	0%
Other:	23%

Weather††

Average annual precipitation: 71 centimeters (28
  inches)
Average temperature in January: 32°C (90°F)
Average temperature in July: −7°C (19°F)

†*Arable land:* Land used for temporary crops, like
meadows for mowing or pasture, gardens, and greenhouses. *Permanent crops:* Land cultivated with crops
that occupy its use for long periods, such as cocoa,
coffee, rubber, fruit and nut orchards, and vineyards.
Permanent pastures: Land used permanently for forage crops. *Forests:* Land containing stands of trees.
Other: Any land not specified, including built-on
areas, roads, and barren land.

††Temperature variations are greater in the highlands,
where winter temperatures may fall as low as −18°C
(0°F). Annual precipitation varies from 60 centimeters
(24 inches) in the lowlands to 191 centimeters (75
inches) in the mountains.

fall below −7°C (19°F) in the winter. The
range in the highlands is greater; temperatures sometimes fall below −18°C (0°F),
and frost and hail are frequent hazards.
Rainfall, which is mostly concentrated in
the months from October to April, averages 71 centimeters (28 inches) annually.

4 PLANTS AND ANIMALS

Grass is the natural vegetation in this virtually treeless country. The high plateau is
covered with montane or subalpine grass-
land. Red oat grass forms a dry carpet in
much of the Drakensberg foothill region.
The African lammergeier, a bird common
only in Lesotho and in the mountains of
Ethiopia, and the bald ibis, both of which
are near extinction, are found in small
numbers in the Drakensberg Range.

5 ENVIRONMENT

Much of the country has become stripped
of its natural grass cover through uncontrolled grazing and rushing surface water.
Unlike neighboring South Africa, Lesotho
is not rich in game and other wildlife.
After suffering a decline because of ruin-
ous trading practices, overstocking, overgrazing, disease, and drought, the famous
Basuto pony, of almost pure Arabian
stock, has begun to make a comeback
through a selective breeding program and
improved feeding methods. Other vanish-
ing species, like the wildebeest and bles-
bok, have been reintroduced in areas
where they formerly were numerous.

6 POPULATION

In 1998, the population of Lesotho was
estimated at 2.1 million. A population of
2.3 million is projected for the year 2005.
Maseru, the capital city, had an estimated
population of 150,000 in 1995, and a
metropolitan population of 297,000.

7 MIGRATION

In 1996 about 60% of the Lesothan male
labor force worked in the Republic of
South Africa.

8 ETHNIC GROUPS

Lesotho is ethnically homogeneous. At least 93% of the people are of Basotho origin, and about 6% are Nguni.

9 LANGUAGES

The Sesotho language is spoken by virtually all the indigenous population. English shares with Sesotho the position of official language.

10 RELIGIONS

Christian missions have long been active in Lesotho. As a result, according to 1993 estimates, some 90% of the population is Christian, primarily Roman Catholic. The remainder of the indigenous population follows African traditional religions.

11 TRANSPORTATION

In 1993 there were 799 kilometers (496 miles) of tarred roads and 4,525 kilometers (2,811 miles) of gravel, crushed stone, or stabilized soil roads. Lesotho Airways and South African Airways maintain scheduled passenger service between Johannesburg and an international airport 19 kilometers (12 miles) outside of Maseru.

12 HISTORY

What is now Lesotho was inhabited by hunter-gatherers, called the San Bushmen, until about 1600, when refugees from Bantu tribal wars began arriving. In 1818, Moshoeshoe, a minor chief of a northern tribe in what was to become Basutoland, founded the Basotho nation.

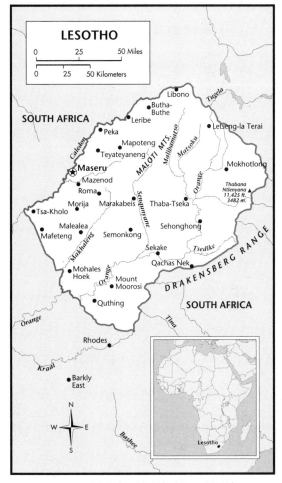

LOCATION: 28°35' to 30°40's; 27° to 29°30'E.

During the early days of its existence, the Basotho had to contend with incursions by Boers, or Dutch settlers, from the Orange Free State in what is now South Africa. Moshoeshoe sought British protection, but not before much land had been lost to white settlers. His urgent appeals for assistance went unheeded until 1868, when Basutoland became a British protectorate. Moshoeshoe died in 1870. The fol-

Photo credit: AP/Wide World Photos.

Rural Basotho horsemen line the streets where Pope John Paul II was expected to drive after arriving in Lesotho. Their waiting was in vain because the Papal plane could not land at Maseru airport due to bad weather conditions. Christian missions have long been active in Lesotho. As a result, 90% of the population is Christian, primarily Roman Catholic.

In 1884, Basutoland was returned to British administration under a policy of indirect rule. Local government was introduced in 1910 which in effect allowed the chiefs to govern for the next 50 years. Under a new constitution that became effective in 1960, an indirectly elected legislative body, the Basutoland National Council, was created. A pre-independence constitution went into effect on 30 April 1965.

Independence

The United Kingdom granted independence to the newly named Kingdom of Lesotho on 4 October 1966; Moshoeshoe II was proclaimed king. The first general election was held in January 1970. As the election progressed, it appeared that the ruling party, the Basotho National Party (BNP), would be defeated by the Basotho Congress Party (BCP). Fearing defeat, Prime Minister Leabua Jonathan, the leader of the BNP, declared a state of emergency and suspended the constitution. King Moshoeshoe II was placed under house arrest.

Through the late 1970s and early 1980s the BCP's military arm, the Lesotho Liberation Army (LLA), continued to struggle against the Jonathan government. They claimed responsibility for periodic bombings in Maseru, ambushes of government officials, and attacks on police stations. The Lesotho government charged that South Africa was allowing the LLA to use its territory as a base of operations.

lowing year, Basutoland was annexed to the Cape Colony, over the protests of both Basotho and Boer leaders.

In 1880, the so-called Gun War broke out between the Basotho and the Boers over the attempt to disarm the Basotho. A high point in Basotho history was the successful resistance waged against the Cape's forces.

Relations with South Africa deteriorated and on 1 January 1986, South Africa imposed a near-total blockade of Lesotho. The blockade resulted in severe shortages of food and essential supplies. Within the month, a military coup led by Major General Justin Metsing Lekhanya overthrew the government. All political activity was banned. There was widespread skepticism about the military government and its links to South Africa.

Many groups within the country called for a return to civilian rule. In November 1990, a new law was announced providing for a constitutional monarchy, but barring Moshoeshoe II from the throne. However, in April 1991, rebel army officers staged a bloodless coup, forcing Lekhanya to resign. He was succeeded by Colonel Elias Ramaema as leader of a military junta.

Finally, on 27 March 1993, in the first democratic elections in 23 years, the BCP won all 65 seats in the Assembly. The BCP formed a new government under Prime Minister Dr. Ntsu Mokhehle. However, on 25 January 1994, army troops mutinied after the government refused their demands for a 100% pay increase. Prime Minister Mokhehle requested military assistance from South Africa, but that request was denied. After three weeks of sporadic fighting, opposing factions within the military agreed to new negotiations.

In September 1994, the king and Prime Minister Mokhehle signed an agreement reestablishing democratic rule and removing King Letsie from the throne and returning his father, the exiled King Moshoeshoe II. In 1996, King Moshoeshoe II was killed in a car crash and his son was returned to power. The move alarmed supporters of democracy because Letsie had suspended parliament when he earlier held power.

13 GOVERNMENT

According to the 1965 constitution and its 1993 replacement, the Kingdom of Lesotho is a monarchy with a bicameral parliament. The parliament consists of a National Assembly of 65 members, and a Senate with 33 members. Until 1993 the king was official chief of state *(motlotlehi)*. The 1993 constitution, however, clearly defines the king's role as ceremonial.

14 POLITICAL PARTIES

Lesotho's government party, the Basotho National Party (BNP), formerly the Basutoland National Party, was founded in 1959 and was in the forefront of Lesotho's independence drive. Also active in the independence drive was the Basotho Congress Party (BCP), founded in 1952. The third major party is the Marematlou Freedom Party (MFP), formed in 1965. The BCP holds all the seats in the National Assembly, although it won just over half the vote in 1993.

15 JUDICIAL SYSTEM

The judicial system consists of the High Court, the Court of Appeal, subordinate courts, and the Judicial Service Commission (JSC). The High Court hears appeals from subordinate courts. There is no trial by jury.

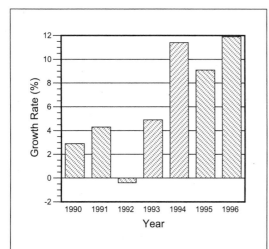

Yearly growth rate of the economy. This economic indicator tells by what percent the economy has increased or decreased when compared with the previous year.

60% of Lesotho's male work force worked in South African coal and gold mines, and their tax payments accounted for 45% of the gross domestic product (GDP).

19 INDUSTRY

Lesotho has a wide variety of light industries, which include, among others, tire retreading, tapestry weaving, diamond processing, and the production of textiles, electric lighting, candles, and ceramics.

20 LABOR

About 70% of the entire Basotho population dwelling in Lesotho is engaged in agriculture and livestock raising. About 60% of the male labor force works in South Africa. The estimated unemployment rate in 1992 was 35%. Child labor is not uncommon in Lesotho.

16 ARMED FORCES

A 2,000-member army has eight combat companies (with United States and United Kingdom weapons) and one air squadron.

17 ECONOMY

Lesotho is an agricultural country, with modest incomes from industry and tourism. Political reforms in South Africa and the involvement of the International Monetary Fund (IMF) have created new opportunities for the Lesotho economy.

18 INCOME

In 1995 Lesotho's gross national product (GNP) was $1,519 million, or about $660 per person. Taxes from Lesotho's migrant labor force working in South Africa constitute a key source of income. In 1996,

21 AGRICULTURE

Crop production in Lesotho is a high-risk, low-yield activity due to poor soil quality and a harsh climate. The principal food crop is corn. Main agricultural production in 1995 included (in tons) corn, 27,000; sorghum, 10,000; wheat, 2,000; peas, 2,000; and beans, 2,000.

22 DOMESTICATED ANIMALS

The raising of livestock is the principal economic undertaking in Lesotho. Lesotho's main exports are wool and mohair.

In 1995 there were an estimated 1.3 million sheep, 670,000 goats, 640,000 head of cattle, 153,000 mules, 120,000

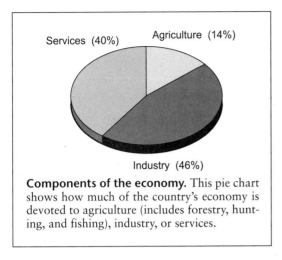

Components of the economy. This pie chart shows how much of the country's economy is devoted to agriculture (includes forestry, hunting, and fishing), industry, or services.

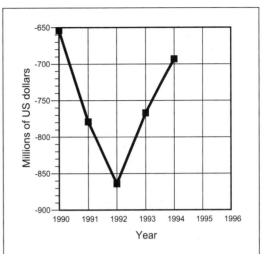

Yearly balance of trade measured in millions of US dollars. The balance of trade is the difference between what a country sells to other countries (its exports) and what it buys (its imports). If a country imports more than it exports, it has a negative balance of trade (a trade deficit). If exports exceed imports there is a positive balance of trade (a trade surplus).

horses, 45,000 hogs, and 1 million chickens.

23 FISHING

There is virtually no commercial fishing. In 1994, the total catch was 35 tons, including 20 tons of carp.

24 FORESTRY

Lesotho is almost devoid of natural woodland. Roundwood production in 1995 was estimated at 709,000 cubic meters (929,000 cubic yards), all nonconiferous logs for fuel.

25 MINING

Geological surveys have revealed a limited variety of exploitable mineral resources, including some alluvial diamonds north of Mokhotlong. Mineral production in 1994 was limited to small amounts of crushed stone, sand and gravel, clay, and diamonds.

26 FOREIGN TRADE

Lesotho has suffered from a severe trade imbalance. Its chief exports are clothing, shoes, electronics, furniture, and wool. The main imports are corn, building materials, clothing, vehicles, machinery, medicines, and petroleum products. South Africa and Swaziland provide almost all of Lesotho's imports.

27 ENERGY AND POWER

About 80% of Lesotho's electrical power is imported from South Africa. Lesotho produces no petroleum and imports virtually all petroleum products from South Africa. The Highlands Water Project calls

Selected Social Indicators

These statistics are estimates for the period 1993 to 1996. For comparison purposes, data for the United States and averages for low-income countries and high-income countries are also given.

Indicator	Lesotho	Low-income countries	High-income countries	United States
Per capita gross national product†	**$660**	$490	$25,870	$28,020
Population growth rate	**2.1%**	1.7%	0.6%	0.9%
Population growth rate in urban areas	**5.4%**	3.8%	0.9%	1.2%
Population per square kilometer of land	**67**	82	30	29
Life expectancy in years	**58**	63	77	77
Number of physicians per 1,000 people	**n.a.**	1.0	2.5	2.5
Number of pupils per teacher (primary school)	**49**	41	17	14
Illiteracy rate (15 years and older)	**29%**	34%	<5%	3%
Energy consumed per capita (kg of oil equivalent)	**n.a.**	393	5,123	7,905

† The gross national product (GNP) is the total dollar value of all goods and services produced by a country in a year. The per capita GNP is calculated by dividing a country's GNP by its population. The World Bank defines low-income countries as those with a per capita GNP of $785 or less. High-income countries have a per capita GNP of $9,636 or more. About 16% of the world's 5.7 billion people live in high-income countries, while almost 56% live in low-income countries.   n.a. = data not available   > = greater than   < = less than

Sources: World Bank, World Development Indicators on CD-ROM, Washington, D.C.: The World Bank, 1998. Central Intelligence Agency, The World Fact Book, Washington, D.C.: Government Printing Office, 1998.

for the construction of a hydroelectric plant that could meet all of Lesotho's power needs.

28 SOCIAL DEVELOPMENT

The Social Welfare Department is administered by the Ministry of Health. The Homemakers' Association, an organization long active in social welfare, has given family-management courses in remote areas under a grant from the Oxford Committee for Famine Relief (Oxfam).

The roles of women are limited by law and tradition, although a few women serve in important government roles.

29 HEALTH

Major health problems include pellagra, kwashiorkor, and other diseases that stem from poor nutrition and inadequate hygiene. In 1989–95, 21% of children under five years of age were considered malnourished. Famines have resulted from periodic droughts.

Tuberculosis and venereal diseases are also serious problems. In 1995, approximately 80% of the population had access to health care service. Estimated life expectancy in 1995 was 58 years.

A Basotho woman working in a grocery store.

30 HOUSING

The Lesotho Housing Corp. builds new housing for sale and rent, and a government-supported development program is building low-cost housing.

31 EDUCATION

In 1994, Lesotho had 1,234 primary schools. That year, there were 366,935 primary school pupils taught by 7,433 teachers, and 61,615 general secondary school students taught by 2,597 teachers. In 1992, 1,590 students were enrolled in vocational training. Education is compulsory between the ages of 6 and 13.

The University of Lesotho, at Botswana and Swaziland, was renamed the National University of Lesotho in 1975 by Prime Minister Leabua Jonathan. In 1993, all higher level institutions totaled 4,001 pupils and 492 teaching staff.

32 MEDIA

The government operates postal and telephone services. There were 12,220 telephones in 1995. Government-owned Radio Lesotho broadcasts in English and

Sesotho, and there is no television station. There were an estimated 60,000 radios and 11,000 television sets in use in 1995.

The *Mochochonono* is a weekly government paper, printed in Sesotho and English. The *Leselinyana la Lesotho* and the *Moeletsi oa Basotho* are weeklies published by the Lesotho Evangelical Church and the Roman Catholic Church.

33 TOURISM AND RECREATION

Although lacking in game, Lesotho has spectacular natural attractions in its mountains, as well as excellent trout-fishing grounds. The rock paintings near Teyateyaneng are also a potentially important tourist site.

In 1994 there were 253,310 foreign visitors, and tourism receipts totaled $17 million.

34 FAMOUS BASOTHO

Moshoeshoe (or Moshesh, 1786–1870) is acclaimed as the founder of the Basotho nation. Moshoeshoe II (1938–96) served as king from October 1966 until January 1996, when he was killed in an automobile accident. Crown Prince Letsie David Mohato (b.1964), who had served as king during his father's 1989–94 exile, returned to the throne in February 1996 as King Letsie III. Chief Leabua Jonathan (1914–87), prime minister of Lesotho from its inception until 1986, was a leader in the drive for independence.

35 BIBLIOGRAPHY

Bardill, John E., and James H. Cobbe. *Lesotho.* Boulder, Colo.: Westview, 1985.
Ferguson, James. *The Anti-politics Machine: "Development," Depoliticization, and Bureaucratic Power in Lesotho.* New York: Cambridge University Press, 1990.

LIBERIA

Republic of Liberia

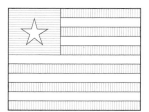

CAPITAL: Monrovia.

FLAG: The national flag, dating from 1847, consists of 11 horizontal stripes, alternately red (6) and white (5), with a single five-pointed white star on a square blue field 5 stripes deep in the upper left corner.

ANTHEM: *All Hail, Liberia, Hail.*

MONETARY UNIT: The Liberian dollar (L$) of 100 cents is established by law as equivalent to the US dollar. There are no Liberian notes. US notes in the denominations of 5, 10, 20, 50, and 100 dollars are in circulation and are legal tender. Both US and Liberian coins of 1, 5, 10, 25, and 50 cents, and 1 dollar are in circulation; in 1982, a $5 Liberian coin was issued.

WEIGHTS AND MEASURES: US and UK weights and measures are used.

HOLIDAYS: New Year's Day, 1 January; Armed Forces Day, 11 February; Decoration Day, 2d Wednesday in March; Birthday of J. J. Roberts (first president), 15 March; Fast and Prayer Day, 2d Friday in April; National Redemption Day, 12 April; Unification Day, 14 May; Independence Day, 26 July; Flag Day, 24 August; Thanksgiving Day, 1st Thursday in November; Anniversary of 1985 Coup Attempt, 12 November; President Tubman's Birthday, 29 November; Christmas, 25 December. Good Friday and Easter Monday are movable religious holidays.

TIME: GMT.

1 LOCATION AND SIZE

Located on the west coast of Africa, Liberia has an area of about 111,370 square kilometers (43,000 square miles), slightly larger than the state of Tennessee. Liberia's capital city, Monrovia, is located on the Atlantic coast.

2 TOPOGRAPHY

There are three distinct belts lying parallel to the coast: a low coastal belt, rolling hills, and a series of low mountains and plateaus. The Nimba Mountains, near the Guinea frontier, rise to 1,380 meters (4,528 feet), and the Wologizi Mountains reach a maximum of about 1,356 meters (4,450 feet). There are six principal rivers, all of which flow into the Atlantic Ocean.

3 CLIMATE

The climate is tropical with a mean temperature of 27°C (81°F). Yearly rainfall is as high as 510 centimeters (200 inches) on the coast. Most of the rainfall occurs between late April and mid-November. Between December and March, a dust-laden wind known as the harmattan blows from the Sahara Desert.

4 PLANTS AND ANIMALS

Liberia includes some of Africa's most impressive evergreen forests. There are

Geographic Profile

Geographic Features

Size ranking: 101 of 192
Highest elevation: 1,380 meters (4,528 feet) at Mount Wutuvi
Lowest elevation: Sea level at the Atlantic Ocean

Land Use†

Arable land:	1%
Permanent crops:	3%
Permanent pastures:	59%
Forests:	18%
Other:	19%

Weather††

Average annual precipitation: 200–510 centimeters (80–200 inches)
Average temperature range in January (Monrovia): 23–30°C (73–86°F)
Average temperature range in July (Monrovia): 22–27°C (72–81°F)

†*Arable land:* Land used for temporary crops, like meadows for mowing or pasture, gardens, and greenhouses. *Permanent crops:* Land cultivated with crops that occupy its use for long periods, such as cocoa, coffee, rubber, fruit and nut orchards, and vineyards. *Permanent pastures:* Land used permanently for forage crops. *Forests:* Land containing stands of trees. *Other:* Any land not specified, including built-on areas, roads, and barren land.

††Yearly rainfall is highest along the coast and decreases in areas farthest inland. The rainy season lasts from late April until mid-November.

about 235 species of trees. Fruit trees include citrus varieties, the alligator apple, papaya, mango, and avocado. Pineapples grow wild.

Elephant and buffalo, once common in Liberia, have largely disappeared, but several species of antelope are found in the interior. Wild pigs and porcupines exist in sparsely settled areas, and several members of the leopard group are also found. Among the birds are the hornbill, wild guinea fowl, cattle egret (cowbird), flamingo, and woodpecker.

5 ENVIRONMENT

Commercial logging, firewood cutting, and a government land-clearing program threaten primary forestland. Hunting and loss of habitat have decimated wildlife along the coastal plain, and there are no longer any large herds of big game in the interior. The rivers are becoming increasingly polluted from the dumping of iron ore tailings, and the coastal waters from oil residue.

6 POPULATION

The population consists of native Africans and descendants of American black settlers (also known as Liberico-Americans or Amerafricans), in a ratio of at least 30 to 1. The 1984 census reported a population of 2.1 million. The estimate for mid-1998 was 2.8 million, and a population of 3.8 million is projected for the year 2005. Monrovia, the capital, had an estimated metropolitan-area population of 962,000 in 1995.

7 MIGRATION

The Liberian civil war caused a great amount of migration in the early 1990s. As of mid-1997, there were still 210,000 Liberian refugees in Côte d'Ivoire, 420,000 in Ghana, 14,000 in Sierra Leone, and 6,000 in Nigeria. At the same time, there were 120,000 refugees from Sierra Leone in Liberia.

8 ETHNIC GROUPS

Liberia is peopled by about 28 ethnic tribes, which may be divided into three main groups based on their languages: the Mande people in the north and far west, the Kru tribes (including the Krahn) in the east and southeast, and the Mel in the northwest. About 5% of the population consists of Americo-Liberians, descendants of former slaves from the United States.

9 LANGUAGES

English is the official language, but only a minority of the people can speak or write it. The tribal people use their own languages, of which there are about 28. Of these, Vai, Bassa, and Loma can be written.

10 RELIGIONS

Liberia is officially a Christian state. The early settlers, freed American slaves, brought with them the religion of the United States' Deep South. Thus, their descendants are followers of the principal Protestant denominations, of which the largest is the Methodist Church. It is estimated that the population is 10% Christian and 20% Muslim; the remainder are followers of native religions.

11 TRANSPORTATION

In 1996 there were 10,087 kilometers (6,268 miles) of public roads and 2,323 kilometers (1,443 miles) of private roads. In 1995 there were 17,400 registered passenger autos, and 10,700 commercial vehicles.

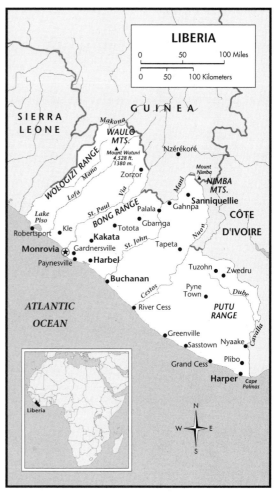

LOCATION: 4°20′ to 8°33′N; 7°22′ to 11°30′W. **BOUNDARY LENGTHS:** Guinea, 563 kilometers (350 miles); Côte d'Ivoire, 716 kilometers (445 miles); Atlantic coastline, 538 kilometers (334 miles); Sierra Leone, 306 kilometers (190 miles). **TERRITORIAL SEA LIMIT:** 200 miles.

Liberia's railways in 1996 were all owned by mining companies and used for transportation of iron ore from mines to the ports of Buchanan and Monrovia. These two deepwater ports handle over 98% of all cargo. Many foreign-owned ships are registered in Liberia because of low fees and lenient labor laws.

12 HISTORY

It is believed that many of the peoples of Liberia migrated there from the north and east between the twelfth and sixteenth centuries AD. Portuguese explorers first visited the coast in 1461, and Europeans traded with coastal tribes during the next three centuries.

Modern Liberia was founded in 1822 by freed black slaves from the United States. They were sent to Africa with the support of the American Colonization Society, a private organization whose purpose was to colonize Africa with freed American slaves. The first settlement was near where the present capital city, Monrovia, is located.

In 1847 the Republic of Liberia was established under a constitution modeled after that of the United States. Black emigration from the United States to Liberia continued until the close of the US Civil War (1861–65). Although they recognized Liberia, various European governments pushed the new country out of areas it had lawfully acquired by purchase or exploration. Pressure on Liberia's borders continued well into the twentieth century. Added to these dangers was Liberia's precarious economic position. The depression of the 1930s brought Liberia to the verge of bankruptcy. In the 1930s, Liberia's political sovereignty was also severely threatened by a scandal involving high government officials, These officials shipped Liberian laborers to the Spanish island of Fernando Póo, under conditions that resembled slave trading.

The establishment of a United States air base in Liberia during World War II (1939–45) and the building of an artificial harbor at Monrovia stimulated the country's development. William V. S. Tubman, elected president in 1944 and reelected for five additional terms, sought to unify the descendants of the original American ex-slaves and the tribal peoples of the interior. Upon Tubman's death in 1971, Vice-President William R. Tolbert, Jr., succeeded to the presidency. Having been elected without opposition in October 1975, Tolbert was inaugurated for an eight-year term in January 1976.

Doe Takes Power

Tolbert and at least 26 supporters were killed in the fighting during a military coup on 12 April 1980; 13 officials were publicly executed ten days later. The People's Redemption Council (PRC), formed to rule the country, was led by Sergeant Samuel K. Doe, who became head of state. The constitution was suspended, but a return to civilian rule was promised for 1985. In the elections held on 15 October 1985, Doe was elected president with 51% of the vote. Foreign observers declared that the elections were rigged, and most of the opposition candidates who were elected refused to take their seats.

Since late December 1989, Liberia has fallen into chaos. Insurgents (people who revolt against authority) led by Charles Taylor began a campaign to overthrow the Doe regime. Thousands of civilians were massacred by gunmen on both sides. Hundreds of thousands fled their homes. By June 1990, Doe was besieged in Monrovia. In an effort to stop the killing, a regional peacekeeping force, known as ECOMOG, entered the country and installed an interim government. Most of the ECOMOG force was supplied by Nigeria. However, on 9 September 1990, rebel forces shot their way into ECOMOG's headquarters and captured Doe, videotaping his torture and execution. On two occasions since entering the country, the ECOMOG forces prevented Charles Taylor's forces from capturing the capital, Monrovia.

The interim government was able to establish authority over most of Monrovia, but the rest of Liberia was in the hands of various factions. Despite three major peace agreements since 1990, fighting continued. Finally, in August 1995 all sides agreed to a ceasefire and set up a council of state to govern the country until elections could be held. The ceasefire only held until the year's end, when fighting resumed. In early 1996, roving gangs of heavily armed teenagers recklessly shot up Monrovia. International relief organizations became the targets of looting, since seven years of war had left the country empty of anything worth stealing.

Liberia's four main militias approved a peace plan on 8 May 1996. In August 1996 West African leaders put together a new ceasefire agreement between the warring factions and selected an interim government. Elections were finally held in July 1997 and were overseen by ECOMOG forces. ECOMOG's presence in

Photo credit: AP/Wide World Photos.

A nine-year-old boy carries his family's ration of water outside the French relief organization's Medecins Sans Frontiers (Doctors without Borders) headquarters in Monrovia.

Liberia was an important factor in ending the civil war that had killed more than 150,000 people over seven years. Charles Taylor, the man who had initially started the uprising, was elected with 66% of the vote.

13 GOVERNMENT

Under the constitution approved on 3 July 1984, Liberia is a republic modeled after the United States. Its constitution provides for a president and vice-president elected jointly by universal vote for a four-year term with a limit of two consecutive terms. The legislature is divided into a 26-member Senate and a 64-member House of Representatives.

14 POLITICAL PARTIES

Charles Taylor's National Patriotic Front of Liberia (NPFL) has gained influence since his election to the presidency in 1997. The United Liberation Movement of Liberia (ULIMO) has been identified with former Doe supporters.

15 JUDICIAL SYSTEM

Most cases originate in magistrates' courts and may be taken for appeal to one of ten circuit courts or to the highest court. More serious cases originate in the circuit courts. Traditional courts are presided over by tribal chiefs. The 1984 constitution provides for the establishment of a Supreme Court consisting of a chief justice and four associate justices. Due to the war, the judiciary did not function in most areas as of early 1997.

16 ARMED FORCES

The regular armed forces (5,000) and police are active only in parts of Monrovia. Liberia no longer has air or naval capabilities. The rebel National Patriotic Forces of Liberia number 15,000. A six-nation African peacekeeping force numbers around 6,000.

17 ECONOMY

Liberia's economy, which is primarily agricultural, is in turmoil as a result of financial mismanagement and the civil war which has divided the country into two economic zones, one centered in and around the major urban centers, the other in the countryside. Even prior to the civil war, however, Liberia faced serious financial problems. In 1988 the World Bank closed its offices in Monrovia. In March of 1990, the International Monetary Fund (IMF) threatened to expel Liberia for non-payment of its debt.

18 INCOME

Liberia's gross domestic product (GDP) in 1995 was $2.3 billion, or about $770 per person.

19 INDUSTRY

Before the civil war, Liberia's industrial sector was dominated by processing plants associated with its key agricultural outputs: rubber, palm oil, and lumber. Liberia also produced cement, plastics, shoes, recycled steel, and refined petroleum products.

During 1990–96, faction leaders and traders exploited the industrial wealth of Liberia. They used forced labor and stolen goods and fuel. The method of manufacture often harmed the environment or the ability to produce in the future. Profits from these enterprises were used to buy more weapons.

20 LABOR

Before the onslaught of civil war, the labor force totaled over 1.3 million persons. In 1997 it was estimated that 90% of the labor force was unemployed.

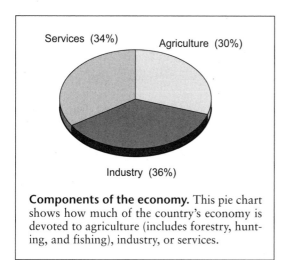

Services (34%)   Agriculture (30%)

Industry (36%)

Components of the economy. This pie chart shows how much of the country's economy is devoted to agriculture (includes forestry, hunting, and fishing), industry, or services.

21 AGRICULTURE

In 1995, agriculture engaged about 70% of the labor force on 4% of the total land area. Estimated production of field crops in 1995 included cassava, 450,000 tons; rice, 50,000 tons; and sugarcane, 234,000 tons. Rubber far outranks all other agricultural products in cash importance. The principal export crops produced by small farmers are coffee, cocoa, oil palm nuts, sugarcane, and fruits. Estimated production in 1995 was palm oil, 38,000 tons; rubber, 31,000 tons; palm kernels, 8,500 tons; and coffee, 3,000 tons. Banana production came to 82,000 tons; plantains, 45,000 tons.

22 DOMESTICATED ANIMALS

The importance of poultry farming and the marketing of eggs has increased in the 1990s. There were an estimated 4 million chickens in 1995. Liberia also has an esti-mated 210,000 sheep, 220,000 goats, 120,000 pigs, and 36,000 cattle.

23 FISHING

The fishing industry is dominated by the oceangoing trawlers of the Mesurado Fishing Co. The total Liberian catch in 1994 was estimated at 7,721 tons.

24 FORESTRY

Forests constituted 47% of the land area in 1994. National forests cover 18% of the total land area. There are about 235 timber species, of which 90 are potentially marketable. Roundwood production was estimated at 6.3 million cubic meters (8.3 million cubic yards) in 1995, with 84% burned as fuel.

25 MINING

Since December 1989, the mining industry has been severely damaged by civil war. Mining revenues came primarily from the export of iron ore. By 1991, a single iron ore mine, operated by the Iron Mining Company of Liberia (LIMCO) was one of only a few industrial operations functioning in the entire country.

26 FOREIGN TRADE

Liberia had a history of trade surpluses before the war. In 1994, exports were led by iron ore sales, accounting for 61% of total exports, followed by rubber (20%) and timber (11%). Imports were led by mineral fuels, chemicals, machinery, transportation equipment, manufactured goods, and rice and other foods. Leading purchasers of Liberian exports (1995) were Belgium-Luxembourg and Ukraine. Liberia's imports came principally from Japan and South Korea.

27 ENERGY AND POWER

The capacity of the country's electric generating plants was 332,000 kilowatts in 1991. Liberia's total production in 1994 was 465 million kilowatt hours, down from 834 million kilowatt hours in 1988. Liberia has no domestic petroleum resources. Wood accounts for about 90% of the total energy requirement. The civil war has caused severe fuel distribution problems and shortages.

28 SOCIAL DEVELOPMENT

In 1976, the National Social Security and Welfare Corp. was established to administer pensions, sickness benefits, and welfare funds. Before the civil war, the Liberian Red Cross was active in child care and welfare, as were the Antoinette Tubman Welfare Foundation and the Catherine Mills Rehabilitation Center. Today, however, virtually no social services are functioning within the country.

An estimated 10% of those who fought in the civil war were under 15 years of age. Massacres of civilians were carried out by all the major fighting factions. Many children were wounded, killed, orphaned, or abandoned.

29 HEALTH

Liberia has an average life expectancy of only 49 years. In 1992 there were an estimated 11 doctors per 100,000 people, and only about 39% of the population had access to health care services. The major causes of death are malaria and gastrointestinal disease. The World Health Organization (WHO) estimates that about 1 million people in sub-Saharan Africa are HIV positive.

30 HOUSING

The typical dwelling of the tribal people in the Liberian interior is the rondavel, a circular, one-room mud-and-wattle thatch-roofed hut, windowless and with a single low door. These rondavels are being replaced by large rectangular huts, also of mud and wattle, subdivided into two or more rooms and equipped with windows. Many of the older corrugated-iron structures in Monrovia have also been replaced with more modern dwellings.

31 EDUCATION

Although education is compulsory from ages 6 to 16, probably fewer than half of all children are in school. The adult illiteracy rate was 62%. There are three institutions of higher learning: the government-operated University of Liberia in Monrovia (established in 1862); Cuttington University College at Monrovia, an Episcopalian institution; and a three-year engineering school, the William V. S. Tubman College of Technology.

32 MEDIA

Many existing newspapers and magazines ceased publication when the Doe regime was overthrown in 1990. Since the following year, a number of new ones have been begun printing, including *The Inquirer,*

Selected Social Indicators

These statistics are estimates for the period 1993 to 1996. For comparison purposes, data for the United States and averages for low-income countries and high-income countries are also given.

Indicator	Liberia	Low-income countries	High-income countries	United States
Per capita gross national product†	$770	$490	$25,870	$28,020
Population growth rate	2.8%	1.7%	0.6%	0.9%
Population growth rate in urban areas	4.1%	3.8%	0.9%	1.2%
Population per square kilometer of land	29	82	30	29
Life expectancy in years	49	63	77	77
Number of physicians per 1,000 people	<0.1	1.0	2.5	2.5
Number of pupils per teacher (primary school)	n.a.	41	17	14
Illiteracy rate (15 years and older)	62%	34%	<5%	3%
Energy consumed per capita (kg of oil equivalent)	40	393	5,123	7,905

† The gross national product (GNP) is the total dollar value of all goods and services produced by a country in a year. The per capita GNP is calculated by dividing a country's GNP by its population. The World Bank defines low-income countries as those with a per capita GNP of $785 or less. High-income countries have a per capita GNP of $9,636 or more. About 16% of the world's 5.7 billion people live in high-income countries, while almost 56% live in low-income countries.   n.a. = data not available   > = greater than   < = less than

Sources: World Bank, *World Development Indicators on CD-ROM,* Washington, D.C.: The World Bank, 1998. Central Intelligence Agency, *The World Fact Book,* Washington, D.C.: Government Printing Office, 1998.

New Times, and *The Patriot.* The number of radio receivers increased from 152,000 in 1969 to 622,000 in 1995. The first television station was opened early in 1964; although government owned, it was partly commercial. In 1995 there were about 51,000 television sets.

33 TOURISM AND RECREATION

Continued civil unrest has had an adverse effect on tourism. Several hotels in or near Monrovia are suitable for tourists, and several missionary organizations accommodate visitors in the interior.

34 FAMOUS LIBERIANS

Joseph Jenkins Roberts (1809–76) was Liberia's first and later its sixth president (1848–56, 1872–76). The national heroine is Matilda Newport, who helped to repel an attack on the first struggling settlement. Among white Americans who went to Liberia to assist the early black settlers were Jehudi Ashmun (1794–1828) and Ralph Randolph Gurley (1797–1872). William Vacanarat Shadrach Tubman (1895–1971) was president of Liberia from 1944 until 1971. William Richard Tolbert, Jr. (1913–80) succeeded Tubman as president. He was killed in the 1980 coup led by Samuel Kanyon Doe (1950–90), who became commander-in-chief. Doe was in turn tortured and killed in 1990 by rebels loyal to Charles G. Taylor (b.1948), the leader of the faction that gained control during the civil war. Taylor was elected president in 1997.

35 BIBLIOGRAPHY

Adibe, Clement. *Managing Arms in Peace Processes: Liberia*. New York: United Nations, 1996.

American University. *Liberia: A Country Study*. 3d ed. Washington, D.C.: Government Printing Office, 1984.

Gershoni, Yekutiel. *Black Colonialism: The Americo-Liberian Struggle for the Hinterland*. Boulder, Colo.: Westview, 1984.

Riley, Stephen P. *Liberia and Sierra Leone: Anarchy or Peace in West Africa?* London, England: Research Institute for the Study of Conflict and Terrorism, 1996.

LIBYA

Socialist People's Libyan Arab Jamahiriya

Al-Jamahiriyah al-'Arabiyah al-Libiyah ash-Sha'biyah al-Ishtirakiyah

CAPITAL: Tripoli (Tarabulus).

FLAG: The national flag is plain green.

ANTHEM: *Almighty God.*

MONETARY UNIT: The Libyan dinar (LD) of 1,000 dirhams is a paper currency. There are coins of 1, 5, 10, 20, 50, and 100 dirhams, and notes of ¼, ½, 1, 5, and 10 dinars. LD1 = $2.75482 (or $1 = LD0.363).

WEIGHTS AND MEASURES: The metric system is the legal standard, but some local weights and measures are used.

HOLIDAYS: UK Evacuation Day, 28 March; US Evacuation Day, 11 June; Anniversary of the Revolution, 1 September; Constitution Day, 7 October. Muslim religious holidays include 'Id al-Fitr, 'Id al-'Adha', the 1st of Muharram, and Milad an-Nabi.

TIME: 2 PM = noon GMT.

1 LOCATION AND SIZE

Situated on the coast of North Africa, Libya is the fourth-largest country on the continent, with an area of 1,759,540 square kilometers (679,362 square miles), slightly larger than the state of Alaska. Libya's capital city, Tripoli, is located on the Mediterranean coast.

2 TOPOGRAPHY

Libya forms part of the North African plateau extending from the Atlantic Ocean to the Red Sea. The highest point is Bette Peak, a 2,266-meter (7,434-foot) peak in the extreme south. The chief geographical areas are a series of terraces along the coastal plain near Tunisia; a rugged coastline in the eastern third of the country; a barren area along the Gulf of Sidra; and a series of depressions, with occasional oases in the southwest.

3 CLIMATE

The climate has marked seasonal variations influenced by both the Mediterranean Sea and the desert. Summer temperatures range between 27–46°C (81–115°F). The ghibli, a hot, dry desert wind, can change temperatures by 17–22°C (30–40°F) in both summer and winter. Rain falls generally in a short winter period and frequently causes floods. Evaporation is high, and severe droughts are common. The Sahara Desert has less than 5 centimeters (2 inches) of rain a year.

4 PLANTS AND ANIMALS

The primary plant is the deadly carrot (*Thapsia garganica*). Other plants are various cultivated fruit trees, date palms, junipers, and olive and mastic trees. Goats and cattle are found in the extreme north. In the south, sheep and camels are numerous.

Geographic Profile

Geographic Features

Size ranking: 16 of 192
Highest elevation: 2,266 meters (7,434 feet) at Bette Peak (Bikku Bitti)
Lowest elevation: −47 meters (−154 feet) at Sabkhat Ghuzayyil

Land Use†

Arable land:	1%
Permanent crops:	0%
Permanent pastures:	8%
Forests:	0%
Other:	91%

Weather††

Average annual precipitation: 25.3 centimeters (10.0 inches)
Average temperature in January: 10.9°C (51.6°F)
Average temperature in July: 27.1°C (80.8°F)

†*Arable land:* Land used for temporary crops, like meadows for mowing or pasture, gardens, and greenhouses. *Permanent crops:* Land cultivated with crops that occupy its use for long periods, such as cocoa, coffee, rubber, fruit and nut orchards, and vineyards. *Permanent pastures:* Land used permanently for forage crops. *Forests:* Land containing stands of trees. *Other:* Any land not specified, including built-on areas, roads, and barren land.

††The measurements for precipitation and average temperature were taken at weather stations closest to the country's largest city. Precipitation and average temperature can vary significantly within a country, due to factors such as latitude, altitude, coastal proximity, and wind patterns.

5 ENVIRONMENT

The depletion of underground water, as a result of overuse in agriculture and water pollution, is a significant environmental problem in Libya. The combined impact of sewage, oil by-products, and industrial waste threatens the nation's coast. The desertification of existing fertile areas is being combated by the planting of trees as windbreaks. In 1994, endangered species in Libya included the Mediterranean monk seal. The leopard and slender-horned gazelle are extinct in Libya.

6 POPULATION

The population at the time of the 1984 census was 3.6 million. The population in 1998 was estimated at 5.7 million by the US Bureau of the Census and at 6 million by the United Nations. A population of 7.3 million was projected for the year 2005 by the US Bureau of the Census, which estimated the average annual growth rate at 3.4% during 1990–2000. The two chief cities, Tripoli and Banghazi, had populations of 1.7 million and 804,000, respectively, in 1995.

7 MIGRATION

In 1992, the foreign population was estimated at 2 million, half of them Egyptian, and 600,000 from South Korea, the Philippines, Thailand, and Vietnam. About 100,000 Libyans were in exile in the mid-1980s. The nomadic inhabitants of Libya follow regular patterns of migration; nomadic tribes in the south normally ignore international frontiers. Libya had about 3,000 refugees in 1996 from Sudan, Somalia, Eritrea, and Ethiopia.

8 ETHNIC GROUPS

Arabs started arriving in the seventh century AD, displacing or assimilating their Berber predecessors. The Fezzan has a mixture of Arabs, Berbers, and black Africans from regions to the south. About 10,000 nomadic Tuareg live in the southwestern desert.

LIBYA

LOCATION: 19°30′ to 33°N; 9°30′ to 25°E. **BOUNDARY LENGTHS:** Mediterranean coastline, 1,770 kilometers (1,100 miles); Egypt, 1,115 kilometers (693 miles); Sudan, 383 kilometers (238 miles); Chad, 1,054 kilometers (655 miles); Niger, 354 kilometers (220 miles); Algeria, 982 kilometers (610 miles); Tunisia, 459 kilometers (285 miles). **TERRITORIAL SEA LIMIT:** 12 miles, but all of the Gulf of Sidra south of 32°30′ is claimed.

9 LANGUAGES

Arabic is the official language; since 1969, its use in daily life, even by foreigners, has been encouraged by government decree. English, which is also used in some government publications, has replaced Italian as the second language. Berber is spoken by small communities.

10 RELIGIONS

In 1990, 97% of Libyans were estimated to be Sunni Muslims. Under the 1969 constitution, Islam is Libya's official religion, but freedom for other religions is guaranteed. There were about 48,000 Orthodox, Roman Catholic, and Protestant Christians in 1985.

11 TRANSPORTATION

Transportation varies from dirt tracks suitable for camels and donkeys to a coastal highway extending for 1,822 kilometers (1,132 miles) from the Tunisian to the Egyptian border. In all, there were 19,189 kilometers (11,923 miles) of roads in 1995. That same year there were 450,000 private cars and 322,000 commercial vehicles registered in the country. Libya's two railway lines were closed down in the early 1960s. The main ports are Tripoli, Banghazi, Qasr Ahmad (the port for Misratah), and Tobruk. Libya's two international airports are Tripoli Airport and Benina Airport.

12 HISTORY

The Berbers entered what is now Libya in about 2000 BC, presumably from southwestern Asia. Phoenician seafarers, who arrived early in the first millennium BC, founded settlements along the coast, including one that became Tripoli. Around the seventh century BC, Greek colonists settled in the Libyan desert known as Cyrenaica. By the fourth century BC, some parts of Libya had fallen to Carthage and others to Egypt. When the Romans defeated Carthage in the Punic Wars of the third and second centuries BC, they occupied the regions around Tripoli. In 96 BC, they forced Egypt to surrender Cyrenaica, and Roman influence later extended far south.

Libya became very prosperous under Roman rule. However, with the decline of Rome, western Libya fell in the fifth century AD to Germanic Vandal invaders, who ruled from Carthage. In the sixth century, the Byzantines conquered the Vandals and ruled the coastal regions of Libya until the Arab conquest of the seventh century. The Arabs intermixed with the Berbers, who were gradually absorbed into the Muslim Arab culture.

Western Libya was administered by Tunisian peoples in the ninth and tenth centuries. During the eleventh century, invasions by two nomadic Arab groups destroyed many of the urban and agricultural areas. Normans from Sicily occupied Tripoli and surrounding regions in 1145 but were soon displaced by the Almohads of Morocco; during the thirteenth century, the Hafsids of Tunisia ruled western Libya. The eastern regions remained subject to Egyptian dynasties. In the sixteenth century, Spanish invaders seized parts of the coast. The Ottoman Turks occupied the coastal regions in 1551, ruling the country until 1711, when Ahmad Qara-

Tens of thousands of Libyan supporters gather at the Green Square in Tripoli, Libya to celebrate the anniversary of the Libyan revolution. One person holds a picture of Libya's leader, Mu'ammar al-Qadhafi.

manli, of Turkish origin, won partially independent status for the region. The Qaramanlis ruled until 1835, when the Ottomans again assumed control.

World War II and Independence

In September 1911, the Italians invaded Libya, meeting fierce resistance from both Turks and indigenous Libyans. The Italian struggle for control of the region continued until 1932, when its conquest was completed. In World War II (1939–45), Libya became a main battleground for Allied and Axis forces, until it was occupied by victorious British and Free French troops. The Treaty of 1947 between Italy and the Allies ended Italian rule in Libya.

When the Allies could not decide upon the country's future, Libya's fate was left to the United Nations. On 21 November 1949, the United Nations General Assembly voted that Libya should become an independent state. On 24 December 1951, Libya gained independence, with Muhammad Idris al-Mahdi as-Sanusi as king.

Qadhafi and the Libyan Revolution

On 1 September 1969, a secret army organization, the Free Unionist Officers, deposed the king and proclaimed a republican regime. On 8 September, the Revolutionary Command Council (RCC) announced the formation of a civilian government. This government resigned on 16

January 1970, and a new cabinet was formed under Colonel Mu'ammar al-Qadhafi, chairman of the RCC.

Qadhafi has sought to make Libya the axis of a unified Arab nation, but relations with many Arab nations, including Egypt and Tunisia, have often been tense. Qadhafi has been equally active in Africa, annexing the disputed Aouzou Strip from Chad in 1973, and supporting the failing regimes of Uganda's Idi Amin in 1979, and Chad's Goukouni Oueddei in 1980. Qadhafi has also been accused of supporting subversive plots in such countries as Morocco, Niger, Sudan, and Egypt. He has also been accused of providing material support to the Irish Republican Army, the Muslim rebels in the Philippines, and to Japanese and German terrorists.

In 1982, the United States charged Qadhafi with supporting international terrorism. In January 1986, the United States ordered all Americans to leave Libya and cut off all economic ties. On 15 April, following a West Berlin bomb attack in which United States servicemen were victims, United States warplanes bombed targets in Tripoli and Banghazi.

Qadhafi has survived several reported assassination and coup attempts (1984 and 1993). Opposition from Islamic groups prompted him to crack down on militants in 1993. His most serious challenge has been the tough sanctions imposed on Libya by the United Nations Security Council. These sanctions were imposed after he refused to surrender two men suspected in the terrorist bombing of a Pan American passenger jet over Lockerbie, Scotland, in 1988.

In September 1995, Libya began deporting thousands of Palestinian, Sudanese, and Egyptian workers. Qadhafi claimed the foreigners were being deported to create jobs for Libyans. However, Qadhafi stated that many of those being deported were Islamic militant "infiltrators" pretending to be migrant workers.

In 1996, it was believed that Libya was almost finished building the world's largest underground chemical weapons plant at Tarhunah near Tripoli. Intelligence officials from the United States claimed that the facility is capable of producing tons of poison gas per day. The Libyan government claimed that the building was a water irrigation system.

13 GOVERNMENT

The people theoretically exercise their authority through a system of people's congresses and committees. Qadhafi, as "Leader of the Revolution," however, is the de facto head of state. He also is the commander of the armed forces and virtually all power is concentrated in him and his close advisers.

14 POLITICAL PARTIES

Political parties have not played an effective role in Libya's history. In 1971, the RCC (Revolutionary Command Council) founded the Libyan Arab Socialist Union as an alternative to political parties. It was viewed as an organization to promote national unity but has functioned in a minor capacity since 1977.

15 JUDICIAL SYSTEM

Minor civil and commercial cases may be heard by a sitting judge in each village and town. Other cases are heard initially by courts of first instance, and appeals may be taken to provincial courts of appeal. There is also a Supreme Court, consisting of a president and judges appointed by the GPC. In 1981, the private practice of law was abolished and all lawyers became employees of the secretariat of justice. Since 1981, revolutionary committees have been encouraged to conduct public trials without legal safeguards.

16 ARMED FORCES

In 1995, the army had 3,500 personnel organized into 28 brigades, about half armored, half infantry; armaments included 2,210 tanks, all made in the former Soviet Union. The navy had 8,000 personnel and 65 vessels, including 4 Russian submarines. The air force had 22,000 personnel, with 420 combat aircraft and 52 combat helicopters. The military budget was estimated at $1.4 billion in 1995, or 7% of the gross domestic product (GDP).

17 ECONOMY

Until the late 1950s, Libya was one of the poorest countries in the world. But with the discovery of the Zaltan oil field in 1959, the economic horizons of the country were dramatically enlarged. Production has fallen since 1970, but its value has increased, and Libya remains one of the world's leading oil producers. Until the late 1950s, about 80% of the population was engaged in agriculture and animal farming; in 1989, however, only 19% of the labor force was engaged in agricultural pursuits.

A massive water pipeline project, called the Great Manmade River (GMR) project began in the early 1990s. The GMR will carry water in a huge 267-mile-long pipeline from 225 underground wells to irrigate 1.2 million acres of land used to grow cereal crops. The public works project is expected to cost $25 billion. There is concern among United States intelligence officials that the GMR might be used to shuttle troops or weapons underground in order to avoid detection.

Since the 1992 UN-imposed air embargo, many large projects have been postponed because of budget restrictions. Libya's isolation has slowed the pace of oil exploration through the absence of major foreign oil companies. Lack of outlets is limiting the development of refineries, petrochemicals, and gas facilities.

18 INCOME

In 1995 Libya's gross national product (GNP) was between $3,036 and $9,385 per person.

19 INDUSTRY

Industry accounts for 55% of the gross domestic product (GDP). Libyan manufacturing industries had been developing significantly since the early 1960s, but have fallen far behind the petroleum sector of the economy. Total refinery capacity in 1996 was about 348,400 barrels per day.

A large methanol, ammonia, and urea plant is at Marsa al-Burayqah, and a major plant producing ethylene, propylene, and butene was opened in 1987. The $6 billion iron and steel complex at Misratah began operations in 1990; crude steel production totaled 874,000 tons in 1994. Libya's other manufacturing industries are small, lightly capitalized, and devoted primarily to the processing of local agricultural products and to textiles, building materials, and basic consumer items.

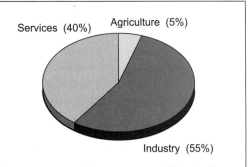

Components of the economy. This pie chart shows how much of the country's economy is devoted to agriculture (includes forestry, hunting, and fishing), industry, or services.

20 LABOR

According to figures for 1996, the total labor force was 1.2 million, plus 161,000 non-Libyans. About 27% were employed in services; 31% in mining, manufacturing, construction, and utilities; 18% in agriculture, forestry, hunting and fishing; and 24% in government. Foreign workers, who do much of the blue-collar and technical work, are not treated with equality under Libyan labor law, and may only stay in the country for the duration of their employment contracts. The largest employer is the government, which operates public utilities, public works, several banks, the port and harbor organizations, and other enterprises.

21 AGRICULTURE

Agriculture is the only economic sector in which private ownership is still important. Virtually all crops are grown for domestic consumption. Nevertheless, most agricultural products must be imported. Estimated agricultural output in 1995, in tons, included tomatoes, 135,000; wheat, 167,000; potatoes, 127,000; barley, 148,000; and onions, 75,000. The 1995 production of fruits, in tons, included watermelons, 180,000; oranges, 80,000; dates, 68,000; and olives, 62,000. A government agency markets farm produce and has authority to operate cooperatives and farms. Libya is investing a significant share of national revenues in agriculture in the hope of someday becoming agriculturally self-sufficient.

22 DOMESTICATED ANIMALS

The livestock population of Libya in 1995 included 4.4 million sheep, 800,000 goats, 100,000 head of cattle, 130,000 camels, 22,000 horses, 55,000 donkeys, and 17 million chickens. Private dairy farms are allowed to operate, but their milk has to be sold to the state. The government maintains large poultry farms. Livestock products in 1995 included 179,000 tons of meat, 33,000 tons of eggs, and 85,000 tons of cow milk.

23 FISHING

Libya's excellent fishing grounds contain tuna, sardines, and other fish, but the industry has failed to meet increasing domestic demand. The catch was 8,503 tons in 1994.

24 FORESTRY

The only important forest areas in Libya are shrubby juniper growths in the east. During the 1980s, reforestation was proceeding at the rate of 32,000 hectares (79,000 acres) per year. In 1995, roundwood removals were estimated at 651,000 cubic meters (853,000 cubic yards), of which 536,000 cubic meters (702,000 cubic yards) were used for fuel.

25 MINING

In addition to oil and natural gas, Libya has large reserves of iron ore. There is also potash, limestone (for cement), and marine salt. Estimated production in 1994 included lime, 260,000 tons; gypsum, 180,000 tons; and sulfur, 14,000 tons.

26 FOREIGN TRADE

Libya has long enjoyed a favorable trade balance because of exports of crude oil. In a typical year, oil production and sales account for 95% of Libya's revenues. Oil exports were valued at $7–8 billion in 1995. The most important imports are foodstuffs, machinery, transport equipment, iron and steel products, and basic manufactured goods.

In 1995, the countries of the European Union purchased 82% of Libya's exports

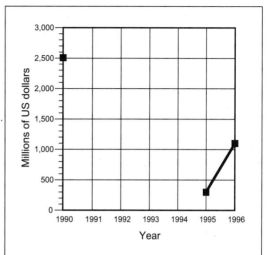

Yearly balance of trade measured in millions of US dollars. The balance of trade is the difference between what a country sells to other countries (its exports) and what it buys (its imports). If a country imports more than it exports, it has a negative balance of trade (a trade deficit). If exports exceed imports, there is a positive balance of trade (a trade surplus).

and provided about 68% of its imports. The United States halted all trade with Libya in January 1986.

27 ENERGY AND POWER

Oil production has fallen since 1970, first because of conservation and political decisions, and later because of falling demand for Libya's high-quality (but also high-cost) oil. From the 1970 peak of 157.4 million tons, production fell to 67.9 million tons by 1995, second highest in Africa. Crude petroleum reserves were estimated at 3.9 billion tons in 1996.

Reserves of natural gas were estimated at 1.3 trillion cubic meters (46 trillion cubic feet). Production was 6.2 billion

Selected Social Indicators

These statistics are estimates for the period 1993 to 1996. For comparison purposes, data for the United States and averages for low-income countries and high-income countries are also given.

Indicator	Libya	Low-income countries	High-income countries	United States
Per capita gross national product†	n.a.	$490	$25,870	$28,020
Population growth rate	2.4%	1.7%	0.6%	0.9%
Population growth rate in urban areas	3.0%	3.8%	0.9%	1.2%
Population per square kilometer of land	3	82	30	29
Life expectancy in years	68	63	77	77
Number of physicians per 1,000 people	n.a.	1.0	2.5	2.5
Number of pupils per teacher (primary school)	13	41	17	14
Illiteracy rate (15 years and older)	24%	34%	<5%	3%
Energy consumed per capita (kg of oil equivalent)	3,129	393	5,123	7,905

† The gross national product (GNP) is the total dollar value of all goods and services produced by a country in a year. The per capita GNP is calculated by dividing a country's GNP by its population. The World Bank defines low-income countries as those with a per capita GNP of $785 or less. High-income countries have a per capita GNP of $9,636 or more. About 16% of the world's 5.7 billion people live in high-income countries, while almost 56% live in low-income countries.   n.a. = data not available   > = greater than   < = less than

Sources: World Bank, World Development Indicators on CD-ROM, Washington, D.C.: The World Bank, 1998. Central Intelligence Agency, The World Fact Book, Washington, D.C.: Government Printing Office, 1998.

cubic meters (219 billion cubic feet) in 1995.

28 SOCIAL DEVELOPMENT

By law, all employees are entitled to sickness, invalid, disability, death, and maternity benefits, unemployment payments, and pensions. Profit sharing, free medical care and education, and subsidized food are other social welfare benefits.

Women were granted full legal rights in 1969, but few women work outside the home.

Under Libyan law, an individual may be arrested and detained without a specific charge. Political dissenters are imprisoned.

Citizens do not have the right to legal counsel or to fair public trials.

29 HEALTH

In 1993, 100% of Libya's population had access to health care services. Widespread diseases include typhoid, venereal diseases, and infectious hepatitis. With the assistance of the World Health Organization (WHO), Libya has eradicated malaria, once a major problem. The average life expectancy was 68 years.

30 HOUSING

Increasing urbanization has created slum conditions in the major cities. There have been slum clearance and building projects since 1954, but the housing deficit has not yet been met. Real estate was the main area of private investment until 1978, when most tenants were made owners of their residences.

31 EDUCATION

The government has invested heavily in education, which is free at all levels. School is compulsory from the age of 6 until 15. Illiteracy was estimated at 24% in 1995 (males, 12.1% and females, 37%). In 1993, primary schools had 1.4 million pupils. Secondary schools had 310,556 pupils in 1992.

In 1976, the University of Libya at Tripoli was renamed Al-Fatah University, and the University of Libya at Banghazi was renamed the University of Garyounis. The Bright Star University of Technology at Marsa al-Brega was founded in 1981. Total enrollment at all higher level institutions was 72,899 in 1991.

Photo credit: Libyan Mission to the UN/EPD Photos.

Libya's leader, Mu'ammar al-Qadhafi.

32 MEDIA

Postal, telephone, and wireless services are government-owned and -operated. In 1995 there were 500,000 telephones, 1.1 million radios, and 485,000 television sets in use.

The major newspaper is *Al-Shams,* a government-owned daily published in Tripoli, with a circulation of about 40,000. *Al-Zahf al-Akhdar,* published by the revolutionary committees, had a 1995 circulation of 35,000.

33 TOURISM AND RECREATION

Tourist attractions in Libya are its good climate, extensive beaches, and magnificent Greek and Roman ruins. However, tourist facilities are not widely available, because tourism has mostly been discouraged during the tenure of Qadhafi. It suffered a further blow with the 1992 imposition of United Nations sanctions related to the 1988 bombing of a Pan Am jet over Lockerbie, Scotland. However, the government has recently taken steps to attract visitors, including plans to build a hotel on the island of Farwa near the Tunisian border. In 1994, Libya had 1.5 million tourist arrivals and receipts of $7 million.

34 FAMOUS LIBYANS

As Roman emperor, Septimius Severus (r.193–211) was responsible for initiating an extensive building program at his native Leptis Magna. Muhammad Idris al-Mahdi as-Sanusi (1890–1983) was Libya's first king, ruling the country from its independence until he was deposed in 1969.

Colonel Mu'ammar Muhammad al-Qadhafi (b.1942) has been the actual ruler of the country since that time.

35 BIBLIOGRAPHY

Ahmida, Ali Abdullatif. *The Making of Modern Libya: State Formation, Colonization, and Resistance, 1830–1932.* Albany: State University of New York Press, 1994.

Brill, M. *Libya.* Chicago: Children's Press, 1987.

Gottfried, Ted. *Libya: Desert Land in Conflict.* Brookfield, Conn.: The Millbrook Press, 1994.

Metz, Helen Chapin, ed. *Libya, a Country Study.* 4th ed. Washington, D.C.: Library of Congress, 1989.

LIECHTENSTEIN

Principality of Liechtenstein

Fürstentum Liechtenstein

CAPITAL: Vaduz.

FLAG: The national flag is divided into two horizontal rectangles, blue above red. On the blue rectangle, near the hoist, is the princely crown in gold.

ANTHEM: *Oben am jungen Rhein (On the Banks of the Young Rhine)*.

MONETARY UNIT: The Swiss franc (SwFr) of 100 centimes, or rappen, has been in use since February 1921. There are coins of 1, 5, 10, 20, and 50 centimes and 1, 2, and 5 francs, and notes of 10, 20, 50, 100, 500, and 1,000 francs. SwFr1 = $0.7092 (or $1 = SwFr1.41).

WEIGHTS AND MEASURES: The metric system is the legal standard.

HOLIDAYS: New Year's Day, 1 January; Epiphany, 6 January; Candlemas, 2 February; St. Joseph's Day, 19 March; Labor Day, 1 May; Assumption, 15 August; Nativity of Our Lady, 8 September; All Saints' Day, 1 November; Immaculate Conception, 8 December; Christmas, 25 December; St. Stephen's Day, 26 December. Movable religious holidays include Good Friday, Easter Monday, Ascension, Whitmonday, and Corpus Christi.

TIME: 1 PM = noon GMT.

1 LOCATION AND SIZE

Liechtenstein is a landlocked country in the Rhine (Rhein) River Valley. The fourth-smallest country in Europe, the principality has an area of 160 square kilometers (61.8 square miles), about 0.9 times the size of Washington, D.C. Liechtenstein's capital city, Vaduz, is located in the western part of the country.

2 TOPOGRAPHY

Liechtenstein is divided into a fairly narrow area of level land bordering the right bank of the Rhine River and an upland and mountainous region occupying the remainder of the country; the level land occupies about two-fifths of the total surface area.

3 CLIMATE

The annual lowland temperature varies between −4.5°C (24°F) in January and 19.9°C (68°F) in July. Late frost and prolonged dry periods are rare. Average annual precipitation is 105 centimeters (41 inches).

4 PLANTS AND ANIMALS

In the higher mountain reaches are such alpine plants as gentian, alpine rose, and edelweiss. Common trees include the red beech, sycamore, maple, alder, larch, and various conifers. Native mammals include the deer, fox, badger, and chamois. Birds, including ravens and eagles, number about 120 species.

5 ENVIRONMENT

All wastewater is purified before being discharged into the Rhine River. The great horned owl is now rare, and the European otter has become extinct.

6 POPULATION

The census of 1990 reported a population of 28,877. The 1998 estimated population was 31,700. The overall population density as of 1998 was 198 persons per square kilometer (513 persons per square mile). In 1995, the Vaduz area had a population of 6,000.

7 MIGRATION

There were 12,000 foreign residents in Liechtenstein in 1996, mostly Swiss. Nearly 6,900 Austrians and Swiss commute to Liechtenstein every day.

8 ETHNIC GROUPS

The native population, accounting for 62.5% of the 1991 total, is described as being chiefly of Alemannic stock. Alemannic describes people from Switzerland and southwestern Germany. German-speakers from Switzerland and Austria are the main immigrant groups.

9 LANGUAGES

German is the official language. The population speaks in the Alemannic dialect that is also heard in Switzerland and southwestern Germany.

10 RELIGIONS

The state religion is Roman Catholicism, to which about 87% of the population

Geographic Profile

Geographic Features

Size ranking: 187 of 192
Highest elevation: 2,599 meters (8,527 feet) at Grauspitz (Vorder-Grauspitz)
Lowest elevation: 430 meters (1,411 feet) at Ruggleller Riet

Land Use

Arable land:	25%
Permanent pastures:	38%
Forests:	19%
Other:	18%

Weather

Average annual precipitation: 105 centimeters (41.3 inches)
Average temperature in January: –4.5°C (24°F)
Average temperature in July: 19.9°C (68°F)

belongs. In 1992, 7.9% of the population was Protestant, while 5.8% was of other denominations.

11 TRANSPORTATION

Postal buses are the chief means of public transportation both within the country and to Austria and Switzerland. A tunnel, 740 meters (2,428 feet) in length, connects the Samina River Valley with the Rhine River Valley.

In 1991, there were some 131 kilometers (81 miles) of main roads. A major highway runs through the principality, linking Austria and Switzerland. The nearest airport is in Zürich, Switzerland.

12 HISTORY

The territory now occupied by the Principality of Liechtenstein was known as Lower Rhaetia in the medieval period. The County of Vaduz (the present-day capital) was formally established in 1342, and the

LIECHTENSTEIN

0   2   4 Miles

0   2   4 Kilometers

Bangs
Ruggell
Salez
Schellenberg
Tisis
Frastanz
Gamprin
Mauren
Eschen
Motten
Gurtis
Planken
AUSTRIA
RHEIN VALLEY
Schaan
Rhein
Haupt Kanal
Vaduz
Samina
SWITZERLAND
ALPS
Triesenberg
Meng
Triesen
Malbun
Rhein
Balzers
Vorder-
Grauspitz
8,527 ft.
2599 m.

SWITZERLAND

Liechtenstein

N
W   E
S

LOCATION: 47°3′ to 47°14′N; 9°29′ to 9°38′E.
BOUNDARY LENGTHS: Austria, 34.9 kilometers (21.7 miles); Switzerland, 41.1 kilometers (25.5 miles).

Lordship of Schellenberg, in the north, was added to the area in 1434.

During the Thirty Years' War (1618–48), the area was invaded first by Austrian troops and then, in 1647, by the Swedes. The principality received its present name when Prince Johann Adam of Liechten- stein purchased first Schellenberg (1699) and then Vaduz (1712) from the ruling von Hohenems family.

The Principality of Liechtenstein was created on 23 January 1719 by act of Holy Roman Emperor Charles VI, who con- firmed the rule of Prince Anton-Florian, Johann Adam's successor, under the title of Prince von und zu Liechtenstein.

In 1815, following the downfall of Napoleon Bonaparte, Liechtenstein joined the newly formed Germanic Confedera- tion. In 1866, the Confederation was dissolved and Liechtenstein's constitu- tional ties to other German states came to an end.

From 1852 to the end of World War I (1914–18), Liechtenstein was closely tied economically to Austria. After Austria's defeat in the war, Liechtenstein sought closer ties with its other neighbor, Switzer- land. A treaty concluded in 1923 provided for a customs union and the use of Swiss currency.

Liechtenstein (like Switzerland) re- mained neutral in World War II, as it had in World War I. The postwar decades have been marked by political stability and out- standing economic growth. On 26 August 1984, Franz Josef II, who succeeded his granduncle, Franz I, in 1938, handed over executive authority to his eldest son and heir, Crown Prince Hans Adam.

Liechtenstein has sought further inte- gration into the world community. The country was admitted to the United Nations in September 1991. In 1995 Liechtenstein became a member of the

European Economic Area (an organization associated with the European Union).

13 GOVERNMENT

Liechtenstein is a constitutional monarchy ruled by the hereditary princes of the house of Liechtenstein. The constitution provides for a single-chamber parliament (Landtag) of 25 members elected for four years. The prince appoints the prime minister on the recommendation of parliament. Liechtenstein is divided into 11 communes (Gemeinden) for administrative purposes.

14 POLITICAL PARTIES

The two principal parties are the Fatherland Union (Vaterländische Union—VU) and the Progressive Citizens' Party (Fortschrittliche Bürgerpartei—FBP).

15 JUDICIAL SYSTEM

Courts that function under sole Liechtenstein jurisdiction are the County Court (Landgericht), which decides minor civil cases and criminal offenses; the juvenile court; and the Schöffengericht, a court for misdemeanors.

16 ARMED FORCES

Since 1868, no military forces have been maintained in Liechtenstein.

17 ECONOMY

Despite its small size and limited national resources, Liechtenstein has developed since the 1940s from a mainly agricultural to an industrialized country and a prosperous center of trade and tourism.

Photo credit: Corel Corporation.
The Alps cover much of eastern Liechtenstein.

18 INCOME

In 1995, Liechtenstein's gross domestic product (GDP) was $630 million in current US dollars, or $22,300 per person.

19 INDUSTRY

The industry of Liechtenstein, limited by shortages of raw materials, is primarily devoted to small-scale production of precision items. The output includes optical lenses, high-vacuum pumps, heating equipment, electron microscopes, and electronic measuring and control devices.

Selected Social Indicators

These statistics are estimates for the period 1993 to 1996. For comparison purposes, data for the United States and averages for low-income countries and high-income countries are also given.

Indicator	Liechtenstein	Low-income countries	High-income countries	United States
Per capita gross national product†	n.a.	$490	$25,870	$28,020
Population growth rate	1.1%	1.7%	0.6%	0.9%
Population growth rate in urban areas	n.a.	3.8%	0.9%	1.2%
Population per square kilometer of land	198	82	30	29
Life expectancy in years	79	63	77	77
Number of physicians per 1,000 people	2.5	1.0	2.5	2.5
Number of pupils per teacher (primary school)	16	41	17	14
Illiteracy rate (15 years and older)	<1%	34%	<5%	3%
Energy consumed per capita (kg of oil equivalent)	n.a.	393	5,123	7,905

† The gross national product (GNP) is the total dollar value of all goods and services produced by a country in a year. The per capita GNP is calculated by dividing a country's GNP by its population. The World Bank defines low-income countries as those with a per capita GNP of $785 or less. High-income countries have a per capita GNP of $9,636 or more. About 16% of the world's 5.7 billion people live in high-income countries, while almost 56% live in low-income countries.   n.a. = data not available   > = greater than   < = less than

Sources: World Bank, *World Development Indicators on CD-ROM,* Washington, D.C.: The World Bank, 1998. Central Intelligence Agency, *The World Fact Book,* Washington, D.C.: Government Printing Office, 1998.

20 LABOR

In 1990, there were 19,905 persons in the labor force, of whom 6,885 commuted to work from Switzerland and Austria. The domestic labor force was estimated at 7,500 in 1994. Unemployment in 1996 was 1.5%.

21 AGRICULTURE

In the Rhine Valley, the chief vegetables are corn, potatoes, and garden produce. On gradual mountain slopes, a variety of grapes and orchard fruits are grown.

22 DOMESTICATED ANIMALS

Alpine pasture covers over 35% of the total land area. In 1995, cattle numbered about 6,000; hogs, 3,000; and sheep, 3,000.

23 FISHING

There is no commercial fishing in Liechtenstein.

24 FORESTRY

Forests cover about 3,000 hectares (7,400 acres). The most common trees are spruce, fir, beech, and pine.

25 MINING

There is no mining of commercial importance in Liechtenstein.

26 FOREIGN TRADE

Important exports include precision instruments, ceramics, textiles, and pharmaceuticals. Liechtenstein imports mainly raw materials, light machinery, and processed foods. In 1996, 40% of total exports went to the countries of the European Economic Area (an organization associated with the European Union).

27 ENERGY AND POWER

Electric power production in 1989 amounted to 150 million kilowatt hours. Supplementary energy is imported from Switzerland, especially in winter.

28 SOCIAL DEVELOPMENT

Accident, old age, and survivors' insurance are compulsory, as are unemployment and health insurance. Family allowances have been granted since 1958. A 1992 constitutional amendment guarantees women equality under the law.

29 HEALTH

Average life expectancy is about 79 years. In 1992, Liechtenstein had an estimated 2.5 physicians per 1,000 population. Regular examinations are provided for children up to the age of 10.

30 HOUSING

Liechtenstein does not have a significant housing problem.

31 EDUCATION

In 1990–91, there were 120 teachers and 1,985 students in the primary schools or about 1 teacher for every 16 students.

That same year, there were 112 secondary school teachers, with 1,190 students enrolled. While there are no universities in Liechtenstein, many students continue their studies at universities in Switzerland, Austria, and Germany.

32 MEDIA

There were 19,000 radios and 10,000 television sets in 1995. The number of telephones in 1995 was 18,920. As of 1995, there were no radio or television broadcasting facilities. Two newspapers are published: the *Liechtensteiner Volksblatt* and the *Liechtensteiner Vaterland*, each with a circulation of about 9,000.

33 TOURISM AND RECREATION

Attractions include mountaineering and nature walks, the castles of Vaduz, and the ruins of several fortresses. The ski resort of Malbun has 10 hotels and 6 ski lifts. In 1994, an estimated 62,000 persons visited Liechtenstein, 90% of them from Europe.

34 FAMOUS LIECHTENSTEINERS

Prince Franz Josef II (1906–89), whose rule began in 1938, was Europe's longest-reigning sovereign of the twentieth century. In 1980, Hanni Wenzel (b.1956) and her brother Andreas (b.1958) won the World Cup international skiing championships.

35 BIBLIOGRAPHY

Kranz, Walter, ed. *The Principality of Liechtenstein: A Documentary Handbook.* 5th edition, revised. Schaan, Liechtenstein: Press and Information Office of Liechtenstein, 1981.

Meier, Regula A. *Liechtenstein.* Santa Barbara, Calif.: Clio Press, 1993.

LITHUANIA

Republic of Lithuania
Lietuvos Respublika

CAPITAL: Vilnius.

FLAG: Three equal horizontal bands of yellow (top), green, and red.

ANTHEM: *Tautiška Giesme (The National Song).*

MONETARY UNIT: The Lithuanian lita of 100 cents has replaced the transitional system of coupons (talonas) which had been in force since October 1992, when the Soviet ruble was demonetized. There are coins of 1, 2, 5, 10, 20, and 50 cents and 1, 2, and 5 litas, and notes of 10, 20, 50, and 100 litas; litas 1 = $0.25 (or $1 = litas 4.0).

WEIGHTS AND MEASURES: The metric system is in force.

HOLIDAYS: New Year's Day, 1 January; Day of the Restoration of the Lithuanian State, 16 February; Good Friday (movable); Anniversary of the Coronation of Grand Duke Mindaugas of Lithuania, 6 July; National Day of Hope and Mourning, 1 November; Christmas, 25–26 December.

TIME: 2 PM = noon GMT.

1 LOCATION AND SIZE

Lithuania is located in eastern Europe, bordering the Baltic Sea, between Latvia and Russia. With a total area of 65,200 square kilometers (25,174 square miles), it is slightly larger than the state of West Virginia. Lithuania's boundary length totals 1,372 kilometers (853 miles).

Lithuania's capital city, Vilnius, is located in the southeastern part of the country.

2 TOPOGRAPHY

The topography of Lithuania features lowland terrain with many scattered small lakes and fertile soil.

3 CLIMATE

Lithuania's climate is transitional between maritime and continental. Yearly, the mean temperature is 6.1°C (43°F). The mean temperature in July is 17.1°C (63°F). Rainfall averages from 54 centimeters (21 inches) to 93 centimeters (37 inches), depending on location.

4 PLANTS AND ANIMALS

The country's plant life is a mixture of coniferous, broadleaf woodlands, arctic, and steppe species. Latvia has rabbit, fox, red deer, roe, elk, wild boar, badger, raccoon, dog, wolf, and lynx. Roach, ruff, bream, and perch can be found in Lithuania's lakes and streams.

5 ENVIRONMENT

In 1992, a United Nations' report on Lithuania stated that air pollution had damaged about 68.4% of the nation's forests. The cement industry produces 62,600 tons of airborne pollutants per year.

Water pollution results from uncontrolled dumping by industries and the lack of adequate sewage treatment facilities. In rural areas, 41.5% of the well water is unsafe.

The 1986 nuclear accident at Chernobyl, a nuclear power plant in the former Soviet Union, contaminated much of Lithuania with excessive radiation.

6 POPULATION

The population of Lithuania was estimated at 3.6 million in 1998. The US Bureau of the Census projects a population of 3.5 million in 2005. The estimated population density was about 57 persons per square kilometer (148 persons per square mile). Vilnius, the capital, had a metropolitan population of 639,000 in 1995.

7 MIGRATION

Many Lithuanians were deported to Siberia following the Soviet occupation in 1940. However, Russian immigration to Lithuania was never as heavy as in the other Baltic republics.

8 ETHNIC GROUPS

In 1989, Lithuanians formed 80% of the population. Russians accounted for 9.4%; Poles, 7%; Belarusans, 1.7%; and Ukrainians, 1.2%. About 90% of all non-

---

Geographic Profile

Geographic Features

Size ranking: 120 of 192
Highest elevation: 292 meters (958 feet) at Juozapines (Juozapine Kalnas)
Lowest elevation: Sea level at the Baltic Sea

Land Use†

Arable land:	35%
Permanent crops:	12%
Permanent pastures:	7%
Forests:	31%
Other:	15%

Weather††

Average annual precipitation: 54–93 centimeters (21.2-36.6 inches)
Average temperature in January: –4.9°C (23.2°F)
Average temperature in July: 17°C (62.6°F)

†*Arable land:* Land used for temporary crops, like meadows for mowing or pasture, gardens, and greenhouses. *Permanent crops:* Land cultivated with crops that occupy its use for long periods, such as cocoa, coffee, rubber, fruit and nut orchards, and vineyards. *Permanent pastures:* Land used permanently for forage crops. *Forests:* Land containing stands of trees. *Other:* Any land not specified, including built-on areas, roads, and barren land.

††Annual precipitation is highest in the uplands. About 75% of Lithuania's precipitation falls as rain, the rest consists of snow and freezing rain. There are between 40 and 100 foggy days each year, and 15 to 30 days with thunderstorms.

Lithuanians had been granted citizenship by 1993.

9 LANGUAGES

Lithuanian is noted for having retained ancient Indo-European language forms and has some remarkable similarities with Sanskrit.

10 RELIGIONS

In 1993, some 80% of the population was Roman Catholic. Lutherans are present and, in 1990, some 9,000 Jews. A number

LOCATION: 56°0′N; 24°0′E. **BOUNDARY LENGTHS:** Total boundary lengths, 1,372 kilometers (858 miles); Latvia, 453 kilometers (282 miles); Belarus, 502 kilometers (312 miles); Poland, 91 kilometers (57 miles); Russia, 227 kilometers (141 miles); Baltic Sea coastline, 99 kilometers (62 miles).

of ethnic Russians belong to the Russian Orthodox church.

11 TRANSPORTATION

Railways extend 2,010 kilometers (1,250 miles) across Lithuania, and there are 44,200 kilometers (27,500 miles) of highways. Kaunas is the principal inland port. In 1995, the merchant fleet consisted of 43 ships (of 1,000 gross registered tons or over) totaling 264,600 gross registered tons. A railway sea ferry from Klaipėda to

Mukran (Germany) began in 1986. Two international airlines serve Lithuania: Lithuanian Airlines and Lietuva. In 1995, 210,000 passengers were carried on scheduled flights.

12 HISTORY

From the fourteenth to the eighteenth centuries, the Grand Duchy of Lithuania was linked to the Kingdom of Poland. What is now Lithuania was annexed to the Russian Empire in 1795. During the nineteenth century, a Lithuanian nationalist movement arose.

On 16 February 1918, Lithuania proclaimed its independence. The new Bolshevik government in Moscow (Russia) attempted to seize power in Lithuania, but failed. In July 1920, Moscow recognized Lithuanian independence. However, the 1939 Nazi-Soviet pact assigned Lithuania to Soviet control, and Soviet forces were stationed on its territory. After proclaiming Lithuania a Soviet Socialist Republic in July 1940, Moscow lost control of the area to Germany in June 1941 but recaptured it in 1944.

Soviet president Mikhail Gorbachev's unrestricted policies allowed Lithuanians to once again seek national self-determination. Lithuanian independence was proclaimed on 11 March 1990 but was not generally recognized until August 1991.

On 14 February 1993, former communist Algirdas Brazauskas was elected president in a general election. In 1997, former US bureaucrat Valdas Adamkus was elected president.

Photo credit: Anne Kalosh.

Headquarters of Lithuania's Independence Party in Vilnius.

13 GOVERNMENT

On 25 October 1992, Lithuanian voters approved a new constitution that called for a 141-member single-chamber legislature (Seimas) and a popularly elected president. Apylinkes (rural settlements) and district towns are the local units.

14 POLITICAL PARTIES

The majority party in the Seimas in the 1992 parliamentary elections was the Lithuanian Democratic Labor Party (LDLP). In the elections of 1996, the Homeland Union Party took 70 of 141 seats. The LDLP only won 12 seats.

15 JUDICIAL SYSTEM

The legal system is being transformed from that of the old Soviet regime to a democratic model. A newly created Constitutional Court began deliberations in 1993. A new civil and criminal procedure code and a court reform law were enacted in 1995.

16 ARMED FORCES

The army numbers 5,100, with 11,000 reserves. There is a small navy and an air force with no combat aircraft. The paramilitary has 4,800 border guards.

17 ECONOMY

Agriculture accounts for roughly 13% of the nation's gross domestic product. Services contribute 55%. During the Soviet years, Lithuania built up a large and inefficient industrial sector that in 1996 accounted for 32% of the economy.

18 INCOME

In 1995, the gross national product (GNP) was $7.1 billion, or about $2,280 per capita.

19 INDUSTRY

Lithuania underwent rapid industrialization during the Soviet era. Major industries include machine building and metalworking, textiles, leather, and agroprocessing. About 65% of the industrial sector is privately owned.

20 LABOR

In 1993, the economically active population was estimated at 1.8 million, with

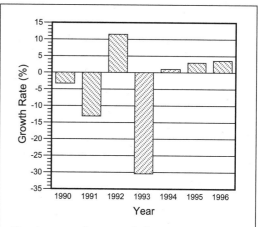

Yearly growth rate of the economy. This economic indicator tells by what percent the economy has increased or decreased when compared with the previous year.

25% working in industry and 20% in agriculture. Use of child labor does not appear to be widespread.

21 AGRICULTURE

Crops of importance in 1995 included potatoes, 1.6 million tons; barley, 1.3 million tons; sugar beets, 800,000 tons; wheat, 750,000 tons; rye, 300,000 tons; vegetables and melons, 280,000 tons; and oats, 90,000 tons.

22 DOMESTICATED ANIMALS

Livestock in 1995 included 1.2 million head of cattle, 1.3 million pigs, 9 million chickens, 40,000 sheep, and 78,000 horses. Meat production in 1995 totaled 377,000 tons.

23 FISHING

Klaipėda's fishing port is the center of the fishing industry. In 1994, production

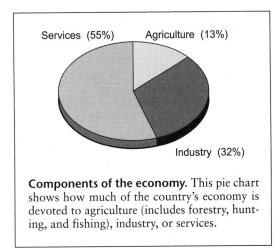

Components of the economy. This pie chart shows how much of the country's economy is devoted to agriculture (includes forestry, hunting, and fishing), industry, or services.

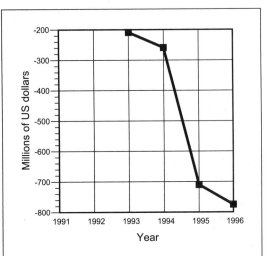

Yearly balance of trade measured in millions of US dollars. The balance of trade is the difference between what a country sells to other countries (its exports) and what it buys (its imports). If a country imports more than it exports, it has a negative balance of trade (a trade deficit). If exports exceed imports, there is a positive balance of trade (a trade surplus).

totaled 51,036 tons of fish and marine products, down from 475,001 tons in 1991.

24 FORESTRY

Forests and woodlands cover about 31% of Lithuania. The timber cut totaled 5.5 million cubic meters (7.2 million cubic yards) in 1995. Chemical timber processing, and the production of furniture, pulp, paper, wood fiber, wood chips, joinery articles, and cardboard are the main activities of the forest sector. Exports of forest products amounted to $170.8 million in 1995.

25 MINING

Cement, clays, dolomite, limestone, and sand and gravel are the primary commodities produced by more than 290 industrial mineral enterprises.

26 FOREIGN TRADE

Lithuania depends heavily on trade, particularly with other republics of the former Soviet Union. However, Lithuania is increasing its trade with western nations while reducing trade with former Soviet republics. Imports were valued at $3 billion in 1995, and exports at $2.7 billion.

27 ENERGY AND POWER

Energy production in Lithuania has long depended on imported oil, natural gas, and coal. In 1994, electrical power production amounted to 9.6 billion kilowatt hours.

28 SOCIAL DEVELOPMENT

A national system of social insurance covers all of Lithuania's residents. Old age, sickness, disability, and unemployment

Selected Social Indicators

These statistics are estimates for the period 1993 to 1996. For comparison purposes, data for the United States and averages for low-income countries and high-income countries are also given.

Indicator	Lithuania	Low-income countries	High-income countries	United States
Per capita gross national product†	**$2,280**	$490	$25,870	$28,020
Population growth rate	**–0.2%**	1.7%	0.6%	0.9%
Population growth rate in urban areas	**0.6%**	3.8%	0.9%	1.2%
Population per square kilometer of land	**57**	82	30	29
Life expectancy in years	**70**	63	77	77
Number of physicians per 1,000 people	**4.0**	1.0	2.5	2.5
Number of pupils per teacher (primary school)	**17**	41	17	14
Illiteracy rate (15 years and older)	**2%**	34%	<5%	3%
Energy consumed per capita (kg of oil equivalent)	**2,291**	393	5,123	7,905

† The gross national product (GNP) is the total dollar value of all goods and services produced by a country in a year. The per capita GNP is calculated by dividing a country's GNP by its population. The World Bank defines low-income countries as those with a per capita GNP of $785 or less. High-income countries have a per capita GNP of $9,636 or more. About 16% of the world's 5.7 billion people live in high-income countries, while almost 56% live in low-income countries.   > = greater than   < = less than

Sources: World Bank, *World Development Indicators on CD-ROM,* Washington, D.C.: The World Bank, 1998. Central Intelligence Agency, *The World Fact Book,* Washington, D.C.: Government Printing Office, 1998.

benefits are paid on an earnings-related basis. Women receive maternity and day-care benefits.

29 HEALTH

Life expectancy was about 70 years in 1995 (75 for females and 63 for males). In 1990, there was 1 physician for every 233 people. There was a 13% increase in diphtheria cases during 1994–95.

30 HOUSING

At the end of 1989, housing floor space totaled 70.8 million square meters (761.8 million square feet). A total of 142,000 families (18% of all families) were on waiting lists for housing.

31 EDUCATION

The adult illiteracy rate is estimated at 2%. Education is free and compulsory for all children between the ages of 6 and 16 years. At the postsecondary level institutions, over 70,863 pupils were enrolled in 1994. Universities include Kaunas University of Technology; Vilnius Technical University; Vilnius University; and Vytautas Magnus University.

32 MEDIA

There are approximately 22 telephones per 100 people. Radio Vilnius broadcasts in Lithuanian, Russian, Polish, and English. There are 39 radio stations and three television stations. In 1995, there were 1.4 million radios and 1.4 million television sets. There were 18 daily newspapers published in 1995, with a total circulation of 836,000.

33 TOURISM AND RECREATION

The capital city of Vilnius has one of the largest historic districts in Eastern Europe. Seaside resort towns are active in the summer. The traveler can participate in tennis, fishing, sailing, rowing, and winter sports. In 1994, an estimated 222,000 tourists visited Lithuania, and tourism receipts amounted to $82 million.

34 FAMOUS LITHUANIANS

Vytautas the Great (1350–1430) was an early Lithuanian national leader. Kristijonas Donelaitis (1714–1780) was a prominent eighteenth-century poet and Mikaljus Konstantinus Ciurlionis (1875–1911) was a famous painter and composer. Valdus Adamkus (b.1927) was elected president in 1997.

35 BIBLIOGRAPHY

Chicoine, Stephen. *Lithuania: The Nation That Would Be Free.* New York: Cobblehill Books, 1995.

Kagda, Sakina. *Lithuania.* New York: Marshall Cavendish, 1997.

Senn, Alfred Erich. *Lithuania Awakening.* Berkeley: University of California Press, 1990.

Senn, Alfred Erich. *The Emergence of Modern Lithuania.* New York: Columbia University Press, 1959.

LUXEMBOURG

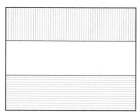

Grand Duchy of Luxembourg
French: *Grand-Duché de Luxembourg*
German: *Grossherzogtum Luxemburg*

CAPITAL: Luxembourg.

FLAG: The flag is a tricolor of red, white, and blue horizontal stripes.

ANTHEM: *Ons Hémecht (Our Homeland).*

MONETARY UNIT: The Luxembourg franc (LFr) of 100 centimes is a paper currency equal in value to the Belgian franc. There are coins of 25 and 50 centimes and ¼, 1, 5, 10, and 20 francs, and notes of 50 and 100 francs. Belgian currency is legal tender in Luxembourg, and bills of 500, 1,000, and 5,000 Belgian francs are regularly circulated. LFr1 = $0.03204 (or $1 = LFr31.21).

WEIGHTS AND MEASURES: The metric system is the legal standard.

HOLIDAYS: New Year's Day, 1 January; Labor Day, 1 May; public celebration of the Grand Duke's Birthday, 23 June; Assumption, 15 August; All Saints' Day, 1 November; Christmas, 25–26 December. Movable religious holidays include Shrove Monday, Easter Monday, Ascension, and Pentecost Monday.

TIME: 1 PM = noon GMT.

1 LOCATION AND SIZE

A landlocked country in Western Europe, Luxembourg has an area of 2,586 square kilometers (998 square miles), slightly smaller than the state of Rhode Island. It has a total boundary length of 356 kilometers (221 miles).

Luxembourg's capital city, also named Luxembourg, is located in the southcentral part of the country.

2 TOPOGRAPHY

The country is divided into two distinct geographic regions: the rugged uplands (Oesling) of the Ardennes in the north and the fertile southern lowlands, called Bon Pays (Good Land). The entire area is crisscrossed by deep valleys. The northern region, comprising one-third of the country, is forested and has poor soil.

3 CLIMATE

Summers are generally cool, with a mean temperature of about 17°C (63°F); winters are seldom severe, average temperature being about 0°C (32°F). Precipitation throughout the country averages about 74 centimeters (29 inches) annually.

4 PLANTS AND ANIMALS

The principal trees are pine, chestnut, spruce, oak, linden, elm, and beech, along with fruit trees. There are many shrubs, such as blueberry and genista, and ferns; a multitude of lovely flowers; and many vineyards. Only a few wild animal species

Geographic Profile

Geographic Features

Size ranking: 165 of 192
Highest elevation: 559 meters (1,835 feet) at
  Burgplatz (Buurgplaatz)
Lowest elevation: 133 meters (436 feet) at the Moselle
  River

Land Use†

Arable land:	24%
Permanent crops:	1%
Permanent pastures:	20%
Forests:	21%
Other:	34%

Weather††

Average annual precipitation: 74 centimeters (29.1
  inches)
Average temperature in January: 0.3°c (32.5°F)
Average temperature in July: 17.4°c (63.3°F)

†*Arable land:* Land used for temporary crops, like
meadows for mowing or pasture, gardens, and greenhouses. *Permanent crops:* Land cultivated with crops
that occupy its use for long periods, such as cocoa,
coffee, rubber, fruit and nut orchards, and vineyards.
Permanent pastures: Land used permanently for forage crops. *Forests:* Land containing stands of trees.
Other: Any land not specified, including built-on
areas, roads, and barren land.

††The measurements for precipitation and average
temperature were taken at weather stations closest to
the country's largest city. Precipitation and average
temperature can vary significantly within a country,
due to factors such as latitude, altitude, coastal proximity, and wind patterns.

13% used in farming. Luxembourg's cities produce 0.2 tons of solid waste and 817.7 tons of toxic substances. Its forest reserves have been severely depleted.

There is one endangered mammal species in Luxembourg, as well as eight bird species and one plant species.

6 POPULATION

The population was estimated at 425,000 in 1998. A population of 446,000 is projected for the year 2005. Average density in 1998 was 164 persons per square kilometer (426 persons per square mile). The city of Luxembourg, the capital, had a metropolitan population of 74,000 in 1995.

7 MIGRATION

In recent years, both emigration and immigration have been comparatively light. Since 1992, 1,700 former Yugoslavs have received temporary protection. Many residents of Luxembourg are foreigners, chiefly "guest workers" from Portugal, Italy, France, Belgium, and other European countries.

8 ETHNIC GROUPS

Native-born descendents of Luxembourgers consider themselves a distinct nationality. There are also native-born residents of French, Belgian, and German ancestry, as well as a substantial immigrant population (33% of the total in 1996).

(deer, roe deer, and wild boar) remain, but birds are plentiful, and many varieties of fish are found in the rivers, including perch, carp, bream, trout, pike, and eel.

5 ENVIRONMENT

Luxembourg produces 3.3 tons of particulate emissions and 22 tons of hydrocarbon emissions per year. The nation has 0.8 cubic kilometers (0.2 cubic miles) of water, with 45% used for industrial activity and

9 LANGUAGES

Luxembourgers are a trilingual people who speak Letzeburgesch, the original dialect of the country, as well as French and German. All three are official languages. Letzeburgesch is a Germanic dialect related to the Moselle Frankish language that was once spoken in western Germany. It rarely appears in written form.

10 RELIGIONS

In 1993, the population was estimated as 95% Roman Catholic, with 5% Protestant or other religions.

11 TRANSPORTATION

Railway lines, totaling 275 kilometers (170 miles) in 1995, provide direct links with Belgium, France, and Germany. There is direct service to Paris and other points in France.

In 1995, there were 5,108 kilometers (3,174 miles) of state and local roads. As of 1995, 231,600 cars and 16,655 commercial vehicles were registered. A program to link Luxembourg's highways to those of Belgium, France, and Germany is being carried out.

The only river available for industrial transport is the Moselle. In 1995, the merchant fleet comprised 36 ships with 825,496 gross registered tons. The country's only airport is Findel, near the city of Luxembourg. In 1995, 570,000 passengers were carried on scheduled flights.

LOCATION: 49°26'52" to 50°10'58"N; 5°44'10" to 6°31'53"E. **BOUNDARY LENGTHS:** Germany, 135 kilometers (84 miles); France, 73 kilometers (45 miles); Belgium, 148 kilometers (92 miles).

Photo credit: © The Stock Shop/D&J Heaton.

Luxembourg city.

12 HISTORY

The land now known as Luxembourg fell under the successive domination of the Celts, Romans, and Franks before its founding as the County of Luxembourg in 963 by Sigefroid, count of the Ardennes. John, count of Luxembourg (r.1309–46) and king of Bohemia, became the national hero, laying the foundations for a powerful dynasty before he fell in the Battle of Crécy during the Hundred Years' War (1337–1453). His son Charles (1316–78) was the second of four Luxembourgian princes to become Holy Roman emperor.

Luxembourg came under Burgundian rule in 1443 and remained in foreign hands for more than 400 years. It passed to Spain for most of the seventeenth century, Austria for most of the eighteenth, and France from 1795 to 1815. The Congress of Vienna in 1815 made Luxembourg a grand duchy and assigned it to the king of the Netherlands as an independent state, after ceding to Prussia Luxembourgian territory east of the Moselle, Sûre, and Our Rivers.

Luxembourg lost more than half its territory to Belgium in 1839, but gained a larger measure of self-rule. By the Treaty of London in 1867, Luxembourg was declared an independent and neutral state. In 1890, the house of Nassau-Weilbourg, in the person of Grand Duke Adolphe (r.1890–1905), became the ruling house of Luxembourg. The country was occupied by German troops in World War I (1914–18). In 1919, Grand Duchess Charlotte succeeded to the throne. In 1921, Luxembourg formed an economic union with Belgium.

The Germans again invaded the country in May 1940, but the royal family and most members of the government escaped to safety. Under the Nazi occupation, the people suffered severely, particularly when their revolt in 1942 protesting compulsory service in the German army was savagely repressed. Luxembourg was liberated by Allied forces in September 1944.

The government agreed to form an economic union with Belgium and the Netherlands. The first phase, the Benelux Customs Union, took effect in 1948. In

February 1958, a treaty of economic union was signed by representatives of the three countries. During the postwar decades, Luxembourg also became an active member of the North Atlantic Treaty Organization (NATO) and the European Community.

In April 1963, Luxembourg celebrated its 1,000th anniversary as an independent state. On 12 November 1964, Grand Duchess Charlotte abdicated in favor of her son, Jean, who became grand duke and who remained so as of 1994. His reign was marked by continued prosperity, as Luxembourg's economy shifted from dependence on steel to an emphasis on services, notably international banking.

In July 1992, Luxembourg approved the Maastrecht Treaty that agreed upon closer European union.

13 GOVERNMENT

Luxembourg is a constitutional monarchy, with hereditary power passed down through the house of Nassau-Weilbourg. Legislative power is vested in the Chamber of Deputies, the 60 members of which are elected for five-year terms. In addition, the Council of State, composed of 21 members appointed for life by the sovereign, acts as a consulting body in legislative, administrative, and judicial matters and has the right of suspensive veto.

Executive power rests jointly in the sovereign, who may initiate legislation, and a prime minister (president of the government) who is appointed by the monarch, and who in turn selects a cabinet.

Voting is compulsory, and eligibility begins at age 18.

Luxembourg is divided into 3 districts subdivided into 12 cantons, which in turn are divided into 118 communes.

14 POLITICAL PARTIES

Since 1947, the country has been governed by shifting coalitions among the three largest parties, The Christian Social Party (Parti Chrétien Social—PCS), which favors progressive labor legislation and protection for farmers and small business; the Socialist Party (Parti Ouvrier Socialiste Luxembourgeois—POSL), which supports expanding social welfare programs; and the Democratic Party (Parti Démocratique—PD), which favors minimal government activity in the economy.

15 JUDICIAL SYSTEM

Minor cases generally come before a justice of the peace. On a higher level are the two district courts, one in the city of Luxembourg and the other in Diekirch. The Superior Court of Justice acts as a court of appeal. The Court of Assizes, within the jurisdiction of the Superior Court, deals with criminal cases. Luxembourg is the site of the European Court of Justice.

16 ARMED FORCES

In 1967, Luxembourg abolished conscription and created a volunteer military force that is part of the North Atlantic Treaty Organization (NATO). In 1995 its army consisted of one infantry battalion of 800, and a police force of 560. Luxembourg has no air force or navy. Budgeted defense expenditures in 1995 were $141.3 million.

17 ECONOMY

In relation to its size and population, Luxembourg is one of the most highly industrialized countries in the world. Its standard of living rivals that of any country in Europe. Steelmaking has declined since the 1970s. Plastics, rubber, chemicals, and other light industries have been developed. The gross domestic product increased by 3.9% in 1996. The unemployment rate was 3.7% in mid-1997. Although unemployment is low by international standards, it was at its highest since the end of World War II (1939–45).

18 INCOME

In 1995, Luxembourg's gross national product (GNP) was $10 billion, or $45,360 per person. For the period 1985–95 the average inflation rate was 4.7%, resulting in a real growth rate in GNP of 1% per person.

19 INDUSTRY

Massive reorganization of the steel industry and continuing diversification of industries characterized the 1980s. Chemicals, rubber, metal processing, glass, and aluminum gained growing importance. Production of steel in 1995 was 2.6 million tons; and rolled steel products, 3.7 million tons.

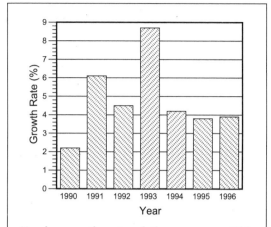

Yearly growth rate of the economy. This economic indicator tells by what percent the economy has increased or decreased when compared with the previous year.

20 LABOR

In 1995, domestic employment amounted to 213,100, including 16,000 self-employed persons. Of the 197,100 wage earners, 1,600 were employed in agriculture and forestry; 1,700 in energy and water industries; 32,500 in mining and manufacturing; 22,100 in construction; 18,600 in banking and insurance; 29,400 in distributive trades and repairs; 59,100 in other services; and 31,800 in other areas.

21 AGRICULTURE

Almost 50% of the land (126,865 hectares/313,483 acres) was devoted to agriculture and grazing in 1995. The majority of agricultural land consisted of meadows and pastures. Farms are generally small and highly mechanized, although average farm size has been increasing. Wine and clover seeds are the important agricultural exports. In addition, millions of rose-bushes, a major speciality crop, are exported annually. Chief fruits produced include apples, plums, and cherries.

22 DOMESTICATED ANIMALS

Livestock breeding is important because of Luxembourg's dairy product exports. In 1995, livestock included 213,887 head of cattle, 72,640 pigs, 7,552 sheep, and 2,164 horses. A total of 24,800 tons of meat and 268,600 tons of milk were produced in 1995.

23 FISHING

There is some fishing for domestic consumption and much private fishing for sport. The rivers contain perch, carp, trout, pike, eel, and bream.

24 FORESTRY

About 88,620 hectares (218,980 acres) were covered by forests in 1993. Forestry production in 1993 included 158,932 cubic meters (207,875 cubic yards) of round wood from broad-leaved trees and 146,312 cubic meters (191,369 cubic yards) from conifers. Chief commercial woods are spruce and oak.

25 MINING

Slate quarrying is carried on primarily for export, and a few nonmetallic minerals (dolomite, gypsum, limestone, and sand and gravel) are mined for use in construction.

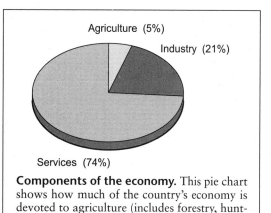

Components of the economy. This pie chart shows how much of the country's economy is devoted to agriculture (includes forestry, hunting, and fishing), industry, or services.

26 FOREIGN TRADE

The leading exports are base metals, mechanical and electrical equipment, plastics, rubber and tires, textiles and clothing, and chemical products. Base metals, mechanical and electrical equipment, and transport equipment are the leading imports.

Trade with European nations accounted for 92.9% of imports and 89.8% of exports in 1995. With 29% of the total trade volume in 1995, Germany was Luxembourg's most important trading partner. Belgium ranked second, with 27%.

27 ENERGY AND POWER

Production of electrical energy in 1994 amounted to 596 million kilowatt hours, of which 472 million kilowatt hours were produced by thermal power and 124 million kilowatt hours by three hydroelectric

Selected Social Indicators

These statistics are estimates for the period 1993 to 1996. For comparison purposes, data for the United States and averages for low-income countries and high-income countries are also given.

Indicator	Luxembourg	Low-income countries	High-income countries	United States
Per capita gross national product†	$45,360	$490	$25,870	$28,020
Population growth rate	1.5%	1.7%	0.6%	0.9%
Population growth rate in urban areas	1.9%	3.8%	0.9%	1.2%
Population per square kilometer of land	164	82	30	29
Life expectancy in years	77	63	77	77
Number of physicians per 1,000 people	2.1	1.0	2.5	2.5
Number of pupils per teacher (primary school)	14	41	17	14
Illiteracy rate (15 years and older)	<1%	34%	<5%	3%
Energy consumed per capita (kg of oil equivalent)	n.a.	393	5,123	7,905

† The gross national product (GNP) is the total dollar value of all goods and services produced by a country in a year. The per capita GNP is calculated by dividing a country's GNP by its population. The World Bank defines low-income countries as those with a per capita GNP of $785 or less. High-income countries have a per capita GNP of $9,636 or more. About 16% of the world's 5.7 billion people live in high-income countries, while almost 56% live in low-income countries.   n.a. = data not available   > = greater than   < = less than

Sources: World Bank, *World Development Indicators on CD-ROM*, Washington, D.C.: The World Bank, 1998. Central Intelligence Agency, *The World Fact Book*, Washington, D.C.: Government Printing Office, 1998.

facilities. Petroleum accounted for 54% of Luxembourg's total energy consumption in 1995; coal, 11.9%; natural gas, 17.8%; and other sources, 16.3%.

28 SOCIAL DEVELOPMENT

A broad system of social insurance covers practically all employees and their families. In the late 1980s, Luxembourg ranked second in the world after Sweden in spending on social security and housing as a percentage of the national budget. Sickness, maternity, old age, disability, and survivors' benefits are paid.

Although women are legally entitled to equal pay for equal work, their salaries on average are only 55% of men's earnings.

29 HEALTH

Luxembourg has an advanced national health service. In 1995, there were 870 physicians and 217 dentists. In 1994, there were 34 hospitals with 4,560 beds (11.3 per 1,000 inhabitants).

Average life expectancy was 77 years. Leading causes of death in 1992 were circulatory/heart diseases (1,686); cancer (996); road accidents (76); and suicides

(59). There were 107 cases of AIDS in 1996.

30 HOUSING

The immediate post-World War II housing shortage has been relieved by large-scale construction of private homes and apartment buildings. In 1995, 2,676 new dwellings were built, down from 4,452 in 1991.

31 EDUCATION

There is practically no adult illiteracy. School attendance is compulsory between the ages of 6 and 15. Pupils attend primary schools for six years and then enter secondary schools for a period of up to seven years. In 1994, school enrollment included 27,595 elementary pupils. In 1995, there were 9,012 pupils in secondary schools. Luxembourg had 1,911 primary teachers and 2,115 secondary and university professors in 1994. The Central University of Luxembourg has about 500 students; most advanced students attend institutions of higher learning in Belgium and France.

32 MEDIA

Radio-Télé-Luxembourg broadcasts on five radio channels (in Letzeburgesch, French, German, English, and Dutch) and two television channels (Letzeburgesch and French). Within Luxembourg, licensed radio sets totaled about 240,000 and television sets some 101,000 in 1995. In the same year, there were 214,800 telephones.

There were five daily newspapers in 1995, including the *Luxemburger Wort* (German and French) (1991 circulation, 81,500); *Tageblatt* (German and French) (24,500); and *La Républicaine Lorraine* (French) (24,000).

33 TOURISM AND RECREATION

Picturesque Luxembourg, with approximately 130 castles, has long been a tourist attraction. Among the points of greatest attraction are Vianden; Clervaux, with its castle of the De Lannoi family, forebears of Franklin Delano Roosevelt; the famous abbey of Clervaux; Echternach, an ancient religious center; the Moselle region; and the fortifications of the capital. More than 5,000 American soldiers are buried at the American Military Cemetery near the capital, including General George S. Patton.

In 1994, there were 762,000 tourist arrivals. Popular sports include swimming, hiking, rock climbing, cycling, and golf.

34 FAMOUS LUXEMBOURGERS

Count Sigefroid founded the nation in 963, and Countess Ermesinde (r.1196–1247) tripled the extent of the country. The Grand Duke Adolphe (1817–1905) founded the present dynasty, the house of Nassau-Weilbourg. Grand Duchess Charlotte (1896–1985) abdicated in 1964 in favor of her son Grand Duke Jean (b.1921), who has reigned since then. The heir apparent is Crown Prince Henri (b.1955).

An artist of note was the expressionist painter Joseph Kutter (1894–1941). Gabriel Lippmann (1845–1921) was awarded the Nobel Prize in physics (1908) for his pioneering work in color photography.

35 BIBLIOGRAPHY

Clark, Peter. *Luxembourg*. New York: Routledge, 1994.

Dolibois, John. *Pattern of Circles: An Ambassador's Story*. Kent, Ohio: Kent State University Press, 1989.

Kurian, George Thomas. *Facts on File National Profiles: The Benelux Countries*. New York: Facts on File Publications, 1989.

Lepthien, E. *Luxembourg*. Chicago: Children's Press, 1989.

MACEDONIA

Former Yugoslav Republic of Macedonia

Republika Makedonija

CAPITAL: Skopje.

FLAG: The flag consists of a gold sun with eight rays on a red field.

ANTHEM: *Denec Nad Makedonija (Today over Macedonia)*

MONETARY UNIT: The currency in use is the denar (Den). Denominations from smallest to largest are fifty deni, one denar, two denari, and five denari. In 1995, US$1 = Den38.8 (Den1 = US$0.0256), but exchange rates are likely to fluctuate.

WEIGHTS AND MEASURES: The metric system is in effect in Macedonia.

HOLIDAYS: Orthodox Christmas, 7 January; national holiday, 2 August; Day of Referendum, 8 September.

TIME: 1 PM = noon GMT.

1 LOCATION AND SIZE

Macedonia is a landlocked nation located in southeastern Europe. With a total area of 25,333 square kilometers (9,781 square miles), Macedonia is slightly larger than the state of Vermont. It has a total boundary length of 748 kilometers (465 miles). Macedonia's capital city, Skopje, is located in the northwestern part of the country.

2 TOPOGRAPHY

The topography of Macedonia features a mountainous landscape covered with deep basins and valleys. There are two large lakes, each divided by a frontier line. Macedonia suffers from a high incidence of earthquakes.

3 CLIMATE

Macedonia's climate features hot summers and cold winters. The mean temperature is between 20 and 23°C (68 and 73°F) in July and between –20 and 0°C (–4 and 32°F) in January. Rainfall averages 48 centimeters (19 inches) a year. Snowfalls can be heavy in winter.

4 PLANTS AND ANIMALS

Macedonia is home to European bison, fox, rabbits, brown bears, and deer. Ducks, turtles, frogs, raccoons, and muskrats inhabit the country's waterways.

5 ENVIRONMENT

Air pollution from metallurgical plants is a problem in Macedonia, as in the other former Yugoslav republics. Earthquakes are a natural hazard.

6 POPULATION

The population of Macedonia was estimated at 2.1 million in 1998. It was projected by the US Bureau of the Census to remain about the same in 2005. The popu-

Geographic Profile

Geographic Features

Size ranking: 145 of 192
Highest elevation: 2,764 meters (9,068 feet) at Korab
Lowest elevation: 50 meters (164 feet) at the Vardar River

Land Use†

Arable land:	24%
Permanent crops:	2%
Permanent pastures:	25%
Forests:	39%
Other:	10%

Weather††

Average annual precipitation: 48 centimeters (19 inches)
Average temperature range in January: –20°C to 0°C (–4°F to 32°F)
Average temperature range in July: 20°C to 23°C (68°F to 73°F)

†*Arable land:* Land used for temporary crops, like meadows for mowing or pasture, gardens, and greenhouses. *Permanent crops:* Land cultivated with crops that occupy its use for long periods, such as cocoa, coffee, rubber, fruit and nut orchards, and vineyards. *Permanent pastures:* Land used permanently for forage crops. *Forests:* Land containing stands of trees. *Other:* Any land not specified, including built-on areas, roads, and barren land.

††The measurements for precipitation and average temperature were taken at weather stations closest to the country's largest city. Precipitation and average temperature can vary significantly within a country, due to factors such as latitude, altitude, coastal proximity, and wind patterns.

lation density in 1998 was about 78 persons per square kilometer (202 persons per square mile). Skopje, the capital, had a population of 466,000 in 1995.

7 MIGRATION

In 1995, Macedonia sheltered 12,800 Bosnian refugees and 2,000 Croatian refugees. There were about 1,000 Macedonian refugees scattered elsewhere in the former Yugoslavia. The net emigration rate in 1996 was 0.2 emigres per 1,000 population.

8 ETHNIC GROUPS

Slavic Macedonians comprised 66.5% of the population in 1994. Another 22.9% were Albanians. Other groups included Turks, Roma (Gypsies), Serbs, Greeks, and Bulgarians.

9 LANGUAGES

Macedonian is a southern Slavic tongue that was not officially recognized until 1944. It is the primary language of 70% of the population. Bulgarians claim it is merely a dialect of their own language. Minority languages are officially recognized at the local level. Albanian is spoken by 21% of the population.

10 RELIGIONS

As of 1993, 59% of the population was Eastern Orthodox, 26% Muslim, 4% Roman Catholic, and 1% Protestant. The remaining 10% belonged to other faiths or had no religious preference. The Macedonian Orthodox Church broke from the Serbian Orthodox Church in 1967.

11 TRANSPORTATION

A railway connects Skopje with Serbia to the north and Greece to the south. In 1991, there were 10,591 kilometers (6,581 miles) of highways, of which 48% were paved, 13% were gravel, and 39% were dirt roads. There are 14 airports with paved runways.

12 HISTORY

Macedonia is an ancient name, historically related to Philip II of Macedon, whose son became Alexander the Great, founder of one of the great empires of the ancient world. Beginning in the fifth century AD, Slavic tribes began settling in the Balkan area, and by 700 they controlled most of the Central and Peloponnesian Greek lands, including Macedonia.

Through most of the later Middle Ages, Macedonia was an area contested by the Byzantine Empire, the Bulgarian Kingdom, and the Serbian empire of Dušan the Great. Following the defeat of the Serbs at the Kosovo Field in 1389, the Turks conquered the Macedonian area over the next half century and kept it under their control until the 1912 Balkan War.

In the second half of the nineteenth century, while still under the weakening rule of the Turks, Macedonia became the object of territorial claims by its Greek, Serb, and Bulgarian neighbors. In 1893, the Internal Macedonian Revolutionary Organization (IMRO) was formed with the goal of overthrowing the Turks and establishing an independent Macedonia.

On 2 August 1903, rebels took over the town of Kruševo and proclaimed a Socialist Republic. After initial defeats of the local Turkish forces, the rebels were subdued by massive Ottoman attacks, including wholesale massacres of the population over a three-month period. In 1912, Serbia, Greece, Bulgaria, and Montenegro formed the Balkan League, and agreed on the division of Turkish Balkan territory among themselves. They declared war on

LOCATION: 41°50′N; 22°0′E. **BOUNDARY LENGTHS:** Total boundary lengths, 748 kilometers (465 miles); Albania, 151 kilometers (94 miles); Bulgaria, 148 kilometers (92 miles); Greece, 228 kilometers (142 miles); Serbia and Montenegro, 221 kilometers (137.3 miles).

Turkey in October after Turkey refused their requests.

A Country Divided

The Balkan League's quick defeat of the Turks stunned the European powers. Turkey signed a treaty in London on 30 May 1913 giving up almost all its European possessions. Internal conflicts between Serbia, Bulgaria, and Greece led to a second Balkan War, which ended with the partitioning of Macedonia between those three countries.

On 1 December 1918, Prince Alexander of Serbia declared the unification of the "Kingdom of Serbs, Croats, and Slovenes," a kingdom in which Macedonian nationhood had no place. Southern Macedonia belonged to Greece, while most of Macedonia was annexed to the Serbs.

During World War II (1939–45), Macedonia was occupied by Bulgaria and Albania. By the summer of 1943, Josip Tito, the leader of the Yugoslav Partisans, took over control of the Communist Party of Macedonia after winning its agreement to form a separate Macedonian republic as part of a Yugoslav federation.

After the war, Macedonia became one of the co-equal republics of the Federal Socialist Yugoslavia under the communist regime of Marshal Tito. The Macedonian language became its official language and was used as the language of instruction in schools.

A Macedonian University was established in Skopje, the capital city, and cultural, political, social, and economic institutions were developed within the framework of the Yugoslav Socialist system of self-management. All the republics of the former Federal Socialist Republic of Yugoslavia share a common history between 1945 and 1991, the year of Yugoslavia's break-up.

A conflict erupted between Tito and the Russian leader Joseph Stalin in 1948, and Tito was expelled from the Soviet Bloc.

Photo credit: A/P Wide World Photos.

Ann Hansen, 24, from Horten, Norway, is one of five women in a 700-person-strong Nordic/UN Battalion. She is in Macedonia as part of a UN peacekeeping force.

Yugoslavia then developed its own brand of Marxist economy based on workers' councils and self-management of enterprises and institutions, and became the leader of the nonaligned group of nations.

Being more open than the Soviet bloc to Western influences, the Yugoslav Communist regime relaxed its central controls somewhat. The 1974 constitution shifted much of the decision-making power from the federal level to the republics, further decentralizing the political process.

Rising Tensions

Following Tito's death in 1980, there was an economic crisis. Severe inflation and inability to pay the nation's foreign debts led to tensions between the different republics. There were demands for a reorganization of the Yugoslav federation into a confederation of sovereign states.

Pressure towards individual autonomy for the regions and demand for a market economy grew stronger. These demands led to the formation of non-communist political parties. By 1990, the non-communists were able to win majorities in multiparty elections in Slovenia and Croatia. These defeats ended the era of Communist Party monopoly of power.

In the wake of developments in Slovenia and Croatia, Macedonia held its first multiparty elections in November/December 1990, with the participation of over 20 political parties. In January 1991, the Macedonian Assembly passed a declaration of sovereignty.

Independence

When the dissolution of Yugoslavia took place in 1990–91, Macedonia refused to join Serbia and Montenegro and instead opted for independence on 20 November 1991. Greece refused to recognize the newly independent Macedonia for fear of unrest among Slav Macedonians in Northern Greece. Greece also objected to the use of "Macedonia" for the name of the country. In April 1993, Macedonia gained membership in the United Nations, but only under the name of "Former Yugoslav Republic of Macedonia."

Greece proclaimed a trade embargo against Macedonia in 1994. In the fall of 1995, a preliminary agreement was reached between the two nations. Greece agreed to lift its blockade and assume diplomatic relations with Macedonia, while Macedonia agreed to restrict the use of certain national symbols in its flag and currency. However, the issue of the new nation's name was still unresolved.

In October 1995, Macedonian President Kiro Gligorov narrowly survived a car-bomb attack that killed his driver. Stojan Andov became interim president until early 1996, when Gligorov was able to resume his duties.

Ethnic violence erupted in July 1997 in Gostivar when police sent in forces to remove the illegal Albanian, Turkish, and Macedonian flags from the town hall. Thousands of protesters had gathered in a stalemate with police. During the confrontation, police killed three ethnic Albanians and several policemen were shot. Tensions between ethnic Albanians and Macedonians in the country are increasing.

13 GOVERNMENT

Macedonia became independent of the former Yugoslavia on 20 November 1991, having adopted its constitution on 17 November 1991. Macedonia has a single-chamber assembly of 120 seats, an executive branch consisting of a President (Kiro Gligorov) and a Council of Ministers (in 1994, the Prime Minister was Branko Crvenkovski).

Macedonia's 34 local governments are still based on the preexisting Yugoslav system.

14 POLITICAL PARTIES

After the 1994 elections, party representation in the 120-seat Sobranje was as follows: the Social Democratic Alliance of Macedonia (former Communist Party), 58; Liberal Party, 29; Socialist Party of Macedonia, 8; Party for Democratic Prosperity, 10; National Democratic Party, 4; independents, 7; and others, 4.

15 JUDICIAL SYSTEM

The judicial system is comprised of three levels: municipal courts, district courts, and the Supreme Court. A Constitutional Court handles issues of constitutional interpretation, including protection of individual rights.

16 ARMED FORCES

In January 1992, the Macedonian Assembly approved the formation of a standing army of 25,000–30,000 troops. However, the actual size of the military is estimated to be 10,400 regular soldiers. Reservists total 100,000.

17 ECONOMY

Although the poorest of the six former Yugoslav republics, Macedonia is capable of meeting its food and energy needs using its own agricultural and coal resources. Due to the shortage of fertile land in the Vardar River Valley and other valleys in the west, the employment of Macedonians

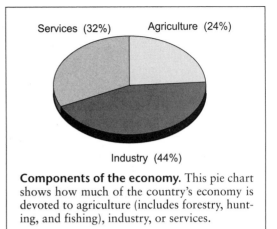

Components of the economy. This pie chart shows how much of the country's economy is devoted to agriculture (includes forestry, hunting, and fishing), industry, or services.

in Serbia and Germany has become more common.

In August 1992, because it resented the use of "Macedonia" as the republic's name, Greece imposed a partial blockade on Macedonia. This blockade, combined with the United Nations sanctions on Serbia and Montenegro, cost the Macedonian economy some $2 billion by the end of 1994. Greece ended the embargo in 1995 after the European Union threatened to take legal action.

In 1995, mining and industry accounted for 44% of the domestic economy; agriculture and fishing, 24%; and services and trade, 32%.

18 INCOME

In 1995, Macedonia's gross national product (GNP) was $1.8 billion, or about $990 per person. In 1996, about 47% of disposable income went to buy food. In 1995, the inflation rate was 14.8%, and the real

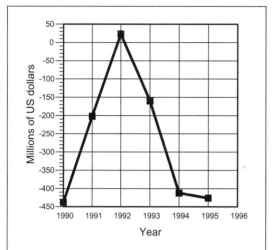

Yearly balance of trade measured in millions of US dollars. The balance of trade is the difference between what a country sells to other countries (its exports) and what it buys (its imports). If a country imports more than it exports, it has a negative balance of trade (a trade deficit). If exports exceed imports, there is a positive balance of trade (a trade surplus).

growth rate in the domestic economy was 4%.

19 INDUSTRY

Steel and chemical production, along with textiles, furniture, and ceramics are important industries. Industry suffers from low levels of technology and overstaffing. The production of food, beverages, and textiles, accounted for 29% of the manufacturing sector's value in 1994.

20 LABOR

Most employment is in agriculture, mining, and light industry. Economic collapse was aggravated by regional warfare and the trade embargo against Serbia and Montenegro that lasted until November 1995. In 1996, there were 356,000 employed persons. At that time, 35% of the labor force could not find work. There is a 42-hour workweek and a minimum employment age of 15 years.

21 AGRICULTURE

Estimated grain production in 1995 included: wheat, 381,000 tons; barley, 98,000 tons; and corn, 85,000 tons, Rye, rice, and oats are grown in smaller quantities. Other important crops produced in 1995 included (in tons): tomatoes, 134,000; potatoes, 154,000; sunflower seeds, 22,000; sugar beets, 55,000; and walnuts, 2,800. In 1995, 191,000 tons of grapes and 90,000 tons of wine were produced.

22 DOMESTICATED ANIMALS

Meadows and pastures accounted for 25% (635,000 hectares/1.6 million acres) of the total area in 1994. Livestock in 1996 consisted of 2.2 million sheep, 259,622 head of cattle, 108,777 pigs, and 3.1 million chickens. Production in 1995 included (in tons): mutton, 10,000; pork, 9,300; beef, 6,900; poultry, 1,900; and milk, 197,000.

23 FISHING

Inland fishing occurs on Lake Ohrid (Ohridsko Jezero), Lake Prespa (Prespansko Jezero), and the Vardar River. Macedonia has no direct access to the sea for marine fishing.

Selected Social Indicators

These statistics are estimates for the period 1993 to 1996. For comparison purposes, data for the United States and averages for low-income countries and high-income countries are also given.

Indicator	Macedonia	Low-income countries	High-income countries	United States
Per capita gross national product†	$990	$490	$25,870	$28,020
Population growth rate	0.7%	1.7%	0.6%	0.9%
Population growth rate in urban areas	1.4%	3.8%	0.9%	1.2%
Population per square kilometer of land	78	82	30	29
Life expectancy in years	72	63	77	77
Number of physicians per 1,000 people	2.3	1.0	2.5	2.5
Number of pupils per teacher (primary school)	20	41	17	14
Illiteracy rate (15 years and older)	n.a.	34%	<5%	3%
Energy consumed per capita (kg of oil equivalent)	1,308	393	5,123	7,905

† The gross national product (GNP) is the total dollar value of all goods and services produced by a country in a year. The per capita GNP is calculated by dividing a country's GNP by its population. The World Bank defines low-income countries as those with a per capita GNP of $785 or less. High-income countries have a per capita GNP of $9,636 or more. About 16% of the world's 5.7 billion people live in high-income countries, while almost 56% live in low-income countries. n.a. = data not available > = greater than < = less than

Sources: World Bank, *World Development Indicators on CD-ROM*, Washington, D.C.: The World Bank, 1998. Central Intelligence Agency, *The World Fact Book*, Washington, D.C.: Government Printing Office, 1998.

24 FORESTRY

About 39% of the total area consisted of forests and woodlands in 1994, mostly in the eastern and southern regions. Bitola is the center for the wood products industry.

25 MINING

Chrome, iron ore, marble, and zinc are found in Macedonia. Zinc, lead, copper, chromite, nickel, iron, and silver are mined.

26 FOREIGN TRADE

In 1995, exports amounted to $916.2 million, and imports totaled $199 million. Manufactured goods and machinery are the leading exports. Fuel is the leading import.

In 1994, the leading export markets were Germany, Italy, and Russia. The principal sources of imports were Germany, Italy, and Slovenia.

27 ENERGY AND POWER

In 1994, 5.2 billion kilowatt hours of electricity were generated. Macedonia's only domestic mineral fuel is coal.

28 SOCIAL DEVELOPMENT

Macedonia, historically the poorest of the former Yugoslav republics, suffered further from the imposition of international

Houses on a hillside overlooking a river.

sanctions against its trading partner Serbia, the rising tide of refugees, and increasing unemployment. Many of the state's social welfare programs for children have been inoperative due to the region's political and economic crises.

Although women have the same legal rights as men, the traditional cultures of both Christian and Muslim communities have limited their advancement in society.

29 HEALTH

Life expectancy in 1990–95 was 72 years. Physicians are adequately trained, but there is a shortage of medicines and medical equipment. Patients who are seriously ill must often go to another country for medical help.

30 HOUSING

During the years of the former Yugoslav SFR, there was a chronic shortage of housing. Since independence, the ability to find housing had improved. Bank loans are now available to finance building new housing.

31 EDUCATION

Education at the elementary level is free and compulsory for eight years. There are many secondary level schools. At the postsecondary level, there are two universities:

Bitola University, founded in 1979, and the University of Skopje, founded in 1949.

32 MEDIA

The Macedonian media remain mostly free of government influence. An independent television station, A–1, broadcasts from Skopje. State-sponsored newspapers include the Albanian-language *Flaka e Vlazerimit* and the Turkish-language *Birlik*. In 1994, *Delo,* a new weekly with reportedly nationalist leanings, began publication. There were 92 Internet hosts in 1996.

33 TOURISM AND RECREATION

As a republic of the former Yugoslavia, tourism-related activities were not traditionally emphasized in Macedonia. There were 185,000 tourist arrivals in 1994.

34 FAMOUS MACEDONIANS

Kiro Gligorov (b.1917) has been the president of Macedonia since January 1991 and was reelected in 1994. Branko Crvenkovski was made prime minister in September 1992. Mother Teresa (Agnes Gonxha Bojaxhiu, 1910–97) was from Skopje, Macedonia, but left at age 17 to join a convent in Calcutta, India. In 1948, Mother Teresa left the convent to found the Missionaries of Charity. She won the Nobel Peace Prize in 1979.

35 BIBLIOGRAPHY

Borowiec, Andrew. *Yugoslavia After Tito.* New York: Praeger, 1977.

Danforth, Loring M. *The Macedonian Conflict: Ethnic Nationalism in a Transitional World.* Princeton, N.J.: Princeton University Press, 1995.

Poulton, Hugh. *Who are the Macedonians?* Bloomington, Ind.: Indiana University Press, 1995.

Shea, John. *Macedonia and Greece: The Struggle to Define a New Balkan Nation.* Jefferson, N.C.: McFarland, 1997.

MADAGASCAR

Democratic Republic of Madagascar
République Démocratique de Madagascar
Repoblika Demokratika n'i Madagaskar

CAPITAL: Antananarivo.

FLAG: The flag consists of a white vertical stripe at the hoist flanked at the right by two horizontal stripes, the upper in red, the lower in green.

ANTHEM: *Ry Tanindrazanay Malala O (Our Beloved Country).*

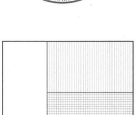

MONETARY UNIT: The Malagasy franc (FMG) is a paper currency. There are coins of 1, 2, 5, 10, 20, 25, 50, 100, and 250 Malagasy francs and notes of 50, 100, 500, 1,000, 2,500 5,000, 10,000 and 25,000 Malagasy francs. FMG1 = $0.00025 (or $1 = FMG3,999.4).

WEIGHTS AND MEASURES: The metric system is generally used.

HOLIDAYS: New Year's Day, 1 January; Commemoration of 1947 Rebellion, 29 March; Labor Day, 1 May; Independence and National Day, 26 June; All Saints' Day, 1 November; Christmas, 25 December; Anniversary of the Democratic Republic of Madagascar, 30 December. Movable religious holidays include Good Friday, Easter Monday, Ascension, and Pentecost Monday.

TIME: 3 PM = noon GMT.

1 LOCATION AND SIZE

Situated off the southeast coast of Africa, Madagascar is the fourth-largest island in the world, with an area of 587,040 square kilometers (226,657 square miles), slightly less than twice the size of Arizona. It is separated from the coast of Africa by the Mozambique Channel, where it claims a number of small islands covering about 28 square kilometers (11 square miles), which are administered by France. The coastline of Madagascar is 4,828 kilometers (3,000 miles). Madagascar's capital city, Antananarivo, is located near the center of the island.

2 TOPOGRAPHY

Madagascar consists mainly of a block of crystalline rocks. It is generally described as a plateau, rising sharply from the east coast and descending in a series of steps to the west coast. The highest point is Mount Maromokotro, 2,876 meters (9,436 feet) in the Tsaratanana Massif (Massif du Tsaratanana). The island's major rivers flow westward and are navigable for about 160 kilometers (100 miles) inland.

3 CLIMATE

The climate of the eastern and northwestern coasts is dominated by the almost constant blowing of the southeasterly trade winds, which carry heavy rains from May to September, and from which the central plateau, the western coast, and the southern part of the island are sheltered. The central plateau enjoys a tropical mountain climate with well-differentiated seasons. Generally speaking, the climate throughout the island is moderated by altitude, with the coast being hotter (average tem-

Geographic Profile

Geographic Features

Size ranking: 44 of 192
Highest elevation: 2,876 meters (9,436 feet) at Mount Maromokotro
Lowest elevation: Sea level at the Indian Ocean

Land Use†

Arable land:	4%
Permanent crops:	1%
Permanent pastures:	41%
Forests:	40%
Other:	14%

Weather††

Average annual precipitation: 127 centimeters (50 inches)
Average temperature in January: 19.3°C (66.7°F)
Average temperature in July: 13°C (55.4°F)

†*Arable land:* Land used for temporary crops, like meadows for mowing or pasture, gardens, and greenhouses. *Permanent crops:* Land cultivated with crops that occupy its use for long periods, such as cocoa, coffee, rubber, fruit and nut orchards, and vineyards. *Permanent pastures:* Land used permanently for forage crops. *Forests:* Land containing stands of trees. *Other:* Any land not specified, including built-on areas, roads, and barren land.

††The measurements for precipitation and average temperature were taken at weather stations closest to the country's largest city. Precipitation and average temperature can vary significantly within a country, due to factors such as latitude, altitude, coastal proximity, and wind patterns.

peratures 21–27°C, or 70–80°F) and wetter than the plateau (average temperatures 13–19°C, or 55–67°F).

4 PLANTS AND ANIMALS

Madagascar is the home of over 200,000 species of plants and animals, which developed in isolation from those of mainland Africa. There are a few small patches of deciduous, or nonevergreen, forest in the northwest and west. Mangrove swamps are generally found along the northwest and west coasts. Most of Madagascar is covered with tropical grasslands, green in the wet season, but brown and red in the summer.

The animals are remarkable chiefly because of the presence of 28 species of lemur, a lower primate largely confined to Madagascar. The island has 32 species of chameleon. Among the 238 species of birds, 106 are found nowhere else in the world. The same is true for 80% of the island's flowering plants and more than 95% of its reptiles. Madagascar is also unusual in its lack of poisonous snakes.

5 ENVIRONMENT

Erosion is a serious problem in Madagascar. Many farmers burn off their old crops at the end of winter and damage surrounding forests. By 1994, 75% of Madagascar's forests had been eliminated. Water pollution caused mainly by sewage is also a significant environmental problem in Madagascar. The nation's cities produce 0.6 million tons of solid waste per year. In addition to 50 of its mammal species and 28 of its bird species, 194 of Madagascar's plant species are threatened with extinction.

6 POPULATION

In 1998, the estimated population of Madagascar was 14.5 million. A population of 17.6 million was projected for the year 2005. The average population density in 1998 was estimated at about 24 persons per square kilometer (62 per square mile). Antananarivo (Tananarive), the capital and largest city, had about 876,000 inhabitants in 1995.

7 MIGRATION

Since independence, government policy has been uniformly opposed to immigration in any form. In the early 1970s, the government started taking over foreign businesses, causing many foreign residents to leave. Rural-to-urban migration is nearly 6% a year.

8 ETHNIC GROUPS

The original immigrants to Madagascar are believed to have been members of an Afro-Malagasy race that lived in East Africa. Later arrivals were Africans, Arabs, and, much more recently, immigrants from Europe, China, and India. There are 18–20 distinct African ethnic groups now recognized on the island. The major ethnic groups are the Merina, Betsimisaraka, Betsileo, Tsimihety, Sakalava, Antandroy, Antaisaka, and Tanala. The Merina have been the most powerful group since the late eighteenth century. The course that colonialism took in Madagascar strengthened their domination of the island. Resentment of the Merina by the other ethnic groups is still a source of social unrest. In 1988 there were about 18,000 French in Madagascar. The number of Indians and Pakistanis was estimated at 17,000 and the number of Chinese at 9,000.

9 LANGUAGES

The principal languages are French and Malagasy. The Merina dialect has come to be considered the standard literary form of the language. Instruction in French is preferred by the coastal peoples, who do not accept Merina cultural dominance.

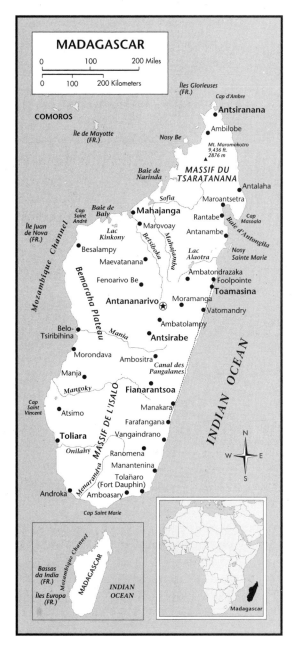

LOCATION: 43°12′ to 50°17′E; 11°57′ to 25°38′S.
TERRITORIAL SEA LIMIT: 12 miles.

Photo credit: Susan D. Rock.

A young Malagasy boy with his lemur.

10 RELIGIONS

Although there are many variations in detail, nearly all Malagasy share certain basic religious ideas, the central one being belief in the soul and its immortality. Besides the almighty (Andrianahary or Zanahary), secondary divinities are recognized, especially the earliest inhabitants of the island (Vazimba), legendary kings and queens, and other great ancestors. The burial places and other places of special significance in the lives of these secondary deities are objects of veneration (profound respect) and pilgrimages, during which special rites are performed.

According to a 1993 estimate, some 43% of the population was Christian, with Roman Catholics slightly more numerous than Protestants. The Merina tend to be Protestant and the coastal peoples Catholic. Over half of the Malagasy follow tribal religions, and about 1.7%, mostly on the northwest coast, follow Islam. There are small numbers of Baha'is, Hindus, Buddhists, and Jews.

11 TRANSPORTATION

Although physical features of the land make railway building difficult and expensive, there are four main railroads. All are publicly operated, covering 883 kilometers (548 miles). There are about 34,750 kilometers (21,592 miles) of motor roads on the island. In 1995 there were 47,700 passenger automobiles and 34,300 trucks and buses in use.

The three major ports are Toamasina, Nosy Be, and Mahajanga. The merchant fleet consisted of 12 vessels, with gross weight of 22,132 tons at the end of 1995. The principal international airport is at Ivato, near Antananarivo. Air Madagascar (the national airline), Air France, Alitalia, Aeroflot, Air Mauritius, and Air Tanzania also provide international service. In all there are 105 usable airports, 68 with permanent-surface runways.

12 HISTORY

The original inhabitants of Madagascar probably came from Indonesia via the African coast between 500 BC and 500 AD.

A Malagasy mother and her children at home.

The earliest written histories of the Malagasy are the *sorabe,* in the Malagasy language using Arabic script. While the Portuguese named the island Madagascar in 1502, attempts by the Portuguese, British, Dutch, and French to settle the island in the sixteenth and seventeenth centuries were unsuccessful.

Under King Andrianampoinimerina (r.1787–1810), the foundations were laid for the primacy of the Merina kingdom, which retained its dominance through the reigns of his successors. The French claimed a protectorate over parts of the kingdom by virtue of treaties made in 1840, and disputes over this claim and over French properties on the island resulted in a war in 1883. It was ended in 1885 by a treaty giving the French control over Merina foreign policy. The French annexed Madagascar in 1896, although Malagasy resistance was not overcome until 1904.

During World War II (1939–45), Madagascar was occupied by British troops to prevent its naval facilities from being used by the Japanese. In 1943, French administration was restored under General Charles de Gaulle's Free French government. Madagascar became a French overseas territory in 1946.

The Malagasy Republic became an independent nation on 26 June 1960 and on 20 September 1960 was elected to United Nations membership.

The constitution that was adopted in October 1958 and amended in June 1960 provided Madagascar with a strong presidential form of government. The president, Philibert Tsiranana, remained in power until 18 May 1972, when political protests throughout Madagascar led to the fall of his government. General Gabriel Ramanantsoa was immediately asked to form a nonpolitical "government of national unity." Ramanantsoa raised the minimum wage, provided strike pay, prosecuted corrupt officials, and introduced price and currency controls. The new government also broke diplomatic ties with South Africa, established relations with the Communist countries, and arranged for the withdrawal of French military forces under new cooperation agreements with France.

In December 1975, the Second Malagasy Republic, to be called the Democratic Republic of Madagascar, was proclaimed, and Admiral Didier Ratsiraka was installed as president on 4 January 1976. The new regime accelerated growing state control of the economy, and Madagascar turned to the former Soviet Union and the Democratic People's Republic of Korea for military aid. By 1979, however, growing economic difficulties forced Ratsiraka to develop closer ties with the West. Ratsiraka was elected to a new term as president on 7 November 1982. By early 1987, the governing coalition appeared to be unraveling. On May Day, four of the parties called for the resignation of the government and early elections. By November,

Ratsiraka agreed to share power with a transitional government headed by Albert Zafy, his main rival. Ratsiraka's Revolutionary Supreme Council stepped down from power.

On 19 August 1992, a new constitution was approved by national referendum. By the end of 1993, however, some of the provisions in the new constitution had not been met, such as the establishment of a senate and an independent judiciary. Territorial elections, the first step in the creation of the senate, were held in November 1995.

President Zafy was impeached in September 1995, and Ratsiraka defeated Zafy in a runoff election that December.

13 GOVERNMENT

The first government of the Third Republic was formed in late August 1993. Its August 1992 constitution provides for a two-chamber legislature—a 138-deputy National Assembly and a Senate. The National Assembly alone has the authority to choose the prime minister. Two-thirds of the senators are chosen indirectly by electors representing geographical areas and various economic and social sectors of the population, and one-third are appointed by the president.

14 POLITICAL PARTIES

After the democratic changes of 1992 and 1993, some 30 parties operate in Madagascar. Albert Zafy, the leader of the National Union for Democracy and Development (UNDD), heads a coalition of a dozen groups under the collective name of

Comité des Forces Vives. Following his defeat in the presidential elections of 1993, Admiral Didier Ratsiraka created a new party, the Vanguard for Economic and Social Recovery (ARES—Avant Gardes pour le Redressement Économique et Social). It was a federalist party seeking to deny central government control of the provinces. There are four other functioning parties.

15 JUDICIAL SYSTEM

At the top of the judicial system is the Supreme Court in Antananarivo. Other courts include the Court of Appeal, also in Antananarivo; courts for first trials of civil and criminal cases; ordinary and special criminal courts; and military courts. There are also a High Court of Justice to try high officials and a Constitutional Court. Military courts presided over by civilian magistrates hear cases involving national security.

The traditional courts (dina) continue to handle some civil disputes and recently have been used in criminal cases because of inconvenience and inadequacy of the formal court system.

16 ARMED FORCES

The armed forces of Madagascar were composed in 1995 of about 21,000 personnel, including an army of 20,000, a navy of 500 (100 marines), and an air force of 500. The navy had 2 ships and the air force 12 combat aircraft. Manpower is provided by conscription of all men from 20 to 50 for 18-month periods, but most servicemen are volunteers.

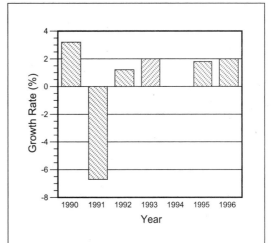

Yearly growth rate of the economy. This economic indicator tells by what percent the economy has increased or decreased when compared with the previous year.

The paramilitary Gendarmerie National, which had a strength of 7,500 in 1995, is the main force for the maintenance of public order and internal security. Military spending was estimated at $49 million in 1995.

17 ECONOMY

Madagascar has an agriculture-based economy that supports 76% of the country's labor force. There are also substantial mineral deposits. Industry is centered on food processing and accounted for 15% of the gross domestic product (GDP) in 1995. Madagascar has made important investments in tourism.

18 INCOME

In 1995 Madagascar's gross national product (GNP) was $3.2 billion, or about $250 per person. For the period 1985–95

A beachfront fish market.

Photo credit: Susan D. Rock.

the average inflation rate was 17.9%, resulting in a decline in GNP of 2% per person.

19 INDUSTRY

Industrialization has been severely hampered by inadequate internal transportation and a restricted local market. The majority of industrial enterprises process agricultural products: rice, sugar, flour, tobacco, tapioca, and sisal. In addition, there are some meat-packing plants. Urea- and ammonia-based fertilizers are produced in a plant that opened in 1985. Other industrial enterprises include two cement plants, a paper pulp factory, cotton spinning and weaving mills, and three automobile assembly plants. Industrial

output grew by 2.5% annually during 1990–95.

20 LABOR

The labor force in 1996 was estimated at 5 million persons. In 1996, agriculture (especially production of rice, vanilla, and coffee) employed 80% of the work force, with unionized labor making up less than 5% of the total.

The law provides for collective agreements between employers and trade unions, basic minimum wages fixed by the government on the advice of advisory committees, paid annual leave, maternity and children's allowances, and compensation for industrial injuries.

21 AGRICULTURE

Agriculture generates about 80% of export earnings and employs about 80% of the work force. Large-scale plantations dominate the production of sisal, sugarcane, tobacco, bananas, and cotton, but, overall, Malagasy agriculture is dependent mainly on small-scale subsistence farmers.

A wide variety of food crops is grown. Rice is the staple of the Malagasy diet; production was an estimated 2.6 million tons in 1995. Other important food crops (with 1995 production figures) include cassava, 2.4 million tons; sugarcane, 2 million tons; sweet potatoes, 560,000 tons; potatoes, 270,000 tons; bananas, 210,000 tons; corn, 169,000 tons; and oranges, 80,000 tons.

The major Malagasy export is coffee. Production was 79,000 tons in 1995. Vanilla is the second-ranking agricultural export, with exports of 698 tons of extract in 1992. Madagascar is the world's major natural vanilla producer, accounting for about 73% of production in 1992. Cloves are the third main export crop, grown mostly by small farmers. Production figures for cash crops in 1995 include seed cotton, 33,000 tons; peanuts, 28,000 tons; sisal, 17,000 tons; and cocoa, 4,000 tons.

22 DOMESTICATED ANIMALS

Only since the end of World War I (1914–18) has the consumption of meat become widespread among Malagasy, and now beef consumption is relatively high compared with other African countries. Estimates of the size of livestock herds vary

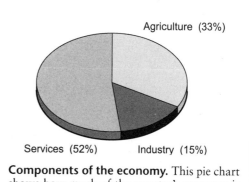

Components of the economy. This pie chart shows how much of the country's economy is devoted to agriculture (includes forestry, hunting, and fishing), industry, or services.

considerably. Estimates for 1995 were cattle, 10.3 million head; hogs, 1.6 million; sheep, 740,000; and goats, 1.3 million. Total meat production was about 289,000 tons.

23 FISHING

Despite the island's long coastline, fishing is relatively undeveloped as an industry in Madagascar. In the northwest, sardine and tuna are caught, and dried fish find a ready market. The catch in 1994 was estimated at 104,768 tons, of which 30,120 tons were caught in inland waters. Ships from the European Union nations are allowed to take up to 11,000 tons of tuna and prawns a year. French investment helped to establish a tuna cannery.

24 FORESTRY

In 1991, the woodland area of Madagascar was estimated to cover more than 23.2 million hectares (about 57.3 million acres), or about 40% of the land. Forestry

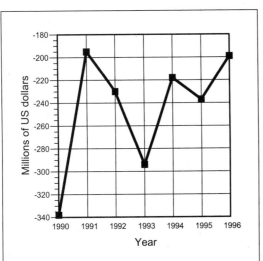

Yearly balance of trade measured in millions of US dollars. The balance of trade is the difference between what a country sells to other countries (its exports) and what it buys (its imports). If a country imports more than it exports, it has a negative balance of trade (a trade deficit). If exports exceed imports there is a positive balance of trade (a trade surplus).

policy has tried to stop further destruction of the woodlands. Roundwood removals were estimated at 10.9 million cubic meters (14.3 million cubic yards) in 1995, with 96% used as fuel.

25 MINING

The mining of chromite and graphite is the principal mineral activity. In 1994, a reported 91,000 tons of chromite and 8,000 tons of graphite were extracted. Deposits of gem and ornamental stones, and stones for electrical geodes (quartz and celestine) have also been mined. Marine-salt production was about 30,000 tons in 1994.

26 FOREIGN TRADE

Madagascar consistently runs a trade deficit. Exports consist mainly of unprocessed agricultural products and some extracted minerals. Leading exports in 1994 were textiles, coffee, and vanilla. Principal imports that year were petroleum products, chemicals, road vehicles, and telecommunications equipment.

France is by far Madagascar's leading trade partner, accounting for 41.4% of exports and 39.5% of imports in 1995. Germany accounted for 9.6% of exports and 4.4% of imports. Other export clients were the United States (9.6%) and Japan (5.4%). Imports likewise came from Japan (6.6%), Singapore (5.2%), and Iran (4.1%).

27 ENERGY AND POWER

An estimated 80 million tons of oil are thought to be extractable from bituminous sand deposits near Mahajanga, but it was not economically feasible.

Installed electrical capacity in 1994 amounted to 220,000 kilowatts, of which 85% was public. Annual output of power in 1994 was 587 million kilowatt hours, 60% of this amount was hydroelectrically produced.

28 SOCIAL DEVELOPMENT

There is a National Social Security Fund that provides family allowances and workers' compensation for wage earners. Women in urban areas enjoy a highly visible and influential—although secondary—position in society. Women hold many posts in business and government. Rural

Selected Social Indicators

These statistics are estimates for the period 1993 to 1996. For comparison purposes, data for the United States and averages for low-income countries and high-income countries are also given.

Indicator	Madagascar	Low-income countries	High-income countries	United States
Per capita gross national product†	$250	$490	$25,870	$28,020
Population growth rate	3.0%	1.7%	0.6%	0.9%
Population growth rate in urban areas	5.3%	3.8%	0.9%	1.2%
Population per square kilometer of land	24	82	30	29
Life expectancy in years	58	63	77	77
Number of physicians per 1,000 people	n.a.	1.0	2.5	2.5
Number of pupils per teacher (primary school)	40	41	17	14
Illiteracy rate (15 years and older)	20%	34%	<5%	3%
Energy consumed per capita (kg of oil equivalent)	36	393	5,123	7,905

† The gross national product (GNP) is the total dollar value of all goods and services produced by a country in a year. The per capita GNP is calculated by dividing a country's GNP by its population. The World Bank defines low-income countries as those with a per capita GNP of $785 or less. High-income countries have a per capita GNP of $9,636 or more. About 16% of the world's 5.7 billion people live in high-income countries, while almost 56% live in low-income countries.   n.a. = data not available   > = greater than   < = less than

Sources: World Bank, *World Development Indicators on CD-ROM,* Washington, D.C.: The World Bank, 1998. Central Intelligence Agency, *The World Fact Book,* Washington, D.C.: Government Printing Office, 1998.

women face greater hardships, engaging in subsistence labor while raising a family.

29 HEALTH

All medical services in Madagascar are free. Each province has a central hospital, and local clinics, dispensaries, and maternity-care centers are supplemented by mobile health units. Approximately 65% of the population has access to health care services. In 1993, there was one doctor for every 8,385 people. The most widespread diseases are malaria, leprosy, schistosomiasis, and tuberculosis. In 1994–95, 32% of the population had access to safe water, and only 17% had adequate sanitation. The average life expectancy is 58 years in 1995.

30 HOUSING

Malagasy houses, although constructed of varying materials in different parts of the island (brick and wood in the plateau, thatch and leaves in the west, and often on stilts in the east), are always rectangular, sited north–south, with the doorway opening to the west. The rapid growth of towns after the end of World War II in 1945 created grave housing and sanitation problems, especially in Antananarivo.

31 EDUCATION

Although education is free and compulsory between the ages of 6 and 12, there is still a considerable degree of illiteracy, estimated at 20%. In 1992, there were 1.6

million pupils attending 13,791 primary schools, secondary school enrollment was 340,191 pupils, and there were 35,824 students enrolled in higher education. The University of Madagascar in Antananarivo has several campuses. Also in Antananarivo are the Rural College of Ambatobe and the National Institute of Telecommunications and Posts.

32 MEDIA

The government owns and operates all major communications services. In 1995 there were 34,800 telephone subscribers. Radio-Télévision Malagasy broadcasts in French, Malagasy, and English, and telecasts in French and Malagasy; Radio Madgasi Kara broadcasts in French and Malagasy. In 1995 there were about 2.5 million radios and 260,000 television sets.

The principal daily newspapers are *Journal de Madagascar*—formerly *Madagascar-Matin*—(1995 circulation 13,000) and *Midi-Madagascar* (1995 circulation 23,000) in French; *Atrika* in French and Malagasy; and *Maresaka* and *Imongo Vaovao*, all published in Antananarivo. Despite prior censorship of all print media, the press is independent and quite outspoken.

33 TOURISM AND RECREATION

Since the mid-1980s, the government has encouraged tourism as a source of foreign exchange, and the industry grew until 1991, when there was a decline due to civil unrest. In 1994, there were 66,136 tourist arrivals (up from 34,891 in 1991). Of these, nearly half were either French or German. Tourism receipts totaled $54 million.

34 FAMOUS MALAGASY

Jacques Rabémananjara (b.1914), is well known for his verse play, *Les Dieux Malgaches*. Philibert Tsiranana (1910–78), a Tsimihety teacher, became Madagascar's first president in May 1959. Admiral Didier Ratsiraka (b.1936) became head of state in June 1975 and president of the republic in January 1976.

35 BIBLIOGRAPHY

Bradt, Hilary. *Madagascar*. Santa Barbara, Calif.: Clio, 1993.

Jolly, Alison. "Madagascar: A World Apart." *National Geographic*, February 1987, 148–183.

Madagascar in Pictures. Minneapolis: Lerner Publications, 1988.

Preston-Mafham, Ken. *Madagascar: A Natural History*. New York: Facts on File, 1991.

MALAWI

Republic of Malawi

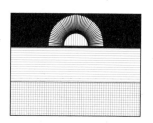

UNITY AND FREEDOM

CAPITAL: Lilongwe.

FLAG: The national flag is a horizontal tricolor of black, red, and green, with a red rising sun in the center of the black stripe.

ANTHEM: Begins "O God, Bless Our Land of Malawi."

MONETARY UNIT: The kwacha (κ) of 100 tambala (t) is the national currency; it replaced the Malawi pound (м£) on 28 August 1970 and was linked with the pound sterling until November 1973. There are coins of 1, 2, 5, 10, and 20 tambala, and notes of 50 tambala and 1, 5, 10, 20, and 50 kwacha. κ1 = $0.06536 (or $1 = κ15.3).

WEIGHTS AND MEASURES: The metric system is the legal standard.

HOLIDAYS: New Year's Day, 1 January; Martyrs' Day, 3 March; Kamuzu Day, 14 May; Republic or National Day, 6 July; Mothers' Day, 17 October; National Tree Planting Day, 21 December; Christmas, 25 December; Boxing Day, 26 December. Movable holidays include Good Friday and Easter Monday.

TIME: 2 PM = noon GMT.

1 | LOCATION AND SIZE

A landlocked country in southeastern Africa, Malawi (formerly Nyasaland) has an area of 118,480 square kilometers (45,745 square miles), slightly larger than the state of Pennsylvania, with a total boundary length of 2,768 kilometers (1,720 miles). Malawi's capital city, Lilongwe, is located in the southwestern part of the country.

2 | TOPOGRAPHY

Malawi lies at the southern end of the Great Rift Valley system, an area which extends south from the valley of the Jordan River to Mozambique. Lake Malawi, a body of water 580 kilometers (360 miles) long and about 460 meters (1,500 feet) above sea level, is the country's most prominent physical feature. About 75% of the land surface is plateau at an elevation between 750 meters and 1,350 meters (2,460 and 4,430 feet) above sea level.

3 | CLIMATE

Precipitation is heaviest along the northern coast of Lake Malawi, where the average is more than 163 centimeters (64 inches) per year. The average daily minimum and maximum temperatures in November, the hottest month, are 17°C (63°F) and 29°C (84°F); those in July, the coolest month, are 7°C (45°F) and 23°C (73°F).

4 | PLANTS AND ANIMALS

About half of the land area is classified as forest. There are native softwoods in the better-watered areas, with bamboo and cedars on Mt. Sapitwa; evergreen conifers also grow in the highlands. There are

Geographic Profile

Geographic Features

Size ranking: 97 of 192
Highest elevation: 3,000 meters (9,843 feet) at Mount Sapitwa
Lowest elevation: 37 meters (121 feet) at the junction of the Shire River and the international boundary with Mozambique

Land Use†

Arable land:	18%
Permanent crops:	0%
Permanent pastures:	20%
Forests:	39%
Other:	23%

Weather††

Average annual precipitation: 84.9 centimeters (33.4 inches)
Average temperature in January: 21.2°C (70.2°F)
Average temperature in July: 15°C (59.0°F)

†*Arable land:* Land used for temporary crops, like meadows for mowing or pasture, gardens, and greenhouses. *Permanent crops:* Land cultivated with crops that occupy its use for long periods, such as cocoa, coffee, rubber, fruit and nut orchards, and vineyards. *Permanent pastures:* Land used permanently for forage crops. *Forests:* Land containing stands of trees. *Other:* Any land not specified, including built-on areas, roads, and barren land.

††The measurements for precipitation and average temperature were taken at weather stations closest to the country's largest city. Precipitation and average temperature can vary significantly within a country, due to factors such as latitude, altitude, coastal proximity, and wind patterns.

many varieties of animal life. The elephant, giraffe, hippopotamus and buffalo are found in certain areas. Other mammals in Malawi are the baboon, monkey, hyena, wolf, zebra, lion, nocturnal cat, badger, warthog, porcupine, and several varieties of antelope. There are at least 600 species of birds. Reptiles are plentiful, including many varieties of snakes. Fish include bream, bass, catfish, mudfish, perch, carp, and trout.

5 ENVIRONMENT

Cultivation and continued population pressure raise the threat of soil erosion, and the demand for firewood has significantly depleted the timber stock. One-third of city dwellers and about half of the rural population lack pure water. Some of the nation's fish population is threatened with extinction due to pollution from sewage, industrial waste, and agricultural chemicals. Malawi has four national parks and three game reserves; about 11% of the nation's total area is protected from development.

6 POPULATION

According to a 1998 estimate by the United States Census Bureau, the population was 9.8 million; the projection for the year 2005 was 10.8 million. The estimated population density was 107 persons per square kilometer (277 per square mile), one of the highest in Africa. Lilongwe, the capital, had about 437,000 people in 1995.

7 MIGRATION

During the early 1990s, the annual urban growth rate was about 6%. During 1992–96, 1.3 million Mozambican refugees returned from Malawi.

8 ETHNIC GROUPS

The people of Malawi belong mainly to various Central Bantu groups. About half belong to the Chewa and Nyanja groups, known collectively as Malawi (or Maravi) before the nineteenth century. About 15% are Lomwe (Alomwe), who live south of Lake Chilwa. The Ngoni and Yao arrived in the nineteenth century; together they constitute about 15% of the population. There are a few thousand Europeans, mainly of British origin, including descendants of Scottish missionaries.

9 LANGUAGES

Numerous Bantu languages and dialects are spoken. Chichewa is spoken by more than half the population, but the Lomwe, Yao, and Tumbuka have their own widely spoken languages. English and Chichewa are the official languages.

10 RELIGIONS

It was estimated in the early 1990s that about 50% of the population belonged to various Christian denominations. Tribal religions account for as much as 15% of the population and Islam 20%.

11 TRANSPORTATION

In 1996, Malawi had 789 kilometers (490 miles) of railways. There were 27,294 kilometers (16,959 miles) of roads in 1995, and 34,000 motor vehicles, of which about half were passenger cars. Until 1982, about 95% of Malawi's foreign trade passed through Mozambican ports, but because of fighting and instability in Mozambique, most exports are shipped from Zambia. Kamuzu International Airport, at Lilongwe, opened in 1982. In 1995, 149,000 passengers were carried on scheduled flights.

12 HISTORY

Malawi has been inhabited for at least 12,000 years; its earliest peoples were nomadic hunter-gatherers. By the thir-

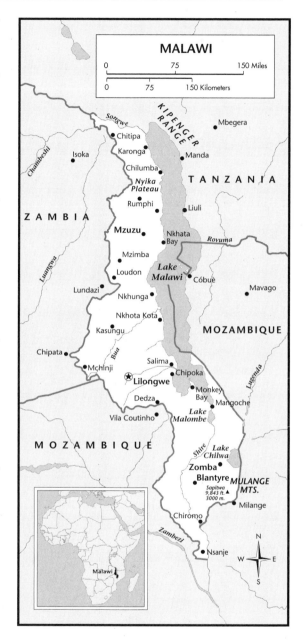

LOCATION: 9°27' to 17°10's; 32°20' to 36°E. **BOUNDARY LENGTHS:** Tanzania, 451 kilometers (280 miles); Mozambique, 1,497 kilometers (930 miles); Zambia, 820 kilometers (510 miles).

Photo credit: Cory Langley.

The average life expectancy for the children pictured above is only 43 years of age. In comparison, children living in the United States can expect to live until age 77.

teenth century AD, Bantu-speaking migrants had entered the region, and the Chewa peoples had become dominant by the early sixteenth century. The first European to explore the area extensively was David Livingstone, in the 1850s and 1860s. In 1878, the African Lakes Company was formed by Scottish businessmen, and the British government annexed the whole of the territory (then known as Nyasaland) in 1891.

Between World Wars I (1914–18) and II (1939–45), Nyasaland seemed headed for eventual independence. In 1953, however, it was joined with the two Rhodesias—Northern Rhodesia (now Zambia) and Southern Rhodesia (now Zimbabwe)—in the Central African Federation.

When African citizens expressed angry opposition to the federation in 1959, a state of emergency was declared. In 1960, the Malawi Congress Party (MCP), headed by Dr. Hastings Kamuzu Banda, stepped up the campaign against federation rule. At a constitutional conference held in London in November 1962, it was agreed that Nyasaland should become fully self-governing early in 1963, and that Banda, who headed the MCP, should become prime minister.

The Banda Era

On 6 July 1964, Nyasaland became a fully independent member of the British Commonwealth of Nations, and adopted the name Malawi. On 6 July 1966, Banda assumed the presidency. During the first decade of Banda's presidency, Malawi's relations with its neighbors, ruled by blacks, were sometimes stormy. In addition to claiming extensive territories outside the present boundaries of Malawi, Malawi became the first black African country to establish diplomatic relations with white-ruled South Africa; moreover, Banda became the first black African head of state to be officially received in South Africa, which supplied arms and development funds to Malawi.

Banda continued to rule Malawi with an iron hand through the 1970s and into the late 1980s. During his rule his opponents were treated severely. Several thousand people were imprisoned for political offenses at one time or another, and leaders of opposition groups were persecuted.

Opposition to Banda's harsh rule strengthened and Banda's grip on the country began to weaken. Under mounting pressure, Banda agreed to hold a referendum early in 1993 on whether Malawi should remain a one-party state. On 14 June 1993, 63% of those voting favored adopting multiparty democracy. Banda agreed to hold elections in 1994 and to draft a new constitution. Parliament adopted laws ending one-party rule and imprisonment without trial, and allowing dissidents to return home.

Post-Banda Malawi

In the 17 May 1994 elections, Bakili Muluzi, a former cabinet minister, was elected president over Banda and two other candidates. Muluzi immediately ordered the release of political prisoners and the closing of the most notorious jails. The transition of power was fairly smooth, and an atmosphere of relative tolerance prevails.

13 GOVERNMENT

Malawi officially became a republic on 6 July 1966. The new constitution took effect on 18 May 1995. The president is the head of state and supreme executive authority. Legislative power is vested in the single-chamber National Assembly, and all adults may vote. Parliamentary elections are to occur every five years unless the president dissolves the National Assembly before then. In March 1995, the National Assembly voted to establish a second chamber of parliament (a senate of 80 seats) in 1999.

14 POLITICAL PARTIES

Malawi was officially a one-party state from October 1973 until July 1993. The Malawi Congress Party (MCP) was the national party and Hastings Kamuzu Banda was its president for life. In a referendum on 14 June 1993, voters rejected single-party rule by a margin of 63% to 35%, and opposition parties and coalitions blossomed. Elections were held on 17 May 1994, with seven parties participating. The United Democratic Front (UDF) won, trailed by the MCP and two other parties.

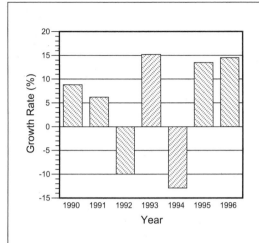

Yearly growth rate of the economy. This economic indicator tells by what percent the economy has increased or decreased when compared with the previous year.

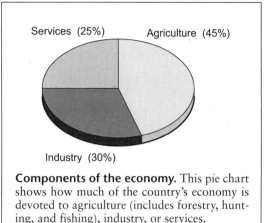

Components of the economy. This pie chart shows how much of the country's economy is devoted to agriculture (includes forestry, hunting, and fishing), industry, or services.

15 JUDICIAL SYSTEM

The constitution provides for an independent judiciary, and the government respects this provision. Defendants have the right to public trial, to have an attorney, to challenge evidence and witnesses, and to an appeal. There are numerous local courts throughout Malawi, with a chain of appeals from the local courts up to a Supreme Court of Appeal.

In 1993, the attorney general suspended the operation of regional and national level traditional courts. Traditional courts at the local level may survive the recent reforms and continue to hear cases involving small claims and customary law.

16 ARMED FORCES

In 1995, Malawi had an army of 9,800 men, organized into 3 infantry battalions and 1 support battalion. The air wing had 80 men and 6 transports. A 220-member naval force had 1 lake patrol craft. In 1995 Malawi spent $21 million on defense.

17 ECONOMY

Malawi's agricultural economy has been troubled in recent years by drought and financial instability. It is dependent for most of its income on the export sales of tobacco, tea, peanuts, coffee, and sugar. International aid donors, concerned about human rights abuses in Malawi, have tied future support to human rights reforms.

18 INCOME

In 1995, Malawi's gross national product (GNP) was $1.6 billion, or $180 per person. During 1985–95, the average annual

Fishermen working their nets.

decline of the GNP was 0.7% per person, and the inflation rate averaged 22%.

19 INDUSTRY

Malawi's manufacturing sector is diverse. The processing of tea, tobacco, sugar, coffee, and cotton accounts for most of its output. Factories manufacture soap, detergents, cigarettes, furniture, cookies, bread, blankets and rugs, clothing, and mineral waters. Other operations include a gin distillery, a cotton mill, and two textile plants.

20 LABOR

At the end of 1991, the labor force totaled 594,360, including 211,080 in agriculture, forestry, and fishing; 63,870 in manufacturing; 80,930 in community and personal services; and 43,710 in building and construction. The average monthly wage in 1990 was $26.50.

21 AGRICULTURE

Malawi is self-sufficient in food production (except during droughts), but the population increased more rapidly than the food supply in the 1980s. Tea, a major export crop, is produced mostly on estates. Production in 1995 was 34,000 tons. Production of tobacco, the chief export, amounted in 1996 to 160,014 tons. Sugarcane production was about 2.2 million tons in 1995; the output of refined

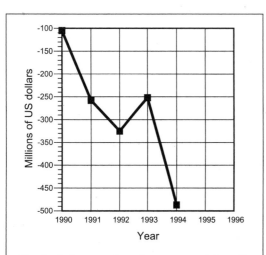

Yearly balance of trade measured in millions of US dollars. The balance of trade is the difference between what a country sells to other countries (its exports) and what it buys (its imports). If a country imports more than it exports, it has a negative balance of trade (a trade deficit). If exports exceed imports there is a positive balance of trade (a trade surplus).

sugar reached 237,000 tons. Other cash crops produced in 1995 include peanuts, 32,000 tons, and seed cotton, 68,000 tons.

Corn is the staple food crop; about 1.7 million tons were produced in 1995. Other food crops, with 1995 estimated production figures, include cassava, 200,000 tons; potatoes, 376,000 tons; pulses (beans, peas, or lentils), 273,000 tons; sorghum, 45,000 tons; plantains, 200,000 tons; bananas, 91,000 tons; and paddy rice, 52,000 tons.

22 DOMESTICATED ANIMALS

In 1995 there were an estimated 890,000 goats, 980,000 head of cattle, and 247,000 hogs, and 196,000 sheep. The number of poultry was estimated at 9 million. About 88,000 head of cattle were slaughtered in 1995, yielding 18,000 tons of beef. Milk production was estimated at 42,000 tons.

23 FISHING

The growing commercial fishing industry is concentrated mainly in Lake Malawi. Fish farming is carried on in the south. The total catch in 1994 was estimated at 58,800 tons.

24 FORESTRY

Natural forests are extensive, and in the high-altitude regions, the Forestry Department is engaged in a softwood planting program. Roundwood removals in 1995 were estimated at 10.5 million cubic meters (13.8 million cubic yards), of which 95% went for fuel.

25 MINING

Quarrying for limestone and other building materials is the only current mining activity; in 1994, about 140,000 tons of limestone were quarried for the manufacture of cement. Coal production began in 1985 at the Kaziwiziwi mine in the northern region; production was 55,000 tons in 1994.

26 FOREIGN TRADE

Malawi's chief export crops are tobacco, tea, and sugar, followed by groundnuts, coffee, cassava, rice, cotton, and sunflower seeds. Principal imports are petroleum products, vehicles, piece goods, medicine, and agricultural machinery. In 1995, Malawi's exports were sent primarily to South Africa (14.6%), Germany

Selected Social Indicators

These statistics are estimates for the period 1993 to 1996. For comparison purposes, data for the United States and averages for low-income countries and high-income countries are also given.

Indicator	Malawi	Low-income countries	High-income countries	United States
Per capita gross national product†	$180	$490	$25,870	$28,020
Population growth rate	2.6%	1.7%	0.6%	0.9%
Population growth rate in urban areas	5.4%	3.8%	0.9%	1.2%
Population per square kilometer of land	107	82	30	29
Life expectancy in years	43	63	77	77
Number of physicians per 1,000 people	<0.1	1.0	2.5	2.5
Number of pupils per teacher (primary school)	63	41	17	14
Illiteracy rate (15 years and older)	44%	34%	<5%	3%
Energy consumed per capita (kg of oil equivalent)	38	393	5,123	7,905

† The gross national product (GNP) is the total dollar value of all goods and services produced by a country in a year. The per capita GNP is calculated by dividing a country's GNP by its population. The World Bank defines low-income countries as those with a per capita GNP of $785 or less. High-income countries have a per capita GNP of $9,636 or more. About 16% of the world's 5.7 billion people live in high-income countries, while almost 56% live in low-income countries.   n.a. = data not available   > = greater than   < = less than

Sources: World Bank, *World Development Indicators on CD-ROM,* Washington, D.C.: The World Bank, 1998. Central Intelligence Agency, *The World Fact Book,* Washington, D.C.: Government Printing Office, 1998.

(13%), and Japan (10%). Imports came primarily from South Africa (36.2%), Zimbabwe (16.2%), and Germany (4.3%).

27 ENERGY AND POWER

Both the consumption and the production of electric power are small, even by African standards. In 1994, 793 million kilowatt hours of power were sold by the Electric Supply Commission of Malawi; in addition, 16,000 kilowatt hours were produced privately. Almost 98% of power production was hydroelectric that year.

28 SOCIAL DEVELOPMENT

The Ministry of Community Services is responsible for social welfare generally.

Government hospitals and clinics provide some medical services to residents without charge.

Beginning in 1992, a gradual improvement in Malawi's human rights record was evident. However, the use of excessive force and mistreatment of prisoners are still reported. Vigilante killings (executions conducted by a group of citizens that have taken the law into their own hands) are increasing.

29 HEALTH

Health services in Malawi rank among the poorest in Africa. The major health threats are malnutrition, malaria, and tuberculosis.

In addition, there are thousands of acquired immune deficiency syndrome (AIDS) cases in Malawi. In 1994, an estimated 13.6% of all adults were infected with HIV, the virus that causes AIDS. There were 43,067 new cases of AIDS reported in 1996. Life expectancy averages 43 years. From 1988–93, there was one physician for approximately 50,360 people.

30 HOUSING

Government-built houses are either rented or sold. The Malawi Housing Corp. has also developed housing plots in order to relocate urban squatters.

31 EDUCATION

School attendance is compulsory for eight years at the primary level. In 1994, Malawi's 3,425 primary schools had 2.9 million pupils; secondary schools had 49,412 students. The University of Malawi has three campuses. In 1993 there were 309 teachers and 3,684 pupils at all higher level institutions.

32 MEDIA

Radio broadcasting services are provided in English and Chichewa, and there are no television broadcast facilities. In 1991 there were 2.2 million radio sets and 32,800 telephones in use. The *Daily Times*, published in English in Blantyre, had a circulation of 25,000 in 1991. The *Malawi News*, published in English and Chichewa, had a circulation of 35,000.

33 TOURISM AND RECREATION

The major tourist attractions in Malawi are Mount Mulanje, Mount Zomba, and the nation's game parks. In 1994, 154,000 foreign tourists visited Malawi, and receipts were estimated at $5 million.

34 FAMOUS MALAWIANS

The dominant political figure was Dr. Hastings Kamuzu Banda (1906–97), who became Malawi's first president in 1966 and held the office until 1994. Bakili Muluzi (b.1943) was elected president in 1994.

35 BIBLIOGRAPHY

Lane, M. *Malawi*. Chicago: Children's Press, 1990.

O'Toole, Thomas. *Malawi in Pictures*. Minneapolis: Lerner Publications Co., 1988.

Reinthal, Peter. "The Living Jewels of Lake Malawi." *National Geographic*, May 1990, 42–51.

Theroux, Paul. "Malawi: Faces of A Quiet Land." *National Geographic*, September 1989, 371–390.

MALAYSIA

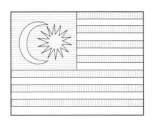

CAPITAL: Kuala Lumpur.

FLAG: The national flag consists of 14 alternating horizontal stripes, of which 7 are red and 7 white; a gold 14-pointed star and crescent appear on a blue field in the upper left corner.

ANTHEM: *Negara Ku (My Country).*

MONETARY UNIT: The Malaysian ringgit (M$), or dollar, is divided into 100 sen, or cents. There are coins of 1, 5, 10, 20, and 50 sens and 1 ringgit, and notes of 1, 5, 10, 20, 100, 500, and 1,000 ringgits. M$1 = US$0.3741 (or US$1 = M$2.6730).

WEIGHTS AND MEASURES: The metric system became the legal standard in 1982, but some British weights and measures and local units are also in use.

HOLIDAYS: National Day, 31 August; Christmas, 25 December. Movable holidays include Vesak Day, Birthday of His Majesty the Yang di-Pertuan Agong, Hari Raya Puasa, Hari Raya Haji, the 1st of Muharram (Muslim New Year), Milad an-Nabi, Dewali, Thaipusam, and the Chinese New Year. Individual states celebrate the birthdays of their rulers and other holidays observed by native ethnic groups.

TIME: 7 PM = noon GMT.

1 LOCATION AND SIZE

Situated in Southeast Asia, Malaysia, with an area of 329,750 square kilometers (127,581 square miles), consists of two separate, nonadjoining areas: Peninsular Malaysia on the Asian mainland, and the states of Sarawak and Sabah, known together as East Malaysia, on the island of Borneo. Comparatively, the area occupied by Malaysia is slightly larger than the state of New Mexico.

Peninsular Malaysia, protruding southward from the mainland of Asia, comprises an area of 131,587 square kilometers (50,806 square miles), with a total boundary length of 2,574 kilometers (1,608 miles). In east Malaysia, Sarawak covers an area of 124,449 square kilometers (48,050 square miles); and Sabah, situated at the northern end of Borneo, has an area of 74,398 square kilometers (28,725 square miles). East Malaysia's boundary length is 4,716 kilometers (2,947 miles). The total boundary length of Malaysia is 7,290 kilometers (4,555 miles).

Malaysia's capital city, Kuala Lumpur, is located in the western part of Peninsular Malaysia.

2 TOPOGRAPHY

Four-fifths of Peninsular Malaysia is covered by rainforest, jungle, and swamp. The northern regions are divided by a series of mountain ranges that rise abruptly from the wide, flat coastal plains. The western

Geographic Profile

Geographic Features

Size ranking: 65 of 192
Highest elevation: 4,101 meters (13,455 feet) at
  Mount Kinabalu
Lowest elevation: Sea level at the Indian Ocean

Land Use†

Arable land:	3%
Permanent crops:	12%
Permanent pastures:	0%
Forests:	68%
Other:	17%

Weather††

Average annual precipitation: 249.9 centimeters (98.4
  inches)
Average temperature in January: 26.8°C (80.2°F)
Average temperature in July: 27.1°C (80.8°F)

†*Arable land:* Land used for temporary crops, like
meadows for mowing or pasture, gardens, and greenhouses. *Permanent crops:* Land cultivated with crops
that occupy its use for long periods, such as cocoa,
coffee, rubber, fruit and nut orchards, and vineyards.
Permanent pastures: Land used permanently for forage crops. *Forests:* Land containing stands of trees.
Other: Any land not specified, including built-on
areas, roads, and barren land.

††The measurements for precipitation and average
temperature were taken at weather stations closest to
the country's largest city. Precipitation and average
temperature can vary significantly within a country,
due to factors such as latitude, altitude, coastal proximity, and wind patterns.

the Crocker Mountains, which rise to 4,101 meters (13,455 feet) at Mount Kina-balu, the highest point in Malaysia. Most of the interior is covered with tropical forest, while the western coastal area makes up the main rubber and rice land.

3 CLIMATE

The climate of Peninsular Malaysia is characterized by fairly high but uniform temperatures (ranging from 23° to 31°C/ 73° to 88°F throughout the year), high humidity, and heavy rainfall, averaging about 250 centimeters (100 inches) annually. There are seasonal variations in rainfall, with the heaviest rains from October to December or January. The nights are usually cool because of the nearby seas. The climate of East Malaysia is relatively cool for an area so near the equator.

4 PLANTS AND ANIMALS

About 70% of Malaysia consists of tropical rainforest. In Peninsular Malaysia, camphor, ebony, sandalwood, teak, and many varieties of palm trees abound. Jungle animals include seladang (Malayan bison), deer, wild pigs, tree shrews, honey bears, forest cats, civets, monkeys, crocodiles, huge lizards, and snakes. The seladang weighs about a ton and is the largest wild ox in the world. An immense variety of insects, particularly butterflies, and some 575 species of birds are found.

On Sabah and Sarawak, lowland forests contain some 400 species of tall hardwoods and semihardwoods; fig trees abound, and groves are formed by the extensive aerial roots of warangen (a sacred tree to native peoples). As altitude

coastal plain contains most of the country's population and the main seaports, George Town and Keluang. The eastern coastal plain is mostly jungle and lightly settled.

Sarawak consists of a swampy coastal plain, an area of rolling country alternating with mountain ranges, and a mountainous interior. Rainforests cover the greater part of Sarawak. Many of the rivers are navigable. Sabah is split in two by

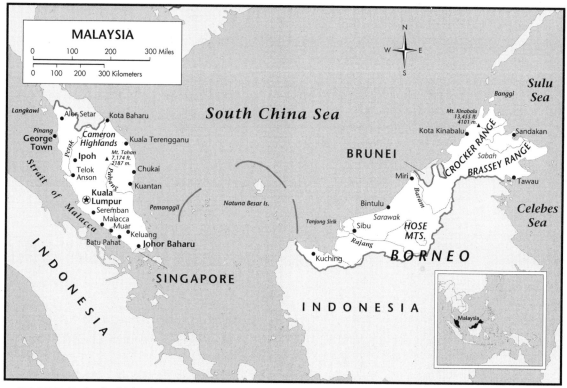

MALAYSIA

0   100   200   300 Miles

0   100   200   300 Kilometers

South China Sea

Sulu Sea

Langkawi

Alor Setar ● Kota Baharu

Pinang
George Town ●

Cameron Highlands
Kuala Terengganu

Ipoh ▲ *Mt. Tahan 7,174 ft. 2,187 m.*

Telok Anson ● Chukai

● Kuantan

Kuala Lumpur ✪

Pemanggil   *Natuna Besar Is.*

Seremban ●
Malacca ●
● Muar
● Keluang
Batu Pahat ● **Johor Baharu** ●

I N D O N E S I A

Strait of Malacca

SINGAPORE

BRUNEI

Mt. Kinabalu 13,455 ft. 4101 m. ▲
Kota Kinabalu ●

Banggi

● Sandakan

CROCKER RANGE

Sabah

BRASSEY RANGE

Miri ●

● Tawau

Celebes Sea

Bintulu ●

Tanjong Sirik   *Sarawak*
Sibu ● **HOSE MTS.**

Rajang

B O R N E O

● Kuching

I N D O N E S I A

Malaysia

LOCATION: Peninsular Malaysia: 1°17′ to 6°43′N; 99°38′ to 104°39′E. Sarawak: 0°52′ to 4°59′N; 109°38′ to 155°43′E. Sabah: 4°6′ to 7°22′N; 115°7′ to 119°17′E. **BOUNDARY LENGTHS:** Peninsular Malaysia: Thailand, 506 kilometers (316 miles); coastline, 2,068 kilometers (1,292 miles). East Malaysia: Brunei, 381 kilometers (238 miles); Indonesia, 1,728 kilometers (1,080 miles); coastline, 2,607 kilometers (1,629 miles). Total boundary length, land and coastline: 7,290 kilometers (4,555 miles). **TERRITORIAL SEA LIMIT:** 12 miles.

increases, herbaceous plants—buttercups, violets, and valerian—become more numerous, until moss-covered evergreen forests are reached from 1,520 to 1,830 meters (5,000–6,000 feet). Large butterflies, brilliantly colored birds of paradise, and a great wealth of other insect and bird species inhabit the two states.

5 ENVIRONMENT

Discharge of untreated sewage accounted for one-quarter of all water pollution in the mid-1980s, the most heavily polluted areas being along the west coast. The nation has 455.8 cubic kilometers (109.4 cubic miles) of water with 47% used for farming and 30% used for industrial activity. Of the people in rural areas, 34% do not have pure water. Malaysia's cities produce 1.5 million tons of solid waste per year. Clean-air legislation, limiting industrial and automobile emissions, was adopted in 1978. Discharge of oil by vessels in Malaysian waters is prohibited.

In 1994, 23 of the nation's mammal species and 35 bird species were endangered.

6 POPULATION

The population of Malaysia totaled 17.6 million at the 1991 census, of whom 82.3% lived in Peninsular Malaysia, 9.4% in Sarawak, and 8.3% in Sabah. The estimated 1998 population was 20.9 million and the projection for 2005 was 24.1 million. The overall population density was 63 persons per square kilometer (164 per square mile).

Approximately 37% of the total population was under 15 years of age in 1998.

The population of Peninsular Malaysia is concentrated along the west coast. Kuala Lumpur, the capital, with a population (1995 estimate) of 1.2 million, is the largest city.

7 MIGRATION

By 1953, native Malays were a minority in their own territory, due to immigration by Chinese, Indian, and nonnative Indonesians and Borneans. The government enacted legislation restricting further immigration, and by 1968 the Malays formed slightly more than 50% of the population. Between 1975–89, more than 250,000 Vietnamese refugees found asylum in Malaysia; the vast majority later migrated to other countries. Between May 1989 and the end of 1993, all 10,495 Vietnamese arriving were denied entry. Nevertheless, an estimated 1 million illegal immigrants are believed to be in Malaysia.

8 ETHNIC GROUPS

The population of Malaysia consists of three main ethnic groups—Malays, Chinese, and peoples of the South Asian subcontinent (Asian Indians, Pakistanis, Bangladeshis, and Sri Lankans). Malays and other native groups are known as Bumiputras ("sons of the soil"). Estimates for 1990 reported the following distribution: Malays and other native groups (Bumiputras), 61.7%; Chinese, 29.7%; persons of Indian, Pakistani, and Bangladeshi descent, 8.1%; and other groups, 0.5%. Hostility between the Malays and Chinese has occasionally erupted into violence. The non-Malay native groups on the peninsula are collectively called the Orang Asli (aborigines) and number about 50,000.

9 LANGUAGES

Bahasa Malaysia, or Malay, is the national language and the common language of all Malaysia. Bahasa Malaysia is traditionally written using Jawi, which derives from Arabic script, but Rumi, based on the Roman alphabet, is officially used in government, education, and business. English is widely employed in government and commerce and is a compulsory subject in all schools. Chinese (notably the Mandarin, Cantonese, Hokkien, and Hakka dialects), Arabic, Tamil, Hindustani, Punjabi, Kadazan, and many other languages and dialects are spoken. Most Malaysians are bilingual or multilingual (able to speak two or more languages fluently).

10 RELIGIONS

Islam is the official religion, and about 53% of all Malaysians are Muslims. The head of state, the yang di-pertuan agong, is also the national leader of the Islamic faith. Religious lines generally follow ethnic lines. Almost all Malays are Muslims; most Indians are Hindus, with a sizable minority of Muslims, Sikhs, and Parsees; and most Chinese are Confucian-Buddhists, with a minority Muslim representation. Christianity has won some followers among the Chinese and Indians. The native peoples of Sabah and Sarawak largely follow traditional tribal religions, although many have become Christian. Roman Catholics were estimated at 3% of the population in 1993.

11 TRANSPORTATION

In 1992, the highway system of Peninsular Malaysia consisted of 92,545 kilometers (57,504 miles) of roads, of which 69,409 kilometers (43,128 miles) were paved. In 1995, registered vehicles included 2.6 million automobiles and 35,000 commercial vehicles.

The national Malayan Railway Administration operates over some 1,665 kilometers (1,035 miles) of Peninsular Malaysia, providing links to Thailand, Singapore, and eastern parts of the peninsula. Sabah State Railways provides diesel service along the west coast and in the interior for 136 kilometers (85 miles). There are no railroads in Sarawak.

The three leading ports, all located on the busy Strait of Malacca, are Keluang, Johor Baharu, and George Town. Kuching

Photo credit: Susan D. Rock.
Malaysians at a local bus stop.

is the main port for Sarawak, and Kota Kinabalu the main port for Sabah.

Most international flights enter or leave Malaysia through Kuala Lumpur Sabang International Airport; other international airports serve George Town and Kota Kinabalu. In 1995, 15.4 million passengers were carried on scheduled flights in Malaysia. The Malaysian Airline System (MAS) provides domestic service to most major cities of the peninsula and to Sarawak and Sabah.

12 HISTORY

The ancestors of the Malays came down from South China and settled in the Malay

Peninsula about 2000 BC. Sri Vijaya, a strong Indo-Malay empire with headquarters at Palembang in southern Sumatra (in Indonesia), rose about AD 600 and came to dominate both sides of the Strait of Malacca, levying tolls on the ships faring between China and India. In the fourteenth century, however, Sri Vijaya fell, and Malaysia became part of the Majapahit Empire centered in Java, an island of Indonesia east of Sumatra.

The British East India Company first entered Malaya (as the region was then called) in 1786. Throughout the following century, Britain established protectorates in the area by gaining control of, and combining, groups of several states at a time. British control was extended to Sabah in 1882, and, six years later, to North Borneo and Sarawak. Tin mining and rubber grew rapidly under British rule, and large numbers of Chinese and Indian laborers were imported, respectively, for these industries.

Japanese forces invaded Malaya and the Borneo territories in December 1941 and occupied them throughout World War II (1939–45). Within a year after the Japanese surrender in September 1945, the British formed the Malayan Union, succeeded by the Federation of Malaya on 1 February 1948. Over the next decade, Malaya progressed toward self-government. On 31 August 1957, the Federation of Malaya became an independent member of the Commonwealth of Nations.

On 16 September 1963, the Federation of Malaya, the State of Singapore, and the newly independent British colonies of Sarawak and Sabah merged to form the Federation of Malaysia, but by 1965, Singapore seceded from the Federation and established an independent republic. Internal disorders stemming from hostilities between Chinese and Malay communities in Kuala Lumpur disrupted the 1969 national elections and prompted the declaration of a state of emergency lasting from mid-1969 to February 1971. Successive governments managed to sustain political stability until 1987, when racial tensions between Chinese and Malay increased over a government plan to assign non-Mandarin-speaking administrators to Chinese-language schools.

The rise of Dayak nationalism in Sarawak was also considered a threat to political stability after the 1987 state elections, but it had been diffused by the 1991 elections, when The Sarawak Native People's Party (PBDS, Parti Bansa Dayak Sarawak) retained only 7 of the 15 seats it had won in 1987. In 1991, Malaysia's ruling party, the United Malays National Organization (UMNO) raised the issue of the alleged abuse of privilege by Malaysia's nine hereditary rulers, and in January 1993 proposed Constitutional amendments which passed, limiting their powers and removing their immunity from legal prosecution. In 1994, the government moved to ban the Islamic sect, Al-Arqam.

13 GOVERNMENT

Malaysia is a constitutional monarchy consisting of 13 states. The constitution of 1957, subsequently amended, provides for the election of a royal head of state, the yang di-pertuan agong (or "paramount ruler"), for a single term of five years. He is elected by the Conference of Rulers, nine hereditary sultans whose consent must be obtained for any law that alters state boundaries; affects the rulers' privileges or honors; or extends any religious observances or ceremonies to the country as a whole.

The yang di-pertuan agong, who must be one of the hereditary sultans, is commander-in-chief of the armed forces and has the power to designate judges for the Federal Court and the High Courts on the advice of the prime minister, whom he appoints.

Executive power rests with the cabinet, chosen by the prime minister, who is the leader of the majority party or coalition of the House of Representatives (Dewan Rakyat), the lower house of Parliament. The 180 members of the House of Representatives must be at least 21 years old; they are elected by universal adult vote. Their term is five years unless the House is dissolved earlier.

The 70-member Senate (Dewan Negara) consists of 26 elected members (2 from each state); 4 members appointed by the paramount ruler to represent the Federal Territories of Kuala Lumpur and the island of Labaun; and 40 members appointed by the paramount ruler on the basis of distinguished public service or their eligibility to represent an ethnic minority. Senators, who serve six-year terms, must be at least 30 years old.

In August 1995, the House of Representatives increased its parliamentary districts from 180 to 192. Members are elected to represent states and territories, or are appointed. Members must be at least 21 years of age, and serve a five-year term.

Of the thirteen Malaysian states, nine are headed by sultans; the other four are headed by federally appointed governors.

14 POLITICAL PARTIES

As of 1992 there were more than 30 registered parties, 13 of which are represented in the federal parliament. Some of the main parties are: the Barisan Nasional (National Front), a broad coalition comprising the United Malays National Organization (UMNO) and 12 other parties, most ethnically based; DAP (the Chinese-based Democratic Action Party); Parti Se-Islam Malaysia (PAS); Parti Bersatu Sabah (PBS); the Malaysian Chinese Association (MCA); and Semangat 46. In the election held on 25 April 1995, of the 192 seats the results were: National Front (162 seats), DAP (9), PBS (8), PAS (7), Semangat 46 (6).

15 JUDICIAL SYSTEM

Most cases come before magistrates and sessions courts. Religious courts decide questions of Islamic law and custom. The Federal Court, the highest court in Malaysia, reviews decisions referred from the High Court of Peninsular Malaysia, the High Court of Sabah and Sarawak, and subordinate courts. The Federal Court, of which the *yang di-pertuan agong* (paramount ruler) is lord president, has original jurisdiction in disputes among states, or between a state and the federal government.

16 ARMED FORCES

In 1995, the all-volunteer armed forces numbered 114,500. The total strength of the army was 90,000, including 36 infantry and armored battalions, 5 artillery regiments, and supporting air defense, signal, engineer, special forces, and administrative units. Contingents of the Malaysian army patrol the Malaysia-Thailand border against communist guerrillas and provide four United Nations observer teams.

The navy had 12,000 personnel, 4 frigates, 8 missile-equipped fast-attack craft, and 29 large patrol craft. The air force had 12,500 personnel and 79 combat aircraft. Paramilitary forces numbered 20,100, and the People's Volunteer Corps had 240,000. There are 35,800 reserves. Malaysian arms and equipment are a mixture of domestic, United Kingdom, and United States material.

17 ECONOMY

Malaysia is one of the most prosperous nations in Southeast Asia. Until the 1970s, Malaysia's economy was based chiefly on its plantation and mining activities, with rubber and tin the principal exports. Since then, however, Malaysia has added palm oil, tropical hardwoods, petroleum, natural gas, and manufactured items to its export list. Malaysia is the world's third largest producer of semiconductors (after the United States and Japan).

In 1985–86 Malaysia's long period of high growth abruptly halted as oil and palm oil prices were halved. Recovery began in late 1986–87; growth was

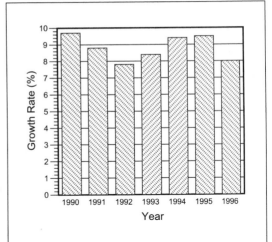

Yearly growth rate of the economy. This economic indicator tells by what percent the economy has increased or decreased when compared with the previous year.

spurred by foreign demand for exports. Growth rates continued on the average in the 8–9% range from 1987–92. As of 1997, the economy had annually grown by an average of nearly 9% for eight years.

Sarawak's basic economy is based on agriculture, supplemented by petroleum production and refining, the collection of forest produce, fishing, and the cultivation of cash crops, primarily rubber, timber and pepper. Sabah's economy rests on logging, petroleum production, rubber, pepper, and timber.

18 INCOME

In 1995, Malaysia's gross national product (GNP) was US$78 billion at current prices, or about US$4,370 per person. For the period 1985–95 the average inflation rate was 3.3%, resulting in a real growth rate in GNP of 5.7% per person.

19 INDUSTRY

The leading manufacturing industries include rubber processing, the manufacture of tires and other rubber products, palm oil processing, and tin smelting. Other manufactured goods include electrical/electronic machinery and appliances; textiles, clothing and footwear; chemicals and petroleum products; other machinery and transport equipment; and iron and steel products. Malaysia is the world's largest exporter of semiconductor devices.

Malaysia is developing what it calls the "multimedia super corridor" (MSC), an area it hopes will become a world-class research and development site for industry. The MSC is composed of several projects: the completion of the Petronas Twin Towers in Kuala Lumpur (the tallest building in the world); the building of an $8 billion city and technology center; a $3.6 billion international airport; and a massive fiber-optic telecommunications system linking them all.

20 LABOR

In 1995, Malaysia's total civilian employment was estimated at 7.9 million. Of these, 20% were in agriculture and mining; 23% in industry; and the remaining 57% in services. Unemployment in 1995 was 2–3%.

Trade unions are generally organized along ethnic lines. The Malaysian Trade Unions Congress had 410,000 members in 1994.

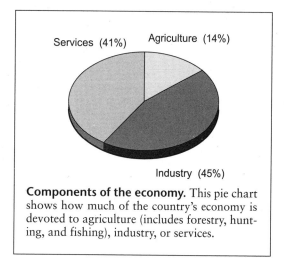

Components of the economy. This pie chart shows how much of the country's economy is devoted to agriculture (includes forestry, hunting, and fishing), industry, or services.

There is no national minimum wage, but minimum wages are set by an employment sector or on a regional basis. Only 150,000 workers in Malaysia were covered by minimum wages in 1996.

21 AGRICULTURE

Agriculture is no longer the most important sector of the Malaysian economy. It accounted for only 14% of the domestic economy in 1995. Development of such newer crops as oil palm, cocoa, and pineapples is promoted by the government. Much of Sabah and Sarawak is covered with dense jungle and is not conducive to farming. Peninsular Malaysia, however, is predominantly an agricultural region, with cultivation carried out on the coastal plains, river valleys, and foothills.

Domestically grown rice furnishes Peninsular Malaysia with about 80% of its requirements; most of the rice supply for Sabah and Sarawak, however, must be imported. Milled rice production for 1995 totaled 1.3 million tons, of which about 70% came from Peninsular Malaysia. Rubber production totaled 1.1 million tons in 1995. Malaysia produced 18% of the world's rubber in 1995, and typically accounts for over one-third of the world's rubber exports. However, competition from Thailand and Indonesia has recently diminished the Malaysian share of the rubber market.

Production of palm oil totaled 8.8 million tons in 1995, more than any other country in the world. More than 90% of all palm oil is produced in Peninsular Malaysia. Black and white peppers are grown on Sarawak; 15,000 tons were produced in 1995. Output of lesser agricultural products in 1995 included copra (dried coconut meat for coconut oil), 23,000 tons; coconut oil, 12,000 tons; and canned pineapple, 38,000 tons. Cocoa production in 1995 was an estimated 122,000 tons.

22 DOMESTICATED ANIMALS

Peninsular Malaysia is free of most infectious and contagious diseases that plague livestock in the tropical zone. The livestock population in 1995 included 2.5 million hogs, 659,000 head of cattle, 229,000 goats, 204,000 sheep, and 103,000 buffalo. Hog raising and export are handled mainly by non-Muslim Chinese.

23 FISHING

Fishing is being developed both as a means of reducing unemployment and as a primary source of protein in the country's diet. The total catch in 1994 was 1.2 million tons, as compared with 296,300 tons in 1966; the increase has been largely the result of expanded and improved marketing facilities. Exports of fish products totaled $324.8 million in 1994. Freshwater fishing in paddy fields and irrigation ditches is integrated with rice farming and hog production.

24 FORESTRY

In 1996, Malaysia produced 31 million cubic meters (40.6 million cubic yards) of roundwood from a forest area of 18.3 million hectares (45.2 million acres). About 31.8% of the forest is located on Peninsular Malaysia, 22.5% in Sabah, and 45.7% in Sarawak.

To maintain the nation's forests as a resource, the government reduced the amount of land it planned to develop during 1991–95. Log output is expected to drop during 1997–2000. Exports of logs are being phased out in order to focus on the development of veneer, plywood, furniture, and other wood-using industries. In 1995, Malaysia was the world's leading producer of veneer sheets, and ranked fourth in the production of plywood.

25 MINING

Malaysia was the world's seventh largest tin producer in 1995. That year, Malaysia mined and processed some 6,402 tons of tin metal and concentrates. Continued low prices and sluggish world demand for the metal are the main reasons for the slump since the mid-1980s.

Iron ore production increased markedly after World War II under the stimulus of Japanese demand. Production fell from

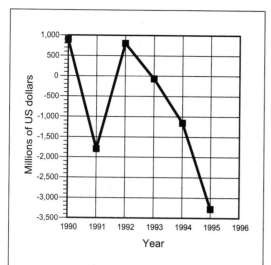

Yearly balance of trade measured in millions of US dollars. The balance of trade is the difference between what a country sells to other countries (its exports) and what it buys (its imports). If a country imports more than it exports, it has a negative balance of trade (a trade deficit). If exports exceed imports there is a positive balance of trade (a trade surplus).

a peak of 3.9 million tons in 1965 to 181,600 tons in 1985, but rose back to 202,000 tons in 1995. The output of bauxite for export was 184,000 tons in 1995. Output of copper, of which there are large reserves on Sabah, was 21,900 tons in 1995.

Other minerals extracted include gold, columbite, monazite, tungsten, manganese, kaolin, and ilmenite.

26 FOREIGN TRADE

Malaysia's main exports are electronic equipment, petroleum and petroleum products, palm oil, wood and wood products, rubber, and textiles. The principal imports for domestic consumption are foodstuffs, machinery, and transport equipment.

Singapore, the United States, and Japan were Malaysia's largest export markets in 1995. Japan, the United States, Singapore, and Taiwan were the leading import suppliers that year.

27 ENERGY AND POWER

Malaysia's electrical energy production increased to 37.9 billion kilowatt hours in 1994. In that year, 5.5 billion kilowatt hours were hydrogenerated, and 32.4 billion kilowatt hours were of thermal origin. The National Electricity Board, a state-owned corporation, supplies the greater part of the nation's power.

Crude oil, developed in the 1970s, is now the chief mineral produced, with reserves estimated at 4.3 billion barrels in 1996. Output averages 735,000 barrels per day. Of new and increasing importance are large offshore natural gas deposits, with reserves estimated at more than 1.9 trillion cubic meters (67 trillion cubic feet). Production in 1995 totaled 29 billion cubic meters (1 trillion cubic feet). Malaysia also produced 12.9 million cubic meters (450 million cubic feet) of liquefied natural gas that year. Since reserves of oil are limited and local coal is of an inferior grade, the government has greatly expanded efforts to harness the country's hydroelectric potential and natural gas as alternative energy sources.

Selected Social Indicators

These statistics are estimates for the period 1993 to 1996. For comparison purposes, data for the United States and averages for low-income countries and high-income countries are also given.

Indicator	Malaysia	Low-income countries	High-income countries	United States
Per capita gross national product†	$4,370	$490	$25,870	$28,020
Population growth rate	2.3%	1.7%	0.6%	0.9%
Population growth rate in urban areas	3.7%	3.8%	0.9%	1.2%
Population per square kilometer of land	63	82	30	29
Life expectancy in years	72	63	77	77
Number of physicians per 1,000 people	0.4	1.0	2.5	2.5
Number of pupils per teacher (primary school)	20	41	17	14
Illiteracy rate (15 years and older)	17%	34%	<5%	3%
Energy consumed per capita (kg of oil equivalent)	1,655	393	5,123	7,905

† The gross national product (GNP) is the total dollar value of all goods and services produced by a country in a year. The per capita GNP is calculated by dividing a country's GNP by its population. The World Bank defines low-income countries as those with a per capita GNP of $785 or less. High-income countries have a per capita GNP of $9,636 or more. About 16% of the world's 5.7 billion people live in high-income countries, while almost 56% live in low-income countries.   > = greater than   < = less than

Sources: World Bank, World Development Indicators on CD-ROM, Washington, D.C.: The World Bank, 1998. Central Intelligence Agency, The World Fact Book, Washington, D.C.: Government Printing Office, 1998.

28 SOCIAL DEVELOPMENT

Public financial assistance is provided within the framework of Malaysian society's highly developed sense of family and clan responsibility. The government has generally encouraged volunteer social welfare activities and has subsidized programs of private groups. The government's program of public assistance takes the form of cash, commodities, and institutional care.

Children's services, begun in 1952, provide case-work services and administer children's homes. A probation service provides care and assistance for juvenile delinquents and dependents, and a handicapped persons' service aids the deaf, mute, and blind. In addition, care is provided for the aged and chronically ill.

Women make up more than 40% of the nation's total labor force, but except in teaching and nursing, are underrepresented in professional occupations. In family and religious matters, Muslim women are subject to Islamic law, which allows polygyny (multiple wives) and favors men in matters of inheritance.

29 HEALTH

Malaysia enjoys a comparatively high standard of health, due to the government's long-established health and medical services. The country has improved its

Malaysian ox-cart transport.

health care and social conditions, and is considering a national health insurance plan. As of 1990, the government paid for three-fourths of health care expenses. About 80% of the population had access to health care facilities in 1993.

In 1994–95, 90% of the population had access to safe water and 94% had adequate sanitation. In 1989–95, 23% of children under five years of age were considered malnourished. Life expectancy has risen over the last decade and was 72 years in 1995.

30 HOUSING

The need for urban housing is acute: an estimated 24% of Kuala Lumpur's population consists of recently arrived squatters living in overcrowded shantytowns with few urban amenities. The total number of housing units is about 3.4 million units: 92% of all housing units are detached houses, 7% are apartments, and 1% are single rooms.

31 EDUCATION

Six years of free primary education is followed by three years of comprehensive general and prevocational education. A two-year preuniversity course prepares students for admission to the universities. Malay is the language of instruction in primary and secondary schools, with English a compulsory second language.

School enrollment in Malaysia in 1993 was 2.8 million pupils instructed by

140,342 teachers in 6,965 primary schools. In all secondary schools, there were 84,744 teachers and 1.6 million pupils. In 1993, 170,145 students were enrolled in institutions of higher education, which include the University Kebangsaan Malaysia (the National University of Malaysia), the University of Malaya, and the Technological University of Malaysia, all in or near Kuala Lumpur, and the University of Science Malaysia.

32 MEDIA

The government owns and operates a well-developed and well-equipped telecommunications system servicing 2.4 million telephones.

Radio-Television Malaysia (RTM) operates radio and television stations in Kuala Lumpur, Sabah, and Kuching. There is a commercial station, Sistem TV-3 Berhad, in Kuala Lumpur as well. Broadcasts are in English, Malay, five Chinese dialects, Tamil, and numerous local languages and dialects.

Malaysia generally enjoys a large measure of press freedom. In October 1987, however, the government closed four newspapers in an effort to end criticism of its policies. There are about 80 English, Malay, Chinese, and Tamil daily and weekly newspapers. The Malay-language press is the largest segment, followed by English, Chinese, Tamil, Punjabi, and Kadazan. The leading Kuala Lumpur dailies are: *Utusan Malaysia* (cirrculation 300,000); *Berita Harian* (300,000); *New Straits Times* (260,000); *New Life Post* (175,000); and *Star* (152,000).

33 TOURISM AND RECREATION

In 1996, Malaysia had 1,265 hotels with 99,144 rooms. Most large hotels are in Kuala Lumpur and George Town. One of the best-known hill resort areas is Cameron Highlands. Island resorts off the coast of the peninsula include Langkawi. Tourists numbered 7.2 million in 1994, of which 90% came from eastern Asia.

Horse racing, soccer, rugby, cricket, and *sepak raga* (a form of badminton) are popular spectator sports. Kite flying and top spinning are traditional pastimes for children and adults, and *silat* (a Malay martial art) is popular in rural areas.

34 FAMOUS MALAYSIANS

Among the foremost Malaysian leaders of the past was Sultan Mahmud, sixteenth-century ruler of Malacca. A great figure in Malay culture was 'Abdallah bin 'Abd al-Kabir (surnamed Munshi', 1796–1854), sometimes called the greatest innovator in Malay letters. The best-known figure in the political life of modern Malaysia is Tunku Abdul Rahman Putra bin Abdul Hamid Halimshah (b.1903), first prime minister of the Federation of Malaysia.

35 BIBLIOGRAPHY

American University. *Malaysia: A Country Study.* Washington, D.C.: Government Printing Office, 1984.

Major, John S. *The Land and People of Malaysia and Brunei.* New York: HarperCollins Publishers, 1991.

Spruit, Ruud. *The Land of the Sultans: An Illustrated History of Malaysia.* Amsterdam, Netherlands: Pepin Press, 1995.

Wright, D. *Malaysia.* Chicago: Children's Press, 1988.

MALDIVES

Republic of Maldives

Dhivehi Raajjeyge Jumhooriyyaa

CAPITAL: Malé.

FLAG: The national flag consists of a white crescent at the center of a green field which, in turn, is at the center of a red field.

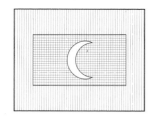

MONETARY UNIT: The Maldivian rupee, or rufiyaa (MR), is a paper currency of 100 laris. There are notes of 1/2, 1, 2, 5, 10, 50, and 100 rufiyaa. The dollar circulates freely and is the only currency accepted at some resorts. MR1 = $0.08496 (or $1 = MR11.770).

WEIGHTS AND MEASURES: The metric system has been adopted, but some local units remain in use.

HOLIDAYS: National Day, 7 January; Independence Day, 26 July; Republic Day, 11 November; Fishermen's Day, 10 December. 'Id al-Fitr, 'Id al-'Adha', and Milad an-Nabi are some of the Muslim religious holidays observed.

TIME: 5 PM = noon GMT.

1 LOCATION AND SIZE

The smallest country in Asia, the Republic of Maldives consists of an archipelago (a large group of islands) of nearly 1,200 coral islands and sand banks in the Indian Ocean, about 200 of which are inhabited. The area occupied by Maldives is slightly more than 1.5 times the size of Washington, D.C.

Maldives' capital, Malé, is situated on the largest island in the entire chain, in the Malé Atoll.

2 TOPOGRAPHY

Some of the islands are in process of formation and are constantly increasing in size; others are gradually washing away. The islands are level and extremely low-lying, with elevations rarely exceeding 1.8 meters (6 feet) above sea level. Many contain freshwater lagoons.

3 CLIMATE

The Maldives' equatorial climate is generally hot and humid, with a mean temperature of about 27°C (81°F). Annual rainfall in the south averages about 380 centimeters (150 inches); in the north, 250 centimeters (100 inches).

4 PLANTS AND ANIMALS

Coconut, breadfruit, plantain, papaya, mango, and banyan trees flourish. Shrubs and flowers are widespread. Rats, rabbits, and flying foxes are the only native mammals. Birds include ducks, bitterns, crows, curlews, snipes, and various sea birds. Small scorpions, beetles, and land crabs are common. Inland lagoons and coastal reefs contain tropical ocean fish, crustaceans, and turtles; the surrounding waters contain sharks, swordfish, and porpoises.

5 ENVIRONMENT

Environmental issues in the Maldives include a dwindling freshwater supply and inadequate sewage treatment. There is also concern that rising sea levels, as an effect of global warming, may someday cover some of the low-lying atolls. Environmental preservation is complicated by the unique problems of a nation consisting of 1,190 islands spread over 820 kilometers (510 miles) of the Indian ocean.

6 POPULATION

In 1998, the population was estimated at 290,000. The population density was about 852 persons per square kilometer (2,207 per square mile). Malé, the capital and sole urban settlement, had a population of 68,000 in 1995.

7 MIGRATION

People migrate between islands mainly to settle in Malé; between 1967 and 1990, population in the capital rose from one-tenth to over one-quarter of the national total.

8 ETHNIC GROUPS

The original inhabitants of the Maldives are thought to have been of south Indian and Arab origin. The people of the northern atolls have to some extent intermarried with peoples from western India, Arab nations, and North Africa. Inhabitants of the southern islands show stronger physical affinities with the Sinhalese of Sri Lanka.

9 LANGUAGES

The Maldivian language, called Divehi, is similar to the old Sinhala (Elu) of Ceylon.

Geographic Profile

Geographic Features

Size ranking: 184 of 192
Highest elevation: 24 meters (79 feet) at an unnamed location
Lowest elevation: Sea level at the Indian Ocean

Land Use†

Arable land:	10%
Permanent crops:	0%
Permanent pastures:	3%
Forests:	3%
Other:	84%

Weather††

Average annual precipitation: 250–380 centimeters (100–150 inches)
Average temperature in January: 27°C (81°F)
Average temperature in July: 27°C (81°F)

†*Arable land:* Land used for temporary crops, like meadows for mowing or pasture, gardens, and greenhouses. *Permanent crops:* Land cultivated with crops that occupy its use for long periods, such as cocoa, coffee, rubber, fruit and nut orchards, and vineyards. *Permanent pastures:* Land used permanently for forage crops. *Forests:* Land containing stands of trees. *Other:* Any land not specified, including built-on areas, roads, and barren land.

††The measurements for precipitation and average temperature were taken at weather stations closest to the country's largest city. Precipitation and average temperature can vary significantly within a country, due to factors such as latitude, altitude, coastal proximity, and wind patterns.

Thaana, developed during the seventeenth century, is the corresponding script, written from right to left.

10 RELIGIONS

With few exceptions, the people are Sunni Muslims, and both land ownership and citizenship are limited to followers of this faith.

11 TRANSPORTATION

Malé, the capital, and some other islands have fairly good streets. Most people travel by bicycle or on foot. Interatoll transportation still depends mostly on local sailing boats, called *batheli* and *odi*.

Oceangoing shipping has been increasing. At the outset of 1995, the Maldives had a fleet of 20 vessels serving worldwide destinations. Hulule, Malé's international airport, is a mile away over water from the capital. In 1995, the airport served 93,000 passengers.

12 HISTORY

Indo-European-speaking Sinhalese from Ceylon entered the Maldives in the fourth and fifth centuries BC. Maldivians were converted to Sunni Islam from Buddhism by Arab traders from east Africa and the Middle East in the middle of the twelfth century. From 1153, an unbroken line of 92 sultans served as local rulers for 800 years until 1953.

During the sixteenth century, the Maldives were occupied by the Portuguese. In the seventeenth century, the

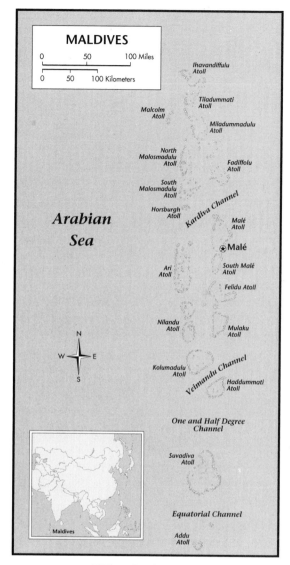

LOCATION: 7°7′N to 0°43′S; 72°31′ to 73°46′E.
TERRITORIAL SEA LIMIT: 12 miles.

Dutch, who controlled neighboring Ceylon (now Sri Lanka), concluded a treaty with the sultanate. When Ceylon fell to the British in the nineteenth century, so did

Photo credit: Susan D. Rock.

Boats in Malé harbor.

the protection arrangements of the Maldives.

When Ceylon gained independence in 1948, the Maldives remained under the protection of Great Britain. In 1959, government forces crushed rebellions in two of the southernmost atolls. The Sultanate of the Maldive Islands achieved complete independence on 26 July 1965. A new republican constitution came into force on 11 November 1968, establishing the Republic of Maldives. Britain left the Gan air base on 31 December 1975, and the United Kingdom-Maldivian protection accord was formally terminated the following year.

In November 1988, President Maumoon Abdul Gayoom successfully resisted an attempt to overthrow him by hired soldiers from Sri Lanka. He was helped by an Indian military contingent flown to the Maldives at his request. Gayoom was reelected for a fourth term as president in August 1993.

13 GOVERNMENT

Under the 1968 constitution, the president is elected to a five-year term by the Citizens' Majlis (parliament) but must be confirmed in office by popular referendum. The president heads the executive branch and appoints the cabinet. The Majlis has 48 members, 40 directly elected and 8 appointed by the president.

The Maldives is divided into 19 districts, each headed by a government-appointed *verin*, or chief.

14 POLITICAL PARTIES

There are no organized political parties. Candidates run for election as independents and campaign based on their personal and family reputations.

15 JUDICIAL SYSTEM

Justice is carried out according to traditional Islamic law *(Shari'a)* by the High Court and lower courts appointed for that purpose by the president. Civil law is also applied but remains subordinate to Shari'a.

On the capital island, Malé, there is a High Court and eight lower courts. On the other islands, there is one all-purpose

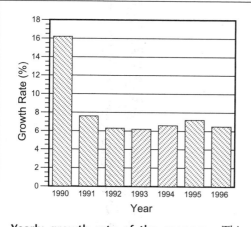

Yearly growth rate of the economy. This economic indicator tells by what percent the economy has increased or decreased when compared with the previous year.

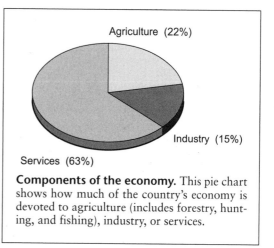

Components of the economy. This pie chart shows how much of the country's economy is devoted to agriculture (includes forestry, hunting, and fishing), industry, or services.

lower court, and complex cases are referred to the appropriate specialized court in Malé.

16 ARMED FORCES

The armed forces of the Maldives consist of a paramilitary National Security Service and Militia of only a few hundred. Defense spending may reach $1.8 million a year.

17 ECONOMY

The Maldives is among the least developed countries in the world. Fishing, tourism, and shipping are the mainstays of the economy. The government is seeking to diversify the economy through further promotion of tourism, processing industries, and garment production.

18 INCOME

In 1995, Maldives's gross national product (GNP) was $251 million at current prices, or about $1,080 per person. For the period 1985–95 the average inflation rate was 9.2%, resulting in a real growth rate in GNP of 6.7% per person.

19 INDUSTRY

After the fishing industry, important traditional industries in the Maldives include the manufacture of coir (a rope made from dried coconut fibers) and lacemaking.

20 LABOR

The fishing industry employed 20% of the labor force in 1996. The total employed work force in 1996 was 60,000. About one-third of the work force consisted of foreigners.

21 AGRICULTURE

Millet, corn, pumpkins, sweet potatoes, pineapples, sugarcane, almonds, and many kinds of tropical vegetables and fruits are successfully grown. Coconut palms provide copra and coir, the most important exports after fish. Production in 1995 included 13,000 tons of coconuts.

22 DOMESTICATED ANIMALS

Fodder (animal feed) is insufficient for more than a few head of cattle, but there are many goats and chickens.

23 FISHING

Fishing is the chief industry, with the main catch being skipjack and yellowfin tuna. The fish catch in 1994 totaled 104,110 tons. Exports of fish were valued at $36.5 million that year. On a per person basis, Maldivians eat more fish than any other nation in the world.

24 FORESTRY

There are no forests. Coconut wood, however, is used in the building of boats and the construction of houses.

25 MINING

There are no known mineral resources.

26 FOREIGN TRADE

In 1994, fish products accounted for 77% of total exports. Apparel and clothing accessories are also important exports. In 1995, leading trade partners included the

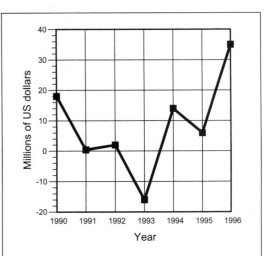

Yearly balance of trade measured in millions of US dollars. The balance of trade is the difference between what a country sells to other countries (its exports) and what it buys (its imports). If a country imports more than it exports, it has a negative balance of trade (a trade deficit). If exports exceed imports, there is a positive balance of trade (a trade surplus).

United Kingdom, Sri Lanka, the United States, Thailand, and Germany.

27 ENERGY AND POWER

The power plant in Malé provided 43 million kilowatt hours of electricity for the island in 1994.

28 SOCIAL DEVELOPMENT

There is no organized social welfare system. Assistance is traditionally provided through the extended family. In spite of traditional Islamic restrictions on women, they have increased their participation in public life.

Selected Social Indicators

These statistics are estimates for the period 1993 to 1996. For comparison purposes, data for the United States and averages for low-income countries and high-income countries are also given.

Indicator	Maldives	Low-income countries	High-income countries	United States
Per capita gross national product†	$1,080	$490	$25,870	$28,020
Population growth rate	2.6%	1.7%	0.6%	0.9%
Population growth rate in urban areas	3.6%	3.8%	0.9%	1.2%
Population per square kilometer of land	852	82	30	29
Life expectancy in years	64	63	77	77
Number of physicians per 1,000 people	n.a.	1.0	2.5	2.5
Number of pupils per teacher (primary school)	n.a.	41	17	14
Illiteracy rate (15 years and older)	7%	34%	<5%	3%
Energy consumed per capita (kg of oil equivalent)	141	393	5,123	7,905

† The gross national product (GNP) is the total dollar value of all goods and services produced by a country in a year. The per capita GNP is calculated by dividing a country's GNP by its population. The World Bank defines low-income countries as those with a per capita GNP of $785 or less. High-income countries have a per capita GNP of $9,636 or more. About 16% of the world's 5.7 billion people live in high-income countries, while almost 56% live in low-income countries.　　n.a. = data not available　　> = greater than　　< = less than

Sources: World Bank, World Development Indicators on CD-ROM, Washington, D.C.: The World Bank, 1998. Central Intelligence Agency, The World Fact Book, Washington, D.C.: Government Printing Office, 1998.

29 HEALTH

In 1993, the Maldives had 15 physicians and 6 midwives. There is an 86-bed hospital in Malé, backed by a 12-bed regional hospital and medical rescue services in the outlying atolls. Life expectancy was 64 years.

30 HOUSING

Most houses have coral or coconut-wood walls; the roofs are tiled or made of corrugated galvanized iron. The poorer houses are walled from the street with mats, called *cadjan,* or palm leaves.

31 EDUCATION

An estimated 7% of the adult population was illiterate in 1995. In 1993 there were 48,321 students in primary schools, and secondary schools had 18,678 students.

32 MEDIA

The Voice of Maldives transmits radio broadcasts in Dhivehi and English. Television Maldives is the country's only TV station. In 1995, 27,000 radio receivers and 6,000 television sets were counted; in addition, 10,000 telephones were in operation. There are two newspapers, *Aafathis* (1995 circulation 2,000) and *Haveeru* (2,500).

[33] TOURISM AND RECREATION

Tourism is the principal industry and leading foreign exchange earner. There were 279,436 visitors in 1994, 70% from Europe, and 16% from East Asia. Income from tourism was $181 million.

Natural attractions are crystal-clear lagoons and white beaches that are ideal for swimming, fishing, snorkeling, and scuba diving.

[34] FAMOUS MALDIVIANS

Sultan Iskandar Ibrahim I built the Hukuru Miskit, the principal mosque on Malé Atoll, in 1674. Modern-day leaders include Amir Ibrahim Nasir (b.1926) and Maumoon Abdul Gayoom (b.1937).

[35] BIBLIOGRAPHY

Heyerdahl, Thor. *The Maldives Mystery*. Bethesda, Md.: Adler & Adler, 1986.
Reynolds, C. H. B. *Maldives*. Santa Barbara, CA: Clio Press, 1993.

MALI

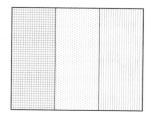

Republic of Mali
République du Mali

CAPITAL: Bamako.

FLAG: The flag is a tricolor of green, yellow, and red vertical stripes.

ANTHEM: National Anthem begins "At thy call, O Mali."

MONETARY UNIT: The Malian franc (MF), a paper currency that had been floating with the French franc, was replaced in June 1984 by the French Community Franc (CFA Fr) at a ratio of MF2 = CFA Fr1. There are coins of 1, 2, 5, 10, 25, 50, and 100 CFA francs and notes of 50, 100, 500, 1,000, 5,000, and 10,000 CFA francs. CFA Fr1 = $0.0018 (or $1 = CFA Fr571).

WEIGHTS AND MEASURES: The metric system is the legal standard.

HOLIDAYS: New Year's Day, 1 January; Armed Forces Day, 20 January; Democracy Day, 26 March; Labor Day, 1 May; Africa Day, 25 May; Independence Day, 22 September; Christmas, 25 December. Movable religious holidays include 'Id al-Fitr, 'Id al-'Adha', Milad an-Nabi, and Easter Monday.

TIME: GMT.

1 LOCATION AND SIZE

A landlocked country in West Africa, Mali has an area of about 1.2 million square kilometers (479,000 square miles), slightly less than twice the size of the state of Texas. Its total boundary length is 7,501 kilometers (4,661 miles). Mali's capital city, Bamako, is located in the southwestern part of the country.

2 TOPOGRAPHY

There are few prominent surface features in Mali, which is crossed by two river systems—the Niger and the Sénégal. The republic is divided into three natural zones: the Sudanese, an area of cultivation in the south and in the inland delta; the semiarid Sahel; and the Sahara Desert.

3 CLIMATE

Southern and western Mali, the Sudanese zone, has a climate with a short rainy season when rainfall averages 140 centimeters (55 inches). To the north is the Sahelian zone, a semiarid region along the southern border of the Sahara, with about 23 centimeters (9 inches) of rainfall a year. Continuing north, one gradually enters into a Saharan climate, marked by the virtual absence of rain and an extremely dry atmosphere.

The year is divided into three main seasons varying in length according to latitude: a cool and dry season; a hot and dry season; and a season of rains characterized by lower temperatures and an increase in humidity.

Geographic Profile

Geographic Features

Size ranking: 23 of 192
Highest elevation: 1,155 meters (3,789 feet) at
  Hombori Tondo
Lowest elevation: 23 meters (75 feet) at the Senegal
  River

Land Use†

Arable land:	2%
Permanent crops:	0%
Permanent pastures:	25%
Forests:	6%
Other:	67%

Weather††

Average annual precipitation: 109.9 centimeters (43.3
  inches)
Average temperature in January: 25.5°C (77.9°F)
Average temperature in July: 26.9°C (80.4°F)

†*Arable land:* Land used for temporary crops, like
meadows for mowing or pasture, gardens, and greenhouses. *Permanent crops:* Land cultivated with crops
that occupy its use for long periods, such as cocoa,
coffee, rubber, fruit and nut orchards, and vineyards.
Permanent pastures: Land used permanently for forage crops. *Forests:* Land containing stands of trees.
Other: Any land not specified, including built-on
areas, roads, and barren land.

††The measurements for precipitation and average
temperature were taken at weather stations closest to
the country's largest city. Precipitation and average
temperature can vary significantly within a country,
due to factors such as latitude, altitude, coastal proximity, and wind patterns.

4 PLANTS AND ANIMALS

The Saharan zone of Mali contains thick-
leaved and thorny plants (mimosas and
gum trees). The Sahelian zone also has
thorny plants, as well as shrubby tropical
grasslands, or savannas. Trees of the
Sudanese zone include mahogany, kapok,
baobab, and shea.

In the Saharan, or desert zone, animal
life includes the cheetah and the maned

wild sheep. In the Sahelian region there
are gazelles, giraffes, wart hogs, ostriches,
red monkeys, and cheetahs, as well as
lions, jackals, foxes, and hyenas. In the
Sudanese zone there are large and small
antelopes, buffalo, elephants, lions, and
monkeys, plus such water birds as the
duck, teal, and sandpiper. Other birds
include the pelican, heron, eagle, and vul-
ture.

5 ENVIRONMENT

The major environmental problem in Mali
is desertification—growing amounts of
land turning to desert. Mali also has an
inadequate water supply: 59% of city
dwellers and 96% of people living in rural
areas do not have pure water. Mali's cities
produce 0.4 million tons of solid waste.

The nation's wildlife is threatened by
drought, illegal hunting, and the destruction of the environment. Mali has a
national park and four animal reserves
that cover a total of 808,600 hectares (2
million acres), as well as six forest reserves
covering 229,400 hectares (566,900
acres). In 1994, 16 of Mali's mammal species and 4 bird species were endangered,
and 15 species of plants were threatened
with extinction.

6 POPULATION

The population of Mali was estimated by
the United States Census Bureau at 10.1
million in 1998. The United Nations,
however, gave a figure of 11.8 million for
1998. Projected population by the US
Census Bureau for 2005 is 12.5 million. In
1998 there were about 8 inhabitants per
square kilometer (21 per square mile).

LOCATION: 10°10′ to 25°N; 4°15′E to 12°15′W. **BOUNDARY LENGTHS:** Algeria, 1,376 kilometers (855 miles); Niger, 821 kilometers (510 miles); Burkina Faso, 1,202 kilometers (747 miles); Côte d'Ivoire, 515 kilometers (320 miles); Guinea, 932 kilometers (579 miles); Senegal, 418 kilometers (260 miles); Mauritania, 2,237 kilometers (1,390 miles).

Population growth was estimated at 2.7% a year during 1990–2000. Bamako, the capital, had an estimated population of 919,000 in 1995.

7 MIGRATION

As many as 2 million nomadic Malians migrate seasonally to Côte d'Ivoire, Senegal, and Libya. Additional nomads fled to Algeria, Burkina Faso, and Mauritania in the early 1990s to escape government persecution. At least 55,000 remain in Burkina Faso. There is also increasing migration from rural to urban areas. In mid-1997, 15,000 Mauritanians were refugees in Mali.

Photo credit: Corel Corporation.

Ancient style mosque in Djénné.

8 ETHNIC GROUPS

The main ethnic groups of Mali are the Bambara (about 30–35%), mostly farmers occupying central Mali, and the Fulani (10–13%), who are found mainly in the region of Mopti. Other groups include the Marka (Sarakolé or Soninké), Songhai, Malinké, Tuareg, Minianka, Sénoufo, and Dogon. The majority of the peoples in Mali are Negroid; the Tuareg are classified as Caucasoid; and the Fulani are of mixed origin.

9 LANGUAGES

French, the official language, is used in government and education. There are practically as many languages as there are ethnic groups. The Semitic-speaking Arabs and Hamitic-speaking Tuareg are the only groups with a traditional written language. Bambara, Fulani, and Songhai are all widely spoken.

10 RELIGIONS

The constitution provides for religious freedom. In the early 1990s, it was estimated that 80% of the people were Muslims; 18% followed native religion; and 1.2% were Roman Catholics and other Christians.

11 TRANSPORTATION

Mali has 642 kilometers (399 miles) of railroad, served by diesel electric locomotives. Mali's road network includes about 15,700 kilometers (9,750 miles) of highways, of which 1,700 kilometers (1,050 miles) were paved as of 1995. In 1991 there were about 31,000 vehicles in Mali.

Mali is landlocked; it is served by the port of Dakar in Senegal. The Niger, Bani, and Sénégal rivers are all navigable. Mali, Senegal, and Mauritania make up the Senegal River Development Organization. An international airport is at Senou, 14 kilometers (9 miles) from Bamako. In 1992, Mali joined the ten other signatories of the Yaoundé Treaty and became a partner in Air Afrique.

12 HISTORY

The recorded history of the area now called Mali begins with the empire of Ghana, which is said to date from the fourth century AD. It disintegrated by the thirteenth century and was succeeded by the Mali Empire, from which the independent republic takes its name.

The Mali Empire which reached its peak in the fourteenth century under Mansa Musa (r.1312–37), ended by the seventeenth century, and the Tuareg took much of the northern area. Meanwhile, to the east, the Songhai Empire, founded around AD 700, held sway for nearly a thousand years until 1591, when the Songhai fell to an invading Moroccan army. Under Moroccan rule, a military caste controlled the countryside, but by 1780, the area had become fragmented into small states.

Around 1880, the French began their advance into what was to become the Republic of Mali. Under French administration, the area became known as French Sudan (Soudan Français) and was a part of French West Africa. In 1946, the Sudanese became French citizens, with representation in the French parliament. In 1958, under the constitution of the Fifth French Republic, French Sudan became an autonomous republic, called the Sudanese Republic, within the French Community. Achievements under French rule included the building of a railway, and development of the Niger River delta.

Independence

In June 1960, the new Mali Federation, consisting of the Sudanese Republic and Senegal, became a sovereign state. However, disagreements soon arose. On 22 September 1960, the Sudan declared itself independent as the Republic of Mali, and

Photo credit: Brian Mantrop and Pierre St. Jacques.
Popular transportation in Mali.

all ties between Senegal and Mali were soon severed as well.

The one-party dictatorship led by President Modibo Keita evolved into a socialist regime modeled on that of the People's Republic of China. However, by 1968, economic problems and discontent became severe. On 19 November, Keita was overthrown in a bloodless coup led by Lieutenant (later General) Moussa Traoré. The 1960 constitution was abolished, and a 14-member Military Committee for National Liberation took command. Lieutenant Traoré became president in 1969. The military regime's efforts to improve the economic situation in Mali were frustrated by the prolonged period of drought that began in 1968 and peaked in 1973.

Traoré was elected president in 1979 under a new constitution, which also confirmed Mali as a one-party state. He was reelected in 1985. However, on 26 March 1991, Lieutenant Colonel Amadou Toumani Touré engineered a coup that toppled the Traoré government.

After the coup, a National Conference drafted new electoral rules, party statutes and a new constitution. The new constitution was adopted by referendum in January 1992. It established an agenda for the transition to a multi-party state. New elections were held and in April 1992 Dr. Alpha Oumar Konaré, the leader of the Alliance for Democracy in Mali (ADEMA), became Mali's first democratically elected president with 69% of the vote, and The Third Republic was launched.

One of the last acts of the Touré transitional government was to negotiate (with Algerian mediation) a peace treaty in April 1992 with rebel members of the ethnic Tuaregs in the north. The government acknowledged the northerners' special status, and the Tuaregs renounced their claims to independence. Student unrest continued and in April 1993, the government was forced to resign. Abdoulaye Sekou Sow replaced Younoussi Touré as prime minister, but his government fell from power in February 1994, as violence continued among students and the unemployed. In January 1996, the government cracked down, arresting several leaders of student groups that had been protesting mostly for economic reasons.

13 GOVERNMENT

The 1979 constitution was replaced by a new constitution adopted by referendum in January 1992. The National Assembly now has 116 deputies with 10 parties represented. The president, elected by popular vote, chooses the prime minister who selects a cabinet (currently 22 ministers, including five from opposition parties).

14 POLITICAL PARTIES

The Democratic Union of Malian People (Union Démocratique de Peuple Malien—UDPM) was created as the sole legal political party in 1979. Shortly after the military coup in March 1991, some 48 parties were functioning, of which 23 contested the 1992 elections and ten elected deputies to the National Assembly. The Alliance for Democracy in Mali (ADEMA) is the majority party, but the prime minister and government formed on 12 April 1993, brought opposition parties into the cabinet. The UDPM, the former ruling party, relaunched itself in mid-1993.

15 JUDICIAL SYSTEM

A Supreme Court was established in Bamako in 1969. It is made up of 19 members, nominated for five years. The judicial section has three civil chambers and one criminal chamber. The administrative section deals with appeals and fundamental rulings. The Court of Appeal is also in Bamako. There are two magistrate courts, courts for labor disputes, and a special court of state security. The 1992 Constitution established a separate constitutional court and a High Court of Justice charged with responsibility for trying senior government officials accused of treason.

16 ARMED FORCES

Armed forces' strength was 7,350 in 1995: 6,900 were in the ground forces, 50 in the marine forces, and 400 in the air forces, (all considered part of the army). Overall, the army consisted of 13 mixed battalions and an air defense missile battery. The air force was equipped with 16 aircraft, and the navy possessed 3 river patrol boats. In 1995 Mali spent $56 million on defense, or 2.5% of the gross domestic product (GDP).

17 ECONOMY

Economic activity in Mali centers on domestic agricultural and livestock production. Vast stretches of Sahara desert limit Mali's agricultural potential and subject the country to severe, prolonged, recurrent drought (1968–74, 1982–85). In periods of adequate rainfall, Mali approaches food self-sufficiency.

In January 1994 France devalued the CFA franc, cutting its value in half overnight. Mali did not benefit very much from the devaluation because it has few exports. Inflation reached 35% after the devaluation but dropped off to 8% in 1995.

18 INCOME

In 1995 Mali's gross national product (GNP) was $2.4 billion, or about $240 per person. For the period 1985–95 the average inflation rate was 151.9%, resulting in

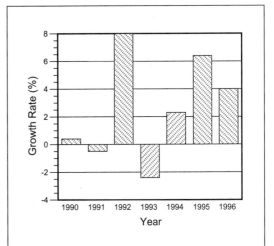

Yearly growth rate of the economy. This economic indicator tells by what percent the economy has increased or decreased when compared with the previous year.

a real growth rate in GNP of 0.6% per person.

19 INDUSTRY

Mali has a very small industrial sector, mostly government-owned plants producing textiles and consumer goods. Textiles account for about 50% of the industrial output's value. Ground nut (peanut) oil, rice polishing, fruit preserving, sugar distilling, tea, and cottonseed oil and cottonseed cake plants are in operation, as are three slaughterhouses. Other industrial facilities include a vinegar factory, a cigarette factory, a soft-drink plant, a flour mill, a shoe factory, a tannery, and two textile plants. There are a few construction related facilities, including a cement works, a brick factory, and a ceramics factory.

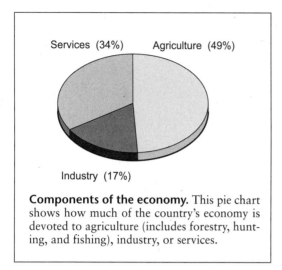

Services (34%) Agriculture (49%)

Industry (17%)

Components of the economy. This pie chart shows how much of the country's economy is devoted to agriculture (includes forestry, hunting, and fishing), industry, or services.

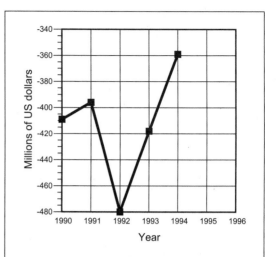

Yearly balance of trade measured in millions of US dollars. The balance of trade is the difference between what a country sells to other countries (its exports) and what it buys (its imports). If a country imports more than it exports, it has a negative balance of trade (a trade deficit). If exports exceed imports, there is a positive balance of trade (a trade surplus).

20 LABOR

Of the total estimated work force of 2.9 million in 1991, 75% were engaged in agriculture or livestock raising, which accounted for about half of the gross domestic product (GDP). Wage workers are given extensive protection under the labor laws, including a maximum work-week, a minimum wage, and a specified number of days of paid annual leave. The constitution allows workers to form and join unions and provides for the right to strike.

21 AGRICULTURE

Only the southern part of Mali is suited to farming, and less than 2% of Mali's area is cultivated. Millet, rice, and corn are the basic food crops. Peanuts are grown in the Sudanese zone, as are cotton, fruits, vegetables, and henna. The shea tree nut, which grows wild, is exploited by Malians for its oil.

Output fluctuates widely as a result of the amount and distribution of rainfall. In 1995, cereal production reached 2.4 million tons. Cotton is Mali's main foreign exchange earner. In 1995, Mali had a record production of 400,000 tons. Production estimates in 1995 for principal agricultural crops grown for domestic use included millet 858,000 tons; sorghum, 746,000 tons; sugarcane, 262,000 tons; corn, 322,000 tons; cassava, 2,000 tons; and sweet potatoes, 10,000 tons. The rice production figure was 469,000 tons.

22 DOMESTICATED ANIMALS

In 1995 there were an estimated 7.4 million goats, 5.2 million sheep, 5.5 million head of cattle, 611,000 donkeys, 260,000 camels, 101,000 horses, 63,000 hogs, and 23 million chickens in Mali. Total meat production was estimated at 185,000 tons in 1995. Livestock exports are the second largest source of foreign exchange after cotton. Milk production was estimated at 377,000 tons, and the production of hides and skins at 22,225 tons.

23 FISHING

The Niger River and its tributaries are extensively fished. About 90% of the fishing catch is dried or smoked for domestic consumption and export. The total catch was 62,950 tons in 1995.

24 FORESTRY

Forest and woodland are estimated to cover some 12 million hectares (29.6 million acres), or about 9.8% of the total land area. A total of 6 forest reserves cover 229,400 hectares (566,900 acres). Wood is Mali's primary energy source, and overcutting for fuel is a serious problem. Roundwood production in 1995 amounted to 6.5 million cubic meters (8.5 million cubic yards), 94% used for fuel.

25 MINING

Mining activity at present includes a marble quarry, a limestone quarry, a phosphate complex, and small-scale extraction of salt. Large-scale gold mining began in December 1984 at Kalana, southwest of Bougouni, with aid from the former Soviet Union. In 1995, total gold output was 7,800 kilograms (17,200 pounds). The gold production accounted for 95% of the mineral value and 20% of Mali's exports

Photo credit: Brian Mantrop and Pierre St. Jacques.
Woman at market in Niono.

that year. All mines are owned by the state, but quarries may be privately owned.

Mali also has manganese, bauxite, and phosphate deposits. Two salt caravans (strings of pack animals), each including thousands of camels, annually transport salt in bars of 30 to 40 kilograms (60–80 pounds) each from the famous salt city of Taoudenni. Annual production is about 5,000 tons.

26 FOREIGN TRADE

Cotton, livestock, and gold are Mali's leading exports. Vehicles, machinery, electronics, telecommunications, mining

Circular mud huts with thatched roofs are characteristic of native villages in Mali.

equipment, and most other manufactured items are imported. Exports totaled $319.7 million in 1995, and imports amounted to $421.6 million.

In 1995, Mali's leading export markets were China, Belgium-Luxembourg, Brazil, and Portugal. Imports came principally from Côte d'Ivoire and France.

27 ENERGY AND POWER

In 1994, total production of electricity reached 283 million kilowatt hours (78% hydroelectric). Installed capacity was 87,000 kilowatts (48% thermal).

28 SOCIAL DEVELOPMENT

Social welfare is basically an extension of the labor code, which includes provisions for medical care, workers' compensation, and retirement benefits. A system of family allowances for wage earners provides small maternity and children's allowances, along with classes in prenatal and infant care. Traditionally, the individual's basic welfare needs were cared for by the tribal organization. This system, however, is breaking down as the country develops.

29 HEALTH

Most health care is provided by the public medical services. The number of private doctors and well-equipped medical institutions is small. In 1993, the population per physician was about 18,376. In 1985–95, only 30% of the population had access to health care services.

Selected Social Indicators

These statistics are estimates for the period 1993 to 1996. For comparison purposes, data for the United States and averages for low-income countries and high-income countries are also given.

Indicator	Mali	Low-income countries	High-income countries	United States
Per capita gross national product†	$240	$490	$25,870	$28,020
Population growth rate	3.0%	1.7%	0.6%	0.9%
Population growth rate in urban areas	5.3%	3.8%	0.9%	1.2%
Population per square kilometer of land	8	82	30	29
Life expectancy in years	50	63	77	77
Number of physicians per 1,000 people	<0.1	1.0	2.5	2.5
Number of pupils per teacher (primary school)	66	41	17	14
Illiteracy rate (15 years and older)	69%	34%	<5%	3%
Energy consumed per capita (kg of oil equivalent)	21	393	5,123	7,905

† The gross national product (GNP) is the total dollar value of all goods and services produced by a country in a year. The per capita GNP is calculated by dividing a country's GNP by its population. The World Bank defines low-income countries as those with a per capita GNP of $785 or less. High-income countries have a per capita GNP of $9,636 or more. About 16% of the world's 5.7 billion people live in high-income countries, while almost 56% live in low-income countries.   n.a. = data not available   > = greater than   < = less than

Sources: World Bank, *World Development Indicators on CD-ROM,* Washington, D.C.: The World Bank, 1998. Central Intelligence Agency, *The World Fact Book,* Washington, D.C.: Government Printing Office, 1998.

The principal diseases are malaria, leprosy, tuberculosis, enteritis and other intestinal diseases, cholera, pneumonia, and infectious and parasite-related diseases, such as schistosomiasis, onchocerciasis, and trypanosomiasis. Anemia, malnutrition, and tetanus are also widespread. In 1990–95, only 37% of the population had access to safe water and 31% had adequate sanitation. The average life expectancy was 50 years.

30 HOUSING

Housing structures in Bamako are mainly like those of a European city. Elsewhere, housing ranges from typical urban structures to the tents of Tuareg nomads, the circular mud huts with thatched roofs characteristic of native African villages, and traditional Sudanese architecture whose buildings resemble those in North Africa and the Middle East.

Since World War II (1939–45), the growth of Bamako and other towns has been rapid, with government activity largely concentrated on improvement of urban housing and sanitation. The Real Estate Trust, a public corporation established in 1949, provides housing loans to persons wishing to build on their own land.

31 EDUCATION

In 1995, 69% of the adult population of Mali was illiterate (60.6% of males and

76.9% of females). In 1994, there were 1,732 primary schools with 8,274 teachers and 542,891 pupils. In the general secondary schools, there were 99,379 pupils. In addition, vocational schools had 11,876 pupils.

Located in Koulikoro is the Rural Polytechnic Institute of Katibougou. There are schools of business, administration, engineering, medicine and dentistry, and education in Bamako.

32 MEDIA

Virtually all media are owned by the state. Radio Mali broadcasts in French, English, and seven local languages. There were 27,000 radios and 6,000 television sets in use in 1995. A television service financed by Libya began broadcasting for two hours a week in 1983. In 1993 there were 13,800 main telephone lines in Mali.

A daily newspaper, *L'Essor*, is published in Bamako; circulation was about 10,000 in 1995. Also published daily is the bulletin of the Chamber of Commerce and Industry of Mali.

33 TOURISM AND RECREATION

A government tourist organization was created in April 1974 to develop hunting, fishing, and sightseeing in Mali, particularly in the areas around Mopti, Tombouctou, and Gao. There are modern motels in Bamako and in Tombouctou, the ancient capital of Muslim learning and culture, previously forbidden to foreigners. Also of interest to the tourist are Mali's national park and game reserves. Football (soccer) is a popular sport. In 1994 there were 28,000 tourist arrivals in hotels and other establishments, 36% from Africa, and 32% from Europe.

34 FAMOUS MALIANS

Early figures associated with the area of present-day Mali include Mansa Musa (r.1312–37), ruler of the Mali Empire, and Sonni 'Ali Ber (r.1464–92) and Askia Muhammad I (r.1492–1528), rulers of the Songhai Empire. Samory Touré, (1835–1900), fought the French at the head of a Malinké (Mandingo) army for 16 years (1882–98). Modibo Keita (1915–77) became the first president of the Republic of Mali in 1960. Moussa Traoré (b.1936) was president of Mali from 1969 to 1991. Alpha Oumar Konaré (b.1947) was elected president in 1992.

35 BIBLIOGRAPHY

Imperato, Pascal James. *Historical Dictionary of Mali*. 3rd edition. London: Scarecrow Press, 1996.

Imperato, Pascal J., ed. *Mali: A Search for Direction*. Boulder, Colo.: Westview Press, 1989.

Imperato, Pascal J. and Eleanor M. *Mali: A Handbook of Historical Statistics*. Boston: G. K. Hall, 1982.

Jenkins, Mark. *To Timbuktu*. New York: W. Morrow, 1997.

MALTA

The Republic of Malta
Repubblika Ta' Malta

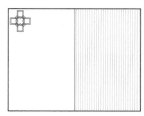

CAPITAL: Valletta.

FLAG: The national flag consists of two equal vertical stripes, white at the hoist and red at the fly, with a representation of the Maltese Cross, edged with red, in the canton of the white stripe.

ANTHEM: *L'Innu Malti (The Maltese Hymn).*

MONETARY UNIT: The Maltese lira (LM) consists of 100 cents, with each cent divided into 10 mils. There are coins of 2, 3, and 5 mils and of 1, 2, 5, 10, 25, and 50 cents, and notes of 2, 5, 10, and 20 lira. Gold and silver coins of 1, 2, 4, 5, 10, 20, 25, 50, and 100 lira are also in circulation. ML1 = $0.357 (or $1 = M2.80112).

WEIGHTS AND MEASURES: The metric system is the legal standard, but some local measures are still in use.

HOLIDAYS: New Year's Day, 1 January; National Day, 31 March; May Day, 1 May; Assumption, 15 August; Republic Day, 13 December; Christmas, 25 December. Movable holidays include Good Friday.

TIME: 1PM = noon GMT.

1 LOCATION AND SIZE

Malta lies in the central Mediterranean Sea. There are three main islands—Malta, Gozo, and Comino—as well as two small uninhabited islands, Cominotto and Filfla. Malta's total area is 320 square kilometers (124 square miles), slightly less than twice the size of Washington, D.C. The total coastline of the inhabited islands is 140 kilometers (87 miles).

Malta's capital city, Valletta, is located on the east coast of the island of Malta.

2 TOPOGRAPHY

The islands of Malta are a rocky formation (chiefly limestone) rising from east to northeast to a height of 240 meters (786 feet), with clefts that form deep harbors, bays, creeks, and rocky coves.

3 CLIMATE

The climate is typically Mediterranean. The average winter temperature is 9°C (48°F); the average summer temperature, 31°C (88°F). Rainfall averages about 64 centimeters (25 inches) per year.

4 PLANTS AND ANIMALS

Vegetation is scarce and stunted. Carob and fig are widespread, and the grape, bay, and olive have been cultivated for centuries. There are some rock plants.

The weasel, hedgehog, and bat are native to Malta. Many types of turtles, tortoises, and butterflies and several varieties of lizard also are found. Common varieties of Mediterranean fish, as well as the seal and porpoise, inhabit the surrounding waters.

Geographic Profile

Geographic Features

Size ranking: 183 of 192
Highest elevation: 240 meters (787 feet) at Dingli Cliffs
Lowest elevation: Sea level at the Mediterranean Sea

Land Use†

Arable land:	38%
Permanent crops:	3%
Permanent pastures:	0%
Forests:	0%
Other:	59%

Weather††

Average annual precipitation: 64 centimeters (25.2 inches)
Average temperature range in January (Valletta): 10–14°C (50–57°F)
Average temperature range in July (Valletta): 22–29°C (72–84°F)

†*Arable land:* Land used for temporary crops, like meadows for mowing or pasture, gardens, and greenhouses. *Permanent crops:* Land cultivated with crops that occupy its use for long periods, such as cocoa, coffee, rubber, fruit and nut orchards, and vineyards. *Permanent pastures:* Land used permanently for forage crops. *Forests:* Land containing stands of trees. *Other:* Any land not specified, including built-on areas, roads, and barren land.

††The measurements for precipitation were taken at weather stations closest to the country's largest city. Precipitation and average temperature can vary significantly within a country, due to factors such as latitude, altitude, coastal proximity, and wind patterns.

5 ENVIRONMENT

Malta's most significant environmental problems include inadequate water supply, deforestation, and danger to its wildlife. Malta was one of the first countries to ratify the 1976 Barcelona Convention for the protection of the Mediterranean from pollution. In cooperation with the World Wildlife Fund, the Ghadira wetland area was made a permanent nature reserve in 1980.

6 POPULATION

The total resident population at the time of the 1985 census was 340,907, of whom 315,913 lived on Malta and 24,994 on Gozo and Comino. The estimated population in 1998 was 380,000 and the projected population for 2005 was 390,000. The estimate of 1,166 persons per square kilometer (3,020 persons per square mile) makes Malta one of the most densely populated countries in the world. Valletta, the capital and chief port, had an estimated 1995 area population of 99,000.

7 MIGRATION

High population and unemployment have led to emigration. Most emigrants go to Australia, the United States, Canada, or the United Kingdom. Most foreigners living in Malta are British nationals and their families.

8 ETHNIC GROUPS

Most Maltese are believed to be descended from the ancient Carthaginians, but there are elements of Italian and other Mediterranean ancestries.

9 LANGUAGES

Maltese, a Semitic language with Romance-language elements, is the national language and the language of the courts. Maltese and English are both official languages.

10 RELIGION

In 1993, an estimated 98% of the population was Catholic; religious minorities include some 3,900 Anglicans.

11 TRANSPORTATION

Malta has no railways. In 1993 there were 1,471 kilometers (914 miles) of paved roads. Passenger cars in 1995 totaled 116,700; taxis, trucks, and buses, 14,600.

The harbors of Valletta, among the finest in the Mediterranean, are a port of call for many lines connecting northwestern Europe and the Middle and Far East. Roughly 3,000 ships dock at Valletta each year. The principal airport is at Luqa. The national air carrier is Malta Airlines.

12 HISTORY

The strategic importance of the island of Malta was recognized in ancient times, when it was occupied by the Phoenicians, Greeks, Carthaginians, and Romans. The apostle Paul was shipwrecked at Malta in AD 58, and the islanders were converted to Christianity within two years. With the official split of the Roman Empire in AD 395, Malta was assigned to Byzantium, and in AD 870 it fell under the domination of the Saracens.

Over the following centuries, Malta had several more occupiers, including the French and, finally, the British, who ousted Napoleon's forces in 1800. British possession of Malta was confirmed in 1814 by the Treaty of Paris.

During almost the entire nineteenth century, a British military governor ruled the colony. The Maltese remained loyal to Britain in World War I (1914–18) and World War II (1939–45). For gallantry under heavy fire during the German-Italian siege (1940–43), the entire population was awarded the George Cross.

LOCATION: 35°48′ to 36°N; 14°10′30″ to 14°35′E.
TERRITORIAL SEA LIMIT: 12 miles.

Although the Maltese enjoyed a great degree of self-government, they wanted complete independence, except in matters of defense and foreign affairs. Malta became a sovereign and independent nation within the British Commonwealth of Nations on 21 September 1964. At the same time, mutual defense and financial agreements were signed with the United Kingdom.

On 13 December 1974, Malta formally adopted a republican form of government, and the former governor-general, Sir Anthony Mamo, became the first president. Dom Mintoff, leader of the Malta Labour Party and prime minister from 1971 through 1984, adopted socialist measures domestically and initiated a non-aligned policy in foreign affairs. The Nationalists, under Eddie Fenech Adami, have been in power since 1987.

Maltese politics has revolved around foreign policy issues, in particular, Malta's relationship with Europe. The Nationalist Party government has been a strong advocate of European Union membership. Malta has applied for full membership in the European Union. However, since the Labor Party won the 1996 elections, the government's stance has shifted towards maintaining neutrality. The government has begun to renegotiate Malta's relationship with the European Union but has not withdrawn its application.

13 GOVERNMENT

The single-chamber parliament, the House of Representatives, consists of 65 members (1994) elected for a five-year term by universal adult suffrage. The House elects the head of state, called the president of the republic, who in turn appoints the prime minister.

14 POLITICAL PARTIES

There are two major political parties, the Nationalist Party (PN) and the Malta Labour Party (MLP), which have alternated in political power. The MLP regained a majority in 1996 after nine years of PN control.

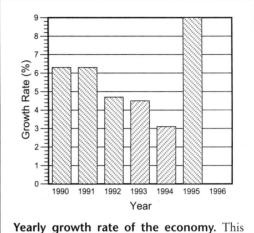

Yearly growth rate of the economy. This economic indicator tells by what percent the economy has increased or decreased when compared with the previous year.

15 JUDICIAL SYSTEM

The superior courts consist of the Constitutional Court, the court of appeal, the court of criminal appeal, two civil courts, the criminal court, and the commercial court.

16 ARMED FORCES

The volunteer army of 1,950 has one infantry battalion and a mixed air and naval battalion. Malta spends $31 million on defense (1995).

17 ECONOMY

Until 1964, the dominant factor in the economy was the presence of British military forces. Malta's economy now relies on light industry, tourism, and other service industries.

Photo credit: AP/World Wide photos.

A woman walks along merchant-lined St. Paul's street in Valletta, Malta. Narrow streets are characteristic of the small Mediterranean island.

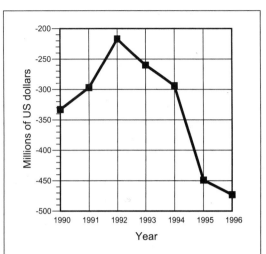

Yearly balance of trade measured in millions of US dollars. The balance of trade is the difference between what a country sells to other countries (its exports) and what it buys (its imports). If a country imports more than it exports, it has a negative balance of trade (a trade deficit). If exports exceed imports, there is a positive balance of trade (a trade surplus).

18 INCOME

In 1995, Malta's gross national product (GNP) was about $8,650 per person. For the period 1985–95 the average inflation rate was 2.9%, resulting in a real growth rate in GNP of 5.1% per person.

19 INDUSTRY

Malta's principal industries are shipbuilding (including maintenance and repairs), food processing, electronics, and textiles and clothing. Industry (including ship building and repair) accounts for 34% of the gross domestic product (GDP).

20 LABOR

As of 1993, Malta's labor force was about 132,260, of which 96,810 were men and 35,450 were women. Unemployment stood at 4.5% at the end of 1993.

21 AGRICULTURE

Wheat, barley, and grapes are the principal crops for domestic consumption, while potatoes, onions, wine, cut flowers, seeds, and fruit are the chief export crops. The total value of agricultural crops exported in 1995 was estimated at $22.2 million.

22 DOMESTICATED ANIMALS

Malta's livestock population in 1995 included 19,000 head of cattle, 104,000 pigs, 17,000 sheep, 9,000 goats, and 1 million poultry.

23 FISHING

Fishing is for local consumption.

24 FORESTRY

There are no forests on the islands.

25 MINING

In 1994, Malta's mineral industry produced 30 metric tons of salt. Limestone, used in domestic construction, was also produced.

26 FOREIGN TRADE

Since it relies on external sources for much of its food, fuel, raw materials, and manufactured items, Malta imports more than it exports. In 1995, total exports amounted to nearly $1.9 billion, while imports came to over $2.9 billion. The United Kingdom

Selected Social Indicators

These statistics are estimates for the period 1993 to 1996. For comparison purposes, data for the United States and averages for low-income countries and high-income countries are also given.

Indicator	Malta	Low-income countries	High-income countries	United States
Per capita gross national product†	$8,650	$490	$25,870	$28,020
Population growth rate	0.5%	1.7%	0.6%	0.9%
Population growth rate in urban areas	0.8%	3.8%	0.9%	1.2%
Population per square kilometer of land	1,166	82	30	29
Life expectancy in years	77	63	77	77
Number of physicians per 1,000 people	2.5	1.0	2.5	2.5
Number of pupils per teacher (primary school)	20	41	17	14
Illiteracy rate (15 years and older)	n.a.	34%	<5%	3%
Energy consumed per capita (kg of oil equivalent)	2,262	393	5,123	7,905

† The gross national product (GNP) is the total dollar value of all goods and services produced by a country in a year. The per capita GNP is calculated by dividing a country's GNP by its population. The World Bank defines low-income countries as those with a per capita GNP of $785 or less. High-income countries have a per capita GNP of $9,636 or more. About 16% of the world's 5.7 billion people live in high-income countries, while almost 56% live in low-income countries.   n.a. = data not available   > = greater than   < = less than

Sources: World Bank, *World Development Indicators on CD-ROM,* Washington, D.C.: The World Bank, 1998. Central Intelligence Agency, *The World Fact Book,* Washington, D.C.: Government Printing Office, 1998.

was Malta's principal trade partner in the 1970s but was outstripped by Italy and Germany during the 1980s. Principal trade partners in 1995 were Italy, Germany, the United Kingdom, and France.

27 ENERGY AND POWER

Production of electrical energy was 1.4 billion kilowatt hours in 1994. Malta is totally dependent on imported fuel for its energy requirements.

28 SOCIAL DEVELOPMENT

The National Insurance Act of 1956 provides benefits for sickness, unemployment, old age, widowhood, orphanhood, disability, and industrial injuries. A constitu-

tional amendment in 1993 requires government protection of all groups against economic, social, and political discrimination.

29 HEALTH

British, Belgian, and other foreign nationals work in Malta's eight hospitals. Average life expectancy is 77 years.

30 HOUSING

At the end of 1983, there were approximately 111,700 dwellings on Malta. New housing units completed during 1983 totaled roughly 2,400.

[31] EDUCATION

Primary education is compulsory between the ages of 6 and 16. Maltese law requires that the teachings of the Roman Catholic Church be included in the public school curriculum. In 1993, there were 35,366 students in primary schools, 34,955 in secondary schools, 5,873 in vocational schools, and 5,177 enrolled in higher level institutions.

[32] MEDIA

In 1995, there were 267,000 television sets, 189,000 radios, and 157,500 telephones. The press includes two Maltese daily newspapers, one English daily, two Maltese Sunday newspapers, and one English Sunday newspaper.

[33] TOURISM AND RECREATION

Tourism is a major industry, with 1.2 million visitors in 1994 and gross earnings of $639 million. About 45% of Malta's visitors that year came from the United Kingdom, 17% from Germany, and 8% from Italy.

[34] FAMOUS MALTESE

The city of Valletta is named after Jehan Parisot de la Vallette (1494–1568), who withstood a great Turkish siege in 1565. Agatha Barbara (b.1923), a former cabinet minister, was elected the first female president of Malta on 16 February 1982. Alfred Sant (b.1948) became prime minister in 1996.

[35] BIBLIOGRAPHY

Berg, Warren G. *Historical Dictionary of Malta.* Lanham, Md.: Scarecrow Press, 1995.

Blouet, Brian. *A Short History of Malta.* New York: Praeger, 1967.

Clews, Hilary A., ed. *The Year Book, 1987.* Sliema: De La Salle Brothers, 1987.

Dobie, Edith. *Malta's Road to Independence.* Norman: University of Oklahoma Press, 1967.

Ellis, William S. "Malta: The Passion of Freedom." *National Geographic,* June 1989, 700–717.

MARSHALL ISLANDS

Republic of the Marshall Islands

CAPITAL: Majuro, Majuro Atoll.

FLAG: The flag, adopted in 1979, is blue, with two diagonal strips of orange over white; in the canton is a white star with 4 large rays and 20 shorter ones.

ANTHEM: *Ij iokwe lok aelon eo ao ijo iaar lotak ie (I Love My Island, Where I Was Born).*

MONETARY UNIT: The US dollar is the official medium of exchange.

WEIGHTS AND MEASURES: British units are used, as modified by US usage.

HOLIDAYS: The government has not legislated official holidays.

TIME: 11 PM = noon GMT.

1 LOCATION AND SIZE

The Marshall Islands is located in the central Pacific Ocean, just north of the equator. The country consists of 29 atolls (ring-shaped coral islands) and 5 islands extending over a sea area exceeding 1.9 million square kilometers (750,000 square miles), but a land area of only about 181 square kilometers (70 square miles), slightly larger than Washington, D.C.

The capital city of the Marshall Islands, Majuro, is located on the island of Majuro.

2 TOPOGRAPHY

The majority of islands are in typical atoll formations, consisting of low-lying narrow strips of land enclosing a lagoon. Soils are porous, sandy, and of low fertility. Kwajalein Atoll is the largest atoll in the world.

3 CLIMATE

The climate is hot and humid, with little seasonal temperature change. Daily variations generally range between 21° and 34°C (70° and 93°F). Rainfall averages about 30–38 centimeters (12–15 inches) per month.

4 PLANTS AND ANIMALS

Native plants consist of species resistant to porous soils, salt spray, and relatively strong wind force. The dominant tree species include coconut palms, pandanus, breadfruit, and citrus trees. Native animals include rodents and native species of pig.

Geographic Profile

Geographic Features

Size ranking: 186 of 192
Highest elevation: 10 meters (33 feet) at an unnamed
  location on Likiep
Lowest elevation: Sea level at the Pacific Ocean

Land Use

Permanent crops: 60%
Other: 40%

Weather

Average annual precipitation: 178–432 centimeters
  (70–170 inches)

5 ENVIRONMENT

Environmental problems include water pollution due to lack of adequate sanitation facilities. Any rise of sea level due to global warming is a threat to the island nation. The Bikini, Enewetak, Rongelap, and Utirik atolls were contaminated by nuclear testing in 1946–1958.

6 POPULATION

The 1998 population was estimated at 63,000. During 1990–2000, the yearly population increase averaged 3.9%. About 60% of the total population resided in two urban areas on two atolls, Majuro on Majuro Atoll and Ebeye on Kwajalein Atoll. Majuro had about 28,000 inhabitants in 1995.

7 MIGRATION

Population has been steadily migrating from the outer atolls to the urban concentrations in Majuro and Ebeye. The Compact of Free Association with the United States permits unrestricted entry into the United States.

8 ETHNIC GROUPS

The Marshallese people are Micronesians, who are physically similar to the Polynesian peoples.

9 LANGUAGES

Both English and Marshallese (Kajin Majol) are spoken and used in official communications and in commerce. Marshallese is a Malayo-Polynesian language and the common source of each of the atolls' dialects.

10 RELIGIONS

The people are almost entirely Christian, primarily Protestant. Some 90% of the population belongs to the United Church of Christ. In 1993 there were 3,440 Roman Catholics. Other religious denominations include Assemblies of God, Seventh Day Adventists, Baptists, Baha'i, Mormons, and Jehovah's Witnesses.

11 TRANSPORTATION

There are 56 kilometers (35 miles) of paved road on the Majuro Atoll and 3.7 kilometers (2.3 miles) on the Kwajalein Atoll. On the outer islands, roads consist primarily of cleared paths. Two ports in Majuro and one in Ebeye are used for international shipping. The merchant fleet consists of 78 ships with a capacity totaling 3.1 million gross registered tons.

The government-owned Airline of the Marshall Islands (AMI) provides service to all outer islands with airstrips. Air Micronesia/Continental Airlines links Majuro with major foreign destinations via Majuro International Airport.

12 HISTORY

The British captain John Marshall, after whom the islands are named, explored them in 1788. Throughout the late 1800s and early 1900s, foreign powers ruled the islands, attracted by the potential for trade, missionary work, mining, and control of sea routes. Spain claimed the islands in 1874, but sold them to Germany in 1899. At the outbreak of World War I (1914–18), Japanese naval squadrons took possession of the Marshalls and began formal administration under a League of Nations mandate in 1920.

In World War II (1939–45), after bitter fighting between United States and Japanese forces, the islands came under US control. In 1947, the Marshalls became part of a United Nations trusteeship administered by the United States. The United States used Bikini and Enewetak atolls as nuclear testing sites from 1946 to 1958, exploding 66 atomic and nuclear tests during this period and displacing the native people.

In 1979, the Republic of the Marshall Islands became a self-governing territory, and Amata Kabua was elected its first president. A Compact of Free Association with the United States, providing for full self-government except for defense, was ratified by the United States in 1986 and went into effect the same year.

In February 1990, the United States agreed to pay $45 million to the victims of

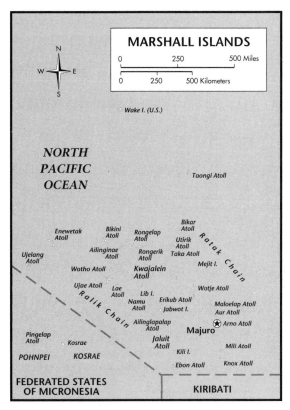

LOCATION: 4° to 14°N; 160° to 173°E.

the nuclear testing program. The Republic became an independent state and joined the United Nations in September 1991.

In the late 1990s, global warming and the possibility of rising sea levels have raised concern over the long-term prospects for the low-lying islands in the middle of the Pacific Ocean.

13 GOVERNMENT

The Marshall Islands is an independent republic. The constitution provides for three main branches of government: the legislature, the executive, and the judiciary. Legislative power is vested in the 33-member Parliament, or Nitijela. Executive power is vested in the cabinet, headed by the president, who is also head of state.

There are 24 local governments for the inhabited islands and atolls.

14 POLITICAL PARTIES

The Our Island's Party has been in power since 1979. The Ralik Ratak Democratic Party, founded in June 1991, acts as the opposition to the majority.

15 JUDICIAL SYSTEM

The judiciary consists of the Supreme Court, the High Court, the District Court, and 22 community courts. The Supreme Court has final appellate jurisdiction. Community courts in local government areas rule on civil and criminal cases.

16 ARMED FORCES

There are no armed forces. Under the Compact of Free Association, the United States provides defense for a minimum 15-year period and operation of the missile range on Kwajalein Atoll for 30 years.

17 ECONOMY

The commercial economy, concentrated in Majuro and Ebeye, is sustained largely by the government and Kwajalein Missile Range employees. Copra (dried coconut meat) production provides a source of income for outer-atoll families engaged in agriculture.

In 1994, the United States government provided grants of $50 million. The grants accounted for 55% of the Marshallese gross domestic product and 74% of the budget.

18 INCOME

In 1995, the Marshall Islands' gross domestic product (GNP) was between $766 and $3,035 per person. During 1985–95, the average annual inflation rate was 5.4%.

19 INDUSTRY

The economy's small manufacturing sector is centered largely in Majuro. The largest industrial operation is a copra-processing mill. Other manufacturing consists of small-scale operations, such as coir making, furniture making, handicrafts, and boat making.

20 LABOR

The government is the largest source of employment, followed by service and construction jobs. Tourism employs about 10% of the labor force. Unemployment was about 16% in 1991; there is a high and rising number of unemployed youth.

21 AGRICULTURE

Dried coconut meat, known as copra, is produced on almost all islands and atolls; some 6,500 hectares (16,000 acres) of coconut palm were productive.

22 DOMESTICATED ANIMALS

Livestock on the islands consists of pigs and poultry. Most families raise pigs for subsistence and for family and community feasts.

Photo credit: Susan D. Rock.

A sunny beach on the Majuro Atoll.

23 FISHING

The total catch in 1994 amounted to 290 tons. Principal marine resources include tuna, prawns, shrimp, seaweed, sponges, black pearls, and giant clams.

24 FORESTRY

Some 8,900 hectares (22,000 acres) are planted with coconut palm. In 1984, a sawmill was purchased for processing coconut trunks and other tree species as lumber.

25 MINING

There is no mining. However, phosphate and manganese have been found within the territorial waters.

26 FOREIGN TRADE

Over 90% of the value of exports is accounted for by coconut oil and copra cake, made of dried coconut meat. The total value of exports in 1995 was $21.3 million. The total value of imports that year was $69.9 million. The United States and Japan are the main sources of imports.

27 ENERGY AND POWER

The Marshall Islands is dependent on imported fossil fuels for electric-power generation. The urban centers of Majuro and Ebeye have major generating facilities. The power requirements in the outer islands are met by solar-powered systems.

28 SOCIAL DEVELOPMENT

The Ministry of Social Services is involved in five major areas: housing, women's and youth development, feeding programs, aging, and other community development welfare programs. A social security system provides old age, disability, and survivor benefits.

The Marshallese society has a matrilineal structure. Each person belongs to the *bwij*, or clan, of his or her mother, through whom traditional rank and property are inherited.

29 HEALTH

The leading causes of death after infancy are respiratory diseases, diarrhea and other intestinal diseases, diabetes, and heart disease. Alcoholism and drug abuse are common, and there is a relatively high incidence of sexually transmitted diseases. There are two hospitals: the Armer Ishoda Hospital in Majuro and a recently renovated hospital in Ebeye. In 1991, there were 20 doctors, 130 nurses, and 4 midwives. Health care on the outer atolls is provided through 69 dispensaries.

30 HOUSING

Houses in the urban centers are simple wooden or cement-block structures, with corrugated iron roofs; because of the limited land availability, houses are heavily crowded. In 1988, there were 4,943 dwellings on the Marshall Islands.

31 EDUCATION

About 93% of the Marshallese are literate. The public elementary education provides eight years of basic education to those aged 7–14.

The Majuro campus of the College of Micronesia opened its School of Nursing and Science Center in 1986. In 1991, Marshall Islands became a member of the University of the South Pacific.

32 MEDIA

Fifty-three shortwave, outer-island radio stations link all major islands and atolls. There is one government radio broadcast station, two privately owned radio stations, and one television station. In 1995 there were 2,300 telephones throughout the islands.

A weekly newspaper, *The Marshall Islands Journal* (1995 circulation 3,000), is published in Majuro in English and Marshallese. *The Marshall Island Government Gazette* is a free four-page government newsletter, printed in English.

33 TOURISM AND RECREATION

Tourist attractions include the sandy beaches on the atolls, protected lagoons, underwater coral reefs, and abundant marine life, including large gamefish. However, tourism remains undeveloped, and the outer atolls do not have any accommodations for visitors.

34 FAMOUS MARSHALLESE

Amata Kabua (1928–96), president from 1979 until his death, guided his country to self-governing status under the United States-administered United Nations trusteeship.

35 BIBLIOGRAPHY

Dibblin, Jane. *Day of Two Suns: US Nuclear Testing and the Pacific Islanders.* New York: New Amsterdam, 1990.
Trust Territory of the Pacific Islands, 1986. Washington, D.C.: US Department of State, 1986.

MAURITANIA

Mauritanian Islamic Republic
[French:] *République Islamique de Mauritanie*
[Arabic:] *Al-Jumhuriyah al-Islamiyah al-Muritaniyah*

CAPITAL: Nouakchott.

FLAG: The flag consists of a gold star and crescent on a light green field.

ANTHEM: *Mauritania* (no words).

MONETARY UNIT: The ouguiya (UM), a paper currency of 5 khoums, issued by the Central Bank of Mauritania, replaced the Communauté Financière Africaine franc on 29 June 1973. There are coins of 1 khoum and 1, 5, 10, and 20 ouguiyas, and notes of 100, 200, 500, and 1,000 ouguiyas. UM1 = $0.00715 (or $1 = UM139.86).

WEIGHTS AND MEASURES: The metric system is the legal standard.

HOLIDAYS: New Year's Day, 1 January; Labor Day, 1 May; African Liberation Day, 25 May; Anniversary of the Proclamation of the Republic, 28 November. Movable religious holidays include Laylat al-Miraj, 'Id al-Fitr, 'Id al-'Adha', 1st of Muharram (Muslim New Year), and Milad an-Nabi.

TIME: GMT.

1 LOCATION AND SIZE

Situated in West Africa, Mauritania has an area of over 1 million square kilometers (almost 398,000 square miles), slightly larger than three times the size of the state of New Mexico. Its total estimated boundary length is 5,828 kilometers (3,622 miles). The capital city, Nouakchott, is located on the Atlantic Coast.

2 TOPOGRAPHY

There are three distinct geographic regions in Mauritania: a narrow belt along the Senegal River valley in the south; north of this valley, a broad east-west band of sandy plains and dunes held in place by sparse grass and scrub trees; and a large northern arid region bordering the Sahara Desert. The country is generally flat.

3 CLIMATE

Although conditions are generally desert-like, three climatic regions can be distinguished. Southern Mauritania has one rainy season from July to October. Annual rainfall averages 66 centimeters (26 inches) in the far south; at Nouakchott the annual average is 14 centimeters (5.5 inches). The coastal region is arid, with an average maximum temperature for October of 32°C (90°F) and an average minimum of 13°C (55°F) for January. Most of Mauritania north of Atar has a desert climate with daytime temperatures exceeding 38°C (100°F) in most areas for over six months of the year.

4 PLANTS AND ANIMALS

In the desert there are some cacti and related species; oases have relatively luxuriant growth, notably date palms. In the south are the baobab tree, palms, and acacias. The far south, in the Senegal River valley, has willows, jujube, and acacias. Lions, panthers, jackals, crocodiles, hippopotami, hyenas, cheetahs, otters, and monkeys survive in the south; in the north there are antelopes, wild sheep, ostriches and other large birds, and ducks.

5 ENVIRONMENT

Deforestation, expansion of the desert into agricultural lands, and grazing on land formerly restricted to wildlife are all severe environmental problems in Mauritania. The nation also has a problem with water pollution, resulting from the leakage of petroleum and industrial waste along with sewage into the nation's ports and rivers. In 1994, 14 of Mauritania's mammal species and five bird species were endangered, as well as three of its plant species.

6 POPULATION

The total population in 1998 was estimated at 2.5 million. The US Bureau of the Census projection for 2005 was 3.9 million. Estimates in 1995 placed the population of Nouakchott, the capital, at 694,000.

7 MIGRATION

The population was 12% nomadic in 1988, compared to 83% in 1963. Since June 1995, 13,000 Malian refugees in Mauritania have returned home, but 6,782 remained in Mauritania as of mid-1997. At that time, there were 64,000

Geographic Profile

Geographic Features

Size ranking: 28 of 192
Highest elevation: 915 meters (3,002 feet) at Kediet ej Jill
Lowest elevation: –3 meters (–10 feet) at Sebkha de Ndrhamcha

Land Use†

Arable land:	<1%
Permanent crops:	0%
Permanent pastures:	38%
Forests:	4%
Other:	57%

Weather††

Average annual precipitation (Nouakchott): 14 centimeters (5.5 inches)
Average temperature range in January (Nouakchott): 14–29°C (57–84°F)
Average temperature range in July (Nouakchott): 23–32°C (73–90°F)

†*Arable land:* Land used for temporary crops, like meadows for mowing or pasture, gardens, and greenhouses. *Permanent crops:* Land cultivated with crops that occupy its use for long periods, such as cocoa, coffee, rubber, fruit and nut orchards, and vineyards. *Permanent pastures:* Land used permanently for forage crops. *Forests:* Land containing stands of trees. *Other:* Any land not specified, including built-on areas, roads, and barren land.

††Annual rainfall averages 66 centimeters (26 inches) in the far south, while most of central and northern Mauritania is arid desert, receiving less than 10 centimeters (4 inches) of rain per year.

Mauritanian refugees in Senegal and 15,000 in Mali.

8 ETHNIC GROUPS

Moors (Maurs), the main ethnic group, constitute between three-fifths and four-fifths of the population. Other groups include the Tukulor, Sarakolé, Fulani (Fulbe), Wolof, and Bambara. The black population is found largely in southern Mauritania and in the cities. There are

MAURITANIA

MAURITANIA

0   75   150   225   300 Miles

0   75   150   225   300 Kilometers

ALGERIA

Dayet el Khadra

Al Bir Lahlou

Erg Iguidi

ATLANTIC OCEAN

Agmar

Bîr Mogreïn

Chegga

'Ayoûn 'Abd el Mâlek

WESTERN SAHARA

S A H A R A   D E S E R T

Fdérik   Zouérat

▲ *Kediet ej Jill* 3,002 ft. 915 m.

MALI

Awaday

El Moueïla

El Mrâyer

Bir Gandús

Cap Blanc Nouadhibou

Ouadane

El Djouf

Baie de Lévrier

Atar   Chinguetti

Île Tidra

Tánoudert

Cap Timiris Nouamrhar

Akjoujt

Nouakchott

Tidjikdja   Tîchît

Tijti

Boutilimit

Qualâta

Lac Rkiz

Aleg

'Ayoûn el 'Atroûs

Néma

Rosso

Bogué

Kîfa

Diadé   Lemoïlé

Senegal

Kaédi

Mbout

Médala

Maghama

Nioro du Sahel

Sélibaby

Bakel   Kayes

Niono

Mauritania

S E N E G A L

M A L I

Bafoulabé

N W E S

LOCATION: 14°42′ to 27°N; 4°30′ to 17°7′w. **BOUNDARY LENGTHS:** Algeria, 463 kilometers (288 miles); Mali, 2,237 kilometers (1,390 miles); Senegal, 813 kilometers (505 miles); Atlantic coastline, 754 kilometers (468 miles); Western Sahara, 1,561 kilometers (970 miles). **TERRITORIAL SEA LIMIT:** 12 miles.

also small numbers of Europeans. Freed slaves and their descendants are known as *haratin* and make up 40% of the population.

9 LANGUAGES

The Arabic spoken in Mauritania, called Hassaniyah, is the official language. Wolof, Peular, and Soninké are spoken in southern Mauritania. French is widely used, although its status as an official language was eliminated in 1991.

10 RELIGIONS

The state religion is Islam, and about 99% of the population is Sunni Muslim. The few thousand Christians are mostly foreigners.

11 TRANSPORTATION

In 1995, of some 7,525 kilometers (4,676 miles) of roads, 22% were paved. Mauritania had about 8,000 passenger cars and 5,700 commercial vehicles in 1995.

The 652-kilometer (405-mile) railway links the iron mines at Zouérat, near Fdérik, with the port at Point-Central, 10 kilometers (6 miles) south of Nouadhibou. There is a wharf at Nouakchott. The only airports that can handle long-distance jets are at Nouakchott and Nouadhibou.

12 HISTORY

The Portuguese were the first Europeans to arrive in Mauritania, attracted in the fifteenth century by the trade in gold and slaves, and later by the gum arabic trade. Competition for control was keen among Portuguese, French, Dutch, and English traders. In 1815 Senegal, Mauritania's neighbor to the south, was awarded to France in the post-Napoleonic war settlement. During the nineteenth century, the French explored the inland regions of West Africa and signed treaties with Moorish chieftains. Mauritania was established as a colony in 1920, becoming one of the eight territories that constituted French West Africa.

In 1946, a Mauritanian Territorial Assembly was established, with some control over internal affairs. Complete independence was attained on 28 November 1960. Since independence, the government of Mauritania has enjoyed considerable stability. Two problems that have dominated internal politics are conflicts between regions and trade union pressures for pro-labor policies and higher wages. Mauritania joined the Arab League in 1973, but ties with Europe, especially France and the United States, remain strong. The disastrous drought that struck Mauritania and the rest of the region during 1968–74 elicited substantial aid from the European Community (EC), the United States, Spain, France, and the Arab countries.

Saharan War and Military Rule

In 1976, forces supported by Algeria launched a war in neighboring Western Sahara following the end of Spanish control over the region. Guerrilla raids on the Mauritanian railway, iron mines, and coastal settlements forced Mauritania to call French and Moroccan troops to its defense. The effects of the war weakened the government both economically and

Photo credit: Jason Laure.

A family of nomads in their tent. Today, about 10% of Mauritania's population lives a nomadic lifestyle, compared to over 80% in 1963.

politically, and in July 1978 Moktar Ould Daddah, Mauritania's president since 1961, was overthrown by a military coup. Lieutenant–Colonel Khouna Ould Haydalla became chief of state in January 1980. A military coup on 12 December 1984 brought Colonel Moaouia Ould Sidi Mohamed Taya to power.

Many problems, including an unsuccessful coup attempt in 1987, are linked to ethnic conflict. It is estimated that Moors account for between 60–80% of the population. The remainder are blacks, concentrated along the Senegal River border. Mass deportations of blacks have fueled charges that Mauritania is trying to eliminate its non-Moorish population. On 26 January 1992, Taya was elected in Mauritania's first multiparty presidential election, with 63% of the vote. A new cabinet was formed in January 1993.

13 GOVERNMENT

The July 1991 constitution delegates most powers to the executive branch. The president is to be elected by universal suffrage (vote) for a six-year term. The prime minister is appointed. Parliament, composed of a directly elected National Assembly and an indirectly elected Senate, is controlled by the president's party. Competing political parties were legalized in July 1991.

14 POLITICAL PARTIES

The Front for the Liberation of Africans in Mauritania (FLAM) played a major role in stirring the 1989 unrest that led to multi-party elections in 1993. Coup leader Colonel Moaouia Ould Sidi Mohamed Taya formed the Democratic and Social Republican Party (Parti Republicain et Democratique Social—PRDS). Chief among 14 opposition parties has been the Union of Democratic Forces (UFD).

15 JUDICIAL SYSTEM

The 1991 Constitution completely revised the judicial system. The revised judicial system includes lower, middle, and upper level courts, each with specialized jurisdiction. Department-level tribunals now bridge the traditional and modern court systems. These courts are staffed by *qadis,* traditional magistrates trained in Koranic law. General civil cases are handled by 10 regional courts. Three regional courts of appeal hear challenges to decisions at the department level. A supreme court reviews appeals taken from decisions of the regional courts of appeal.

16 ARMED FORCES

The army had 15,000 men in 1993; the navy, 500 men and 11 patrol boats; and the air force, 150 men and 7 combat aircraft.

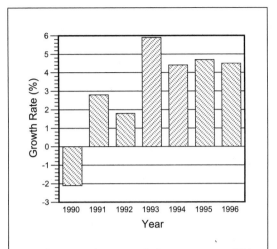

Yearly growth rate of the economy. This economic indicator tells by what percent the economy has increased or decreased when compared with the previous year.

17 ECONOMY

While Mauritania is an agricultural country dependent on livestock production, its significant iron ore deposits have been the backbone of the export economy in recent years. The droughts of the 1970s and 1980s transformed much of Mauritania, as the herds died off and the population shifted to urban areas. Droughts have led to a build up of foreign debt, leaving the country dependent on financial aid flows from international donors.

18 INCOME

In 1995, Mauritania's gross national product (GNP) was $1.05 billion, or about $470 per person. During 1985–95, the average annual growth of the GNP per person was 0.5%. During the same period,

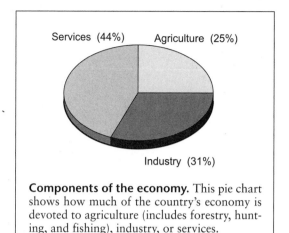

Services (44%)   Agriculture (25%)

Industry (31%)

Components of the economy. This pie chart shows how much of the country's economy is devoted to agriculture (includes forestry, hunting, and fishing), industry, or services.

the average annual inflation rate was 6.9%.

19 INDUSTRY

Fish processing, the principal industrial activity, is carried out in Nouadhibou. A rolling mill at Nouadhibou produces small quantities of iron rods and steel. A petroleum refinery with an annual capacity of 1 million tons resumed operation in 1987 with help from Algeria. It produced 2 million barrels of refined petroleum products in 1995.

20 LABOR

The estimated labor force numbered about 659,000 in 1992, with some 175,000 Mauritanians unemployed. The labor law of 1963 guarantees trade union rights, sets up a framework for collective bargaining, and provides for a 40-hour workweek.

21 AGRICULTURE

Only 0.2% of Mauritania's land is used to grow crops. Millet and sorghum production reached 8,000 and 157,000 tons, respectively, in 1995. Other crop production in 1995 included paddy rice, 79,000 tons; and corn, 1,000 tons.

22 DOMESTICATED ANIMALS

The drought years of 1968–74 reduced the cattle population from 2.6 million head in 1970 to 1.6 million in 1973. There were only 1.1 million head in 1995, when sheep and goats numbered 8.8 million and camels 1.1 million.

23 FISHING

Since the mid-1980s, depletion of the stocks has made Mauritanian fishing increasingly uneconomical. Traditional fishing is carried out along the Senegal River, with sea fishing at Nouakchott and Nouadhibou. The national catch was estimated at 85,000 tons in 1994. Principal species caught included octopus, sardine, squid, and grouper.

24 FORESTRY

The principal forest product is gum arabic, which is extracted from wild acacia trees that grow in the south. Much of the gum is smuggled across the borders, particularly to Senegal. Roundwood removals were estimated at 14,000 cubic meters (18,300 cubic yards) in 1995, 57% for fuel.

25 MINING

Iron deposits play a significant role in the economy. Production was reported at 11.4 million tons in 1994.

26 FOREIGN TRADE

Fish products were 53% of exports in 1995; iron ore, 40%. Mauritania's main export markets in 1995 were Japan (23%), Italy (15%), France (14%), and Spain (13%). The main suppliers of imports were France (30%), China (10%), Japan (9%), and Spain (8%).

27 ENERGY AND POWER

National installed electrical power capacity was 105,000 kilowatts in 1994, 42% of it thermal; production increased from 49.9 million kilowatt hours in 1969 to 141 million kilowatt hours in 1994. Offshore oil exploration is being carried on by Texaco and Amoco.

28 SOCIAL DEVELOPMENT

Slavery has been abolished several times in Mauritania, most recently in 1980. However, there are an estimated 90,000 slaves held in Mauritania, but it is illegal to suggest that a slave trade exists in the country. Slavery is based on race, with lighter-skinned Moors from the north enslaving darker-skinned farmers from the south. Some black groups however, such as the Soninké and Fulani, practice a more concealed form of slavery.

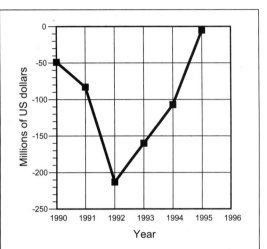

Yearly balance of trade measured in millions of US dollars. The balance of trade is the difference between what a country sells to other countries (its exports) and what it buys (its imports). If a country imports more than it exports, it has a negative balance of trade (a trade deficit). If exports exceed imports there is a positive balance of trade (a trade surplus).

29 HEALTH

Mauritania's public health system consists of administrative units and health facilities organized in pyramid style. The only major hospital is in Nouakchott. Although medical services is available free to those unable to pay, only about 63% of the population has access to health care services. The main health problems include malaria, tuberculosis, measles, dysentery, and influenza.

30 HOUSING

The phenomenal growth of Nouakchott and the effects of rural migration, impelled by drought, have strained housing

Selected Social Indicators

These statistics are estimates for the period 1993 to 1996. For comparison purposes, data for the United States and averages for low-income countries and high-income countries are also given.

Indicator	Mauritania	Low-income countries	High-income countries	United States
Per capita gross national product†	$470	$490	$25,870	$28,020
Population growth rate	2.5%	1.7%	0.6%	0.9%
Population growth rate in urban areas	5.0%	3.8%	0.9%	1.2%
Population per square kilometer of land	2	82	30	29
Life expectancy in years	53	63	77	77
Number of physicians per 1,000 people	0.1	1.0	2.5	2.5
Number of pupils per teacher (primary school)	52	41	17	14
Illiteracy rate (15 years and older)	62%	34%	<5%	3%
Energy consumed per capita (kg of oil equivalent)	102	393	5,123	7,905

† The gross national product (GNP) is the total dollar value of all goods and services produced by a country in a year. The per capita GNP is calculated by dividing a country's GNP by its population. The World Bank defines low-income countries as those with a per capita GNP of $785 or less. High-income countries have a per capita GNP of $9,636 or more. About 16% of the world's 5.7 billion people live in high-income countries, while almost 56% live in low-income countries.   > = greater than   < = less than

Sources: World Bank, *World Development Indicators on CD-ROM,* Washington, D.C.: The World Bank, 1998. Central Intelligence Agency, *The World Fact Book,* Washington, D.C.: Government Printing Office, 1998.

resources. As of 1990, 67% of urban and 65% of rural dwellers had access to a public water supply.

31 EDUCATION

Education is compulsory, but only a minority of school-age children attend school. In 1994, there were 268,216 students in primary schools. In 1993, 45,810 students were enrolled in secondary schools. All higher level institutions had a total of 266 teachers and 7,501 pupils in 1992; these include the National Institute of Higher Islamic Studies and the University of Nouakchott.

32 MEDIA

By 1995 there were 7,600 telephones in use. The government-owned national radio and television networks broadcast in French, Arabic, and several African languages. There were an estimated 309,000 radios and 50,000 television sets in 1995. A government-operated daily, *El Chaab,* is published in French and Arabic.

33 TOURISM AND RECREATION

There are few facilities for tourists, except in the capital, and travel outside it is difficult. Tourists are attracted to Atar, the ancient capital of the Almoravid kingdom, and Chinguetti, with houses and mosques dating back to the thirteenth century.

34 FAMOUS MAURITANIANS

Yusuf ibn Tashfin conquered Morocco in 1082 and most of Spain in 1091. The best-known contemporary Mauritanian is Moktar Ould Daddah (b.1924), president from 1961 until 1978.

35 BIBLIOGRAPHY

Calderini, Simonetta. *Mauritania*. Santa Barbara, Calif.: Clio Press, 1992.

Handloff, Robert E., ed. *Mauritania, a Country Study*. 2d ed. Washington, D.C.: Library of Congress, 1990.

MAURITIUS

Republic of Mauritius

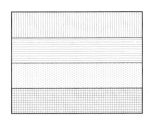

CAPITAL: Port Louis.

FLAG: The national flag consists of four horizontal stripes of red, blue, yellow, and green.

ANTHEM: *Glory to Thee, Motherland, O Motherland of Mine.*

MONETARY UNIT: The Mauritius rupee (R) is a currency of 100 cents. There are coins of 1, 2, 5, 10, 25, and 50 cents and 1 rupee, and notes of 5, 10, 20, 50, 100, 200, 500, and 1,000 rupees. R1 = $0.05629 (or $1 = R17.764).

WEIGHTS AND MEASURES: The metric system is in general use; traditional weights and measures are also employed.

HOLIDAYS: New Year, 1–2 January; National Day, 12 March; Labor Day, 1 May. Christian, Hindu, and Muslim holidays are also observed.

TIME: 4 PM = noon GMT.

1 LOCATION AND SIZE

Mauritius, situated in the Indian Ocean, off the African coast, includes the island of Rodrigues, the two islands of Agelega, and the St. Brandon Group (Cargados Carajos Shoals). Comparatively, the area occupied by Mauritius is slightly less than 10.5 times the size of Washington, D.C. It has a coastline of 177 kilometers (110 miles). The capital city of Mauritius, Port Louis, is located on the island's northwest coast.

2 TOPOGRAPHY

Mauritius was mostly formed by volcanoes and is almost entirely surrounded by coral reefs. Petite Rivière Noire Peak is the highest peak, and the longest river is the Grand South East River, extending about 39 kilometers (24 miles).

3 CLIMATE

The climate of Mauritius is humid, with temperatures ranging from 18° to 30°C (64–86°F) at sea level, and from 13° to 26°C (55–79°F) at an elevation of 460 meters (1,500 feet). The central plateau and windward slopes have a yearly average rainfall of over 500 centimeters (200 inches). On the coast, rainfall averages about 100 centimeters (40 inches) annually.

4 PLANTS AND ANIMALS

Mauritius originally was covered by dense rainforest, but its present vegetation consists mostly of species brought by settlers. The now extinct dodo bird was native to Mauritius. European settlers introduced dogs, cats, rats, monkeys, wild pigs, sambur deer, and mongoose.

5 ENVIRONMENT

The main environmental problems facing Mauritius are water pollution, soil erosion, and preservation of its wildlife. Mauritian cities produce 0.1 million tons of solid waste annually.

In 1992 Mauritius ranked third in the world on the list of countries with the most endangered species. Of 30 species native to the country, only 11 were surviving in the mid-1990s.

6 POPULATION

The total population of Mauritius was estimated at 1.2 million in 1998; only about 2% of the population lives on the island of Rodrigues. A total population of 1.3 million was projected for the year 2005. Port Louis, the capital, had 165,000 inhabitants in 1995.

7 MIGRATION

A small number of Mauritians emigrate each year, principally to Australia, Europe, and Canada.

8 ETHNIC GROUPS

The largest group on Mauritius—about 68%—is Indo-Mauritian, consisting of immigrants from India and their descendants. About 23% of the islanders are Creole (mixed European and African).

9 LANGUAGES

English is the official language; however, Creole, derived from French, is most widely spoken. Bhojpuri and other Indian languages are also spoken.

Geographic Profile

Geographic Features

Size ranking: 167 of 192
Highest elevation: 828 meters (2,717 feet) at Petite Rivière Noire Peak
Lowest elevation: Sea level at the Indian Ocean

Land Use†

Arable land:	49%
Permanent crops:	3%
Permanent pastures:	3%
Forests:	22%
Other:	23%

Weather††

Average annual precipitation: 196.5 centimeters (77.4 inches)
Average temperature in January: 26°C (78.8°F)
Average temperature in July: 20.7°C (69.3°F)

†*Arable land:* Land used for temporary crops, like meadows for mowing or pasture, gardens, and greenhouses. *Permanent crops:* Land cultivated with crops that occupy its use for long periods, such as cocoa, coffee, rubber, fruit and nut orchards, and vineyards. *Permanent pastures:* Land used permanently for forage crops. *Forests:* Land containing stands of trees. *Other:* Any land not specified, including built-on areas, roads, and barren land.

††The measurements for precipitation and average temperature were taken at weather stations closest to the country's largest city. Precipitation and average temperature can vary significantly within a country, due to factors such as latitude, altitude, coastal proximity, and wind patterns.

---

10 RELIGIONS

In 1990, Hindus constituted about 54% of the population, Roman Catholics 29%, and Muslims 17%.

11 TRANSPORTATION

Mauritius had some 1,800 kilometers (1,115 miles) of roads in 1995, more than 90% of which were paved. As of 1995, there were 14,000 commercial vehicles and 54,000 passenger cars. Air Mauritius operates out of the main airport.

12 HISTORY

The Dutch, under Admiral Wybrandt van Warwijck, first arrived in Mauritius in 1598, and settlers followed in 1638. In 1715, however, the French took possession of Mauritius. The island was governed by the French East India Company until 1767, and by the French government for the next 43 years.

During the Napoleonic wars, French-held Mauritius became a major threat to British shipping in the Indian Ocean, and Britain occupied it in 1810. Although under British rule, Mauritius, which now was a sugar-producing island, remained French in culture.

When slavery was abolished in the British Empire in the 1830s, many former slaves left Mauritius for Africa, causing a labor shortage. From 1837 to 1907, indentured workers were imported to Mauritius from India. About 450,000 Indians went to Mauritius under this system. Since 1948, politicians of Indian descent have dominated the government.

Mauritius became independent on 12 March 1968. Sir Seewoosagur Ramgoolam, chief minister in the colonial government, became the first prime minister after independence. Ramgoolam's Mauritius Labor Party (MLP) held power alone, or in coalition with others, until June 1982, when a coalition known as the Militant Socialist Movement (MSM) formed a government. Its leader, Aneerood Jugnauth, became prime minister.

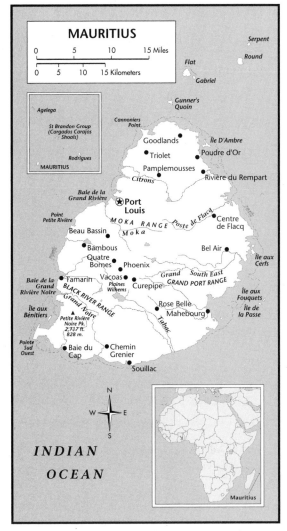

LOCATION: 19°50′ to 20°5′s; 57°18′ to 57°48′e.
TERRITORIAL SEA LIMIT: 12 miles.

Elections in August 1983 produced a clear mandate for a new coalition forged by Jugnauth, which won clear-cut electoral victories in August 1987 and September 1991. The new alliance amended the constitution making Mauritius a republic within the British Commonwealth. Since

Photo credit: © Larry Tackett/Tom Stack & Associates.

A Mauritian man at a mosque in Port Louis.

In the 1982 elections, the MMM (Mauritian Militant Movement) captured 42 seats in parliament and joined the Mauritian Socialist Party (Parti Socialiste Mauricien—PSM) in a ruling coalition under Aneerood Jugnauth. Jugnauth's government fell apart in the early months of 1983, and he then formed the Mauritian Socialist Movement (Mouvement Socialiste Mauricien—MSM).

A MMM/MLP coalition won 60 of 66 seats in the December 1995 elections.

15 JUDICIAL SYSTEM

The Supreme Court has a chief justice and six other judges who also serve on the Court of Criminal Appeal, the Court of Civil Appeal, the Intermediate Court, the Industrial Court, and ten district courts.

16 ARMED FORCES

The National Police Force, which includes a military Special Mobile Force, is responsible for defense. In 1995, it had some 1,800 members.

17 ECONOMY

The Mauritius economy is based on export-oriented manufacturing (mainly clothing), sugar, and tourism. Economic growth declined in 1990 as the economy started to experience labor shortages, rising inflation, and capacity constraints. In the early 1990s, the economy showed modest recovery. In 1995, economic growth was estimated at 5%.

March 12, 1992, Queen Elizabeth II has been replaced by a Mauritian chief of state.

13 GOVERNMENT

The Mauritian government is parliamentary, with executive power vested under the constitution in a president and a prime minister, who is leader of the majority party in parliament.

14 POLITICAL PARTIES

The Mauritius Labor Party (MLP) received popular support during 1947–82.

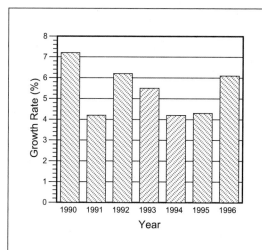

Yearly growth rate of the economy. This economic indicator tells by what percent the economy has increased or decreased when compared with the previous year.

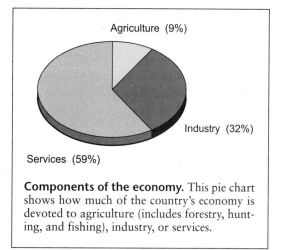

Components of the economy. This pie chart shows how much of the country's economy is devoted to agriculture (includes forestry, hunting, and fishing), industry, or services.

18 INCOME

In 1995 Mauritius's gross national product (GNP) was $3.8 billion, or about $3,710 per person. For the period 1985–95 the average inflation rate was 8.8%, and the average annual real growth rate of the GNP per person was 5.7%.

19 INDUSTRY

Manufacturing centers on the processing of agricultural products, especially sugar cane and its by-products, including molasses and rum. Local tobacco is made into cigarettes, and four factories are maintained to process tea. Other small industries produce goods for local consumption, such as beer and soft drinks, shoes, metal products, and paints.

The Export Processing Zone (EPZ) is an important part of Mauritius' industrial development. Imported goods are processed for export in the EPZ, which gives investors special tax breaks and duty exemption. Textiles generate 80% of exports from the EPZ. EPZ industries also produce sunglasses, toys, nails, razor blades, tires, and audio cassettes.

20 LABOR

There were 289,570 workers employed in business establishments with over 10 employees as of March 1995. The main areas of employment were manufacturing, 30%; services (mostly government), 19%; and agriculture and fishing, 16%. There were 90,000 workers employed within the Export Processing Zone in 1996. Unemployment (excluding Rodrigues) was 8,453 in 1995—down nearly ten-fold from 73,042 in 1983. Minimum wages are set by the government, and cost-of-living allowances are mandatory.

21 AGRICULTURE

Sugarcane is the major crop. In 1995, 5.2 million tons of cane were produced (third largest in Africa), from which 540,000 tons of raw sugar were produced. Sugarcane occupies 36% of Mauritius' total land area and 70% of all cropland. Tea, tobacco, and cut flowers are other export items. Potatoes, tomatoes, bananas, corn, peanuts, and coconuts are grown for local consumption. Almost any crop can be grown on Mauritius, but the shortage of land means that almost all cereals must be imported.

22 DOMESTICATED ANIMALS

In 1995, Mauritius had 34,000 head of cattle, 3 million chickens, 17,000 pigs, and 98,000 goats. That year, 25,000 tons of cow milk, 22,000 tons of meat, and 4,500 tons of hen eggs were produced.

23 FISHING

The total catch in 1994 was 18,969 tons. About 55% of the catch consisted of skipjack tuna.

24 FORESTRY

Roundwood removals were an estimated 12,400 cubic meters (16,200 cubic yards) in 1995, and sawn wood production was about 2,400 cubic meters (3,100 cubic yards).

25 MINING

There are few mineral resources in Mauritius. Small amounts of lime, salt, and coral sand are produced.

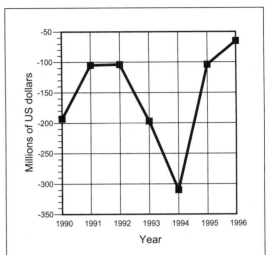

Yearly balance of trade measured in millions of US dollars. The balance of trade is the difference between what a country sells to other countries (its exports) and what it buys (its imports). If a country imports more than it exports, it has a negative balance of trade (a trade deficit). If exports exceed imports there is a positive balance of trade (a trade surplus).

26 FOREIGN TRADE

In 1995, clothing accounted for 51.5% of total exports. Sugar exports contributed 23.6%. Mauritius had exports of goods totaling $1.5 billion in 1995, and imports amounted to $1.8 billion. Principal imports in 1994 included manufactured goods, capital equipment, food, petroleum products, and chemicals.

In 1995, 34% of exports went to the United Kingdom, 21% to France, and 15.2% to the United States. The main sources of imports were France (19.9%), South Africa (10.6%), and the United Kingdom (6.4%).

Selected Social Indicators

These statistics are estimates for the period 1993 to 1996. For comparison purposes, data for the United States and averages for low-income countries and high-income countries are also given.

Indicator	Mauritius	Low-income countries	High-income countries	United States
Per capita gross national product†	**$3,710**	$490	$25,870	$28,020
Population growth rate	**1.1%**	1.7%	0.6%	0.9%
Population growth rate in urban areas	**1.5%**	3.8%	0.9%	1.2%
Population per square kilometer of land	**559**	82	30	29
Life expectancy in years	**71**	63	77	77
Number of physicians per 1,000 people	**0.9**	1.0	2.5	2.5
Number of pupils per teacher (primary school)	**21**	41	17	14
Illiteracy rate (15 years and older)	**17%**	34%	<5%	3%
Energy consumed per capita (kg of oil equivalent)	**388**	393	5,123	7,905

† The gross national product (GNP) is the total dollar value of all goods and services produced by a country in a year. The per capita GNP is calculated by dividing a country's GNP by its population. The World Bank defines low-income countries as those with a per capita GNP of $785 or less. High-income countries have a per capita GNP of $9,636 or more. About 16% of the world's 5.7 billion people live in high-income countries, while almost 56% live in low-income countries.   n.a. = data not available   > = greater than   < = less than

Sources: World Bank, World Development Indicators on CD-ROM, Washington, D.C.: The World Bank, 1998. Central Intelligence Agency, The World Fact Book, Washington, D.C.: Government Printing Office, 1998.

27 ENERGY AND POWER

Power plant production was 945 million kilowatt hours in 1994, when hydroelectric plants supplied 11% of the total. About half of all primary energy consumed comes from bagasse, or sugarcane waste.

28 SOCIAL DEVELOPMENT

Mauritius has a universal system of pensions that supplements an earnings related pension system. Women do not face significant legal discrimination, but most remain limited to traditional roles in the household and workplace.

29 HEALTH

Mauritius has seven general hospitals, and two private hospitals. There are also 74 maternity, child health, and family planning centers. There is 1 physician per 1,165 people. The average life expectancy is 71 years.

30 HOUSING

There are three basic types of houses: wattle and daub (woven poles or sticks with plaster) construction with thatched roofs; galvanized sheet-iron structures; and houses constructed of wood.

31 EDUCATION

Education is free up to college level and is compulsory between the ages of 5 and 12. The estimated adult illiteracy rate in 1995 was 17%. In 1993, an estimated 281 primary schools had 125,543 pupils and 5,931 teachers, and general secondary schools had 87,661 pupils.

Postsecondary institutions include the University of Mauritius, the Mauritius College of the Air, and the Mahatma Gandhi Institute. In 1993, universities had 2,161 students.

32 MEDIA

All parts of the island are linked by telegraph, telephone, and postal services; in 1995 there were 106,900 telephones in use. The state-owned Mauritius Broadcasting Corp. provides radio and television service in French, English, Hindi, and Chinese; there were 395,000 radios and 239,000 television sets in 1995.

Leading daily newspapers (with 1995 circulations) include *L'Express* (30,000), *Le Mauricien* (30,000), and *The Sun* (20,000), each published in Port Louis.

33 TOURISM AND RECREATION

In addition to the nation's beaches and lagoons, tourist attractions include the colonial architecture of Port Louis, an extinct volcano in Curepipe, the fishing port and naval museum at Mahebourg, and the Botanical Gardens at Pamplemousses. In 1994, 400,526 tourists visited Mauritius, 26% from France, 10% from Germany, 8% from the United Kingdom, and 34% from African nations. Tourist receipts totaled $264 million.

34 FAMOUS MAURITIANS

Sir Seewoosagur Ramgoolam (1900–85), was the first prime minister of independent Mauritius from 1968 to 1982, succeeded by Aneerood Jugnauth (b.1930).

35 BIBLIOGRAPHY

McCarry, John. "Mauritius: Island of Quiet Success." *National Geographic*, April 1993, 110–132.
Selvon, Sydney. *Historical Dictionary of Mauritius*. 2d ed. Metuchen, N.J.: Scarecrow Press, 1991.

MEXICO

United Mexican States

Estados Unidos Mexicanos

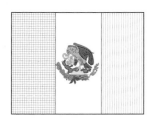

CAPITAL: Mexico City (México).

FLAG: The national flag is a tricolor of green, white, and red vertical stripes; at the center of the white stripe, in brown and green, is an eagle with a snake in its beak, perched on a cactus.

ANTHEM: *Mexicanos, al grito de guerra (Mexicans, to the Cry of War).*

MONETARY UNIT: The peso (P) is a paper currency of 100 centavos. There are coins of 1, 5, 10, 20, 50, 100, 500, 1,000 and 5,000 pesos and notes of 2,000, 5,000, 10,000, 20,000, 50,000 and 100,000 pesos. As of 1 January 1993, a new unit of currency (the new peso) was issued, worth 1,000 of the pesos that were used until 31 December 1992. P1 = $0.12425 (or $1 = P8.048).

WEIGHTS AND MEASURES: The metric system is the legal standard, but some old Spanish units are still in use.

HOLIDAYS: New Year's Day, 1 January; Constitution Day, 5 February; Birthday of Benito Juárez, 21 March; Labor Day, 1 May; Anniversary of the Battle of Puebla (1862), 5 May; Opening of Congress and Presidential Address to the Nation, 1 September; Independence Day, 16 September; Columbus Day, 12 October; Revolution Day (1910), 20 November; Christmas, 25 December. Movable religious holidays include Holy Thursday, Good Friday, and Holy Saturday. All Souls' Day, 2 November, and Our Lady of Guadalupe Day, 12 December, are not statutory holidays but are widely celebrated.

TIME: 6 AM = noon GMT.

1 LOCATION AND SIZE

Situated south of the United States on the North American continent, Mexico has an area of nearly 2 million square kilometers (762,000 square miles), slightly less than three times the size of the state of Texas. It has a total boundary length of 13,857 kilometers (8,610 miles), including the narrow peninsula of Baja California.

Mexico's capital city, Mexico City, is located in the southcentral part of the country.

2 TOPOGRAPHY

Mexico's dominant geographic feature is the great central highland plateau, which extends from the US border to the Isthmus of Tehuantepec. The plateau is enclosed by two high cordilleras (mountain chains), the Sierra Madre Oriental on the east and the Sierra Madre Occidental on the west, both separated from Mexico's coasts by lowland plains.

The Rio Grande (known as the Río Bravo del Norte in Mexico) is a river that extends for about 2,100 kilometers (1,304

Geographic Profile

Geographic Features

Size ranking: 14 of 192
Highest elevation: 5,747 meters (18,856 feet) at
    Orizaba Peak (Pico de Orizaba)
Lowest elevation: –10 meters (–33 feet) at Laguna
    Salada

Land Use†

Arable land:	12%
Permanent crops:	1%
Permanent pastures:	39%
Forests:	26%
Other:	22%

Weather††

Average annual precipitation: 167.2 centimeters (65.8
    inches)
Average temperature in January: 21.1°C (70.0°F)
Average temperature in July: 27.5°C (81.5°F)

†*Arable land:* Land used for temporary crops, like
meadows for mowing or pasture, gardens, and greenhouses. *Permanent crops:* Land cultivated with crops
that occupy its use for long periods, such as cocoa,
coffee, rubber, fruit and nut orchards, and vineyards.
Permanent pastures: Land used permanently for forage crops. *Forests:* Land containing stands of trees.
Other: Any land not specified, including built-on
areas, roads, and barren land.

††The measurements for precipitation and average
temperature were taken at weather stations closest to
the country's largest city. Precipitation and average
temperature can vary significantly within a country,
due to factors such as latitude, altitude, coastal proximity, and wind patterns.

miles) along the boundary with the United States.

3 CLIMATE

The climate varies according to altitude and rainfall. The coastal plains, Yucatán Peninsula, and lower areas of southern Mexico have a mean temperature of 25–27°C (77–81°F). The temperate zone (tierra templada) has a mean temperature of 21°C (70°F). Mexico City and most other important population centers are in the cool zone *(tierra fría)*, with a mean annual temperature of 17°C (63°C). The highest mountain peaks are always covered with snow.

Annual rainfall may exceed 500 centimeters (200 inches) in the Isthmus of Tehuantepec, while in parts of Baja California, practically no rain falls. Precipitation is adequate in central Mexico, while in the northern states desert-like conditions prevail.

4 PLANTS AND ANIMALS

The coastal plains are covered with a tropical rainforest, which merges into subtropical and temperate growth as the plateau rises. In the northern states there is a dry steppe vegetation, with desert flora over much of the area. Oaks and conifers are found in mixed forest regions along the mountain slopes. The Yucatán Peninsula has scrubby vegetation.

Among the wild animals are the armadillo, tapir, opossum, puma, jaguar, bear, and several species of monkey, deer, and boar. Poisonous snakes and harmful insects are found, and in the coastal marshes, malarial mosquitoes pose a problem. The only remaining elephant seals in the world are on an island west of Baja California.

5 ENVIRONMENT

Mexico loses its forest at a rate of (6,151 square kilometers (2,375 square miles) annually to agriculture and industry. Mexico City, located more than 2,250 meters (7,377 feet) above sea level and surrounded by mountains, has chronic smog,

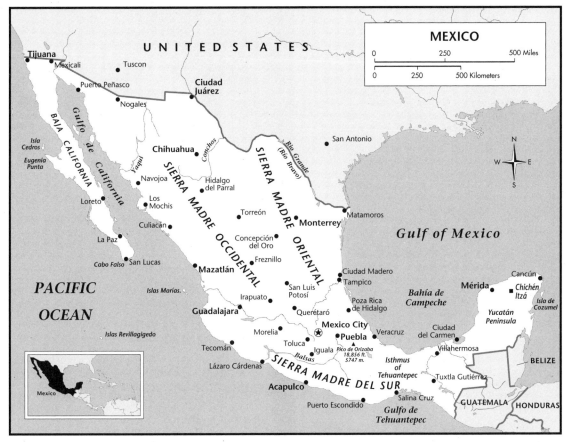

LOCATION: 14°32′ to 32°43′N; 86°42′ to 118°22′W. **BOUNDARY LENGTHS:** US, 3,326 kilometers (2,067 miles); Gulf of Mexico and Caribbean coastline, 2,070 kilometers (1,286 miles); Belize, 251 kilometers (156 miles); Guatemala, 871 kilometers (541 miles); Pacific coastline (including Baja California), 7,339 kilometers (4,560 miles). **TERRITORIAL SEA LIMIT:** 12 miles.

aggravated by some 35,000 factories and more than 2 million motor vehicles, and by slum dwellers' open burning of garbage. Thirty percent of the city's refuse is not regularly collected. Transportation vehicles are responsible for 76% of the air pollution. A severe drought in the spring of 1998 caused thousands of wildfires to burn throughout central Mexico. Smoke and haze covered cities and created health problems.

Mexico's cities produce 12.9 million tons of solid waste per year along with 164 million tons of industrial waste. About 51% of the nation's rural dwellers do not have pure water.

In 1992, United Nations sources reported 242 endangered species in Mex-

Indian weaver, Mexico City, Mexico.

ico. In 1994, 25 mammal species and 35 bird species were endangered. As of 1987, endangered species in Mexico included the Mexican grizzly bear (possibly extinct), southern bald eagle, American peregrine falcon, and ridge-nosed rattlesnake.

6 POPULATION

The 1990 census showed a total population of 81.2 million, more than double the 1960 census total of 34.9 million. The estimated 1998 population was 98.6 million by the US Bureau of the Census and 95.8 million by the United Nations. A population of 110.6 million was projected for 2005 by the US Bureau of the Census.

Population density averages 49 persons per square kilometer (127 persons per square mile).

In 1995, the metropolitan area of Mexico City had a population of over 16.5 million, with 8.5 million within the federal district. Other cities with populations of over 1 million in 1995 included Guadalajara, 1.6 million; Puebla, 1.2 million; Monterrey, 1.1 million; León, 1 million; and Ciudad Juárez, 1 million.

7 MIGRATION

As of 1990, the US Census Bureau estimated that 13.5 million persons of Mexican ancestry were living in the United

States. The United States has banned border crossings of Mexican agricultural laborers, and the 1986 Immigration Act imposes stiff penalties on employers who hire illegal aliens. Nevertheless, hundreds of thousands of illegal crossings still take place annually.

The migration of rural inhabitants to Mexico's already overcrowded cities has created huge urban slums, especially in Mexico City.

Mexico has long had a liberal policy on political asylum. In the 1970s and 1980s, many victims of Latin American military regimes fled to Mexico. By the end of 1993, the number of persons from Guatemala, El Salvador, and other Central American countries living in Mexico was about 400,000, not counting 45,000 Guatemalan refugees living in camps. The largest community of US citizens living outside the United States, estimated at 200,000, is found in Mexico.

In 1996, the net emigration rate was 2.97 emigres per 1,000 population.

8 ETHNIC GROUPS

The people of Mexico are mostly mestizos, a mixture of native Amerindian and Spanish heritage. An estimated 75% of the population was mestizo, 10% Amerindian, 15% European, and 1% had African or other origins. Amerindian influence on Mexican cultural, economic, and political life is very strong.

9 LANGUAGES

Spanish, the official language, is spoken by nearly the entire population. This gives Mexico the world's largest Spanish-speaking community, as more Mexicans speak Spanish than Spaniards. In 1990, 7.5% of the population spoke some Amerindian language. There are at least 31 different Amerindian language groups, the principal languages being Nahuatl, Maya, Zapotec, Otomi, and Mixtec.

10 RELIGIONS

According to estimates in the early 1990s, 93.3% of Mexicans were formally Roman Catholic, and about 5% were Protestant. About 50,000 officially followed native Amerindian religions, but many Mexicans (over 2% of the population) combine elements of native religions with Roman Catholicism. The Jewish population was an estimated 35,000, and there were some 25,000 Buddhists and 25,000 Muslims.

11 TRANSPORTATION

The local, state, and federal Mexican road system amounted to 245,000 kilometers (152,200 miles) in 1993. There were an estimated 12.2 million registered vehicles, including 8.4 million passenger cars and 3.8 million trucks.

In 1994, the total route length of railways was 20,660 kilometers (12,830 miles), consisting of six integrated lines. The Mexico City subway system, totaling 120 kilometers (75 miles) in 1987, suffers from overcrowding.

Mexico's inland waterways and lakes are not important for transportation, but ocean and coastal shipping is significant. Of Mexico's 102 ocean ports, the most important are Tampico and Veracruz, on the Gulf of Mexico; and Mazatlán on the Pacific coast. The merchant marine in 1995 had 51 vessels totaling 875,000 gross registered tons.

Air transportation in Mexico has developed rapidly. In 1991 there were 200 airports with permanent surface runways, 36 of them long enough to accommodate large jets. Mexican commercial aircraft performed 19.4 billion passenger-kilometers of service in 1995. The main airline company is Aeroméxico.

12 HISTORY

The land now known as Mexico was inhabited by many of the most advanced Amerindian cultures of the ancient Americas. The Mayan civilization in the Yucatán Peninsula began about 2500 BC, flourished about AD 300–900, and then declined until its conquest by the Spanish. Skillful in the construction of stone buildings and the carving of stone monuments, the Mayas built great cities at Chichen Itzá, and many other sites.

The Nahua culture of the tribal Toltecs dominated the Valley of Mexico from the early tenth century AD until the early thirteenth century, when the Aztecs, another Nahua tribe, gained control. Skilled in architecture, engineering, mathematics, weaving, and metalworking, the Aztecs had a powerful priesthood and a complex religion dominated by the sun and war god Huitzilopochtli, to whom prisoners captured from other tribes were sacrificed.

The empire was at its height in 1519, when the Spanish, under Hernán Cortés,

landed at present-day Veracruz. With superior weapons and the cooperation of local chieftains, the Spaniards conquered Mexico by 1521. The Spaniards brought Roman Catholicism to Mexico, imposed their legal and economic system on the country, and enslaved many of the inhabitants. The combination of Spanish oppression and the diseases the conquistadores (conquerors) brought with them reduced the Amerindian population from an estimated 5 million in 1500 to 3.5 million a century later.

Evolution of Government

Spain ruled Mexico as the viceroyalty of New Spain for three centuries. Continued political abuses and Amerindian enslavement, combined with the political uncertainty that followed Napoleon's invasion of Spain in 1807 produced a Mexican independence movement. Between 1810 and 1815, several unsuccessful revolts took place. In 1821, independence was finally proclaimed and secured. Agustín de Iturbide proclaimed himself emperor in 1822 but was deposed in 1823, when a republic was established.

In the next 25 years, there were at least 30 changes of government. General Antonio López de Santa Anna, who had participated in the overthrow of Iturbide, become the dominant figure in the 1830s and 1840s and attempted to centralize the new government. Texas gained its independence from Mexico in 1836 as a result of the defeat of Santa Anna at San Jacinto; in 1845, after a period as the Republic of Texas, it joined the United States. Mexico lost the war with the United States that followed (1846–48), which began over a dispute about the border of Texas.

A reform government was established in 1855 after a revolt against Santa Anna, and a new liberal constitution was adopted in 1857. In the 1860s France, under Napoleon III, briefly controlled Mexico, installing Archduke Maximilian of Austria as emperor. Maximilian was executed in 1867, and the republic restored.

In 1876, José de la Cruz Porfirio Díaz seized power and assumed the presidency, a position he held almost continuously until 1911. Under his dictatorship, Mexico modernized by opening its doors to foreign investors and managers. At the same time, all dissent was suppressed, and resentment among the middle classes and the peasantry continued to grow.

After Díaz was once again reelected to the presidency in 1910, the Mexican Revolution erupted. This revolution, which, by 1917, had claimed as many as 1 million lives, was not only a protest by middle-class liberals against the oppressive Díaz regime but also a massive popular rebellion of land-hungry peasants.

Riots in Mexico City forced Díaz to resign in 1911 and leave the country, and liberal politician Francisco Indalecio Madero was elected president. However, popular revolts led by Emiliano Zapata and Pancho Villa, who refused to submit to Madero's authority, led the country into chaos. Madero was ousted and murdered in 1913 by General Victoriano Huerta,

who, in turn, was soon driven from power himself. By July 1914, a full-scale civil war broke out. This phase of the revolution ended in February 1917, when a new constitution was proclaimed.

Political Stability Realized

Venustiano Carranza was elected president in 1917, but for the next decade Mexico was still beset by fighting between various revolutionary groups. Political stability at last came to Mexico with the formation in 1929 of an official government party, known as the Institutional Revolutionary Party (Partido Revolucionario Institucional—PRI) since 1945. Although founded to support the interests of peasants, workers, and other disadvantaged groups, it has also been closely allied with business since the 1940s. The most outstanding political leader of the post-1929 era was Lázaro Cárdenas, president from 1934–40, who sought with some success to realize the social goals of the revolution. His reforms included massive land redistribution, establishment of strong labor unions, extension of education to remote areas of the country, and in 1938, the takeover of foreign petroleum holdings, mostly US-owned.

The years since World War II (1939–45) have been marked by political stability, economic expansion, and the rise of the middle class, but also by general neglect of the poorest segments of the population. An economic boom during the late 1970s, brought about by huge oil export earnings, benefited only a small percentage of the people. Declining world oil prices in 1981 led to a severe financial crisis in 1982.

Mexico City was devastated by a major earthquake in September 1985. The official death toll was 7,000, although unofficial estimates were as high as 20,000. In addition, 300,000 were left homeless. There was widespread protest over the fact that many of the buildings destroyed had been built in violation of construction regulations, and there were claims that foreign emergency aid had been mishandled by the government.

In August 1992, formal negotiations regarding the North American Free Trade Agreement (NAFTA) were concluded, whereby Mexico would join the United States and Canada in the elimination of trade barriers, the promotion of fair competition, and increased investment opportunities. NAFTA went into effect on 1 January 1994.

In January 1994, a primarily Amerindian group calling itself the Zapatista Army of National Liberation resorted to an armed uprising, initially taking control of four municipalities in the state of Chiapas on the Isthmus of Tehuantepec, to protest what it regarded as government failure to deal effectively with regional social and economic problems. Two months later, Mexico had its first high-level assassination in over 60 years when PRI presidential candidate Luis Donaldo Colosio was murdered in Tijuana. His replacement, Ernesto Zedillo, was elected at the end of the year in a closely monitored campaign.

In December 1994, the Mexican peso was devalued. The economy went into its worst recession in over 50 years. During the first five months of 1995, over 1 million Mexicans lost their jobs. The United States offered a multimillion-dollar bailout to keep the economy from getting worse.

The public discontent with the economic crisis, poverty, crime, and corruption led to a rejection of the PRI. Until then, the PRI had ruled in Mexico for about 70 years as a virtual one-party system. In June 1997, the PRI lost its majority in the lower house of the National Congress to the combined power of the Party of the Democratic Revolution (PRD) and the National Action Party (PAN).

In January 1998, tens of thousands of Mexicans supporting the Zapatista movement demonstrated in Mexico City against the December 1997 massacre of 45 Indians by pro-government gunmen in Chiapas.

13 GOVERNMENT

Mexico is a federal republic consisting of 31 states and the Federal District. The president, elected for a six-year term (by universal adult vote beginning at age 18) and not eligible for reelection, appoints the attorney-general and a cabinet, which may vary in number. There is no vice-president. If the president dies or is removed from office, Congress is constitutionally empowered to elect a provisional president.

The two-chamber Congress, also elected by direct universal suffrage, is composed of a Senate (Cámara de Senadores), made up of 128 members (4 from each state and 4 from the Federal District), and a Chamber of Deputies (Cámara de Diputados) made up of 500 members. Senators are elected for six years (half the Senate is elected every three years) and deputies for three years, and both groups are ineligible for immediate reelection.

In an effort to unite various interest groups within the government party, a National Consultative Committee, composed of living ex-presidents of Mexico, was formed in 1961 by President Adolfo López Mateos (1958–64).

Mexico has 2,359 municipalities, which are the principal units of state government.

14 POLITICAL PARTIES

From 1929 to 1997, the majority party and the only political group to gain national importance was the Institutional Revolutionary Party (Partido Revolucionario Institucional—PRI). The PRI includes only civilians and embraces all shades of political opinion. Three large pressure groups operate within the PRI: labor, the peasantry, and the "popular" sector (such as bureaucrats, teachers, and small business people).

In the July 1997 elections, the PRI failed to keep a majority of seats in the 500-member lower house for the first time in nearly 70 years. The Party of Democratic Revolution (PRD) won 125 seats and formed a coalition with the National Action Party (Partido de Acción Nacional—PAN), which won 122 seats. The PRI held 239 seats.

15 JUDICIAL SYSTEM

Federal courts include the Supreme Court, with 21 magistrates; 32 circuit tribunals, and 98 district courts, with 1 judge each.

The jury system is not commonly used in Mexico, but judicial protection is provided by the Writ of Amparo, which allows a person convicted in the court of a local judge to appeal to a federal judge. Low pay and high caseloads increase the possibility of corruption in the judicial system. In 1995, a judicial reform law provided for a competitive examination for selecting most lower court judges.

16 ARMED FORCES

Total full-time strength of the armed forces was 175,000 in 1995. The army had 130,000 personnel. Regular army units included the presidential guard, 3 infantry brigades, 1 armored brigade, an airborne brigade, and support units. The navy, including naval air force and marines, had 37,000 personnel. The air force had 8,000 personnel and 97 combat aircraft. Paramilitary forces included 14,000 rural defense militia; military reserves numbered 300,000. Defense expenditures in 1995 amounted to $2.7 billion.

Under the required military training program, all 18 year-old males must complete one year of part-time basic army training. In 1995, 60,000 draftees were on active duty, drawn by lottery.

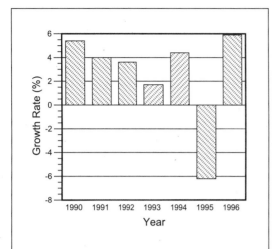

Yearly growth rate of the economy. This economic indicator tells by what percent the economy has increased or decreased when compared with the previous year.

17 ECONOMY

Although Mexico's economy once was mostly agricultural, commerce and industry have long been the nation's chief income earners. A great mining nation, Mexico is the world's leading producer of silver and is well endowed with sulfur, copper, manganese, iron ore, lead, and zinc.

Since 1960 there has been a gradual improvement in social and economic equality, but because of the rapid rate of population increase, many Mexicans still remain in poverty. While peasant wages remained static during the 1960s, industrial wages increased more than 80%, leading to large-scale migration from countryside to city. Mexico City's enormous population growth has been accompanied by mass poverty.

In December 1987, the Pact for Stability and Economic Growth (PECE), a series of price and wage agreements between government, labor, and business, went into effect. The PECE helped curb inflation to 51.6% in 1988 without causing a recession. Gradual recovery has seen the inflation rate fall to 20% in 1991, 11.9% in 1992, and to around 10% in 1993.

The North American Free Trade Agreement (NAFTA), in effect as of 1 January 1994, opened the domestic market to foreign trade by eliminating trade barriers between Mexico, the United States, and Canada over the next 15 years.

Mexico's domestic economy declined by 6.9% in 1995. The problem began with a massive devaluation of the peso in December 1994, which brought on a financial crisis and exposed certain weak spots in the economy. Inflation and interest rates soared, which discouraged foreign investment. The United States provided $20 billion of a $50 billion assistance package, but the Mexican government only used half of that amount for its recovery in 1996.

18 INCOME

In 1995, Mexico's gross national product (GNP) was $304.6 billion, or about $3,670 per person. For the period 1985–95, the average inflation rate was 36.7%, and the real growth rate in per person GNP was 0.1%.

19 INDUSTRY

Mexico is one of the leading manufacturing nations in Latin America. The principal manufacturing industries include automobile and related parts production, steel, textiles, cement and related construction materials, chemicals and petrochemicals, paper and paper products, food processing, breweries, and glass. In 1995, Mexico produced 935,017 vehicles; the leading manufacturers were Ford, Chrysler, General Motors, and Volkswagen.

Maquiladoras, which are facilities engaged in what is known as re-export processing, play an important role in Mexican manufacturing. Usually located near the United States border and owned by a foreign corporation, maquiladoras assemble or process imported goods brought in from the US and then re-export them duty free. In 1992, there were some 2,042 maquiladora factories employing 494,721 workers.

20 LABOR

Mexico's civilian labor force of 35.6 million in 1995 was distributed as follows: government and services, 23%; agriculture, 24.7%; commerce, 23%; industry, 15.3%; building, 5.3%; transportation and communications, 4.3%; mining, 0.4%; and other sectors, 4%.

Underemployment is Mexico's major labor problem. According to official figures, unemployment was 4.7% in 1995, but that figure reflected only the largest metropolitan areas. Rural unemployment

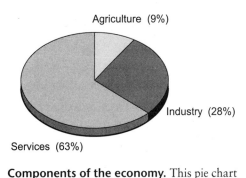

Agriculture (9%)

Industry (28%)

Services (63%)

Components of the economy. This pie chart shows how much of the country's economy is devoted to agriculture (includes forestry, hunting, and fishing), industry, or services.

was believed to be much higher. There is no general unemployment compensation system. About 30% of the labor force was unionized in 1996.

There is a minimum age law of 14 for child employment, which is fairly well enforced at large and middle-sized companies, but not in smaller firms or in agriculture.

21 AGRICULTURE

In 1995, production totals (in tons) for the principal crops were as follows: sugarcane, 41.1 million; corn, 16.2 million; sorghum, 4.3 million; wheat, 3.8 million; dry beans, 1.3 million; soybeans, 239,000; rice, 454,000; and barley, 550,000. Principal exports are coffee, cotton, fresh fruit, sugar, tobacco, and tomatoes. In 1995, the value of agricultural exports amounted to $3.32 billion.

22 DOMESTICATED ANIMALS

More than one-third of the total land area is suitable for pasture. In 1995, the livestock population was estimated at 30.1 million head of cattle, 18 million hogs, 10.5 million goats, 6 million sheep, 6.2 million horses (third in the world), 3.2 million donkeys, 3.2 million mules, and 288 million chickens.

Output of livestock products in 1995 included 6.4 million tons of cows' milk, 143,000 tons of goats' milk, 1.3 million tons of beef and veal, 1.2 million tons of poultry meat, 808,000 tons of pork, and 1.2 million tons of eggs.

23 FISHING

Mexico's principal commercial catches are shrimp, sardines, bass, pike, abalone, Spanish mackerel, and red snapper. The 1994 catch was 1.3 million tons. Among the shellfish caught were shrimp, 78,549 tons; oysters, 36,726 tons; crabs, 16,039 tons; clams, 16,622 tons; and lobsters, 2,239 tons. The main fish caught were California pilchards, 266,135 tons; yellowfin tuna, 114,130 tons; and freshwater cichlids, 80,463.

The fishing industry is largely handled by cooperative societies, which are granted monopolies on the most valuable species of fish. Most fish processed in Mexico's canneries are consumed domestically.

24 FORESTRY

About 48.7 million hectares (120.3 million acres) are classified as forestland. Only about 30% of all forests are utilized,

Photo credit: International Labour Office.

A young boy working at an auto repair shop.

mostly in Chihuahua, Durango, and Michoacán. Trees found include palms, mahogany, cedar, primavera, sapote, oak, copal, and pine. Conifers are found at higher elevations. About 90% of Mexico's forestry production comes from temperate forest, and 10% from tropical forests.

Mexico's forestry policy is designed to protect and renew these resources, so that forests may fulfill their soil-protection functions and timber reserves may be exploited rationally and productively. Roundwood production in 1994 was 22.5 million cubic meters (29.5 million cubic yards). Mexico's ability to supply its own wood products needs are severely restricted by the limited access to timber available in Mexico. Timber is often located in mountainous regions with rough terrain and few all-season roads.

25 MINING

In 1994, Mexico was the world's leading producer of silver and celestite (strontium mineral), second in sodium sulfate, one of the five leading producers of antimony, white arsenic, graphite, bismuth, and fluorospar. Metallic deposits are principally in the Sierra Madre ranges. Copper, gold, and manganese are mined mainly in the northwest; lead, zinc, and silver in central Mexico; and coal and petroleum in the east.

Output of principal minerals in 1994 included silver (metal content of ore), 2.2 million kilograms (4.8 million pounds); gold, 13,900 kilograms (30,600 pounds); iron ore, 7.5 million tons; sulfur, 2.9 million tons; cadmium, 2,580 tons; zinc, 382,000 tons; barite, 86,600 tons; lead, 170,000 tons; and copper, 295,000 tons.

26 FOREIGN TRADE

Of 1994 exports, leading exports included metal manufactures (60.5%), mineral commodities (11.7%), and agricultural products (5%). Merchandise exports in 1992 consisted mostly of crude oil, chemicals, petrochemicals, automobiles, machinery and equipment, iron and steel products, electrical and electronic goods, textiles and clothing, and coffee.

Merchandise imports in 1992 consisted primarily of machinery and transportation equipment, chemicals, electrical and elec-

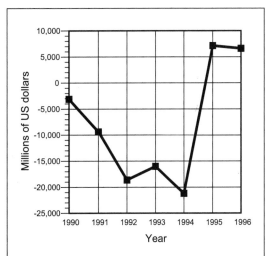

Yearly balance of trade measured in millions of US dollars. The balance of trade is the difference between what a country sells to other countries (its exports) and what it buys (its imports). If a country imports more than it exports, it has a negative balance of trade (a trade deficit). If exports exceed imports there is a positive balance of trade (a trade surplus).

tronic goods, processed foods, beverages and tobacco, iron and steel products, paper printing and publishing, textiles and clothing, oil derivatives, plastics, petrochemicals, maize, and soybeans.

In 1995, an estimated 83.4% of Mexico's exports went to the United States. About 4.2% went to European Union (EU) countries, 2.5% to Canada, and 1% to Brazil. That year, the United States accounted for 74.5% of Mexico's imports; the EU countries, 10.2%; and Japan, 5%.

27 ENERGY AND POWER

The total amount of electricity produced in 1994 was 140.2 billion kilowatt hours, of which 14.1% was hydroelectric and 2.9% was nuclear power. The possibilities for geothermal electrical production are wide-ranging, with over 100 thermal springs available for exploitation.

Mexico's estimated oil reserves as of the beginning of 1996 were 49.8 billion barrels, second in the Western Hemisphere after Venezuela. In 1997, however, Mexican officials suggested that reserves may have been overstated by 30% since the 1970s. Since 1938, the petroleum industry has been operated by a government-owned company, Mexican Petroleum (Petróleos Mexicanos—PEMEX). PEMEX is the world's fifth largest oil company, the largest civilian employer in Mexico, and the single most important business in the Mexican economy.

Crude oil production was about 3.1 million barrels per day during the early 1990s. Mexico exports about half the oil it produces, mostly crude oil to the United States, Spain, and the Far East. In 1995, Mexico produced 29 billion cubic meters (1 trillion cubic feet) of natural gas (mostly from offshore sources). Proven reserves of natural gas were estimated at 1.9 trillion cubic meters (68.4 trillion cubic feet) in 1996.

28 SOCIAL DEVELOPMENT

Mexico's social security system includes old age pensions, disability, medical, and work injury benefits. Insured workers receive medical aid in addition to wage benefits, and the insured worker's family receives first-aid treatment. During pregnancy and childbirth and for a period thereafter, insured women receive obstetrical care, nursing aid, a cash subsidy, and a layette. A worker who has been 60% disabled for at least 12 months is eligible for an invalid's pension, and all residents are eligible for old age pensions at age 60.

Government employees are covered by the Security and Social Services Institute for Civil Workers. Programs for children, including a primary-school breakfast program, are overseen by the National Institute for Child Protection. The Mexican Institution for Child Welfare provides care for neglected, abandoned, or sick children.

Women have held top political and union leadership roles, have the right to file for separation or divorce, and the right to own property in their own name. Domestic violence, however, remains a problem.

Indigenous peoples have full protection under the law, but in practice they face discrimination.

29 HEALTH

Mexico has made slow but measurable progress in public health. Average life expectancy rose from 32.4 years in 1930 to 57.6 in 1965; by 1995, it was estimated at 72 years. Cholera, yellow fever, plague, and smallpox have been virtually eliminated, and typhus has been controlled. Permanent campaigns are waged against malaria, poliomyelitis, skin diseases, tuberculosis, leprosy, onchocercosis, and serious childhood diseases. In 1990–95, 83% of the population had access to safe water, and 50% had adequate sanitation.

Selected Social Indicators

These statistics are estimates for the period 1993 to 1996. For comparison purposes, data for the United States and averages for low-income countries and high-income countries are also given.

Indicator	Mexico	Low-income countries	High-income countries	United States
Per capita gross national product†	$3,670	$490	$25,870	$28,020
Population growth rate	1.7%	1.7%	0.6%	0.9%
Population growth rate in urban areas	2.0%	3.8%	0.9%	1.2%
Population per square kilometer of land	49	82	30	29
Life expectancy in years	72	63	77	77
Number of physicians per 1,000 people	1.6	1.0	2.5	2.5
Number of pupils per teacher (primary school)	29	41	17	14
Illiteracy rate (15 years and older)	10%	34%	<5%	3%
Energy consumed per capita (kg of oil equivalent)	1,456	393	5,123	7,905

† The gross national product (GNP) is the total dollar value of all goods and services produced by a country in a year. The per capita GNP is calculated by dividing a country's GNP by its population. The World Bank defines low-income countries as those with a per capita GNP of $785 or less. High-income countries have a per capita GNP of $9,636 or more. About 16% of the world's 5.7 billion people live in high-income countries, while almost 56% live in low-income countries.   > = greater than   < = less than

Sources: World Bank, *World Development Indicators on CD-ROM*, Washington, D.C.: The World Bank, 1998. Central Intelligence Agency, *The World Fact Book*, Washington, D.C.: Government Printing Office, 1998.

In 1993, there was one doctor for every 615 people, and one hospital bed per 1,704 people. That year, 91% of the population had access to health care services.

30 HOUSING

Mexico's housing shortage was worsened by high population growth in the 1980s. The government allocated $1.93 billion in 1989 to build 250,000 low-cost housing units, and expected to receive an additional $700 million from the World Bank to build more. The 1990 National Housing Plan predicted a shortage of 6.1 million homes, to be felt most severely in the outskirts of urban areas, including Mexico City, Guadalajara, Monterey, and cities in the northern states. In 1992, Mexico had 15.1 million dwellings, of which 49.9% had piped water, 51% had flush toilets, and 87.5% had electric lighting.

31 EDUCATION

A government literacy program helped reduce Mexico's adult illiteracy rate from 37.8% in 1960 to an average of about 10% in 1995 (males: 8.2% and females: 12.6%).

Primary schooling is compulsory and free. In 1995, Mexico had 507,669 teachers and 14.6 million students at the primary level. At the secondary level, there were 448,407 teachers and 7.3 million students.

Major universities include the National Autonomous University (founded in 1551), the National Polytechnic Institute, and Iberoamericana University (private), all in Mexico City. There were 145,789 teachers and 1.4 million students in all higher level institutions in 1993.

The government provides adult education through cultural and motorized missions, community development brigades, reading rooms, and special centers for workers' training, art education, social work, and primary education.

32 MEDIA

In 1995 there were 238 television stations, including 8 cultural stations; and 679 radio stations, 45 of them cultural. In 1995, 22.5 million radios and over 31.1 million television sets were in use. The number of telephones in service in 1995 was 7.6 million. Mexico had over 20,000 Internet hosts in 1996.

As of 1995, some 292 daily newspapers were published in Mexico, with the greatest number coming from Mexico City. Leading newspapers (with their estimated average daily circulations in 1995) include *Esto* (242,383); *El Heraldo* (180,000); *La Prensa* (300,000); *Ovaciones* (130,000); *El Universal* (127,000); *Excélsior* (200,000); *El National* (27,000); and *Novedades* (230,000).

Photo credit: International Labour Office.

Front door of typical Mexican house which is constructed of blocks and dried soil.

33 TOURISM AND RECREATION

In 1994, Mexico was the world's tenth most popular tourist destination. That year 17.1 million tourists entered Mexico, 92% of them from the United States. Receipts from tourism in 1994 were $6.36 billion.

Mexico's tourist attractions range from modern seaside resort areas, such as Tijuana, Acapulco, and Cancún, to the Mayan ruins of Chiapas on the Isthmus of Tehuantepec and the Aztec monuments of the south-central regions. Mexico City, combining notable features from the Aztec, colonial, and modern periods, is itself an important tourist mecca.

Mexico's most popular sports are baseball, soccer, jai-alai, swimming, and volleyball. Bullfights are a leading spectator sport; the Mexico City arena, seating 50,000 persons, is one of the largest in the world, and there are about 35 other arenas throughout the country.

34 FAMOUS MEXICANS

The founder of Spanish Mexico was Hernán Cortés (1485–1547). One of the great heroes in Mexican history is Guatemotzin (Cuauhtémoc, 1495?–1525), the last emperor of the Aztecs, who fought the Spanish after the death of his uncle, Montezuma II (Moctezuma or Motecuhzoma, 1480?–1520). The first years of independence were dominated by Antonio López de Santa Anna (1794–1876). The dictator José de la Cruz Porfirio Díaz (1830–1915) dominated Mexico from 1876 to 1911. He was overthrown largely through the efforts of Francisco Indalecio Madero (1873–1913), called the Father of the Revolution.

Two revolutionary leaders—Doroteo Arango, known as Pancho Villa (1878–1923), and Emiliano Zapata (1879?–1919)—achieved almost legendary status. The foremost political leader after the revolution was Lázaro Cárdenas (1895–1970). Luis Echeverría Álvarez (b.1922), who held the presidency during 1970–76, made Mexico one of the leading countries of the developing world in international forums.

The painter Diego Rivera (1883–1957), is renowned for his murals. Painter Frida Kahlo (1907–1954), who married Rivera in 1929, has received attention in recent years by both the art world and by feminists. Juana Inés de la Cruz (1651–1695), a nun, was a poet and proponent of women's rights. Well-known contemporary authors include Octavio Paz (1914–98) and Carlos Fuentes (b.1928). The outstanding figure in recent Mexican literary life is the diplomat, dramatist, poet, essayist, and critic Alfonso Reyes (1889–1959). Anthropologist Carlos Castaneda (b.Brazil, 1931) is widely known for his studies of mysticism among the Yaqui Amerindians. Carlos Chávez (1899–1978) is a well-known Mexican composer. Significant figures in the motion picture industry are the comedian Cantinflas (Mario Moreno, b.1911), Mexican-born actor Anthony Rudolph Oaxaca Quinn (b.1916), and Spanish-born director Luis Buñuel (1900–83).

Notable Mexican sports figures include Fernando Valenzuela, (b.1960), a pitcher for the Los Angeles Dodgers who won the Cy Young Award as a rookie.

35 BIBLIOGRAPHY

Barry, Tom, ed. *Mexico: A Country Guide.* Albuquerque, N.M.: Inter-Hemispheric Education Resource Center, 1992.

Bazant, Jan. *A Concise History of Mexico.* New York: Cambridge University Press, 1977.

Cobb, Charles E., Jr. "Mexico's Bajio—The Heartland." *National Geographic,* December 1990, 122–143.

Dibble, Sandra. "The Song of Oaxaca." *National Geographic,* November 1994, 38–63.

Grayson, George W. *The North American Free Trade Agreement.* Ithaca, N.Y.: Foreign Policy Association, 1993.

Mexico in Pictures. Minneapolis, Min.: Lerner, 1988.

Meyer, Michael C. *The Course of Mexican History.* 5th edition. New York: Oxford University Press, 1995.

Nagel, Rob, and Anne Commire. "Emiliano Zapata." In *World Leaders, People Who Shaped the World.* Volume III: North and South America. Detroit: U*X*L, 1994.

Nagel, Rob, and Anne Commire. "Juana Ines de la Cruz." In *World Leaders, People Who Shaped the World.* Volume III: North and South America.

ica. Detroit: U*X*L, 1994.

Nagel, Rob, and Anne Commire. "Moctezuma II." In *World Leaders, People Who Shaped the World.* Volume III: North and South America. Detroit: U*X*L, 1994.

Oster, Patrick. *The Mexicans: A Personal Portrait of a People.* New York: W. Morrow, 1989.

Ruiz, Ramón Eduardo. *Triumphs and Tragedy: A History of the Mexican People.* New York: W.W. Norton, 1992.

Stein, R. *Mexico.* Chicago: Children's Press, 1984.

MICRONESIA

Federated States of Micronesia

CAPITAL: Palikir, Pohnpei Island.

FLAG: Adopted in 1978, the flag is light blue, bearing four five-pointed stars arranged in a diamond in the center.

MONETARY UNIT: The US dollar is the official medium of exchange.

WEIGHTS AND MEASURES: British units are used, as modified by US usage.

HOLIDAYS: New Year's Day, 1 January; Federated States of Micronesia Day, 10 May; Independence Day, 3 November; Christmas Day, 25 December.

TIME: In Pohnpei and Kosrae, 10 PM = noon GMT; in Yap and Truk, 9 PM = noon GMT.

1 LOCATION AND SIZE

The Federated States of Micronesia (FSM) is located in the western Pacific Ocean within a large group of islands known as the Carolinian archipelago. The four states—Kosrae, Pohnpei, Truk, and Yap—consist of 607 islands with a total area of 7,866 square kilometers (3,037 square miles), comprising 702 square kilometers (271 square miles) of land, and 7,164 square kilometers (2,766 square miles) of lagoons. Comparatively, the area occupied by the Federated States of Micronesia is slightly less than four times the size of Washington, D.C.

The capital city of the Federated States of Micronesia, Palikir, is located on the island of Pohnpei.

2 TOPOGRAPHY

The 607 islands constituting the four states include large, mountainous islands of volcanic origin. Coral atolls comprise most of the outer islands of all states.

3 CLIMATE

There is little seasonal or daily variation in temperature, which averages 27°C (80°F). The islands are subject to typhoons. Annual average rainfall ranges from 305 centimeters (120 inches) in Yap to 508 centimeters (200 inches) in Pohnpei.

4 PLANTS AND ANIMALS

There is tropical vegetation, with trees including tropical hardwoods on the higher volcanic islands and coconut palms on the coral atolls. The only native land mammal is the tropical bat. A rich marine fauna inhabits the area.

5 ENVIRONMENT

Solid waste disposal and mining operations threaten the land. Micronesia's water

Geographic Profile

Geographic Features

Size ranking: 172 of 192
Highest elevation: 791 meters (2,595 feet) at Totolom
Lowest elevation: Sea level at the Pacific Ocean

Weather

Average annual precipitation: 305–508 centimeters (120–200 inches)

supply is threatened by industrial and agricultural pollutants, as well as untreated sewage. The fish population is endangered by water-borne toxins and explosives used in commercial fishing.

6 POPULATION

The population was estimated in 1998 at 130,000. About 7% live in Kosrae, 30% in Pohnpei, 50% in Truk, and 13% in Yap. During the 1990s, the yearly population growth rate averaged 2%.

7 MIGRATION

Most emigration has been undertaken temporarily for higher education.

8 ETHNIC GROUPS

The islanders are classified as Micronesians of Malayo-Mongoloid origins. The people of the Nukuoro and Kapingamarangi atolls in southwestern Pohnpei are of Polynesian descent.

9 LANGUAGES

English is the official language and is taught in the schools. The native languages are of the Malayo-Polynesian family. Yapese, Ulithian, Woleaian, Trukese, Pohnpeian, and Kosraean are classed as Malaysian. Kapingamarangi and Nukuoro, spoken on two isolated atolls in Pohnpei, are Polynesian languages.

10 RELIGIONS

In 1993, Roman Catholics comprised 42.4% of the population. Protestantism is predominant in Kosrae. Other churches represented are Assembly of God, Seventh-day Adventist, and United Church of Christ.

11 TRANSPORTATION

There were approximately 39 kilometers (24 miles) of paved roads on the major islands. International and interstate scheduled airline services are provided by Continental/Air Micronesia, Air Nauru, and Pacific Missionary Aviation.

12 HISTORY

The string of islands known as the Carolinian archipelago was sighted by European navigators in the sixteenth century. Until the end of the nineteenth century, the islands were under Spanish colonial administration.

In 1899, following the Spanish-American War, Spain sold the islands to Germany. The Japanese took control at the end of World War I (1914–18). Following the defeat of Germany and Japan by the Allies in World War II (1939–45), the four states of the Federated States of Micronesia (FSM) came under United States administration as part of the United Nations Trust Territory of the Pacific Islands.

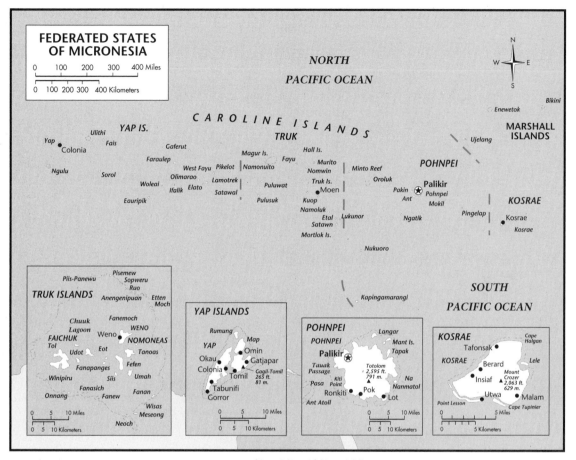

FEDERATED STATES OF MICRONESIA

0   100   200   300   400 Miles

0   100 200 300   400 Kilometers

NORTH
PACIFIC OCEAN

N
W — E
S

Bikini
Enewetok

CAROLINE ISLANDS

YAP IS.
TRUK

Yap
Colonia
Ulithi
Fais
Gaferut
Faraulep
Ngulu
Sorol
Woleai
Olimarao
Ifalik Elato
Eauripik
West Fayu Pikelot
Lamotrek
Satawal
Magur Is.
Fayu
Namonuito
Puluwat
Pulusuk
Hall Is.
Murito
Nomwin
Truk Is.
Moen
Kuop
Namoluk
Etal
Satawn
Mortlok Is.
Minto Reef
Oroluk
Lukunor
Nukuoro

Ujelang

MARSHALL
ISLANDS

POHNPEI

Palikir
Pakin
Ant
Pohnpei
Mokil
Ngatik
Pingelap

KOSRAE

Kosrae
Kosrae

Pils-Panewu
Pisemew
Sopweru
Ruo
Anengenipuan Etten
Moch

TRUK ISLANDS

Fanemoch
Chuuk
Lagoon
FAICHUK
Tol
Udot
Fanapanges
Winipiru
Fanasich
Onnang
Fanew
Weno
Eot
Siis
Fanan
WENO
NOMONEAS
Tanoas
Fefen
Umah
Wisas
Meseong
Neoch

Kapingamarangi

SOUTH
PACIFIC OCEAN

YAP ISLANDS

Rumung
YAP
Okau
Colonia
Tomil
Tabunifi
Gorror
Map
Omin
Gatjapar
Gagil-Tomil
265 ft.
81 m.

POHNPEI

POHNPEI
Palikir
Tauak
Passage
Pasa
Point
Ronkiti
Ant Atoll
Langar
Mant Is.
Tapak
Totolom
2,595 ft.
791 m.
Kiti
Point
Pok
Lot
Na
Nanmatol

KOSRAE

KOSRAE
Tafonsak
Berard
Insiaf
Utwa
Point Lesson
Cape
Halgan
Lele
Mount
Crozer
2,063 ft.
629 m.
Malam
Cape Tupinier

0   5   10 Miles
0   5   10 Kilometers

0   5   10 Miles
0   5   10 Kilometers

0   5   10 Miles
0   5   10 Kilometers

0   5 Miles
0   5 Kilometers

LOCATION: 0° to 14°N; 135° to 166° E.

On 10 May 1979, a constitution drafted by a popularly elected constitutional convention went into effect. The United Nations Security Council voted in December 1990 to terminate the FSM's status as a United Nations Trust Territory. A capital, Palikir, was built in the Palikir Valley; it has served the FSM since 1990. The FSM became an independent state and joined the United Nations in September 1991. Its congress last met in march 1995.

13 GOVERNMENT

The national executive branch includes the president and vice-president, who serve four-year terms. The judiciary consists of a Supreme Court which applies criminal and civil laws and procedures that are similar to those of the United States. The legislature consists of a single-chamber Congress of 14 senators.

Each of Micronesia's four states has a legislature, governor, and lieutenant-governor.

14 POLITICAL PARTIES

There are no formal political parties.

15 JUDICIAL SYSTEM

The national judiciary consists of a Supreme Court, headed by a chief justice, and subordinate courts established by statute. The Supreme Court has both trial and appellate divisions and reviews cases that require interpretation of the Constitution, national law, or treaties.

16 ARMED FORCES

The Federated States of Micronesia (FSM) maintains no armed forces. External security is the responsibility of the United States.

17 ECONOMY

The gross domestic product (GDP) in 1994 was $205 million—$100 million of it was grant aid from the United States. The economy faces serious disadvantages, including shortages of technical and managerial skills, and large trade deficits. Grants from the United States are scheduled to end in 2002. The Asian Development Bank helped put together an economic development plan for Micronesia in 1995. Privatization, reduction of government employment, and the development of tourism and fisheries were recommended.

18 INCOME

In 1995, Micronesia's gross national product (GNP) was estimated to be between $766 and $3,035 per person. During 1985–95, the average annual inflation rate was 4.5%.

19 INDUSTRY

Handicrafts and small-scale processing are carried out in all states. A clothing plant in Yap is the country's largest private-sector industrial enterprise. Truk has a garment factory, a coconut-processing plant, a boat-building plant, and a breadfruit flour plant. Industry in other states includes a coconut–processing and soap and oil plant, a feedmill, an ice production plant, a brick-manufacturing plant, and a wood-processing plant.

20 LABOR

The national labor force was estimated at about 50,000 in 1990. While unemployment remains high, the economy faces shortages of skilled personnel since over 50% of the population is under 16 years of age.

21 AGRICULTURE

Staple crops include taros, sweet potatoes, bananas, cassavas, and breadfruit. Yams, as well as other fruits and vegetables, are also produced. The coconut palm has a wide range of uses, and copra (dried coconut meat that yields oil) is the main cash crop and the nation's leading export. Black and white peppers are both grown on Pohnpei for export.

22 DOMESTICATED ANIMALS

Livestock includes pigs, cattle, poultry, and goats.

23 FISHING

Although Micronesia's territorial waters contain the world's most productive tuna fishing grounds, there is practically no national participation in their exploitation. The tuna catch is valued at about $200 million annually. The total catch in 1994 was 1,650 tons.

24 FORESTRY

The nation has approximately 45,200 hectares (112,000 acres) of woodland, with some 26,700 hectares (66,000 acres) suitable for harvesting. However, most lumber used in construction is imported. Mangrove timber is used for handicrafts and furniture making.

25 MINING

Clays, coral, sand, rock aggregate, and quarry stone works supply construction materials.

26 FOREIGN TRADE

In 1993, exports totaled $49.3 million, while imports came to $109.5 million. Exports include copra, marine products, handicrafts, and a limited amount of farm produce sold to Guam and the Marshall Islands. Major imports include food, beverages, and tobacco; petroleum products; and machinery and transportation equipment.

The United States, Singapore, and Japan are the major trading partners.

27 ENERGY AND POWER

Imported petroleum supplies about 80% of the total energy requirements. Fuel wood provides most of the other 20%. Diesel fuel accounts for over two-thirds of petroleum imports.

28 SOCIAL DEVELOPMENT

Rapid changes in society have resulted in increasing juvenile delinquency, drug and alcohol abuse, and crime. National and state social programs are addressing these trends. A social insurance system includes old age, disability, and survivor benefits. Sex discrimination and violence against women are serious problems.

29 HEALTH

A community health center was established in Pohnpei in 1986. In the outer islands, medical services are provided through dispensaries. Life expectancy was 68 years in 1998. The entire population has access to safe water and sanitation.

30 HOUSING

In 1980, the total housing consisted of 11,562 units. There has been a movement away from traditional construction materials toward imported lumber, plywood, and corrugated metal roofing.

31 EDUCATION

The state governments are responsible for the provision of education. Secondary education is provided through five public and five private high schools. The Community College of Micronesia is in Pohnpei.

32 MEDIA

There are no private newspapers. Newsletters are published by the national government—*The National Union* (twice monthly)—and the four state governments—*Mogethin* (Yap), *Uss Me Auus*,

(Truk), *Pohnpei Reports,* and *Kosrae State Newsletters.*

In 1995, there were a total of six radio stations, six television stations, and one shortwave station. In the same year, there were 17,000 radios and 1,290 television sets. In 1995 there were 6,100 telephones.

33 TOURISM AND RECREATION

There were 30,000 visitors in 1993. Tourist attractions include the spectacular beauty of the high islands; World War II artifacts, including sunken Japanese ships in the Truk lagoon; and ancient remains on Yap Island.

34 FAMOUS MICRONESIANS

John Haglelgam was the president of the Federated States of Micronesia from 1987 to 1991.

35 BIBLIOGRAPHY

Ashby, Gene, ed. *Some Things of Value: Micronesian Customs and Beliefs.* Eugene, Ore.: Rainy Day Press, 1985.
Karolle, Bruce G. *Atlas of Micronesia.* 2d ed. Honolulu, Hawaii: Bess Press, 1993.
Kluge, P. F. *The Edge of Paradise: America in Micronesia.* New York: Random House, 1991.

MOLDOVA

Republic of Moldova

Republica Moldoveneasca

CAPITAL: Chişinău.

FLAG: Equal vertical bands of blue, yellow, and red; emblem in center of yellow stripe is Roman eagle with shield on its breast.

MONETARY UNIT: The leu is a paper currency, replacing the Russian rouble.

WEIGHTS AND MEASURES: The metric system is in force.

HOLIDAYS: Independence Day, 27 August.

TIME: 2 PM = noon GMT.

1 LOCATION AND SIZE

Moldova is a landlocked nation located in eastern Europe, between Ukraine and Romania. With a total area of 33,700 square kilometers (13,012 square miles), Moldova is slightly more than twice the size of the state of Hawaii. Moldova's boundary length totals 1,389 kilometers (864 miles).

Its capital city, Chisinău, is located in the south central part of the country.

2 TOPOGRAPHY

The topography of Moldova consists of rolling steppe gradually sloping south toward the Black Sea.

3 CLIMATE

The climate is of the humid continental type. The mean temperature is 20°C (68°F) in July and –4°C (24°F) in January. Rainfall averages 58 centimeters (22.8 inches) a year.

4 PLANTS AND ANIMALS

Three-fourths of the country consists of grasslands. Carp, bream, trout, and pike populate the lakes and streams.

5 ENVIRONMENT

The natural environment in Moldova suffers from the heavy use of agricultural chemicals (including banned pesticides such as DDT), which have contaminated soil and groundwater.

6 POPULATION

The population of Moldova was estimated at 4.6 million in 1998. A population of 4.5 million is projected for 2005. The population density in 1998 was about 131 persons per square kilometer (339 persons per square mile). The estimated 1995 population for Chisinău, the capital, was 765,000.

Geographic Profile

Geographic Features

Size ranking: 135 of 192
Highest elevation: 429 meters (1,407 feet) at Mount Balanesti (Balaneshty)
Lowest elevation: 2 meters (7 feet) at the Nistru River

Land Use†

Arable land:	53%
Permanent crops:	14%
Permanent pastures:	13%
Forests:	13%
Other:	7%

Weather††

Average annual precipitation: 58 centimeters (22.8 inches)
Average temperature in January: –4°C (24°F)
Average temperature in July: 20°C (68°F)

†*Arable land:* Land used for temporary crops, like meadows for mowing or pasture, gardens, and greenhouses. *Permanent crops:* Land cultivated with crops that occupy its use for long periods, such as cocoa, coffee, rubber, fruit and nut orchards, and vineyards. *Permanent pastures:* Land used permanently for forage crops. *Forests:* Land containing stands of trees. *Other:* Any land not specified, including built-on areas, roads, and barren land.

††The measurements for precipitation and average temperature were taken at weather stations closest to the country's largest city. Precipitation and average temperature can vary significantly within a country, due to factors such as latitude, altitude, coastal proximity, and wind patterns.

LOCATION: 47°0′N; 29°0′E. **BOUNDARY LENGTHS:** Total boundary lengths, 1,389 kilometers (864 miles); Romania, 450 kilometers (280 miles); Ukraine, 939 kilometers (584 miles).

7 MIGRATION

In 1990, there was a net emigration of 29,800 persons to other former Soviet republics. In 1996, the net emigration rate was 2.77 emigres per 1,000 population.

8 ETHNIC GROUPS

The population was 64.5% Moldovan in 1989. Other groups included Ukrainian, 14%; Russian, 13%; Gagauz, 3.5%; Bulgarians, 2%; and Jews, 1.5%.

9 LANGUAGES

Moldovan is considered a dialect of Romanian rather than a separate language. It is derived from Latin, with a large number of Slavonic-derived words.

10 RELIGIONS

As of 1994, 95% of Moldovans were Eastern Orthodox, 1–5% were Jewish, and 1,000 people were Baptist.

11 TRANSPORTATION

Railroads consisted of 1,328 kilometers (825 miles) of track in 1992. Highways that year totaled 14,500 kilometers (9,000 miles). Access to the sea is through Ukraine or Romania. Moldova has 24 airports.

12 HISTORY

The region that is now Moldova (also called Bessarabia) has historically been inhabited by a largely Romanian-speaking population. It was part of the larger Romanian principality of Moldova in the eighteenth century, which in turn was under Ottoman control. In 1812, the region was ceded to the Russian Empire, which ruled it until March 1918, when it became part of Romania. However, Moscow established a small Moldovian Autonomous Soviet Socialist Republic on Ukrainian territory in 1924.

When World War II (1939–45) broke out in Europe, the 1939 Nazi-Soviet pact assigned Moldova to the Soviet area of control, and Soviet forces seized it in June 1940. After the Nazi invasion of the Soviet Union, Germany helped Romania to regain Moldova, which it held from 1941 until Soviet forces reconquered the area in 1944.

Photo credit: AP/Wide World Photos.

Refugees carry their belongings aboard a cargo carriage in the Transdnister city of Tiraspol in Moldova. This small area of ethnic Russians declared itself an independent republic in opposition to the government of Moldova.

Moldova declared its independence from the Soviet Union on 27 August 1991. Russian forces, however, have remained on Moldovan territory east of the Dnister River and have supported the Russian minority (who form 30% of the population in this small region) in proclaiming an independent "Transdnister Republic." This move prompted fighting until a truce was called by Russia, Moldova, Ukraine, and Romania.

Moldova adopted a new constitution on 28 July 1994, replacing the old Soviet constitution of 1979.

13 GOVERNMENT

Elections to Moldova's first post-independence parliament were held on 27 February 1994. The new parliament consists of a single chamber of 104 seats. The president is elected separately in a popular election. Local administration is divided into 38 districts *(rayons)* and 10 cities.

14 POLITICAL PARTIES

Although 26 parties or coalitions of parties participated in the February 1994 elections, only four received more than the 4% of the national vote required to gain seats.

The Agrarian Party is the largest political group in the parliament, with 46 of 104 seats in 1995. The Socialist/Unity Bloc held 26 seats.

15 JUDICIAL SYSTEM

There are lower-level courts at the city and district *(rayon)* levels with a Supreme Court acting as an appeals court. The Supreme Court is divided into civil and criminal sections. Reforms approved in 1995 include the creation of a court to deal with constitutional issues and a system of appeals courts.

16 ARMED FORCES

The military is organized into the Ground Forces, Air and Air Defense Force, and the Security Forces (internal and border troops). There were about 11,900 personnel in Moldova's armed forces in 1995, including 10,600 army personnel and 900 air force personnel. Defense expenditures in 1995 were $45 million, or 2.5% of the gross domestic product (GDP).

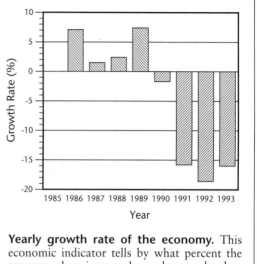

Yearly growth rate of the economy. This economic indicator tells by what percent the economy has increased or decreased when compared with the previous year.

17 ECONOMY

Agriculture is the most important area of Moldova's economy. Manufacturing is concentrated mainly in food processing and other light industry. The country's wide range of crops provides export revenue and employment. Droughts and trade disruptions following the dissolution of the former Soviet Union combined to cause steep declines in the economy during the early 1990s. The Moldovan government has adopted an ambitious economic reform agenda, including a stable convertible currency, price reform, privatization, and the removal of controls over exports and interest rates.

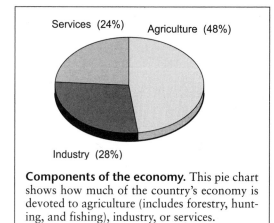

Components of the economy. This pie chart shows how much of the country's economy is devoted to agriculture (includes forestry, hunting, and fishing), industry, or services.

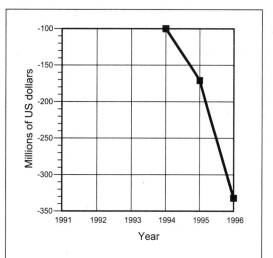

Yearly balance of trade measured in millions of US dollars. The balance of trade is the difference between what a country sells to other countries (its exports) and what it buys (its imports). If a country imports more than it exports, it has a negative balance of trade (a trade deficit). If exports exceed imports, there is a positive balance of trade (a trade surplus).

18 INCOME

In 1995, Moldova's gross national product (GNP) was $4 billion, or about $590 per person. For the period 1985–95, the average decline of the GNP per person was 8.2%.

19 INDUSTRY

Moldova's industry has been concentrated mostly in light manufacturing, including processed food and beverages and cigarettes, but other activities include consumer durables, garments, high-technology electrical motors, precision tools, and farm machinery.

20 LABOR

The total civilian employment in 1992 was 2 million, of which 20.6% were engaged in community, social, and personal services; 19.2% in manufacturing; 40% in agriculture; 5.8% in construction; 5.4% in commerce; and 9% in other areas. Official unemployment was 1% in 1995, but actual rates are much higher.

21 AGRICULTURE

Cropland covers about 66% of the Moldovan land area. Agricultural activities engaged 31% of all employed persons in 1995.

Moldovan crops and their 1995 production amounts include (in tons): sugar beets, 2.1 million; wheat, 1.1 million; grapes, 672,000; corn, 350,000; sunflowers, 203,000; barley, 203,000; potatoes, 400,000; tobacco, 25,300; and soybeans, 4,000. Wine and tobacco products are important agricultural exports.

Selected Social Indicators

These statistics are estimates for the period 1993 to 1996. For comparison purposes, data for the United States and averages for low-income countries and high-income countries are also given.

Indicator	Moldova	Low-income countries	High-income countries	United States
Per capita gross national product†	**$590**	$490	$25,870	$28,020
Population growth rate	**−0.3%**	1.7%	0.6%	0.9%
Population growth rate in urban areas	**1.1%**	3.8%	0.9%	1.2%
Population per square kilometer of land	**131**	82	30	29
Life expectancy in years	**67**	63	77	77
Number of physicians per 1,000 people	**3.6**	1.0	2.5	2.5
Number of pupils per teacher (primary school)	**24**	41	17	14
Illiteracy rate (15 years and older)	**4%**	34%	<5%	3%
Energy consumed per capita (kg of oil equivalent)	**963**	393	5,123	7,905

† The gross national product (GNP) is the total dollar value of all goods and services produced by a country in a year. The per capita GNP is calculated by dividing a country's GNP by its population. The World Bank defines low-income countries as those with a per capita GNP of $785 or less. High-income countries have a per capita GNP of $9,636 or more. About 16% of the world's 5.7 billion people live in high-income countries, while almost 56% live in low-income countries.   > = greater than   < = less than

Sources: World Bank, *World Development Indicators on CD-ROM*, Washington, D.C.: The World Bank, 1998. Central Intelligence Agency, *The World Fact Book*, Washington, D.C.: Government Printing Office, 1998.

22 DOMESTICATED ANIMALS

About 13% of the total area consists of pastureland. In 1995, the livestock population included 832,000 head of cattle, 1.1 million pigs, 1.4 million sheep, 75,000 goats, and 14 million chickens. Pork production amounted to 64,000 tons in 1995, when 45,000 tons of beef were produced. That year, 759,000 tons of milk and 45,000 tons of eggs were also produced.

23 FISHING

With no direct connection to the Black Sea, fishing is limited to the Dnister River. Commercial fishing is not economically significant.

24 FORESTRY

Forested areas account for about 13% of the total land area. Domestic wood and paper production does not meet the demand.

25 MINING

More than 100 deposits of gypsum, limestone, sand, and stone are exploited for industrial mineral production.

26 FOREIGN TRADE

In 1995/96, Moldova's exports amounted to $745 million, while imports totaled $841 million. Exports consisted mostly of foodstuffs, wine, tobacco, textiles, foot-

Photo credit: Valerii Corcimari.

A woman bottling wine, an important agricultural export.

wear, and chemicals. Gas, oil, coal, and steel were the main imports. Russia, Ukraine, and Romania were the major trading partners in 1995/96.

27 ENERGY AND POWER

Moldova imports nearly all of its energy needs. There is only one small hydroelectric power plant at Dubásari that provides domestic production. Refined oil products and natural gas come from Russia, Ukraine, and Belarus.

28 SOCIAL DEVELOPMENT

Moldova has broad legislation for the protection of children, including programs for paid maternity leave and family allowances. There are extensive vaccination and other health care programs for children.

Although women are accorded equal rights under the law, they are underrepresented in government and other leadership positions. There is also higher unemployment among women than among men.

29 HEALTH

Moldova has been working on developing its own standards for health care, among other major programs. Average life expectancy is 67 years. Only half the population had access to sanitation in 1993. That year, there was one doctor for every 250 people and one hospital bed per 80 people.

30 HOUSING

In 1989, 18.2% of all privately owned housing had running water, 16% had sewer lines, and 91.3% had gas. In 1990, Moldova had 17.9 square meters (193 square feet) of housing space per person. A program begun in March 1993 has privatized 80% of all housing units.

31 EDUCATION

While Moldova was a part of the Soviet Union, its education system was based on the Soviet pattern, and Russian was the language of instruction. However, after its separation, large-scale changes were introduced. Expenditures on education amounted to about 5.5% of the country's total gross national product in 1994. The Moldovan State University was founded in 1945 and uses both Moldovan and Russian as languages of instruction.

32 MEDIA

Radio Kishinev and Kishinev Television broadcast in Romanian and Russian. As of 1995, 577,000 telephones were in use.

33 TOURISM AND RECREATION

Civil unrest after Moldova's independence delayed the development of tourism. In 1994 there were 21,000 tourist arrivals, and receipts totaled $2 million.

34 FAMOUS MOLDOVANS

Petru Lucinschi was elected president in December 1996, succeeding Mircea Ion Snegur.

35 BIBLIOGRAPHY

Dima, Nicholas. *From Moldavia to Moldova: The Soviet-Romanian Territorial Dispute.* 2d ed. Boulder, Colo.: East European Monographs, 1991.

Fedor, Helen, ed. *Belarus and Moldova: Country Studies.* Lanham, Md.: Federal Research Division, Library of Congress, 1995.

Moldova. Minneapolis: Lerner Publications Co., 1993.

MONACO

Principality of Monaco
Principauté de Monaco

CAPITAL: The seat of government is at Monaco-Ville.

FLAG: The national flag consists of a red horizontal stripe above a white horizontal stripe.

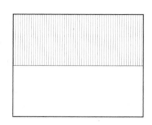

ANTHEM: *Hymne Monégasque,* beginning "Principauté Monaco, ma patrie" ("Principality of Monaco, my fatherland").

MONETARY UNIT: Monaco uses the French franc (Fr), and all monetary restrictions in effect in France apply also in Monaco. Monégasque coins, on a par with French coinage, also circulate; denominations are 10, 20, and 50 centimes, and ½, 1, 2, 5, 10, and 50 francs. Fr1 = $0.19585 (or $1 = Fr5.106).

WEIGHTS AND MEASURES: The metric system is the legal standard.

HOLIDAYS: New Year's Day, 1 January; St. Dévôte, 27 January; Labor Day, 1 May; Assumption, 15 August; All Saints' Day, 1 November; National Day, 19 November; Immaculate Conception, 8 December; Christmas, 25 December. Movable religious holidays include Easter Monday, Ascension, Pentecost Monday, and Fête-Dieu.

TIME: 1 PM = noon GMT.

1 LOCATION AND SIZE

The second-smallest country in both Europe and the world after the Vatican, Monaco is situated in the southeastern part of the French administrative district of Alpes-Maritimes. Its area is 1.9 square kilometers (0.73 square miles), about three times the size of the mall in Washington, D.C. Monaco has a total boundary length of 12.7 kilometers (7.9 miles).

2 TOPOGRAPHY

There are four main areas: La Condamine, the business district around the port; Monte-Carlo, the site of the famous casino, which is at a higher elevation; Monaco-Ville, on a rocky promontory about 60 meters (200 feet) above sea level; and Fontvieille, a 22-hectare (54-acre) industrial area that was reclaimed by landfill in the 1960s and 1970s.

3 CLIMATE

Winters are mild, with temperatures rarely below freezing and a January average of about 8°C (46°F). Summer heat is tempered by sea breezes; the average maximum in July and August is 26°C (79°F). Rainfall averages about 77 centimeters (30 inches) a year.

4 PLANTS AND ANIMALS

Palms, aloes, carobs, tamarisks, mimosas, and other Mediterranean trees, shrubs, and flowers are abundant. Monaco does not have any distinctive native animals.

Geographic Profile

Geographic Features

Size ranking: 191 of 192
Highest elevation: 140 meters (459 feet) at Exotic Garden
Lowest elevation: Sea level at the Mediterranean Sea

Weather

Average annual precipitation: 77 centimeters (30.3 inches)
Average temperature in January: 8°C (46°F)
Average temperature in July: 26°C (79°F)

5 ENVIRONMENT

Monaco is noted for its beautiful natural scenery. The nation has consistently monitored pollution levels in its air and water to ensure the safety of its citizens. The Oceanographic Museum, formerly directed by Jacques Cousteau, is renowned for its work and exhibits on marine life.

6 POPULATION

The 1990 census placed the resident population at 29,876, of whom 6,200 were citizens of Monaco. The estimated population in 1998 was 32,000, with a residential population density estimated at 16,943 per square kilometer (43,883 per square mile), making Monaco the most densely populated country in the world. Monaco-Ville has about 1,500 inhabitants.

7 MIGRATION

There is a long waiting list for Monégasque citizenship. A 1992 law allows Monégasque women (citizens of Monaco) to confer citizenship on their children.

8 ETHNIC GROUPS

The native Monégasques are said to be of Rhaetian stock; they make up 15% of the population. The foreign residents are a highly cosmopolitan group, including more than 50% French and 17% Italians.

9 LANGUAGES

French is the official language. English and Italian are also widely spoken. Many inhabitants speak the Monégasque language, which has its origins in the Genoese dialect of Italian and the Provençal language of southern France.

10 RELIGIONS

Over 90% of the population practices Roman Catholicism, which is the official state religion. Monaco is also part of the diocese of Gibraltar of the Church of England.

11 TRANSPORTATION

In 1995 there were 17,000 passenger cars and 4,000 commercial vehicles. There is frequent bus service. The southeastern network of the French national railroad system serves Monaco with about 1.6 kilometers (1 mile) of track. Monaco is only 10 kilometers (6 miles) from the international airport at Nice, France. The harbor provides access by sea.

12 HISTORY

The ruling family of Monaco, the house of Grimaldi, secured control late in the thirteenth century. The principality was founded in 1338 by Charles I. The first Monégasque coins were minted in the sixteenth century.

France annexed the principality in 1793, but independence was reestablished in 1814. In 1848, the towns of Roquebrune and Menton, which constituted the easternmost part of Monaco, successfully rebelled and established themselves as a republic and, in 1861, became part of France.

The economic development of Monaco proceeded rapidly with the opening of the railroad in 1868 and of the gambling casino. Since that time, the principality has become world famous as a tourist and recreation center.

Monaco has been a constitutional monarchy since the early twentieth century. In 1956 Prince Rainier III married the popular American actress, Grace Kelly, with whom he had three children: Princess Caroline, Prince Albert (the heir to the throne), and Princess Stephanie. Princess Grace was killed in a car accident in 1982.

Monaco joined the United Nations on 28 May 1993. That year, Prince Rainier ordered an investigation of Monaco's principal state-owned company. There had been complaints about threats used to recover loans from gamblers at the casinos.

LOCATION: 43°43′49″N; 7°25′36″E. **BOUNDARY LENGTHS:** France, 5.4 kilometers (3.4 miles); Mediterranean coastline, 7.3 kilometers (4.5 miles).
TERRITORIAL SEA LIMIT: 12 miles.

13 GOVERNMENT

Monaco is a constitutional monarchy ruled by the hereditary princes of the Grimaldi line. A constitution adopted on 17 December 1962 provides for a single-chamber National Council of 18 members elected by direct popular vote every five years; it shares legislative functions with the prince.

14 POLITICAL PARTIES

Monaco does not formally have political parties, but candidates compete on the basis of various lists. The major political groups have been the National and Democratic Union (Union Nationale et Democratique—UNI); Communist Action (Action Communale—AC); Èvolution Communale (EC); and the Movement of Democratic Union (MUD).

Photo credit: Corel Corporation.

A view of Monaco-Ville from the sea. The building in the foreground, one of the largest in Monaco, is the Oceanographic Museum.

15 JUDICIAL SYSTEM

A justice of the peace tries petty cases. Other courts are the Court of First Instance, the Court of Appeal, the Court of Revision, and the Criminal Court. The highest judicial authority is vested in the Supreme Tribunal.

16 ARMED FORCES

France assumed responsibility for the defense of Monaco as part of the Versailles Treaty in 1919. There is no army in the principality. A private guard protects the royal family, and a police force of 390 ensures public safety.

17 ECONOMY

For its livelihood, Monaco depends chiefly on income from tourism, real estate, financial services, and light industry. A substantial part of the principality's revenue from tourist sources comes from the operations of Sea-Bathing Company (Société des Bains de Mer—SBM), in which the government owns 69%. The SBM operates the gambling casino at Monte Carlo as well as several luxury hotels and motion-picture theaters.

18 INCOME

In 1995 the gross domestic product (GDP) was $788 million, or about $25,000 per person, in current United States dollars.

19 INDUSTRY

The tourist industry dominates Monaco's economic life, but small-scale industries produce a variety of items for domestic use and for export, contributing 27% of business turnover in 1990. About 700 small businesses make pottery and glass objects, paper and cards, jewelry, perfumes, dolls, precision instruments, plastics, chemicals and pharmaceuticals, machine tools, watches, leather items, and radio parts.

20 LABOR

There is virtually no unemployment in Monaco. The major employer of the working population is the SBM; others work in industry or in service establishments. As of 1994, the labor force was approximately 30,000. About two-thirds of all employees commute from France and Italy. There were some 35 unions grouped in a union federation, with about 10% of the work force in 1996.

21 AGRICULTURE

There is no agriculture.

22 DOMESTICATED ANIMALS

There is a dairy industry serving local needs.

23 FISHING

Some fishing is carried on to meet domestic requirements. The annual catch was 3,000 tons in 1994.

24 FORESTRY

There are no forests.

25 MINING

There is no mining.

26 FOREIGN TRADE

Foreign trade is included in the statistics for France, with which Monaco has a customs union.

27 ENERGY AND POWER

Power is supplied by France. In 1991, standby electrical capacity totaled 10,000 kilowatts.

28 SOCIAL DEVELOPMENT

Social security benefits are financed by both employers and employees. There is a home for the aged attached to the Princess Grace Polyclinic. There is equal legal treatment of men and women who are born in Monaco.

29 HEALTH

In 1995, Monaco had approximately 42 physicians. There were 432 hospital beds and 16 pharmacies.

30 HOUSING

In 1991, there were 12,000 principal residences in Monaco. In recent years, the government has stressed the construction of luxury housing.

31 EDUCATION

Education is compulsory from age 6 to 16. Attendance is 90%, and nearly all adults are literate. In 1994, Monaco's seven public primary schools had a total of 1,838 students. The public secondary schools had 2,861 students.

Photo credit: Corel Corporation.

Elaborate continental dishes are served to tourists outdoors. Monaco is famous for attracting wealthy and titled tourists. Because of Monaco's lack of an agricultural base, all food must be imported.

once a week, and the *Tribune de Monaco* is published biweekly. International publications are readily available.

33 TOURISM AND RECREATION

Monaco has been famous for attracting wealthy and titled tourists since its gambling casino was established at Monte-Carlo in 1856. Among the many attractions are the Louis II Stadium, several museums and gardens, and the beach. The Monte-Carlo opera house has been the site of many world premiere performances.

34 FAMOUS MONÉGASQUES

Prince Albert (1848–1922), who reigned from 1889 to 1922, was famous as an oceanographer. In 1956, his great-grandson Rainier III (b.1923) married Grace Patricia Kelly (1929–82), a US film actress, whose death on 14 September 1982 following an automobile accident was mourned throughout Monaco. Their son, Prince Albert (b.1958) is the heir apparent; Princess Caroline (b.1957) and Princess Stéphanie (b.1965) are their daughters.

32 MEDIA

The postal and telegraphic services are operated by France, but Monaco issues its own postage stamps. In 1995 there were about 29,820 telephones. Radio Monte Carlo and Télé Monte Carlo provide radio and television services. As of 1995 there were 30,000 radios and 22,000 television sets in homes.

There is no daily press. The *Journal de Monaco*, an official publication, appears

35 BIBLIOGRAPHY

Bernardy, Françoise de. *Princes of Monaco: The Remarkable History of the Grimaldi Family.* London: Barker, 1961.

Englund, Steven. *Grace of Monaco: an interpretive biography.* Garden City, N.Y.: Doubleday, 1984.

Hopkins, Adam. *Essential French Riviera.* Lincolnwood, Ill.: Passport Books, 1994.

Jackson, Stanley. *Inside Monte Carlo.* Briarcliff Manor, N.Y.: Stein & Day, 1975.

MONGOLIA

Mongol Uls

CAPITAL: Ulaanbaatar.

FLAG: The national flag, adopted in 1946, contains a light blue vertical stripe between two red stripes; in gold, on the stripe nearest the hoist, is the *soyombo*, Mongolia's independence emblem.

ANTHEM: *Bügd Nayramdah mongol ard ulsyn töriin duulal (State Anthem of the Mongolian People's Republic).*

MONETARY UNIT: The tugrik (T) of 100 mongos. There are coins of 1, 2, 5, 10, 15, 20, and 50 mongos and notes of 1, 3, 5, 10, 20, 25, 50, and 100 tugriks. T1 = $0.00163 (or $1 = T614.18).

WEIGHTS AND MEASURES: The metric system is the legal standard.

HOLIDAYS: New Year's Day, 1 January; Constitution Day, 13 January; Women's Day, 8 March; Mother and Children's Day, 1 June; Naadam Festival, 11–13 July; Mongolian Republic Day, 26 November. Movable holidays include Mongol New Year's Day, in February or March.

TIME: 8 PM = noon GMT.

1 LOCATION AND SIZE

Situated in east-central Asia, Mongolia has an area of 1,565,000 square kilometers (604,250 square miles), slightly larger than the state of Alaska. The largest landlocked country in the world, Mongolia has a total boundary length of 8,114 kilometers (5,042 miles).

2 TOPOGRAPHY

The vast Mongolian plateau has an average elevation of 1,580 meters (5,184 feet). Mongolia comprises a mountainous section in the extreme west, where Huyten Peak rises to a height of 4,374 meters (14,350 feet). The southern part of the country is occupied by the rocky Gobi Desert.

3 CLIMATE

Mongolia has average January temperatures of −22° to −18°C (−8° to 0°F) and dry, practically snowless winters. Annual precipitation ranges from 25 to 38 centimeters (10 to 15 inches) in mountain areas to less than 13 centimeters (5 inches) in the Gobi Desert.

4 PLANTS AND ANIMALS

Mongolia is divided into several natural regions, including forests, steppes, grasslands, and desert, each with its own type of plant and animal life. Larch and Siberian stone pine are trees of the northern forests, which are inhabited by bear, Manchurian red deer, snow panther, wild boar, and elk. The saiga antelope and the wild horse are typical steppe dwellers.

Geographic Profile

Geographic Features

Size ranking: 18 of 192
Highest elevation: 4,374 meters (14,350 feet) at
  Huyten Peak (Youyi Feng, Tavan Bogd Uul)
Lowest elevation: 518 meters (1700 feet) at Hoh Nuur

Land Use†

Arable land:	1%
Permanent crops:	0%
Permanent pastures:	80%
Forests:	9%
Other:	10%

Weather

Average annual precipitation: 13–38 centimeters (5–
  15 inches). Annual precipitation averages 25–38
  centimeters (10–15 inches) in the mountains but less
  than 13 centimeters (5 inches) in the Gobi Desert.
Average temperature range in January (Ulaanbaatar):
  –32°C to 19°C (–26°F to –2°F)
Average temperature range in July (Ulaanbaatar):
  11°C to 22°C (52°F to 72°F)

†*Arable land:* Land used for temporary crops, like
meadows for mowing or pasture, gardens, and greenhouses. *Permanent crops:* Land cultivated with crops
that occupy its use for long periods, such as cocoa,
coffee, rubber, fruit and nut orchards, and vineyards.
Permanent pastures: Land used permanently for forage crops. *Forests:* Land containing stands of trees.
Other: Any land not specified, including built-on
areas, roads, and barren land.

5 ENVIRONMENT

Mongolia's main environmental problems
are the replacement of forest lands by
desert and an inadequate water supply.
The country has only 24.6 cubic kilometers (5.9 cubic miles) of water, 62% of
which is used for farming. In 1995, 42%
of the people living in rural areas did not
have access to pure water. Air pollution by
local industry, and by the former Soviet
Union and the People's Republic of China,
is also a problem. Nine species of mammals and 13 birds are considered endangered.

After a winter of little snow, wildfires
spread across Mongolia during the spring
of 1996. The fires caused 26 deaths and
800 injuries. About 20% of Mongolia's
pine forest was damaged from the blaze.

6 POPULATION

As of January 1989, the population
totaled 2 million; in 1998, it was estimated at 2.6 million. The projected population for 2005 is 2.8 million. In 1995, the
population of Ulaanbaatar, the principal
city, was 666,000. Average density in 1998
was only about 2 persons per square kilometer (5 per square mile).

7 MIGRATION

Few Mongolians live outside the country,
but 3.4 million persons of Mongolian
descent live in China. About 500,000 live
in Russia. Since the independence of
Kazakstan, a former Soviet Republic,
many Kazaks have emigrated from Mongolia to Kazakstan.

Nomadic herders account for about
half of Mongolia's population. Mongolia
is one of the only developing countries
where people are moving to rural areas
more than they are moving to cities. The
number of families officially registered as
nomadic grew from 74,000 in 1990 to
170,000 in 1995.

8 ETHNIC GROUPS

In 1990, 87% of the population consisted
of Mongols, approximately three-quarters
of them Khalkha. The Kazaks are the lead-

MONGOLIA

| 0 | 100 | 200 | 300 Miles |
| 0 | 100 | 200 | 300 Kilometers |

LOCATION: 87°47′ to 119°54′E 41°31′ to 52°16′N. **BOUNDARY LENGTHS:** Russia, 3,441 kilometers (2,138 miles); China, 4,673 kilometers (2,904 miles).

ing minority group, making up about 6%. People of Chinese origin are also present in substantial numbers (2%).

9 LANGUAGES

Khalkha Mongolian, the official language, is spoken by about 90% of the population. It is a dialect belonging to the Mongolic branch of the Altaic language family.

In 1994, the traditional written alphabet, dating back to the thirteenth century,

was due to replace the modern one, which uses Russian Cyrillic letters. Kazak, Russian, and Chinese are also spoken.

10 RELIGIONS

About two-thirds of the people do not profess any religion or are avowed atheists. Of the remainder, most belong to Lamaist Buddhism, which has been strongly influenced by native religions. Since the new constitution of 1992 estab-

Photo credit: Susan D. Rock.

A Mongolian boy with his dog.

Miat-Air Mongol is the principal airline. There were 34 airfields operating in 1994.

12 HISTORY

The land now known as Mongolia has been inhabited since the Lower Paleolithic period, more than 130,000 years ago. Mongolia first played an important part in world history in AD 1206, when the Mongol tribes united under the leadership of the conqueror Temujin, or Genghis Khan. They established a vast empire extending from the northern Siberian forest to Tibet, and from the Caspian Sea to the Pacific. The Mongols' century of dominance in Asia allowed for great trade and cultural interchange, but it also led to the spread of the bubonic plague to Europe.

During the fourteenth century, the great Mongol states disintegrated, and the Mongols retired to their original steppe homelands, splitting into three major groups: the northern Khalkha Mongols, the southern Chahar Mongols, and the western Oirat Mongols. Buddhism, which had been introduced by Tibetan monks in the fifteenth century, became widespread in the sixteenth and seventeenth centuries.

In the seventeenth and eighteenth centuries, the Mongols were brought under the rule of the Manchu dynasty in China. Following the overthrow of the Manchu dynasty by the Chinese revolution in 1911, Chinese and Russian forces vied for control of Outer Mongolia against Mongol nationalists seeking an autonomous state.

lished freedom of religion, Mahayana Buddhism, the primary religion before communist suppression in the 1930s, has undergone a revival.

11 TRANSPORTATION

The Trans-Mongolian Railway, about 1,500 kilometers (930 miles) in length, connects Mongolia with both China and Russia. The total length of railroads in 1994 was 1,928 kilometers (1,198 miles). Mongolia has about 1,000 kilometers (620 miles) of asphalt or concrete roads. In 1992, Mongolian roads carried 249.3 million passengers and 6.7 million tons of freight.

Photo credit: Susan D. Rock.

Chinese selling goods to Russians at a stop along the Trans-Mongolian Railway.

The People's Republic

The Mongolian People's Republic (MPR), the second communist country in world history, was proclaimed on 26 November 1924. With the support of the former Soviet Union (which formed in 1922 and broke apart in 1991), communist rule was gradually consolidated. Lands of the feudal lords were confiscated, starting in 1929, and those of monasteries in 1938.

On 14 February 1950, the People's Republic of China and the Soviet Union signed a treaty that guaranteed the MPR's independence. In October 1961, the MPR became a member of the United Nations.

In June 1987, the MPR and the United States established diplomatic relations.

Economic and Political Transformation

Following in the footsteps of the former Soviet Union, the MPR initiated its own policy of "openness" *(il tod)* in the late 1980s and began the transition from a centrally planned, collective economy toward a market economy. The ruling Mongolian People's Revolutionary Party (MPRP) opted for political as well as economic reforms. The MPRP's leadership resigned in March 1990 and in May the constitution was amended to allow for new, multiparty elections, which took place in July.

During 1991, the new government issued vouchers to all citizens for the purchase of state property, but economic reform was made more difficult by the economic collapse of the former Soviet Union. Elections in June 1992 created a new legislature, the State Great Hural (SGH), and in June 1993 President Punsalmaagiyn Ochirbat was elected in the first direct presidential elections. By September 1992, some 67,000 former Soviet troops (in the MPR since 1966) completed a process of withdrawal which began in 1990.

In the 1996 parliamentary elections, discontent among younger voters led to the defeat of the MPRP. The winners from the Democratic Union coalition were mostly political novices who promised to intensify market reforms. The election results marked the first smooth transfer of power in Mongolia's modern history.

13 GOVERNMENT

The 1992 constitution went into effect on 12 February, replacing the 1960 constitution and completing Mongolia's transition from a single-party state to a multiparty, parliamentary form of government. At that time, the country's official name was changed from "Mongolian People's Republic" to "Mongolia." The legislature, the State Great Hural (SGH), has 76 members, who are elected by district to four-year terms.

The president, the head of state, is selected by direct, popular vote for a four-year term. The prime minister, the head of government, is nominated by the president and confirmed by the SGH. The prime minister selects a cabinet which must be confirmed by the SGH.

Mongolia consists of 18 provinces (aymag), divided into 299 counties (somon), and three autonomous cities (hot).

14 POLITICAL PARTIES

The Mongolian People's Revolutionary Party (MPRP), the single ruling party between 1924 and 1996, legalized opposition parties in 1990. Other major parties include the Social Democratic Party (SDP), the National Democratic Party (NDP), and the United Party of Mongolia.

In the elections of June 1996, the Democratic Union (which included the NDP, SDP, and two smaller parties) won 50 of 76 seats.

15 JUDICIAL SYSTEM

There is a Supreme Court elected by the People's Great Hural; province and city courts, elected by the corresponding assemblies of people's deputies; and lower courts. Under the 1992 Constitution, the Supreme Court remains the highest judicial body. There is a Constitutional Court that has sole authority for constitutional review.

16 ARMED FORCES

In 1995, the armed forces totaled 21,000. The army had 15,500 personnel (11,000 draftees) in four divisions, and a reserve strength of 200,000. Mongolia spent an estimated $19 million for defense in 1995.

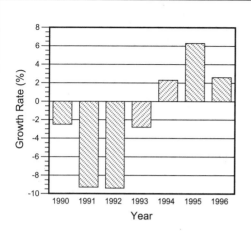

Yearly growth rate of the economy. This economic indicator tells by what percent the economy has increased or decreased when compared with the previous year.

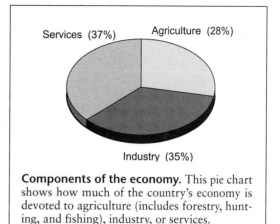

Components of the economy. This pie chart shows how much of the country's economy is devoted to agriculture (includes forestry, hunting, and fishing), industry, or services.

17 ECONOMY

After 70 years as a centrally planned economy, Mongolia has undergone a difficult transition towards a free market system since 1990. A number of factors, including the sudden halt to economic aid from the former Soviet Union and allied countries, the disruption of trade with traditional trading partners, as well as a severe winter in 1990–91, caused a steep decline in the country's economic activity. Despite these difficulties, the government has continued Development of oil and mineral resources is a high priority.

18 INCOME

In 1995 the gross national product (GNP) was $767 million, or about $360 per person.

19 INDUSTRY

Small-scale processing of livestock and agricultural products has historically been the mainstay of Mongolia's industrial sector. Metal processing first became important in the 1970s. In 1996, the leading industries included metals, accounting for 32.6% of industrial output; energy production, 19.1%; and processed foods, 15.8%.

20 LABOR

In 1995, the labor force was estimated at 1.1 million. About half all workers are nomadic herders. There were 55,400 unemployed persons in 1996. Real unemployment exceeds 15%, with about 25% of all unemployed persons living in the Ulaanbaatar area. About 46% of the labor force is female.

21 AGRICULTURE

Mongolia's cultivated area represents only 1% of potential cropland. Principal crops produced in 1995 (in 1,000 tons) included wheat, 257; barley, 4; oats, 1; potatoes, 52; and vegetables, 10. Trade in agricultural products in 1995 consisted of $63.5 million in imports and $44.3 million in exports.

22 DOMESTICATED ANIMALS

Raising livestock is the backbone of Mongolia's economy. Pastures constitute about 75% of the national territory. In 1995 there were 13.7 million sheep, 8.3 million goats, 3.3 million cattle, 2.2 million horses, 390,000 camels, and some 24,000 hogs. The meat produced in 1995 totaled 223,000 tons.

Mongols claim that the Mongolian thoroughbred horse, whose stamina and speed over long distances surpasses Arabian and Akhaltec racers, is the ancestor of many breeds of racehorses worldwide.

23 FISHING

Fishing is not a significant industry in Mongolia.

24 FORESTRY

Forests cover 9% of Mongolia. It is estimated that the country's total timber resources represent at least 1.25 billion cubic meters (1.6 billion cubic yards). In 1995, the timber cut totaled 540,500 cubic meters (708,000 cubic yards), with 70% burned as fuel.

25 MINING

Coal, copper, fluorspar, and molybdenum are heavily mined. Production in 1995 included (in tons) copper, 100,400; fluor-

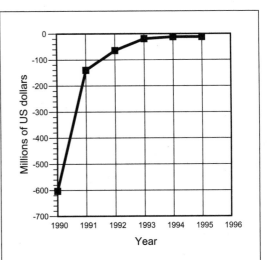

Yearly balance of trade measured in millions of US dollars. The balance of trade is the difference between what a country sells to other countries (its exports) and what it buys (its imports). If a country imports more than it exports, it has a negative balance of trade (a trade deficit). If exports exceed imports there is a positive balance of trade (a trade surplus).

spar, 240,000; gypsum, 25,000; molybdenum, 1,830; tin, 150; and tungsten, 200.

26 FOREIGN TRADE

In 1996, exports totaled $422.9 million, with copper accounting for 50%. Molybdenum is the another leading export. Wool, hides and skins, and manufactured garments are also exported. Imports in 1996 amounted to $438.3 million, led by fuels, rice, wheat flour, tobacco, and lubricants.

In 1996, Switzerland, Russia, China, and South Korea were the leading export markets. The main origins for imports that year were Russia, Japan, China, and Germany.

Selected Social Indicators

These statistics are estimates for the period 1993 to 1996. For comparison purposes, data for the United States and averages for low-income countries and high-income countries are also given.

Indicator	Mongolia	Low-income countries	High-income countries	United States
Per capita gross national product†	$360	$490	$25,870	$28,020
Population growth rate	2.1%	1.7%	0.6%	0.9%
Population growth rate in urban areas	3.0%	3.8%	0.9%	1.2%
Population per square kilometer of land	2	82	30	29
Life expectancy in years	65	63	77	77
Number of physicians per 1,000 people	n.a.	1.0	2.5	2.5
Number of pupils per teacher (primary school)	24	41	17	14
Illiteracy rate (15 years and older)	17%	34%	<5%	3%
Energy consumed per capita (kg of oil equivalent)	1,046	393	5,123	7,905

† The gross national product (GNP) is the total dollar value of all goods and services produced by a country in a year. The per capita GNP is calculated by dividing a country's GNP by its population. The World Bank defines low-income countries as those with a per capita GNP of $785 or less. High-income countries have a per capita GNP of $9,636 or more. About 16% of the world's 5.7 billion people live in high-income countries, while almost 56% live in low-income countries.   n.a. = data not available   > = greater than   < = less than

Sources: World Bank, *World Development Indicators on CD-ROM*, Washington, D.C.: The World Bank, 1998. Central Intelligence Agency, *The World Fact Book*, Washington, D.C.: Government Printing Office, 1998.

27 ENERGY AND POWER

In 1994, electric power production in Mongolia amounted to 3.1 billion kilowatt hours. Oil exploration is underway. Shortages of gasoline are common in the countryside, due to declining deliveries from Russia.

28 SOCIAL DEVELOPMENT

The social insurance program provides for free medical services, benefits for temporary disability, and pensions for permanent disability and old age. Although women receive equal pay for equal work, they fill almost no positions at the highest levels of government or the professions.

29 HEALTH

In 1990, there were 5,625 physicians and, in 1991, 10,340 nurses. There were about 371 people per physician in 1993. In 1990–95, 95% of the population had access to health care services. Average life expectancy was an estimated 65 years in 1995. Pulmonary and bronchial infections, including tuberculosis and brucellosis, are widespread but are being brought under control.

30 HOUSING

The standard housing of the nomadic herders, as well as of many city dwellers, is the yurt—a light, movable, dome-shaped tent consisting of a skin or felt covering stretched over a lattice frame. Large apartment-house complexes with stores, services, and cultural facilities are being built in Ulaanbaatar, as well as in various other cities and towns.

31 EDUCATION

Ten years of schooling is compulsory, starting at age six. In 1995, the United Nations Educational, Scientific and Cultural Organization (UNESCO) estimated the illiteracy rate of 10.9% for males and 21.9% for females. In 1994, there were 6,704 teachers and 158,990 pupils in primary schools. General secondary schools had 12,938 teachers and 229,769 pupils. The Mongolian State University, in Ulaanbaatar, was founded in 1942.

32 MEDIA

In 1995, 89,000 telephones were in use. Radio Ulaanbaatar broadcasts programs in Mongolian, Russian, Chinese, English, French, and Kazakh. Mongel Telev 12 transmits locally produced programs. In 1995 there were 306,000 radios and 93,000 television sets.

The 35 newspapers of Mongolia include *Unen* (with a 1995 circulation of 5,000), the newspaper of the Central Committee of the MPRP; *Novosti Mongoliy,* the newspaper of the Mongolian News Agency; and *Hodolmor,* which represents trade unions.

33 TOURISM AND RECREATION

In 1994, approximately 151,000 travelers visited Mongolia from abroad, with receipts totaling $4 million. Tourist facilities are in short supply (there were 9,989 hotel beds in 1990), and prices are high.

Points of interest include the Gandan Lamasery in Ulaanbaatar and the ruined city of Karakorum, once the capital of the Mongol Empire. Mongolia offers abundant and varied scenery, including forests, steppes, lakes; and deserts, and a wide variety of wildlife. Traditional sports in Mongolia include wrestling, archery, and horse racing.

34 FAMOUS MONGOLIANS

A long line of Mongol khans (rulers) have left their mark on history. Temujin, or Genghis Khan (1162–1227), set up the first Mongol empire in 1206. Kublai Khan (1216–94), a grandson of Genghis, conquered most of China.

The founder of modern Mongolian literature is D. Natsagdorj (1906–37). Jugderdemidiyn Gurragcha (b.1947) became the first Mongolian in space in 1981, when he was carried into orbit aboard the former Soviet Union's *Soyuz 39* spacecraft.

35 BIBLIOGRAPHY

Beall, Cynthia, and Melvyn Goldstein. "Mongolian Nomads." *National Geographic,* May 1993, 127–138.

Brill, M. *Mongolia.* Chicago: Children's Press, 1992.

Major, John S. *The Land and People of Mongolia.* New York: Lippincott, 1990.

Nordby, Judith. *Mongolia.* Santa Barbara, Calif.: Clio Press, 1993.

MOROCCO *

Kingdom of Morocco
Al-Mamlakah al-Maghribiyah

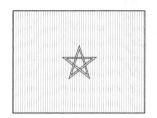

CAPITAL: Rabat.

FLAG: The national flag consists of a green five-pointed star at the center of a red field.

ANTHEM: The *Hymne Chérifien* is a twentieth-century composition without words.

MONETARY UNIT: The dirham (DH) is a paper currency of 100 Moroccan centimes. There are coins of 1, 5, 10, and 20 Moroccan centimes and ½, 1, and 5 dirhams, and notes of 5, 10, 50, 100, and 200 dirhams. DH1 = $0.11515 (or $1 = DH8.684).

WEIGHTS AND MEASURES: The metric system is the legal standard.

HOLIDAYS: New Year's Day, 1 January; Anniversary of the King's Accession, 3 March; Labor Day, 1 May; National Day, 14 August; Anniversary of the Green March, 6 November; Independence Day, 18 November. Movable religious holidays include 'Id al-Fitr, 'Id al-Adha', 1st of Muharram (Muslim New Year), and Milad an-Nabi.

TIME: GMT.

1 LOCATION AND SIZE

Situated at the northwestern corner of Africa, Morocco claims a total area of 446,550 square kilometers (172,414 square miles), of which the Western Sahara comprises 252,120 square kilometers (97,344 square miles). The Western Sahara is claimed and administered by Morocco but, as of 1997, its rulership is under dispute.

Comparatively, the area occupied by Morocco is slightly larger than the state of California. Morocco's total boundary length is 3,837 kilometers (2,389 miles). The capital city, Rabat, is located on the Atlantic coast.

---

*All data include Western Sahara unless otherwise noted.

2 TOPOGRAPHY

Morocco proper is divided into three natural regions: the fertile northern coastal plain along the Mediterranean; the rich plateaus and lowlands lying between the Atlas Mountains, which extend from the Atlantic coast to Algeria and the Mediterranean Sea; and the desert-like area in southern and eastern Morocco. The Atlas Mountains include Mount Toubkal at 4,165 meters (13,665 feet), the highest peak in Africa. Principal rivers flowing northwestward to the Atlantic are the Oumer, Sebou (Sebu), Draa, and Sous (Sus).

3 CLIMATE

The rugged mountain ranges and the Atlantic Ocean moderate the tropical heat of Morocco. Temperatures in Casablanca

Geographic Profile

Geographic Features

Size ranking: 56 of 192
Highest elevation: 4,165 meters (13,665 feet) at
    Mount Toubkal
Lowest elevation: −55 meters (−180 feet) at Sebkha
    Tah

Land Use†

Arable land:	21%
Permanent crops:	1%
Permanent pastures:	47%
Forests:	20%
Other:	11%

Weather††

Average annual precipitation: 42.6 centimeters (16.8
    inches)
Average temperature in January: 12.4°C (54.3°F)
Average temperature in July: 22.5°C (72.5°F)

†*Arable land:* Land used for temporary crops, like
meadows for mowing or pasture, gardens, and greenhouses. *Permanent crops:* Land cultivated with crops
that occupy its use for long periods, such as cocoa,
coffee, rubber, fruit and nut orchards, and vineyards.
Permanent pastures: Land used permanently for forage crops. *Forests:* Land containing stands of trees.
Other: Any land not specified, including built-on
areas, roads, and barren land.

††The measurements for precipitation and average
temperature were taken at weather stations closest to
the country's largest city. Precipitation and average
temperature can vary significantly within a country,
due to factors such as latitude, altitude, coastal proximity, and wind patterns.

range from an average minimum of 7°C
(45°F) to a maximum of 17°C (63°F) in
January and from a minimum of 18°C
(64°F) to a maximum of 26°C (79°F) in
July. Maximum annual rainfall of 75–100
centimeters (30–40 inches) occurs in the
northwest, while other parts of the country receive much less.

4 PLANTS AND ANIMALS

Cork oaks are found in the Atlantic
coastal region, while there are rich ever-

green, oak, cedar, and pine forests on the
slopes of the Atlas mountains. Other areas
contain shrubs, jujube trees, poplars, willows, tamarisks, and olive trees. The
desert has no vegetation except for that
found in occasional oases. Although the
lion has disappeared, panthers, jackals,
foxes, and gazelles are numerous. The surrounding waters abound in sardines,
anchovies, and tuna.

5 ENVIRONMENT

Too much livestock grazing, cutting down
trees for fuel, and poor soil conservation
practices have led to soil erosion and the
replacement of farmland by deserts. Pollution of Morocco's water and land
resources is due to the dumping of
100,000 tons of industrial wastes into the
ocean, 68,000 tons into the country's
inland water sources, and 58,000 tons into
the soil. All of the nation's cities have pure
water. Morocco's cities produce 2.4 million tons of solid waste per year. The
nation's environment is also harmed by
pesticides, insects, and accidental oil spills.
Destruction of wildlife has occurred on a
large scale, despite strict laws regulating
hunting and fishing. Moreover, the drain-
age of marshes to irrigate farm land has
greatly reduced the numbers of crested
coots, purple herons, and marbled and
white-headed ducks. In 1994, the elimination of living areas for Morocco's wildlife
threatened 9 of the nation's mammal species and 14 bird species; 194 plant species
were also endangered.

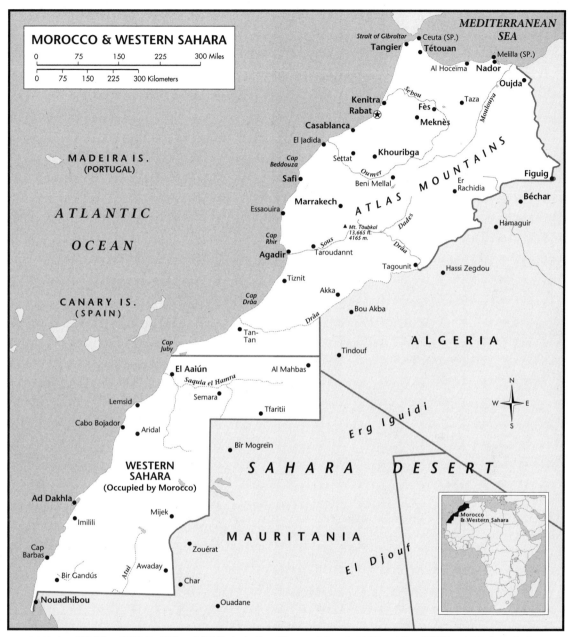

MOROCCO & WESTERN SAHARA

0   75   150   225   300 Miles

0   75   150   225   300 Kilometers

MEDITERRANEAN SEA

Strait of Gibraltar
Ceuta (SP.)
Tangier
Tétouan
Melilla (SP.)
Al Hoceïma
Nador
Oujda
Kenitra
Rabat
Sebou
Taza
Moulouya
Fès
Meknès
Casablanca
El Jadida
Khouribga
Settat
Cap Beddouza
Beni Mellal
Oumer
Er Rachidia
Figuig
Safi
ATLAS MOUNTAINS
Béchar
Essaouira
Marrakech
Dadès
Hamaguir
Cap Rhir
Mt. Toubkal
13,665 ft.
4165 m.
Sous
Drâa
Agadir
Taroudannt
Tagounit
Hassi Zegdou
Tiznit
Akka
Bou Akba
Cap Drâa
Drâa
Tan-Tan
Tindouf
ALGERIA

MADEIRA IS.
(PORTUGAL)

ATLANTIC

OCEAN

CANARY IS.
(SPAIN)

Cap Juby

El Aaiún
Al Mahbas
Saquia el Hamra
Lemsid
Semara
Cabo Bojador
Tfaritii
Aridal
Erg Iguidi
N
W   E
S
Bîr Mogreïn
WESTERN
SAHARA
(Occupied by Morocco)
SAHARA   DESERT
Ad Dakhla
Mijek
Imilili
MAURITANIA
Cap Barbas
Zouérat
El Djouf
Bir Gandús
Atui
Awaday
Nouadhibou
Char
Ouadane

Morocco & Western Sahara

LOCATION: 27°40′ to 35°56′N (23° to 35°56′N including Western Sahara); 0°58′ to 13°w (0°58′ to 16°21′w including Western Sahara). **BOUNDARY LENGTHS:** (excluding Western Sahara): total coastline, 1,835 kilometers (1,140 miles); Algeria, 1,559 kilometers (974 miles); Western Sahara, 443 kilometers (275 miles). **TERRITORIAL SEA LIMIT:** 12 miles.

An ornate entrance to a mosque in Casablanca.

6 POPULATION

The population of Morocco at its 1994 census was 26.1 million, including Western Sahara. The estimated 1998 population of Morocco was 29.1 million. Morocco's projected population for 2005 was 32.9 million. Population density in the late 1990s (excluding Western Sahara) was 61 per square kilometer (158 per square mile). As of 1995, greater Casablanca had a population of about 3.1 million; greater Rabat, the capital (including Salé), had a population of 1.3 million. The US Census Bureau estimated the 1998 population of Western Sahara at 234,000, while the United Nations estimated it at 273,000 that year.

7 MIGRATION

The Moroccan government encourages emigration because the 1.7 million Moroccans living and working abroad typically send money home to their families. In 1990, 584,700 Moroccans lived in France, 141,600 in Belgium, 67,500 in Germany, 156,900 in the Netherlands, and 50,000 in Spain. There is some seasonal migration within Morocco, as workers move into cities and towns after planting and harvesting are finished. Over 200,000 people migrate permanently to the cities each year. The war in Western Sahara has led to much migration, with refugees to Algeria numbering 165,000 at the end of 1992.

8 ETHNIC GROUPS

Berbers make up about 34% of the population, and Arabs, 66%. In the past, the Jewish community played a significant role in the economic life of the country, but its numbers have decreased as many have emigrated to Israel since it was established in 1948. In 1992, some 60,000 foreign citizens, mostly French, Spanish, Italian, and Algerians, were living in Morocco.

9 LANGUAGES

Although classical Arabic is the written and official language, Maghribi Arabic, a dialect unique to Morocco, is widely spoken; it is not understood by most Arabs of the Middle East. Berber dialects are spoken in more remote mountain areas by less than one-third of the population. French and Spanish also are used.

10 RELIGIONS

More than 98% of Moroccans are Sunni Muslims of the Malerte school. Islam was officially declared the state religion in 1961, but full religious freedom is accorded Christians and Jews. In 1993 there were about 69,000 Christians and a diminishing Jewish minority.

11 TRANSPORTATION

The road network in 1995 comprised 29,444 kilometers (18,293 miles) of paved roads suitable for year-round traffic and 31,458 kilometers (19,548 miles) of dry-season tracks. There were 956,000 passenger cars and 321,000 commercial vehicles in use in 1995. The railroad system consists of 1,893 kilometers (1,176 miles) of standard-gauge railways, of which about 51% is electrified; diesel-operated trains are used on the remainder.

Casablanca is by far the most important port, accounting for 55% of the goods loaded and unloaded. Morocco's 37 merchant ships had combined gross tonnage of 175,900 in 1995. Morocco has eight international airports, at Casablanca, Rabat, Tangier, Marrakech, Agadir, Fès, Oujda, and Al Hoceima.

12 HISTORY

The Berbers, the earliest known inhabitants of Morocco, suffered successive waves of invaders in ancient times, including the Phoenicians, Romans (first century BC), and Byzantines (sixth century AD).

Under successive Moorish dynasties (of mixed Arab and Berber descent), beginning with Idris I (Idris bin 'Abdallah) in 788, the Berber tribes were united and the Islamic faith and Arabic language adopted. The Almoravid, and later the Almohad, sect ruled Morocco from 1055 to 1269, when the Marinid (Beni Marin) dynasty came to power. Ahmad al-Mansur, the greatest of the Sa'udi kings, ruled from 1578 to 1603 and inaugurated the golden age of Moroccan history, protecting Morocco from Turkish invasion and adorning his magnificent capital at Marrakech with the treasures captured in Timbuktu. Morocco came under the control of the Filali dynasty, which continued into modern times.

Trade with France and other European countries became increasingly important in the eighteenth and nineteenth centuries. In 1844, France defeated the combined Moroccan and Algerian forces at Isly, becoming the ruling power, although 16 years later it agreed to let Spain invade and occupy northern Morocco. After 45 years of trade rivalry, the Act of Algeciras, signed on 7 April 1906 by representatives of the United States, Germany, the United Kingdom, France, Spain, and others, provided for all countries to trade equally in Morocco and provided for a joint Spanish-French police force in Moroccan ports.

On 30 March 1912, the French made Morocco a protectorate under Marshal Louis Lyautey. The Moroccans sought independence, first in the Rif War (1921–26), in which they were defeated by the combined French and Spanish forces, and later by forming the National Action Bloc in 1934. The Franco-Moroccan agreement of 2 March 1956 granted independence, and Muhammad V became king of Morocco. Incorporated into the new nation was Tangier, formerly a British territory.

After the death of Muhammad V on 26 February 1961, his son was crowned King Hassan II and became head of government. A third constitution, approved on 1 March 1972, transferred many of the king's executive and legislative powers to a parliament which was to have two-thirds of its members directly elected.

In 1975, Spain announced its intention of withdrawing from phosphate-rich Spanish Sahara (now the Western Sahara), and ceded the northern two-thirds of the region to Morocco and the southern third to Mauritania. However, the guerrilla group Polisario, backed by Algeria, challenged the annexation and proclaimed Western Sahara as the Saharan Arab Democratic Republic (SADR). By the early 1980s, Morocco had moved up to 100,000 soldiers into Western Sahara in a costly effort to put down the Polisario revolt.

In 1988, United Nations (UN) Secretary General Perez de Cuellar persuaded Moroccan and Polisario representatives to accept a peace plan which included a ceasefire (effective in September 1991), and a referendum for the territory on independence or integration with Morocco.

Israeli Prime Minister Yitzhak Rabin made a public visit in 1993 as King Hassan continued to play a moderate role in the search for an Arab-Israel settlement.

Photo credit: Gordon Barbery, San Francisco, CA.

Roman ruin in Morocco. The Romans invaded the area now known as Morocco in ancient times.

King Hassan's government maintains close relations with Sa'udi Arabia and the other Gulf states and was the first Arab nation to condemn the Iraqi invasion of Kuwait.

In 1996, King Hassan proposed to make the entire parliament directly elected. Previously, one-third of the deputies were appointed, giving the king power to undermine any opposition majority.

13 GOVERNMENT

The Moroccan crown is hereditary, and the king claims descent from the Prophet Muhammad. He can dismiss the parliament (if in session) and bypass elected institutions by submitting a referendum to the people on any major issue, or whenever parliament rejects a bill he favors. He presides over the cabinet, and, under certain circumstances, may declare a state of emergency. The constitution of 1992, approved by referendum, provides for a constitutional monarchy with increased authority for the prime minister. In 1997, King Hassan proposed revising the constitution to make the entire parliament directly elected and to create a new chamber of appointed ministers. The proposal was accepted in time for the 1997 elections.

14 POLITICAL PARTIES

Morocco has a well-developed multiparty system with 16 officially recognized parties. The National Union of Popular Forces (Union Nationale des Forces Populaires— UNFP), formed in September 1959, formally split into two parties in 1974. The more radical trade union wing called itself the UNFP and the political wing formed the Socialist Union of Popular Forces (Union Socialiste des Forces Populaires— USFP). The program of the Moroccan Communist Party has been similar to that of the UNFP. From 1969 to 1974 it was banned, but since then it has appeared under various names, including the Party for Progress and Socialism (Parti du Progrès et du Socialisme—PPS). The Istiqlal (Independence) Party follows a reformist program and backs the king only on specific issues.

15 JUDICIAL SYSTEM

Morocco has a dual legal system consisting of secular courts based on French legal tradition, and Islamic courts which rule on family and inheritance cases for Moroccan Muslims. The secular system includes district courts, appellate courts, and a Supreme Court. A special court may try officials on charges raised by a two-thirds majority of the full Majlis (legislature). The Islamic court system does not provide for appeals. Cases are decided on the basis of the Koran and derivative Shari'a.

16 ARMED FORCES

Total Moroccan armed strength in 1995 was 194,000. The army had 175,000 men, the navy 6,000, and the air force 13,000. Military hardware included 826 main battle tanks and 100 light tanks; 1 frigate and 27 patrol and coastal combatant ships and boats; and 112 combat aircraft, including 3 jet squadrons. Some 60 Moroccan troops were stationed in Equatorial Guinea and 2,000 in the United Arab Emirates. Polisario, the Western Saharan insurgent force, had 10,000 men. The United Nations has 370 observers in Morocco. The 1996 budget called for defense expenditures of $1.3 billion, or 4.2% of the gross domestic product (GDP).

17 ECONOMY

The major resources of the Moroccan economy are agriculture, phosphates, and tourism. Morocco is the world's third-largest producer of phosphates, and varying prices for phosphates on the interna-

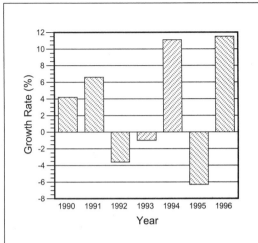

Yearly growth rate of the economy. This economic indicator tells by what percent the economy has increased or decreased when compared with the previous year.

tional market greatly influence Morocco's economy. Tourism and money sent home by Moroccans working abroad have played a critical role since independence.

The high cost of imports, especially of petroleum imports, is a major problem. Another chronic problem is unreliable rainfall, which produces drought or sudden floods. Morocco suffers from unemployment, inflation, a large debt, and a shortage of trained managers and administrators.

18 INCOME

In 1995 Morocco's gross national product (GNP) was $29.5 billion, or about $1,290 per person. For the period 1985–95 the average inflation rate was 4.8%, resulting in a real growth rate in GNP of 0.8% per person.

19 INDUSTRY

The manufacturing sector produces light consumer goods, especially foodstuffs, beverages, textiles, matches, and metal and leather products. Heavy industry is largely limited to petroleum refining, chemical fertilizers, automobile and tractor assembly, foundry work (making objects by pouring metal into a mold), asphalt, and cement. Many of the processed agricultural products and consumer goods are primarily used for local consumption, but Morocco exports canned fish and fruit, wine, leather goods, and textiles, as well as such traditional Moroccan handicrafts as carpets and brass, copper, silver, and wood implements.

There are three oil refineries, several petrochemical plants, a polyvinyl chloride factory, and four phosphate-processing plants. There are four plants assembling cars and small utility vehicles: Renault Moroc, Sopriam, Somaca, and Smeia. Nine cement factories reached a total of 6.35 million tons in 1995. Output of phosphoric acid is typically 1.1 million tons per year.

20 LABOR

The employed work force was estimated in 1992 at 7.6 million, of whom 15% were in the agricultural sector, 26% in commerce, and 59% in services and other sectors. The unemployment rate in urban areas was estimated at more than 19%.

Moroccan trade unions are powerful. In 1993, there were 323 strikes, resulting in the loss of 487,042 working days. The 48-hour workweek is established by law,

Photo credit: Corel Corporation.

A food vendor in Marrakech.

and overtime pay rates apply to all work in excess of 48 hours. At least one day of rest must be granted per week. The minimum wage for industry was $193 per month in 1996; for agricultural workers it was $9.41 per day.

21 AGRICULTURE

The bulk of the native population farms on plots of less than 5 hectares (12 acres). Morocco is essentially self-sufficient in food production. Although there are dams and irrigation projects on most of the country's major rivers, continued widespread variation in rainfall continues to produce serious droughts and occasional flash floods.

The principal export crops are sugar beets, wheat, barley, sugarcane, potatoes, tomatoes, oranges, olives, corn, dates, and beans. Morocco can usually provide itself with enough food. The amount of rainfall for crops can widely vary from year to year.

22 DOMESTICATED ANIMALS

Livestock raising contributes about one-third of agricultural income. There were about 16.5 million sheep, 4.5 million goats, and 2.7 million cattle in 1996. There were 880,000 donkeys, 551,000 mules, 36,000 camels, and 157 million chickens in 1995. In 1996, beef and mutton production was estimated at 310,000 tons; and poultry, 200,000 tons. Output

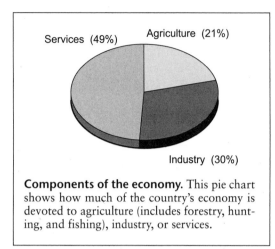

Services (49%)   Agriculture (21%)

Industry (30%)

Components of the economy. This pie chart shows how much of the country's economy is devoted to agriculture (includes forestry, hunting, and fishing), industry, or services.

of cow's milk was about 850 million liters in 1996, along with 2 billion eggs.

23 FISHING

Fishing, which has been a major industry since the 1930s, is centered in Agadir, Safi, and Tan-Tan. In 1995, the fish and marine plant harvest totaled 852,048 tons. Coastal fishing accounted for 85.5%; deep-sea fishing, 13.4%; algae cultivation, 0.9%; and fish farming, 0.2%. In 1995, landings from coastal waters totaled 728,721 tons, with sardines accounting for 570,914 tons. The deep-sea catch included 57,835 tons of octopus and 19,904 tons of squid.

24 FORESTRY

Forests and woodland cover about 20% of the land area and provide subsistence for families engaged in cork gathering, wood cutting, and other forestry occupations. Cork, the principal forest product, is grown on 300,000 hectares (741,000 acres) of state-owned cork oak forests.

Production was about 93,000 tons in 1985, virtually all of it exported. Other commercial trees are evergreen oak, thuja, argan, and cedar. Esparto grass and vegetable fiber are other important forest products. Production of roundwood in 1995 totaled 2.3 million cubic meters (3 million cubic yards).

25 MINING

Morocco has about two-thirds of the world's proved reserves of phosphates and is the world's largest phosphate exporter. Reserves of phosphate rock have been estimated at 88.5 billion tons. Production of lime phosphate was 20.4 million tons in 1995, third in the world after the United States and China.

Morocco also has significant deposits of copper ore. The nation produced an estimated 28,100 tons of copper concentrates in 1995; almost all was exported. Iron ore production decreased from 407,000 tons in 1977 to 35,536 tons in 1995. Jerada, near Oujda, is the only anthracite mine in the Mediterranean area, producing 649,600 tons in 1995. Other minerals include lead (89,700 tons), manganese (23,510 tons), zinc (148,800 tons), barites (163,376 tons), salt (137,910 tons), and fluorspar (105,000 tons).

26 FOREIGN TRADE

Phosphates and phosphoric acid, citrus fruits, clothing, fertilizers, preserved fish, and vegetables are the leading exports. In 1995 food products accounted for 27.9% of total exports; semi-finished products, 27.6%; consumer goods, 24.5%; raw

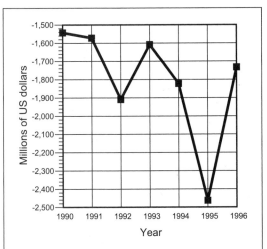

Yearly balance of trade measured in millions of US dollars. The balance of trade is the difference between what a country sells to other countries (its exports) and what it buys (its imports). If a country imports more than it exports, it has a negative balance of trade (a trade deficit). If exports exceed imports there is a positive balance of trade (a trade surplus).

In 1991, Morocco's production of crude petroleum amounted to 15,500 tons. In 1994, 31 million cubic meters (1.1 billion cubic feet) of natural gas were produced. Morocco had an estimated 1.2 million barrels of proven oil reserves and 1.1 billion cubic meters of proven natural gas reserves in 1995. Electricity production has grown rapidly, from 1.9 billion kilowatt hours in 1970, to 10.2 billion kilowatt hours in 1994. Electricity-producing capacity totaled 2.7 million kilowatts (25% hydro) in 1994.

materials, 16.9%; and equipment, 3.4%. Morocco's major imports are crude petroleum and foodstuffs.

France is by far Morocco's leading trade partner, providing 21.8% of imports and trading 29.6% of exports in 1995. Spain took 9.3% of Morocco's exports and supplied 8.5% of imports in 1995. Over 60% of Morocco's merchandise trade is with the European Union countries.

27 ENERGY AND POWER

Morocco is dependent on imported petroleum to satisfy almost 75% of its energy needs; fuel imports cost about $1 billion per year. As of 1994, there were 12 oil wells producing some 200 barrels per day.

28 SOCIAL DEVELOPMENT

The social security system covers employees and apprentices in industrial and commercial fields and the professions, as well as in agriculture and forestry. There is also voluntary coverage for persons leaving covered employment, and voluntary complementary insurance is available. Benefits include maternity allowances, disability pensions, old-age pensions, death allowances, and allowances for illness.

Women comprise about 35% of the work force and are employed mostly in the industrial, service, and teaching sectors. They have the right to vote and run for office (in 1993 two women were elected to parliament). However, women do not have equal status under Islamic family and estate laws. In 1995, women obtained the right to get a passport without the husband's permission.

29 HEALTH

Health conditions are relatively poor, but programs of mass education in child and parent hygiene, as well as government-

Selected Social Indicators

These statistics are estimates for the period 1993 to 1996. For comparison purposes, data for the United States and averages for low-income countries and high-income countries are also given.

Indicator	Morocco	Low-income countries	High-income countries	United States
Per capita gross national product†	$1,290	$490	$25,870	$28,020
Population growth rate	1.9%	1.7%	0.6%	0.9%
Population growth rate in urban areas	3.2%	3.8%	0.9%	1.2%
Population per square kilometer of land	61	82	30	29
Life expectancy in years	66	63	77	77
Number of physicians per 1,000 people	0.4	1.0	2.5	2.5
Number of pupils per teacher (primary school)	28	41	17	14
Illiteracy rate (15 years and older)	56%	34%	<5%	3%
Energy consumed per capita (kg of oil equivalent)	311	393	5,123	7,905

† The gross national product (GNP) is the total dollar value of all goods and services produced by a country in a year. The per capita GNP is calculated by dividing a country's GNP by its population. The World Bank defines low-income countries as those with a per capita GNP of $785 or less. High-income countries have a per capita GNP of $9,636 or more. About 16% of the world's 5.7 billion people live in high-income countries, while almost 56% live in low-income countries.   > = greater than   < = less than

Sources: World Bank, World Development Indicators on CD-ROM, Washington, D.C.: The World Bank, 1998. Central Intelligence Agency, The World Fact Book, Washington, D.C.: Government Printing Office, 1998.

supervised health services in schools and colleges, have helped to raise standards. Campaigns have been conducted against malaria, tuberculosis, venereal diseases, and cancer. However, gastrointestinal infections, malaria, typhoid, trachoma, and tuberculosis remain widespread. The World Health Organization (WHO) and the United Nations Children's Fund (UNICEF) have cooperated in the government's campaigns against eye disorders and venereal diseases.

In 1989–95, 70% of the population had access to health care services. There was one physician per 4,665 people in 1993. The average estimated life expectancy was 66 in 1995.

30 HOUSING

Since the 1950s, significant numbers of Moroccans (estimated at over 4 million) have moved from the countryside to the urban centers to escape rural unemployment. Housing and sanitation, consequently, have become urban problems. The government is engaged in a low-cost housing program to reduce the slum areas, called bidonvilles, that have formed around the large urban centers, especially Casablanca and Rabat. Loans have been available for private home construction, and builders have also received financial and technical assistance from the government to build workers' housing.

Photo credit: Corel Corporation.

A typical bazaar shop in Casablanca's ancient market.

31 EDUCATION

In 1995, the overall illiteracy rate was an estimated 56% (43.4% for men and 69% for women). The school system includes modern secular public institutions, traditional religious schools, and private schools. Nine years of compulsory primary education was made a law in 1962. In 1994, over 3 million pupils were in primary school and 1.3 million in secondary school. In vocational schools, there were 18,762 students. Girls leave school at a younger age than boys and are a minority in secondary, as well as primary, schools; they make up fewer than one-third of university students. The language of instruction in primary schools is Arabic during the first two years, and both Arabic and French are used for the next three years.

Morocco has six universities. Al-Qarawiyin University at Fès, founded in 859, is reputed to be the oldest university in the world. The first modern Moroccan university, the University of Rabat (now the Muhammad V University), was opened in 1957. Other universities are Muhammad bin 'Abdallah (founded 1974), in Fès; Hassan II (1975), Casablanca; Cadi Ayyad (1978), Marrakech; and Muhammad I (1978), Oujda. There are about two dozen colleges and conservatories. In 1994, enrollment at all higher level institutions was 250,919.

32 MEDIA

The postal, telephone, telegraph, radio, and television services are government-operated. In 1995, there were 820,000 telephones. Radiodiffusion Television Marocaine presents programs in Arabic, in Berber dialects, and in English, French, and Spanish. The television service presents daily programs in Arabic and French. A private television station, 2M International, began broadcasting in French and Arabic in 1989. In 1995 there were an estimated 5.5 million radios and 2 million television sets.

Press freedom is guaranteed by the constitution, but criticism of Islam, the king, or Morocco's claim to the Western Sahara is not permitted. Leading daily newspapers published in Rabat include the Arabic-language *Al Anba'a* (1995 circulation 20,000), and the French-language *L'Opinion* (50,000) and *Al-Maghrib* (20,000). The French-language *Le Matin du Sahara* (50,000) and *Maroc Soir* (50,000) are published in Casablanca.

33 TOURISM AND RECREATION

Morocco's scenic variety and beauty, fascinating medieval cities, and favorable climate contribute to a steadily increasing flow of tourists. Tourism is one of the fastest-growing areas of the Moroccan economy and a valuable foreign exchange earner. There were 3.5 million tourists in 1994, of whom 20% were Algerian, 12% French, and 6% Spanish. Income from tourism amounted to $1.26 billion in the same year.

Coastal beach resorts offer excellent swimming and boating facilities. Sports associations are widespread, particularly for soccer, swimming, boxing, basketball, and tennis.

34 FAMOUS MOROCCANS

Yusuf bin Tashfin (r.1061–1106), a religious reformer, conquered much of Spain and northern Africa. Muhammad bin Tumart (1078?–1130) founded the Almohad sect and developed a democratic form of government. Ahmad al-Mansur (r.1578–1603) drove all foreign forces out of Morocco, conquered the western Sudan, and established commercial and other contacts with England and Europe.

The great traveler Ibn Battutah (Abu 'Abdallah Muhammad bin Battutah, 1304–68?) visited and wrote about many countries of Africa, Asia, and Europe. The poetry of Muhammad bin Ibrahim (d.1955) is read throughout the Islamic world.

King Muhammad V (1909–61) gave up his throne as a gesture for independence, was arrested and exiled by the French, and returned in 1955 to become the first ruler of newly independent Morocco.

35 BIBLIOGRAPHY

Cook, Weston F. *The Hundred Years War for Morocco.* Boulder, Colo.: Westview Press, 1994.

Hintz, M. *Morocco.* Chicago: Children's Press, 1985.

Munson, Henry. *Religion and Power in Morocco.* New Haven, Conn.: Yale University Press, 1993.

Park, Thomas K. *Historical Dictionary of Morocco.* London: Scarecrow Press, 1996.

MOZAMBIQUE

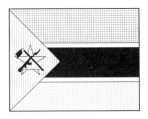

Republic of Mozambique
República Popular de Moçambique

CAPITAL: Maputo (formerly Lourenço Marques).

FLAG: The flag consists of broad stripes of green, black, and yellow, separated by narrow bands of white. Extending from the hoist is a red triangle; centered on the triangle is a yellow five-pointed star upon which is a white book over which are crossed the black silhouettes of a hoe and an AK47 rifle.

ANTHEM: Begins "Viva viva FRELIMO."

MONETARY UNIT: The Mozambique escudo (ME), linked until 1977 with the Portuguese escudo, was in June 1980 renamed the metical (MT); it is a paper currency of 100 centavos. There are coins of ½, 1, 2½, 5, 10, and 20 meticais, and notes of 50, 100, 500, and 1,000 meticais. MT1=$0.00009 (or $1=MT11,478.05).

WEIGHTS AND MEASURES: The metric system is in use.

HOLIDAYS: New Year's Day, 1 January; Heroes' Day, 3 February; Women's Day, 7 April; Workers' Day, 1 May; Independence Day, 25 June; Victory Day, 7 September; Day of Revolution, 25 September; Christmas, 25 December.

TIME: 2 PM = noon GMT.

1 LOCATION AND SIZE

Located on the southeastern coast of Africa, Mozambique (Moçambique) has an area of 801,590 square kilometers (309,496 square miles), slightly less than twice the size of the state of California. It has a total boundary length of 7,003 kilometers (4,351 miles).

2 TOPOGRAPHY

Mozambique is 44% coastal lowlands. The highest mountain is Mount Binga at 2,436 meters (7,992 feet). The most important rivers are the Zambezi, flowing into the Indian Ocean, the Limpopo, the Save (Sabi), and the Lugenda. The most important lake is the navigable Lake Malawi (Lake Niassa).

3 CLIMATE

The wet season has monthly average temperatures between 27°C and 29°C (81°–84°F); the dry season has June and July temperatures averaging 18°–20°C (64°–68°F). The average annual rainfall is greatest, about 142 centimeters (56 inches), over the western hills and the central areas.

4 PLANTS AND ANIMALS

Thick forest covers the wet regions, but the drier interior has little vegetation. Hardwoods, such as ebony, flourish throughout the country. Mozambique has elephants, buffalo, wildebeests, zebras, hippopotamuses, lions, crocodiles, and other southern African game species, as well as over 300 varieties of birds.

5 ENVIRONMENT

Significant environmental problems include the loss of 70% of the nation's forests, and the purity of the water supply. About 60% of the nation's city dwellers and 83% of the rural people do not have pure water. As of 1994, 10 of the nation's mammal species and 11 bird species were endangered, and 89 plant species were threatened with extinction.

6 POPULATION

The 1998 population was estimated at 18.6 million by the US Census Bureau. A population of 22.2 million is projected for 2005. The estimated density is 23 persons per square kilometer (60 per square mile). Maputo, the capital, had an estimated 1995 population of 2.2 million.

7 MIGRATION

Famine and war produced mass migration in the 1980s. Between 1992 (when the civil war ended) and 1996, over 1.3 million refugees returned to Mozambique from Malawi; 241,000 returned from Zimbabwe; 23,000 returned from South Africa; and 32,000 returned from Tanzania.

8 ETHNIC GROUPS

There are 10 major ethnic groups. The largest, residing north of the Zambezi River, is the Makua-Lomwé group, representing about 37% of the total population. Others include the Yao (Ajawa), Makonde, Nguni, Maravi, Tsonga, Chopi, and Shona (or Karanga). There are also smaller numbers of persons of mixed European and African ancestry, Indians, and Europeans.

9 LANGUAGES

Portuguese remains the official language. Different African ethnic groups speak their respective languages and dialects.

Geographic Profile

Geographic Features

Size ranking: 34 of 192
Highest elevation: 2,436 meters (7,992 feet) at Monte Binga
Lowest elevation: Sea level at the Indian Ocean

Land Use†

Arable land:	4%
Permanent crops:	0%
Permanent pastures:	56%
Forests:	18%
Other:	22%

Weather††

Average annual precipitation: 76.8 centimeters (30.2 inches)
Average temperature in January: 25.4°C (77.7°F)
Average temperature in July: 18.4°C (65.1°F)

†*Arable land:* Land used for temporary crops, like meadows for mowing or pasture, gardens, and greenhouses. *Permanent crops:* Land cultivated with crops that occupy its use for long periods, such as cocoa, coffee, rubber, fruit and nut orchards, and vineyards. *Permanent pastures:* Land used permanently for forage crops. *Forests:* Land containing stands of trees. *Other:* Any land not specified, including built-on areas, roads, and barren land.

††The measurements for precipitation and average temperature were taken at weather stations closest to the country's largest city. Precipitation and average temperature can vary significantly within a country, due to factors such as latitude, altitude, coastal proximity, and wind patterns.

MOZAMBIQUE

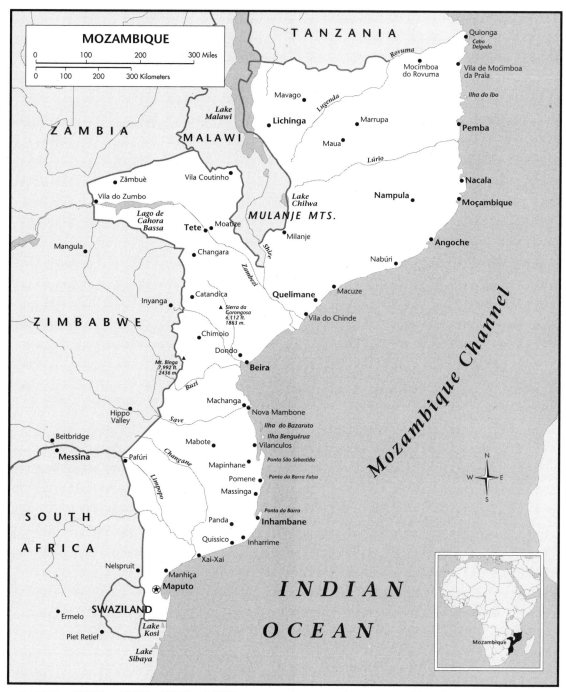

MOZAMBIQUE

0   100   200   300 Miles

0   100   200   300 Kilometers

TANZANIA

Quionga
Cabo Delgado

Rovuma

Mocímboa do Rovuma

Vila de Moçímboa da Praia

Mavago

Lugenda

Ilha do Ibo

Lichinga

Marrupa

Pemba

Lake Malawi

Maua

ZAMBIA

MALAWI

Lúrio

Vila Coutinho

Lake Chilwa

Nampula

Nacala

Zâmbuè

MULANJE MTS.

Moçambique

Vila do Zumbo

Lago de Cahora Bassa

Tete

Moatize

Milanje

Shire

Angoche

Mangula

Changara

Nabúri

Zambezi

Catandica

Quelimane

Macuze

Inyanga

▲ *Sierra da Gorongosa 6,112 ft. 1863 m.*

Vila do Chinde

ZIMBABWE

Chimoio

Dondo

Beira

Mt. Binga ▲ *7,992 ft. 2436 m*

Buzi

Machanga

Nova Mambone

Hippo Valley

Save

Ilha do Bazaruto

Beitbridge

Mabote

Ilha Benguérua

Vilanculos

Messina

Pafúri

Changane

Mapinhane

Ponta São Sebastião

Pomene

Ponta da Barra Falsa

Limpopo

Massinga

SOUTH

Ponta da Barra

Panda

Inhambane

AFRICA

Quissico

Inharrime

Xai-Xai

Nelspruit

Manhiça

⊛ **Maputo**

Mozambique Channel

SWAZILAND

INDIAN

Ermelo

OCEAN

Lake Kosi

Piet Retief

Lake Sibaya

N
W   E
S

Mozambique

LOCATION: 30°12′ to 40°51′E; 10°27′ to 26°52′S. **BOUNDARY LENGTHS:** Tanzania, 756 kilometers (470 miles); Indian Ocean coastline, 2,504 kilometers (1,556 miles); South Africa, 491 kilometers (305 miles); Swaziland, 108 kilometers (67 miles); Zimbabwe, 1,223 kilometers (760 miles); Zambia, 424 kilometers (263 miles); Malawi, 1,497 kilometers (930 miles). **TERRITORIAL SEA LIMIT:** 12 miles.

A young boy in Nampula, Mozambique.

10 RELIGIONS

The population follows African traditional religions, the Christian faith (mainly Roman Catholicism), or Islam. Estimates of the proportions vary, but followers of native religions probably account for 60% of the population. In 1993, there were about 5 million Christians and 4 million Muslims.

11 TRANSPORTATION

Mozambique's landlocked neighbors—Malawi, Zambia, Zimbabwe, and Swaziland—along with South Africa are the main users of the Mozambican transport system. The railways are the most-developed sector, with three good rail links between major Mozambican ports and neighboring countries. The road network totals some 27,287 kilometers (16,955 miles). In 1995 there were 110,800 vehicles, including 84,000 passenger cars.

Maputo, by far the leading port, is a major outlet for South Africa, Swaziland, Zimbabwe, Zambia, Malawi, and eastern Zaire. Maputo and Beira have international airports.

12 HISTORY

Mozambique was occupied by Bantu peoples by about AD 1000. Later, trade developed with Arabs who crossed the Indian Ocean. The first Europeans in the area, the Portuguese, began to settle and trade on the coast early in the sixteenth century. During the seventeenth century, they set up plantations and estates. By the end of the nineteenth century, Portugal had made boundary agreements with its colonial rivals, the United Kingdom and Germany, and had suppressed much of the African resistance in the interior. After the Portuguese revolution of 1926, the influence of trading companies in Mozambique declined, and in 1951 it became an overseas province of Portugal.

On 25 June 1962, the Mozambique Liberation Front (FRELIMO) was formed and on 25 September 1964 began the armed struggle for independence. Samora Machel became president of FRELIMO in December 1970, after its first president, Eduardo Mondlane, was assassinated. Following the Portuguese revolution of 25

A view of the city of Nampula, Mozambique.

April 1974, Portuguese and FRELIMO representatives negotiated an independence agreement, and Mozambique became officially independent at midnight on 24–25 June 1975. Machel, who became the nation's first president, quickly affirmed Mozambique's support of the movement for African control of Rhodesia (now Zimbabwe), and on 3 March 1976, Mozambique closed its border with Rhodesia.

After independence, FRELIMO was transformed from a liberation movement into a Marxist-Leninist party dedicated to the creation of a Socialist state. A newly formed anti-government group opposed to FRELIMO's political stance and sympa-thetic to white interests, the Mozambique National Resistance (RENAMO), began to conduct a guerrilla rebellion with the backing of whites in Rhodesia. These activities continued into the 1980s and turned into a civil war. After the white government in Rhodesia fell and that country became Zimbabwe, RENAMO received substantial aid from South Africa and also had bases in Malawi.

On 19 October 1986, President Machel and 33 others were killed when their Soviet-built jetliner crashed inside South Africa. In August 1989, FRELIMO agreed to allow opposition parties to compete openly and legally. A peace treaty was finally signed on 4 October 1992, and a joint commission of government and RENAMO, along with a small UN monitoring force were named to carry out the agreement. Democratic elections were to be held within a year. In mid-1993, the national election was postponed until October 1994. Joaquim A. Chissano, FRELIMO leader and Mozambique's foreign minister since independence, won with 53.3% of the vote. The elections were monitored by 2,000 international observers for fairness.

13 GOVERNMENT

A revised constitution with a multiparty system of government came into force on 30 November 1990. The name of the country was changed from the People's Republic to the Republic of Mozambique. According to the 1990 constitution, the president is to be elected by universal adult vote for a five-year term. The Assembly of the Republic will replace the People's Assembly. Its deputies (between 200 and 250) are to be elected for five-year terms.

14 POLITICAL PARTIES

The Mozambique Liberation Front (Frente de Libertação de Moçambique—FRELIMO), was the sole legal political party until 1991. The new constitution in force in November 1990 legalized a multiparty system. FRELIMO and RENAMO (created as an armed rebel force) have been the most popular groups. Other parties include the Mozambican National Union (UNAMO), the Democratic Party of Mozambique (PADEMO), and the

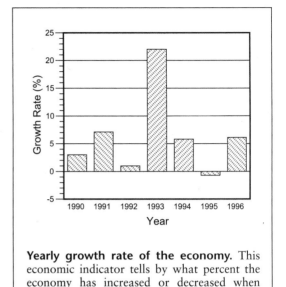

Yearly growth rate of the economy. This economic indicator tells by what percent the economy has increased or decreased when compared with the previous year.

Mozambique National Movement (MONAMO).

15 JUDICIAL SYSTEM

The formal justice system is divided into a civil/criminal system and a separate military justice system under joint supervision of the Ministries of Defense and Justice. The Supreme Court hears appeals from both systems. Local courts, part of the civil/criminal system, handle estate, divorce, and other social and family issues.

16 ARMED FORCES

The armed forces in 1996 included 30,000 army personnel armed with 100 Soviet-made T-34, T-54, and T-55 tanks; a 750-member navy with 3 coastal patrol craft; and an air force of 4,000, with 43 MiG-21s and 4 armed helicopters.

17 ECONOMY

Mozambique is a poverty-stricken country with large debts. Civil war and droughts weakened Mozambique's economy in the 1980s, leaving it heavily dependent on foreign aid. However, recent shifts away from socialism and toward a market economy, as well as a resolution of the civil war, laid the foundation for an economic recovery. The economy grew by an average of 6% yearly between 1990 and 1996. International investment is increasing as stability returns, and an aggressive privatization program continues. Prospects for economic growth will depend heavily on good weather for farmers and a stable political situation.

18 INCOME

In 1992 Mozambique's gross national product (GNP) was $1.35 billion at current prices, or about $80 per person, among the poorest in the world. Inflation was 52.2% per year during 1985–95, and the average annual real growth rate of the GNP per person was 3.6%.

19 INDUSTRY

Mozambique's industrial sector is primarily centered on the processing of locally produced raw materials, especially sugar, cashews, tea, and wheat. Brewing and textile production began in the 1980s, along with cement, fertilizer, and agricultural tool manufacturing.

20 LABOR

Nearly 80% of all Mozambican workers are engaged in agriculture, which accounts for 33% of the gross domestic product

Photo credit: Corel Corporation.

A young woman of Nampula grinds grain at the start of the day.

(GDP). A national minimum wage for farm workers was introduced in 1980. There is a constitutional right to strike, with the exception of employees who provide essential services.

21 AGRICULTURE

Since 1981 Mozambique's agricultural sector has been barely functional due to droughts and flooding. Mozambique's major cash crops are cashew nuts, cotton, copra (dried coconut meat), sugar, tea, and cassava; its major food crops are corn and sorghum.

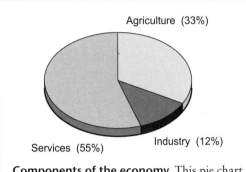

Agriculture (33%)

Services (55%) Industry (12%)

Components of the economy. This pie chart shows how much of the country's economy is devoted to agriculture (includes forestry, hunting, and fishing), industry, or services.

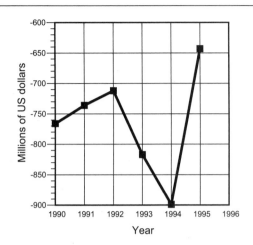

Yearly balance of trade measured in millions of US dollars. The balance of trade is the difference between what a country sells to other countries (its exports) and what it buys (its imports). If a country imports more than it exports, it has a negative balance of trade (a trade deficit). If exports exceed imports there is a positive balance of trade (a trade surplus).

Crop production in 1995 included cassava, 4.7 million tons; sugarcane 300,000 tons; coconuts, 438,000 tons; sorghum, 243,000 tons; peanuts, 102,000 tons; corn, 734,000 tons; bananas, 84,000 tons; citrus fruits, 32,000 tons; cashew nuts, 30,000 tons; rice, 113,000 tons; copra, 74,000 tons; cotton fiber, 16,000 tons; sunflowers, 14,000 tons; and cottonseed, 32,000 tons.

22 DOMESTICATED ANIMALS

In 1995 there were an estimated 1.3 million head of cattle, 385,000 goats, 175,000 hogs, and 121,000 sheep. Beef and veal production was estimated at 38,000 tons; cows' milk, 59,000 tons; and hen eggs, 12 million.

23 FISHING

In 1994, commercial fishery production was 30,000 tons. The potential catch is estimated at 500,000 tons of fish and 14,000 tons of shrimp.

24 FORESTRY

Forests and woodlands occupied about 17.3 million hectares (42.7 million acres) in 1994. About 18.4 million cubic meters (24.1 million cubic yards) of roundwood was produced in 1995, about 94% for fuel. Sawn wood production was 42,000 tons in 1995.

25 MINING

Mozambique is rich in mineral deposits, but little has been done to develop them. In 1994, production included bauxite, 9,620 tons, and gold, 336 kilograms (740 pounds). A significant amount of gold and gemstones are smuggled out of the country.

Selected Social Indicators

These statistics are estimates for the period 1993 to 1996. For comparison purposes, data for the United States and averages for low-income countries and high-income countries are also given.

Indicator	Mozambique	Low-income countries	High-income countries	United States
Per capita gross national product†	$80	$490	$25,870	$28,020
Population growth rate	3.4%	1.7%	0.6%	0.9%
Population growth rate in urban areas	7.1%	3.8%	0.9%	1.2%
Population per square kilometer of land	23	82	30	29
Life expectancy in years	45	63	77	77
Number of physicians per 1,000 people	<0.1	1.0	2.5	2.5
Number of pupils per teacher (primary school)	58	41	17	14
Illiteracy rate (15 years and older)	60%	34%	<5%	3%
Energy consumed per capita (kg of oil equivalent)	38	393	5,123	7,905

† The gross national product (GNP) is the total dollar value of all goods and services produced by a country in a year. The per capita GNP is calculated by dividing a country's GNP by its population. The World Bank defines low-income countries as those with a per capita GNP of $785 or less. High-income countries have a per capita GNP of $9,636 or more. About 16% of the world's 5.7 billion people live in high-income countries, while almost 56% live in low-income countries.   n.a. = data not available   > = greater than   < = less than

Sources: World Bank, *World Development Indicators on CD-ROM,* Washington, D.C.: The World Bank, 1998. Central Intelligence Agency, *The World Fact Book,* Washington, D.C.: Government Printing Office, 1998.

26 FOREIGN TRADE

Agricultural products are Mozambique's leading exports. Principal exports include shrimp, cashew nuts, sugar, and cotton. Food, clothing, farm equipment, and petroleum are the leading imports. Exports of goods totaled $139.3 million in 1995, and imports amounted to $798.5 million. The leading client for Mozambique's exports was South Africa in 1996 (49%), followed by Portugal (16%) and Japan (12%). In that year, South Africa supplied 38% of Mozambique's imports, followed by the United States (7%).

27 ENERGY AND POWER

The coal output was estimated at 60,000 tons in 1995. Natural gas reserves have been estimated at 40 billion cubic meters (1.4 trillion cubic feet). In 1994, electric power production totaled 464 million kilowatt hours, of which 11% was hydroelectric. Mozambique imports all of its petroleum supplies, though oil prospecting is pursued both on and off shore.

28 SOCIAL DEVELOPMENT

FRELIMO and its partner, the Organization of Mozambican Women, have widened educational and occupational opportunities for women and have pushed for a family law protecting women against desertion, abuse, and sexual harassment. Despite official policy and laws requiring equal rights for both sexes, there is still legal and social discrimination against women.

29 HEALTH

In 1985–95, only 39% of the population had access to health care services. The shortage of medical supplies and trained personnel has remained severe throughout Mozambique. In 1993, there was one doctor per 36,225 people. Estimated average life expectancy is only 45 years.

30 HOUSING

As of 1980, 63% of housing units were constructed of woven straw and 14% of cane and woodstick. Nearly 96% were without electricity and over half had no toilet facilities.

31 EDUCATION

Education is compulsory for seven years. In 1995, there were 4,149 primary schools with 24,575 teachers and 1,415,428 pupils. General secondary schools had 171,102 pupils. Eduardo Mondlane University is in Maputo. The country had an estimated adult illiteracy rate of 60% in 1995.

32 MEDIA

There were 62,100 telephones in use in 1995. Radio Moçambique, the official radio service, broadcasts in Portuguese, English, Afrikaans, and local languages.

Televisas Experimental is the government-owned television service. In 1995 there were an estimated 700,000 radios and 44,000 televisions in use. Daily newspapers (with their estimated 1995 circulations) are *Notícias* (Maputo, mornings and Sundays, 45,000) and *Diario do Moçambique* (Beira, evenings, 15,000).

33 TOURISM AND RECREATION

Before independence, tourism, mostly from South Africa and the former Rhodesia (now Zimbabwe), was very important. However, concern for security in the late 1970s and throughout the 1980s, due to the political situation, left the tourist industry at a mere fraction of its previous levels. With stability and an improving economy, the tourism industry may also recover.

34 FAMOUS MOZAMBICANS

Eduardo C. Mondlane (1920–69) was the first president of FRELIMO. His successor, and later the first president of independent Mozambique, was Samora Moïsés Machel (1933–86).

35 BIBLIOGRAPHY

Andersson, Hilary. *Mozambique: A War Against the People.* New York: St. Martin's, 1992.

Darch, Colin. *Mozambique.* Santa Barbara, Calif.: Clio Press, 1987.

James, R. S. *Mozambique.* Philadelphia: Chelsea House, 1999.

Lauré, Jason. *Mozambique.* Chicago: Children's Press, 1995.

Newitt, Malyn D. D. *A History of Mozambique.* Bloomington: Indiana University Press, 1995.

Slater, Mike. *Mozambique.* London, Eng.: New Holland, 1997.

MYANMAR

Union of Myanmar
Pyidaungzu Myanma Naingngandaw

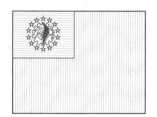

CAPITAL: Yangon (formerly Rangoon).

FLAG: The national flag is red with a blue canton, within which 14 white stars encircle a rice stalk and an industrial wheel.

ANTHEM: *Kaba Makye (Our Free Homeland).*

MONETARY UNIT: The kyat (κ) is a paper currency of 100 pyas. There are coins of 1, 5, 10, 25, and 50 pyas and 1 kyat, and notes of 1, 5, 10, 25, and 100 kyats. κ1 = $0.16804 (or $1 = κ5.951).

WEIGHTS AND MEASURES: Both British and metric weights and measures are in general use, but local units are also employed.

HOLIDAYS: Independence Day, 4 January; Union Day, 12 February; Peasants' Day, 2 March; Defense Services Day, 27 March; Burmese New Year, 17 April; World Workers' Day, 1 May; Martyrs' Day, 19 July; Christmas, 25 December. Movable religious holidays include Full Moon of Tabaung, February or March; Thingyan (Water Festival), April; Full Moon of Kason, April or May; Waso (Beginning of Buddhist Lent), June or July; Thadingyut (End of Buddhist Lent), October; and Tazaungdaing, November.

TIME: 6:30 PM = noon GMT.

1 LOCATION AND SIZE

Situated in Southeast Asia, Myanmar has an area of 678,500 square kilometers (261,970 square miles), slightly smaller than the state of Texas, and a total boundary length of 8,134 kilometers (5,055 miles).

Myanmar's capital city, Yangon (formerly Rangoon), is located in the southern part of the country.

2 TOPOGRAPHY

Myanmar is divided into four topographic regions: (1) a mountainous area in the north and west; (2) the Shan Highlands in the east; (3) central Myanmar, a principal area of cultivation; and (4) the fertile delta and lower valley regions of the Irrawaddy and Sittang rivers in the south.

3 CLIMATE

Myanmar has a largely tropical climate with three seasons. Rainfall ranges from about 76 centimeters (30 inches) in central Myanmar to more than 500 centimeters (200 inches) in upper Myanmar during the monsoon season.

The mean annual temperature is 27°C (81°F); average daily temperatures in Yangon (Rangoon) range from 18° to 32°C (64°–90°F) in January, during the cool season, and from 24° to 36°C (75°–97°F) in April, during the hot season.

Geographic Profile

Geographic Features

Size ranking: 39 of 192
Highest elevation: 5,881 meters (19,294 feet) at Hkakabo Razi
Lowest elevation: Sea level at the Andaman Sea

Land Use†

Arable land:	15%
Permanent crops:	1%
Permanent pastures:	1%
Forests:	49%
Other:	34%

Weather††

Average annual precipitation: 261.8 centimeters (103.1 inches)
Average temperature in January: 24.8°C (76.6°F)
Average temperature in July: 26.6°C (79.9°F)

†*Arable land:* Land used for temporary crops, like meadows for mowing or pasture, gardens, and greenhouses. *Permanent crops:* Land cultivated with crops that occupy its use for long periods, such as cocoa, coffee, rubber, fruit and nut orchards, and vineyards. *Permanent pastures:* Land used permanently for forage crops. *Forests:* Land containing stands of trees. *Other:* Any land not specified, including built-on areas, roads, and barren land.

††The measurements for precipitation and average temperature were taken at weather stations closest to the country's largest city. Precipitation and average temperature can vary significantly within a country, due to factors such as latitude, altitude, coastal proximity, and wind patterns.

4 PLANTS AND ANIMALS

Myanmar has a wide variety of plant and animal life. Teak, representing about 25% of the total forested area, thrives mainly in the mountainous regions; evergreen, bamboo, and palm in the freshwater delta swamps and along the coastlands; mangrove in the salty coastal marshes; temperate forests and rolling grasslands in the Shan Highlands; and scrub vegetation in the dry central area. There are about 12 species of monkeys, as well as tigers, leopards, elephants, and half-wild pariah dogs. Fish abound along the coastline, in the tidal waters of the delta, and in the rivers and streams.

5 ENVIRONMENT

In Myanmar the principal environmental threat comes from cyclones and flooding during the monsoon season, and frequent earthquakes. By 1994, two-thirds of Myanmar's tropical forests had been eliminated. About 64% of the city dwellers and 41% of the rural population do not have pure water.

In 1994, out of a total of 300 species of mammals, 23 were endangered; of 1,000 bird species, 42 were endangered, and 10 reptiles of 360 native species were threatened along with 2 types of freshwater fish. Myanmar also had 23 threatened species of plants in a total of 7,000 as of 1994.

6 POPULATION

In 1998, Myanmar had an estimated population of 47.3 million. The population for 2005 was projected at 52.7 million. Average population density in 1998 was estimated at 70 persons per square kilometer (181 per square mile). Yangon (formerly Rangoon), the capital, had a population of 2.5 million according to the 1983 census, and an estimated population of 3.9 million in 1995.

7 MIGRATION

The government has sought to curtail both immigration and emigration. As many as 500,000 persons may have left Myanmar during the 1960s. About 187,000 Muslims who fled to Bangladesh in 1978 because of alleged atrocities by the military were repatriated with the help of UN agencies by the end of 1981 but lost their citizenship in 1982. About 500,000 poor urban residents were forcibly relocated to rural areas between 1989 and 1992.

In 1995, 116,000 refugees from Myanmar were living in Bangladesh, 82,400 were in Thailand, and 5,100 were in Malaysia.

8 ETHNIC GROUPS

The Burmans, ethnically related to the Tibetans, constituted about 68% of Myanmar's total population in 1992. Although much ethnic fusion has taken place, most other ethnic groups remain distinct cultural entities and have sought to preserve their autonomy, sometimes by violent means.

As of 1992, Karens made up about 6% of the population, Shans 7%, Arikanese, 3.8%, and Chins, Kachins, and Mons, 2.3% each. Indians, Bangladeshis, and Pakistanis made up perhaps another 2% of the population, and Chinese 3%.

9 LANGUAGES

Burmese, the official language, is spoken by at least 80% of the population. Pronunciation varies greatly from area to area. Burmese is the language of government, but the ethnic minorities have their own languages.

10 RELIGIONS

As of 1992, an estimated 89.2% of the people were Hinayana or Theravada Bud-

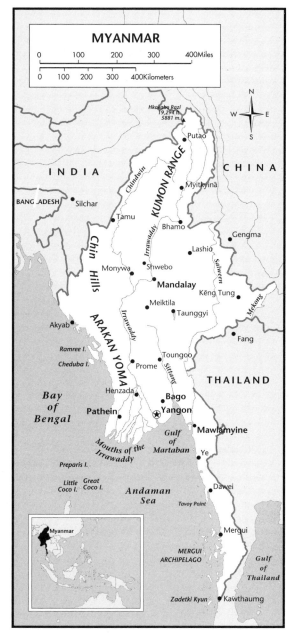

LOCATION: 92°10′ to 101°11′E; 9°35′ to 28°28′N. **BOUNDARY LENGTHS:** China, 2,185 kilometers (1,358 miles); Laos, 238 kilometers (148 miles); Thailand, 1,799 kilometers (1,118 miles); total coastline, 2,276 kilometers (1,414 miles); Bangladesh, 233 kilometers (145 miles); India, 1,403 kilometers (872 miles). **TERRITORIAL SEA LIMIT:** 12 miles.

Photo credit: Corel Corporation.

A golden-roofed temple. It is estimated that almost 90% of the population of Myanmar is Buddhist.

dhists. Many Buddhists are also followers of native religions, believing in powerful spirits called *nats*.

The Chinese in Myanmar practice a traditional mixture of Mahayana Buddhism, Taoism, Confucianism, and ancestor worship; the Indians are Hindus; the Pakistanis are Muslims; and most of the Europeans are Christians. Muslims account for 4% of the population; Hindus, 1%; and Roman Catholics, 1%.

11 TRANSPORTATION

Historically, Myanmar has been dependent on sea and river transport externally and internally, supplemented in modern times by the airplane. There were an estimated 26,861 kilometers (16,690 miles) of roads in 1995, but only 11% were paved. In 1995, Myanmar had about 44,000 passenger cars and 42,000 commercial vehicles. Myanmar's railway system operates 3,569 kilometers (2,217 miles) of track.

Inland waterways are crucial to internal transportation, partly compensating for limited railroad and highway development. Some 500,000 small river craft sail the Irrawaddy, Salween, and Sittang rivers and their numerous tributaries. The state merchant fleet had 40 ships in 1995, with a combined 444,900 gross registered tons.

Yangon is the chief port for ocean shipping, handling over 85% of the country's seaborne trade. Other ports include Akyab (Sittwe), serving western Myanmar; Pathein (Bassein), serving the delta area; and Mawlamyine (Moulmein), Dawei (Tavoy), and Mergui, which handle mineral and timber exports of the southern region.

Mingaladon, outside of Yangon, is the principal airport. In 1995, 334,000 passengers were carried on scheduled domestic and international flights.

12 HISTORY

The founding of a kingdom at Pagan in 1044 AD by Anawrahta marks the beginning of Myanmar's political identity. The kingdom survived until 1287, when it was destroyed by the armies of Kublai Khan, and for the next five centuries conflict reigned. In 1754, however, Alaungpaya

Many people ride buses to get around the cities in Myanmar.

united northern and southern Myanmar and founded the last ruling dynasty, which was in power until the British came in the early nineteenth century.

The British conquest of Myanmar spanned 62 years, from the first Anglo-Burmese War in 1824–26 to 1 January 1886, when total annexation of Myanmar was proclaimed following the territory's defeat in the third war. Incorporated into the British Indian Empire, Myanmar was administered as a province of India until 1937, when it became a separate colony.

National Independence

From 1886 to 1948, the inhabitants fought continually for independence. The nationalists who finally gained freedom for Myanmar were a group of socialist-minded intellectuals, called the Thakins, from the University of Rangoon. At the start of World War II (1939–45), these anti-British nationalists collaborated with the Japanese but were soon disappointed when the Japanese occupied the country. The group was then converted into an anti-Japanese guerrilla force that assisted the British in the liberation of Myanmar.

Photo credit: Susan D. Rock.

Border crossing with northern Thailand.

In 1946, after the end of World War II, the sovereign Union of Burma came into being. In 1951 the nation held its first parliamentary elections. The decade of the 1950s brought an ambitious land reform program and an attempt to forge a neutral foreign policy. However, the country was faced with periodic communist rebellions and an off-and-on border dispute with China.

A coup of 2 March 1962 overthrew the government, and a military regime assumed control. The Socialist Republic of Burma was proclaimed on 3 January 1974. Under a new constitution, a president was elected, but the government continued to be dominated by the military. At this time, the country's only legal political organization was the Burma Socialist Program Party (BSPP). Meanwhile, a guerrilla war in border areas of the north and east continued through the 1980s. It was fought by the underground Burmese Communist Party and rebel ethnic groups.

When the military became dissatisfied with the government and the ruling BSPP party, it staged another military coup. On 18 September 1988 the army abolished the BSPP, took over the government, and imposed military rule under the State Law and Order Restoration Council (SLORC). The SLORC was headed by the army Chief of Staff, General Saw Maung. On 18 June 1989 the Saw Maung regime renamed Burma "Myanmar," the historic ethnic Burman name for the country.

The takeover of the government by the military prompted dissent among the population. Among the most prominent dissidents was Aung San Suu Kyi. She rose to prominence by establishing a coalition party that opposed the military regime. In speeches and interviews she challenged the SLORC's record, characterizing it as one of economic and social degeneration. She also protested the SLORC's repressive laws and actions. Because of her actions, the government placed her under house arrest in 1989.

Multiparty elections were held in May 1990, but the military refused to transfer power to the winning National League for Democracy (NLD). It announced in September 1990 that it intended to remain in power for five to ten more years.

Myanmar Under the SLORC

In the early 1990s, the plight of dissident Aung San Suu Kyi, who was placed under house arrest in 1989, began receiving worldwide attention. In 1991 she was awarded the 1990 Sakharov Prize for Freedom of Thought by the European Parliament. On 10 December 1991 Aung San Suu Kyi's son, Alexander, accepted the 1991 Nobel Peace Prize on her behalf.

Another type of human rights violation in Myanmar that drew international attention was forced labor. It was reported that the SLORC used forced labor on tourist projects such as the reconstruction of the gold palace in Mandalay. Of Mandalay's 500,000 residents, each family had to contribute at least three days of free labor each month. The work lasted from dawn until evening and was so strenuous that it required several days of recovery. Forced labor was also used on many building projects and to carry supplies and munitions into malaria-infested areas for the military. Prison inmates were required to work every day. Many military families could be exempted, as could any family that agreed to pay a monthly fine of $6, about a week's wages for some families. Muslim refugees who fled Myanmar said that Muslims had to pay two to three times as much as others to escape labor.

Ever since Myanmar received its independence in 1948, the government has faced ethnic minorities fighting for autonomy. However, in 1991 the 600-member Palaung State Liberation Army and the 500-member Pa-O National Army rebel group signed truce agreements with SLORC, which served as models for settlements with other rebels. The Karens, Mons, and Karenni along the Thai border began talks with the military regime in early 1994. Eventually, the junta negotiated separate peace treaties with each rebel group.

As of mid-1994 the international community was still debating the most constructive approach to dealing with Myanmar. Many Asian countries argue that maintaining relations with Myanmar is more productive than isolating it. However, the United States has stuck to its hard-line isolationist policy toward Myanmar to press for advancement of democracy and human rights. The United States government still refers to Myanmar as Burma, the country's name prior to the military takeover.

In July 1995, the SLORC released dissident Aung San Suu Kyi from house arrest. She had been detained for six years. Most observers saw the SLORC's action as an attempt to gain international favor, and not as a sign that they were ready to loosen their grip on the country. Upon her release, Suu Kyi confirmed her commitment to democracy. The NLD planned to draft its own version of the constitution, and Suu Kyi planned pro-democracy rallies. Following mass student protests in December 1996, the government blamed Suu Kyi and returned her to house arrest. She was released again in July 1997.

Thousands of political opponents remained in prison during 1995 and 1996. The ruling leaders also faced renewed fighting with border insurgents, particularly the Karen National Union Army.

The Myanmar government has also come under considerable international criticism for its involvement in the country's massive drug trade. Myanmar is the world's largest producer of opium and heroin, and is a major producer of methamphetamines.

13 GOVERNMENT

A military coup in September 1988 brought the State Law and Order Restoration Council (SLORC) to power. SLORC abolished the previous government and the country was placed under martial law. On 18 September 1988 the official title of the state was changed to The Union of Myanmar. SLORC directs, supervises, and coordinates the work of the central and local government institutions.

In a multiparty election held 27 May 1990, the National League for Democracy (NLD) received 59.9% of the total vote and took 396 of the 485 contested seats. However, SLORC refused to hand over power to the NLD, instead insisting that a new constitution be drafted and approved by SLORC prior to the transfer of power.

Myanmar comprises seven states and seven divisions, further divided into 317 townships, which include villages and towns.

14 POLITICAL PARTIES

With the military takeover of September 1988, the ruling Burma Socialist Program Party was formally abolished, and all governing authority was concentrated in the hands of the military. On 24 September 1988 the BSPP was reborn as the National Unity Party (NUP), inheriting the buildings and machinery of the old BSPP.

On 24 September 1988 the National League for Democracy (NLD), a coalition party, was formed in opposition to the military regime. The NLD won the 27 May 1990 elections by a landslide, electing 392 candidates; the NUP took 10 seats. NLD leader Aung San Suu Kyi was placed under house arrest on 20 July 1989 and was released in July 1995. The Democratic Alliance of Burma (DAB) is a coalition of 21 ethnic minorities and political dissident groups formed in 1988.

By March 1993 all but seven political parties had been deregistered by SLORC. Other political or pressure groups were the Kachin Independence Army (KIA), the United Wa State Army (UWSA), the Karen

National Union (KNU), and several Shan factions including the Mong Tai Army (MTA).

15 JUDICIAL SYSTEM

The British-style judicial system with which Myanmar began its independence, including a Supreme Court, was disbanded by the Revolutionary Council. Military tribunals which enforced orders issued by the State Law and Order Restoration Council (SLORC) were abolished in 1992. Ordinary courts now handle such cases. The Supreme Court appoints judges after approval by the SLORC. The judiciary is not independent.

16 ARMED FORCES

The armed forces play the major role in Myanmar's politics and administration; senior members of the government are officers who govern under martial law.

Myanmar's armed forces totaled an estimated 321,000 in 1995; military service for men and women is compulsory. The army, with 300,000 personnel, is organized in infantry battalions chiefly for internal security duties. The navy has 12,000–15,000 members, and the air force 9,000. The navy's ships include 30 gunboats and 36 river patrol craft. The air force has 91 combat aircraft, 10 transports, and 18 armed helicopters. Paramilitary forces total 85,250. Military expenditures were $1.9 billion in 1995.

17 ECONOMY

The military regime, SLORC, which took over Myanmar in 1988, proclaimed a market-oriented economic policy and

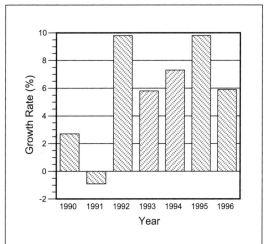

Yearly growth rate of the economy. This economic indicator tells by what percent the economy has increased or decreased when compared with the previous year.

invited foreign investment. Two trends have been apparent in the government's economic policies: the capture of revenues from short-term, quick-turnover sources such as hardwoods, prospecting rights, and taxes on profits from illegal sources; and spending patterns that emphasize defense spending and acquisition of armaments.

Due to Myanmar's inability to stop the flow of drugs from its sector of the Golden Triangle, in February 1989 the United States removed Myanmar from a list of countries eligible to receive aid for combating the drug trade. Myanmar is the world's largest supplier of illegal opiates; in 1995 its opium accounted for 60% of worldwide production. About 60% of the heroin brought into the United States comes from Myanmar. Large quantities of smuggled consumer goods are sold in Myanma cities, where the black market thrives.

Myanmar receives no aid from United States or European Union (EU) programs and aid from Japan is run at a maintenance level. The International Monetary Fund (IMF), the World Bank, and the Asian Development Bank (ADB) extend no credit to Myanmar.

18 INCOME

In 1995 the gross domestic product (GDP) was $47 billion, or about $1,000 per person.

19 INDUSTRY

Industry is geared largely to the processing of agricultural, mineral, and forest products. Principal industrial products are cement, steel, bricks and tiles, fertilizers, and processed foods. Consumer goods that were imported before 1962 and are now manufactured domestically include blankets, paper, glass products, bicycles, and water pumps. Other major consumer items manufactured are aluminum ware, jute and cotton cloth, pharmaceuticals, beverages, matches, and cigarettes. The assembly of television sets and motor vehicles is a recent development in Myanmar's industry.

Industrial products for 1995 included pig iron, 1,500 tons; crude steel, 25,000 tons; refined tin, 190 tons; and refined petroleum products, 5.3 million barrels.

Photo credit: International Labour Office.
A young woman working at a pottery factory.

20 LABOR

In 1992, over two-thirds of Myanmar's civilian wage labor force of 15.7 million was engaged in agriculture, primarily rice cultivation. As of 1992, according to the government, 69% of the labor force worked in agriculture, 8.9% in trade, 10.6% in government and social services, 7.2% in manufacturing, 1.7% in construction, forestry, and mining, 2.5% in transport and communications, and 0.1% in other sectors.

No trade union or independent labor movement activity has occurred since

1988. Forced labor is frequently used by the military for building projects. Wage levels continue to be low and have been eroded by inflation. There were some 502,550 officially unemployed in 1992, although the actual amount is likely to be much higher.

21 AGRICULTURE

Rice, by far the most important agricultural product, in 1995 covered about 6.4 million hectares (16 million acres) of land. Rice production officially totaled 18.8 million tons in 1994/95, although it may have actually been closer to 16 million tons. New high-yield varieties of rice contributed to an increase, as did favorable weather conditions and the completion of new irrigation systems and flood-control dams during the early 1980s.

Other crops in 1995 included 2.2 million tons of sugarcane, 501,000 tons of peanuts, 272,000 tons of corn, and 297,000 tons of sesame. Tobacco and jute are also produced, and rubber is grown on small plantations in the delta regions.

22 DOMESTICATED ANIMALS

Despite Buddhist prohibitions against any kind of animal slaughter, the Myanma eat beef and other meats. Zebu cattle and water buffalo are mainly raised as draft animals; the output of such hides was 23,485 tons in 1995. Dairy farming is confined to the Shan and Kachin states; hogs and poultry are found in virtually every village.

In 1995, Myanmar had an estimated 9.9 million head of cattle, 2.9 million

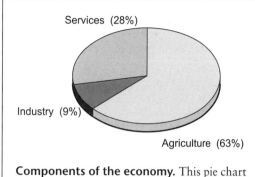

Components of the economy. This pie chart shows how much of the country's economy is devoted to agriculture (includes forestry, hunting, and fishing), industry, or services.

hogs, 2.2 million water buffalo, 1,164,000 goats, 328,000 sheep, 28 million chickens, and 4 million ducks. Milk production was 548,000 tons, and eggs, 46,082 tons.

23 FISHING

Fishing is the most significant nonagricultural source of income in Myanmar. Fish, which supply the main protein element in the Myanma diet, generally are dried and salted before marketing or consumed fresh or as fish paste. To encourage a larger saltwater catch, the government embarked on expanded deep-sea fishing operations and erected a cold-storage plant, a fish cannery, and a fish oil and meal factory. The total fish catch in 1994 was 824,468 tons (73% saltwater, 27% freshwater), up from 686,515 tons in 1986.

24 FORESTRY

Forests and woodland cover nearly half the country. Myanmar has a major share of the world's teak reserves, which constitute about one-third of the forested area.

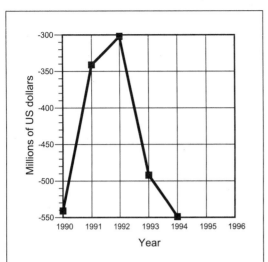

Yearly balance of trade measured in millions of US dollars. The balance of trade is the difference between what a country sells to other countries (its exports) and what it buys (its imports). If a country imports more than it exports, it has a negative balance of trade (a trade deficit). If exports exceed imports there is a positive balance of trade (a trade surplus).

As the world's leading exporter of teak, Myanmar supplies about 75% of the world market. Roundwood production in 1995 totaled 23.3 million cubic meters (30.5 million cubic yards). Other forest products include lac, catechu resin, and bamboo.

The export of forest products increased in value from $115.3 million in 1987 to $307.3 million in 1995.

25 MINING

Metallic ores are mined in small amounts; production in 1995 included (in tons) copper (3,700), lead (2,400), zinc (719), tin (747), and tungsten (531). Industrial mineral production in 1995 included (in tons) barite (34,601), fire clay (2,300), dolomite (3,432), limestone (2.5 million), and gypsum (34,659).

Lead, zinc, silver, copper, nickel, and cobalt are produced at the Baldwin mine in Namtu. Jade, rubies, sapphires, and gold are also extracted, and deposits of iron ore, antimony, and coal have been found. Production of jade and refined silver totaled 702,751 kilograms (1.5 million pounds) and 3,500 kilograms (7,700 pounds), respectively.

26 FOREIGN TRADE

Myanmar's main legal exports are rice, wood products, beans, and garments. Textiles accounted for 82% of reported exports in 1993. Illegal drugs are also a major export, the value of which may be worth as much as all the legal exports combined. The International Monetary Fund estimated exports of goods at $531.3 million in 1995, and imports at $636.2 million.

Major trade partners include Singapore, China, Malaysia, India, Thailand, and Hong Kong.

27 ENERGY AND POWER

Petroleum reserves were estimated at 51.3 million barrels in 1991. Most natural gas comes from the field at Prome. Oil production reached 4.4 million barrels in 1995; in that year, natural gas production totaled 1.5 billion cubic meters (2 billion cubic yards). Coal resources in Myanmar are of relatively low thermal value. About 32,191 tons of coal were mined in 1995.

Selected Social Indicators

These statistics are estimates for the period 1993 to 1996. For comparison purposes, data for the United States and averages for low-income countries and high-income countries are also given.

Indicator	Myanmar	Low-income countries	High-income countries	United States
Per capita gross national product†	$1,000	$490	$25,870	$28,020
Population growth rate	1.7%	1.7%	0.6%	0.9%
Population growth rate in urban areas	3.2%	3.8%	0.9%	1.2%
Population per square kilometer of land	70	82	30	29
Life expectancy in years	56	63	77	77
Number of physicians per 1,000 people	n.a.	1.0	2.5	2.5
Number of pupils per teacher (primary school)	49	41	17	14
Illiteracy rate (15 years and older)	17%	34%	<5%	3%
Energy consumed per capita (kg of oil equivalent)	50	393	5,123	7,905

† The gross national product (GNP) is the total dollar value of all goods and services produced by a country in a year. The per capita GNP is calculated by dividing a country's GNP by its population. The World Bank defines low-income countries as those with a per capita GNP of $785 or less. High-income countries have a per capita GNP of $9,636 or more. About 16% of the world's 5.7 billion people live in high-income countries, while almost 56% live in low-income countries.　　n.a. = data not available　　> = greater than　　< = less than

Sources: World Bank, *World Development Indicators on CD-ROM*, Washington, D.C.: The World Bank, 1998. Central Intelligence Agency, *The World Fact Book*, Washington, D.C.: Government Printing Office, 1998.

Production of electricity totaled 3,369 million kilowatt hours in 1994, of which gas-fired plants provided 50%; hydroelectric power, 44%; and steam and diesel fuel, 6%.

28 SOCIAL DEVELOPMENT

Although considerable advances have been made in health services, Myanmar's goal of establishing a welfare state has been limited by lack of public funds. In 1956, the government inaugurated a social security program that compensates workers for wage losses arising from sickness, injury, and maternity leave, provides free medical care, and establishes survivors' benefits. The program is funded by contributions from employers, employees, and the government. As yet, Myanmar does not have unemployment insurance, but workers are entitled to old-age pensions.

Women have a high status in Myanmar's society and economic life. They may retain their maiden name after marriage, may obtain divorces without undue difficulty, and enjoy equal property and inheritance rights with men.

Myanmar's military government continues to engage in human rights abuses.

Photo credit: Cory Langley.

With less than 50,000 passenger cars to transport almost 50 million people, citizens of Myanmar catch a ride however they can.

The military uses forced labor as porters for the army. There is also widespread mistreatment of prisoners.

29 HEALTH

Until recent decades, few people in rural areas had the benefit of modern medicine. To correct this deficiency, the country's health services were reorganized by sending more doctors to rural areas and increasing the number of rural health centers. Doctors in private practice were inducted for two years of national service.

The progress of the health services is reflected in the reduction of the physician/population ratio from 1 per 15,560 in 1960 to 1 per 3,578 by 1986. In 1986, Myanmar had 635 hospitals with 25,839 beds. There were 12,400 doctors in 1990.

Smallpox and plague have been practically eliminated as health hazards, and programs are under way to eradicate malaria and tuberculosis. However, gastrointestinal diseases such as typhoid, dysentery, and cholera remain widespread. In 1995, only 38% of the population had access to safe water. Another serious health problem is drug addiction, aggravated by the easy availability and low cost of opium. Under a drug-abuse control program financed by the United States and the United Nations, a new 300-bed hospital for addicts was opened in 1982 at Thayetmyo; smaller facilities have been established in two dozen other towns.

Average life expectancy was 56 years in 1996. In 1990–95, 60% of the population had access to health care services.

30 HOUSING

Pre-war housing in Myanmar compared favorably with that in other Southeast Asian nations, but housing conditions have deteriorated. Urban dwellings are overcrowded and often unsafe.

31 EDUCATION

In 1994, Myanmar had 35,744 primary schools with 5.7 million students. Secondary schools had 69,411 teachers and 1.5 million students. Primary education lasts for 5 years, followed by 4 years of secondary education at the first stage and 2 years at the second stage.

Post-secondary institutions, including 18 teacher-training colleges, 6 agricultural institutes, 8 technical institutes, and 35 universities and colleges, enrolled a total of 235,236 students with 5,989 teaching staff in 1993. The Arts and Science Universities at Yangon (Rangoon) and Mandalay together enrolled about 19,500 students in the mid-1980s.

The Mass Education Council has attempted to increase literacy through special programs. The 1995 adult illiteracy rate was estimated at 17% (males, 11.3%; and females, 22.3%).

32 MEDIA

The director-general of posts and telegraphs controls the telephone, telegraph, radio, and postal communications systems. In 1995 there were an estimated 131,000 telephones in use. A satellite communications station that began operating in 1979 links Myanmar with more than 100 countries. The government provides the only radio and television transmissions through Radio Myanmar and TV–Myanmar. As of 1995, there were 3.6 million radios and 88,000 TV sets in use.

The government claims to uphold freedom of the press, but there are no privately owned newspapers, and the print media are government-controlled. Chinese- and Indian-language newspapers are not allowed by the government, but two daily papers are still published in English. Leading newspapers in 1995 included the *Kyemon* (1995 circulation, 220,000), *Myanma Alin* (222,000), and *The New Light of Myanmar* (24,000).

33 TOURISM AND RECREATION

Since the inception of military rule in 1988, tourism has declined sharply, but has risen since 1990. From 1988 to 1995 the number of hotels increased from 19 to 256. There were 80,408 tourist arrivals in 1994. Principal attractions include palaces and Buddhist temples and shrines.

34 FAMOUS MYANMA

Anawrahta, who founded the early Burmese kingdom of Pagan in 1044 and established Hinayana Buddhism as the official religion, is a great figure in Burmese history, as are Bayinnaung (r.1551–

81) and Alaungpaya (r.1752–60), who established the dynasty that ruled Myanmar until 1886.

Great writers of the Burmese past include Bhikkhu Ratthasara, author of the poem *Hatthipala Pyo,* on the life of Gautama Buddha; Nawedegyi and Natshinnaung, poets of the Toungoo dynasties; and Binnyadala, who wrote of the long struggles of the Burmese king of Ava.

In more recent times, U Ba Nyan and U Ba Zaw, well-known painters of the 1920s, introduced Western-style art into Myanmar; both died in the 1940s.

U Nu (Thakin Nu, b.1907) was independent Myanmar's first premier (1948–62) and shares fame as founder of modern Myanmar with Aung San (1916–47), called the Father of the Burmese Revolution. Ne Win (Maung Shu Maung, b.1911) became premier in March 1962 and was president from 1974 to 1981. U

Thant (1909–74) served as UN secretary-general from 1961 through 1971.

Aung San Suu Kyi (b. 1945), daughter of Aung San, is a prominent dissident whose activities have focused international attention on human rights abuses in Myanmar. In 1991 she was awarded both the Sakharov Prize for Freedom of Thought and the Nobel Peace Prize.

35 BIBLIOGRAPHY

American University. *Burma: A Country Study.* Washington, D.C.: Government Printing Office, 1983.

Herbert, Patricia M. *Burma.* Santa Barbara, Calif.: Clio Press, 1991.

Klein, Wilhelm. *Insight Guides Burma Myanmar.* Boston: Houghton Mifflin, 1996.

Orwell, George. *Burmese Days.* New York: Harcourt, Brace, 1935.

Silverstein, Josef. *The Political Legacy of Aung San.* Ithaca, N.Y.: Cornell University, 1993.

Steinberg, David J. *The Future of Burma: Crisis and Choice in Myanmar.* New York: Asia Society, 1990.

Swerdlow, Joel L. "Burma, the Richest of Poor Countries." *National Geographic,* July 1995, 70–97.

Wright, D. *Burma.* Chicago: Children's Press, 1991.

GLOSSARY

abdicate: To formally give up a claim to a throne; to give up the right to be king or queen.

aboriginal: The first known inhabitants of a country. A species of animals or plants which originated within a given area.

acid rain: Rain (or snow) that has become slightly acid by mixing with industrial air pollution.

adobe: A brick made from sun-dried heavy clay mixed with straw, used in building houses. A house made of adobe bricks.

adult literacy: The ability of adults to read and write.

agrarian economy: An economy where agriculture is the dominant form of economic activity. A society where agriculture dominates the day-to-day activities of the population is called an agrarian society.

air link: Refers to scheduled air service that allows people and goods to travel between two places on a regular basis.

airborne industrial pollutant: Pollution caused by industry that is supported or carried by the air.

allies: Groups or persons who are united in a common purpose. Typically used to describe nations that have joined together to fight a common enemy in war.

In World War I, the term Allies described the nations that fought against Germany and its allies. In World War II, Allies described the United Kingdom, United States, the USSR and their allies, who fought against the Axis Powers of Germany, Italy, and Japan.

aloe: A plant particularly abundant in the southern part of Africa, where leaves of some species are made into ropes, fishing lines, bow strings, and hammocks. It is also a symbolic plant in the Islamic world; anyone who returns from a pilgrimage to Mecca (Mekkah) hangs aloe over his door as a token that he has performed the journey.

Altaic language family: A family of languages spoken in portions of northern and eastern Europe, and nearly the whole of northern and central Asia, together with some other regions. The family is divided into five branches: the Ugrian or Finno-Hungarian, Smoyed, Turkish, Mongolian, and Tunguse.

althing: A legislative assembly.

amendment: A change or addition to a document.

Amerindian: A contraction of the two words, American Indian. It describes native peoples of North, South, or Central America.

amnesty: An act of forgiveness or pardon, usually taken by a government, toward persons for crimes they may have committed.

animal husbandry: The branch of agriculture that involves raising animals.

Anglican: Pertaining to or connected with the Church of England.

animism: The belief that natural objects and phenomena have souls or innate spiritual powers.

annex: To incorporate land from one country into another country.

annual growth rate: The rate at which something grows over a period of 12 months.

annual inflation rate: The rate of inflation in prices over the course of a year.

anthracite coal: Also called hard coal, it is usually 90 to 95 percent carbon, and burns cleanly, almost without a flame.

anti-Semitism: Agitation, persecution, or discrimination (physical, emotional, economic, political, or otherwise) directed against the Jews.

apartheid: The past governmental policy in the Republic of South Africa of separating the races in society.

appeasement: To bring to a state of peace.

appellate: Refers to an appeal of a court decision to a high authority.

aquaculture: The culture or "farming" of aquatic plants or other natural produce, as in the raising of catfish in "farms."

aquatic resources: Resources that come from, grow in, or live in water, including fish and plants.

aquifer: An underground layer of porous rock, sand, or gravel that holds water.

arable land: Land that can be cultivated by plowing and used for growing crops.

arbitration: A process whereby disputes are settled by a designated person, called the arbitrator, instead of by a court of law.

archipelago: Any body of water abounding with islands, or the islands themselves collectively.

archives: A place where records or a collection of important documents are kept.

arctic climate: Cold, frigid weather similar to that experienced at or near the north pole.

aristocracy: A small minority that controls the government of a nation, typically on the basis of inherited wealth.

armistice: An agreement or truce which ends military conflict in anticipation of a peace treaty.

artesian well: A type of well where the water rises to the surface and overflows.

ASEAN *see* Association of Southeast Asian Nations

Association of Southeast Asian Nations: ASEAN was established in 1967 to promote political, economic, and social cooperation among its six member countries: Indonesia, Malaysia, the Philippines, Singapore, Thailand, and Brunei. ASEAN headquarters are in Jakarta, Indonesia. In January

1992, ASEAN agreed to create the ASEAN Free Trade Area (AFTA).

asylum: To give protection, security, or shelter to someone who is threatened by political or religious persecution.

atoll: A coral island, consisting of a strip or ring of coral surrounding a central lagoon.

atomic weapons: Weapons whose extremely violent explosive power comes from the splitting of the nuclei of atoms (usually uranium or plutonium) by neutrons in a rapid chain reaction. These weapons may be referred to as atom bombs, hydrogen bombs, or H-bombs.

austerity measures: Steps taken by a government to conserve money or resources during an economically difficult time, such as cutting back on federally funded programs.

Australoid: Pertains to the type of aborigines, or earliest inhabitants, of Australia.

Austronesian language: A family of languages which includes practically all the languages of the Pacific Islands—Indonesian, Melanesian, Polynesian, and Micronesian sub-families. Does not include Australian or Papuan languages.

authoritarianism: A form of government in which a person or group attempts to rule with absolute authority without the representation of the citizens.

autonomous state: A country which is completely self-governing, as opposed to being a dependency or part of another country.

autonomy: The state of existing as a self-governing entity. For instance, when a country gains its independence from another country, it gains autonomy.

average inflation rate: The average rate at which the general prices of goods and services increase over the period of a year.

average life expectancy: In any given society, the average age attained by persons at the time of death.

Axis Powers: The countries aligned against the Allied Nations in World War II, originally applied to Nazi Germany and Fascist Italy (Rome-Berlin Axis), and later extended to include Japan.

Baha'i: The follower of a religious sect founded by Mirza Husayn Ali in Iran in 1863.

Baltic states. The three formerly communist countries of Estonia, Latvia, and Lithuania that border on the Baltic Sea.

Bantu language group: A name applied to the languages spoken in central and south Africa.

Baptist: A member of a Protestant denomination that practices adult baptism by complete immersion in water.

barren land: Unproductive land, partly or entirely treeless.

barter: Trade practice where merchandise is exchanged directly for other merchandise or services without use of money.

bedrock: Solid rock lying under loose earth.

bicameral legislature: A legislative body consisting of two chambers, such as the U.S. House of Representatives and the U.S. Senate.

bill of rights: A written statement containing the list of privileges and powers to be granted to a body of people, usually introduced when a government or other organization is forming.

bituminous coal: Soft coal; coal which burns with a bright-yellow flame.

black market: A system of trade where goods are sold illegally, often for excessively inflated prices. This type of trade usually develops to avoid paying taxes or tariffs levied by the government, or to get around import or export restrictions on products.

bloodless coup: The sudden takeover of a country's government by hostile means but without killing anyone in the process.

boat people: Used to describe individuals (refugees) who attempt to flee their country by boat.

bog: Wet, soft, and spongy ground where the soil is composed mainly of decayed or decaying vegetable matter.

Bolshevik Revolution. A revolution in 1917 in Russia when a wing of the Russian Social Democratic party seized power. The Bolsheviks advocated the violent overthrow of capitalism.

bonded labor: Workers bound to service without pay; slaves.

border dispute: A disagreement between two countries as to the exact location or length of the dividing line between them.

Brahman: A member (by heredity) of the highest caste among the Hindus, usually assigned to the priesthood.

broadleaf forest: A forest composed mainly of broadleaf (deciduous) trees.

Buddhism: A religious system common in India and eastern Asia. Founded by and based upon the teachings of Siddhartha Gautama, Buddhism asserts that suffering is an inescapable part of life. Deliverance can only be achieved through the practice of charity, temperance, justice, honesty, and truth.

buffer state: A small country that lies between two larger, possibly hostile countries, considered to be a neutralizing force between them.

bureaucracy: A system of government that is characterized by division into bureaus of administration with their own divisional heads. Also refers to the inflexible procedures of such a system that often result in delay.

Byzantine Empire: An empire centered in the city of Byzantium, now Istanbul in present-day Turkey.

CACM *see* Central American Common Market.

canton: A territory or small division or state within a country.

capital punishment: The ultimate act of punishment for a crime, the death penalty.

capitalism: An economic system in which goods and services and the means to produce and sell them are privately owned, and prices and wages are determined by market forces.

Caribbean Community and Common Market (CARICOM): Founded in 1973 and with its headquarters in Georgetown, Guyana, CARICOM seeks the establishment of a common trade policy and increased cooperation in the Caribbean region. Includes 13 English-speaking Caribbean nations: Antigua and Barbuda, the Bahamas, Barbados, Belize, Dominica, Grenada, Guyana, Jamaica, Montserrat, Saint Kitts-Nevis, Saint Lucia, St. Vincent/Grenadines, and Trinidad and Tobago.

CARICOM *see* Caribbean Community and Common Market.

carnivore: Flesh-eating animal or plant.

carob: The common English name for a plant that is similar to and sometimes used as a substitute for chocolate.

cartel: An organization of independent producers formed to regulate the production, pricing, or marketing practices of its members in order to limit competition and maximize their market power.

cash crop: A crop that is grown to be sold rather than kept for private use.

cassation: The reversal or annulling of a final judgment by the supreme authority.

cassava: The name of several species of stout herbs, extensively cultivated for food.

caste system: One of the artificial divisions or social classes into which the Hindus are rigidly separated according to the religious law of Brahmanism. Membership in a caste is hereditary, and the privileges and disabilities of each caste are transmitted by inheritance.

Caucasian or Caucasoid: The white race of human beings, as determined by genealogy and physical features.

ceasefire: An official declaration of the end to the use of military force or active hostilities, even if only temporary.

CEMA *see* Council for Mutual Economic Assistance.

censorship: The practice of withholding certain items of news that may cast a country in an unfavorable light or give away secrets to the enemy.

census: An official counting of the inhabitants of a state or country with details of sex and age, family, occupation, possessions, etc.

Central American Common Market (CACM): Established in 1962, a trade alliance of five Central American nations. Participating are Costa Rica, El Salvador, Guatemala, Honduras, and Nicaragua.

Central Powers: In World War I, Germany and Austria-Hungary, and their allies, Turkey and Bulgaria.

centrally planned economy: An economic system all aspects of which are supervised and regulated by the government.

centrist position: Refers to opinions held by members of a moderate political group; that is, views that are somewhere in the middle of popular thought between conservative and liberal.

cession: Withdrawal from or yielding to physical force.

chancellor: A high-ranking government official. In some countries it is the prime minister.

cholera: An acute infectious disease characterized by severe diarrhea, vomiting, and, often, death.

Christianity: The religion founded by Jesus Christ, based on the Bible as holy scripture.

Church of England: The national and established church in England. The Church of England claims continuity with the branch of the Catholic Church that existed in England before the Reformation. Under Henry VIII, the spiritual supremacy and jurisdiction of the Pope were abolished, and the sovereign (king or queen) was declared head of the church.

circuit court: A court that convenes in two or more locations within its appointed district.

CIS *see* Commonwealth of Independent States

city-state: An independent state consisting of a city and its surrounding territory.

civil court: A court whose proceedings include determinations of rights of individual citizens, in contrast to criminal proceedings regarding individuals or the public.

civil jurisdiction: The authority to enforce the laws in civil matters brought before the court.

civil law: The law developed by a nation or state for the conduct of daily life of its own people.

civil rights: The privileges of all individuals to be treated as equals under the laws of their country; specifically, the rights given by certain amendments to the U.S. Constitution.

civil unrest: The feeling of uneasiness due to an unstable political climate, or actions taken as a result of it.

civil war: A war between groups of citizens of the same country who have different opinions or agendas. The Civil War of the United States was the conflict between the states of the North and South from 1861 to 1865.

climatic belt: A region or zone where a particular type of climate prevails.

Club du Sahel: The Club du Sahel is an informal coalition which seeks to reverse the effects of drought and the desertification in the eight Sahelian zone countries: Burkina Faso, Chad, Gambia, Mali, Mauritania, Niger, Senegal, and the Cape Verde Islands. Headquarters are in Ouagadougou, Burkina Faso.

CMEA *see* Council for Mutual Economic Assistance.

coalition government: A government combining differing factions within a country, usually temporary.

coastal belt: A coastal plain area of lowlands and somewhat higher ridges that run parallel to the coast.

coastal plain: A fairly level area of land along the coast of a land mass.

coca: A shrub native to South America, the leaves of which produce organic compounds that are used in the production of cocaine.

coke: The solid product of the carbonization of coal, bearing the same relation to coal that charcoal does to wood.

cold war: Refers to conflict over ideological differences that is carried on by words and diplomatic actions, not by military action. The term is usually used to refer to the tension that existed between the United States and the USSR from the 1950s until the breakup of the USSR in 1991.

collective bargaining: The negotiations between workers who are members of a union and their employer for the purpose of deciding work rules and policies regarding wages, hours, etc.

collective farm: A large farm formed from many small farms and supervised by the government; usually found in communist countries.

collective farming: The system of farming on a collective where all workers share in the income of the farm.

colloquial: Belonging to ordinary, everyday speech: often especially applied to common words and phrases which are not used in formal speech.

colonial period: The period of time when a country forms colonies in and extends control over a foreign area.

colonist: Any member of a colony or one who helps settle a new colony.

colony: A group of people who settle in a new area far from their original country, but still under the jurisdiction of that country. Also refers to the newly settled area itself.

COMECON *see* Council for Mutual Economic Assistance.

commerce: The trading of goods (buying and selling), especially on a large scale, between cities, states, and countries.

commercial catch: The amount of marketable fish, usually measured in tons, caught in a particular period of time.

commercial crop: Any marketable agricultural crop.

commission: A group of people designated to collectively do a job, including a government agency with certain law-making powers. Also, the power given to an individual or group to perform certain duties.

commodity: Any items, such as goods or services, that are bought or sold, or agricultural products that are traded or marketed.

common law: A legal system based on custom and decisions and opinions of the law courts. The basic system of law of England and the United States.

common market: An economic union among countries that is formed to remove trade barriers (tariffs) among those countries, increasing economic cooperation. The European Community is a notable example of a common market.

commonwealth: A commonwealth is a free association of sovereign independent states that has no charter, treaty, or constitution. The association promotes cooperation, consultation, and mutual assistance among members.

Commonwealth of Independent States: The CIS was established in December 1991 as an association of 11 republics of the former Soviet Union. The members include: Russia, Ukraine, Belarus (formerly Byelorussia), Moldova (formerly Moldavia), Armenia, Azerbaijan, Uzbekistan, Turkmenistan, Tajikistan, Kazakhstan, and Kyrgyzstan (formerly Kirghiziya). The Baltic states—Estonia, Latvia, and Lithuania—did not join. Georgia maintained observer status before joining the CIS in November 1993.

Commonwealth of Nations: Voluntary association of the United Kingdom and its present dependencies and associated states, as well as certain former dependencies and their dependent territories. The term was first used officially in 1926 and is embodied in the Statute of Westminster (1931). Within the Commonwealth, whose secretariat (established in 1965) is located in London, England, are numerous subgroups devoted to economic and technical cooperation.

commune: An organization of people living together in a community who share the ownership and use of property. Also refers to a small governmental district of a country, especially in Europe.

communism: A form of government whose system requires common ownership of property for the use of all citizens. All profits are to be equally distributed and prices on goods and services are usually set by the state. Also, communism refers directly to the official doctrine of the former U.S.S.R.

compulsory: Required by law or other regulation.

compulsory education: The mandatory requirement for children to attend school until they have reached a certain age or grade level.

conciliation: A process of bringing together opposing sides of a disagreement for the purpose of compromise. Or, a way of settling an international dispute in which the disagreement is submitted to an independent committee that will examine the facts and advise the participants of a possible solution.

concordat: An agreement, compact, or convention, especially between church and state.

confederation: An alliance or league formed for the purpose of promoting the common interests of its members.

Confucianism: The system of ethics and politics taught by the Chinese philosopher Confucius.

coniferous forest: A forest consisting mainly of pine, fir, and cypress trees.

conifers: Cone-bearing plants. Mostly evergreen trees and shrubs which produce cones.

conscription: To be required to join the military by law. Also known as the draft. Service personnel who join the military because of the legal requirement are called conscripts or draftees.

conservative party: A political group whose philosophy tends to be based on established traditions and not supportive of rapid change.

constituency: The registered voters in a governmental district, or a group of people that supports a position or a candidate.

constituent assembly: A group of people that has the power to determine the election of a political representative or create a constitution.

constitution: The written laws and basic rights of citizens of a country or members of an organized group.

constitutional monarchy: A system of government in which the hereditary sovereign (king or queen, usually) rules according to a written constitution.

constitutional republic: A system of government with an elected chief of state and elected representation, with a written constitution containing its governing principles. The United States is a constitutional republic.

consumer goods: Items that are bought to satisfy personal needs or wants of individuals.

continental climate: The climate of a part of the continent; the characteristics and peculiarities of the climate are a result of the land itself and its location.

continental shelf: A plain extending from the continental coast and varying in width that typically ends in a steep slope to the ocean floor.

copra: The dried meat of the coconut; it is frequently used as an ingredient of curry, and to produce coconut oil. Also written *cobra, coprah,* and *copperah.*

Coptic Christians: Members of the Coptic Church of Egypt, formerly of Ethiopia.

cordillera: A continuous ridge, range, or chain of mountains.

corvette: A small warship that is often used as an escort ship because it is easier to maneuver than larger ships like destroyers.

Council for Mutual Economic Assistance (CMEA): Also known as Comecon, the alliance of socialist economies was established on 25 January 1949 and abolished 1 January 1991. It included Afghanistan*, Albania, Angola*, Bulgaria, Cuba, Czechoslovakia, Ethiopia*, East Germany, Hungary, Laos*, Mongolia, Mozambique*, Nicaragua*, Poland, Romania, USSR, Vietnam, Yemen*, and Yugoslavia. Nations marked with an asterisk were observers only.

counterinsurgency operations: Organized military activity designed to stop rebellion against an established government.

county: A territorial division or administrative unit within a state or country.

coup d'ètat or coup: A sudden, violent overthrow of a government or its leader.

court of appeal: An appellate court, having the power of review after a case has been decided in a lower court.

court of first appeal: The next highest court to the court which has decided a case, to which that case may be presented for review.

court of last appeal: The highest court, in which a decision is not subject to review by any higher court. In the United States, it could be the Supreme Court of an individual state or the U.S. Supreme Court.

cricket (sport): A game played by two teams with a ball and bat, with two wickets (staked target) being defended by a batsman. Common in the United Kingdom and Commonwealth of Nations countries.

criminal law: The branch of law that deals primarily with crimes and their punishments.

crown colony: A colony established by a commonwealth over which the monarch has some control, as in colonies established by the United Kingdom's Commonwealth of Nations.

Crusades: Military expeditions by European Christian armies in the eleventh, twelfth, and thirteenth centuries to win land controlled by the Muslims in the middle east.

cultivable land: Land that can be prepared for the production of crops.

Cultural Revolution: An extreme reform movement in China from 1966 to 1976; its goal was to combat liberalization by restoring the ideas of Mao Zedong.

Cushitic language group: A group of Hamitic languages that are spoken in Ethiopia and other areas of eastern Africa.

customs union: An agreement between two or more countries to remove trade barriers with each other and to establish common tariff and nontariff policies with respect to imports from countries outside of the agreement.

cyclone: Any atmospheric movement, general or local, in which the wind blows spirally around and in towards a center. In the northern hemisphere, the cyclonic movement is usually counter-clockwise, and in the southern hemisphere, it is clockwise.

Cyrillic alphabet: An alphabet adopted by the Slavic people and invented by Cyril and Methodius in the ninth century as an alphabet that was easier for the copyist to write. The Russian alphabet is a slight modification of it.

decentralization: The redistribution of power in a government from one large central authority to a wider range of smaller local authorities.

deciduous species: Any species that sheds or casts off a part of itself after a definite period of time. More commonly used in reference to plants that shed their leaves on a yearly basis as opposed to those (evergreens) that retain them.

declaration of independence: A formal written document stating the intent of a group of persons to become fully self-governing.

deficit: The amount of money that is in excess between spending and income.

deficit spending: The process in which a government spends money on goods and services in excess of its income.

deforestation: The removal or clearing of a forest.

deity: A being with the attributes, nature, and essence of a god; a divinity.

delta: Triangular-shaped deposits of soil formed at the mouths of large rivers.

demarcate: To mark off from adjoining land or territory; set the limits or boundaries of.

demilitarized zone (DMZ): An area surrounded by a combat zone that has had military troops and weapons removed.

demobilize: To disband or discharge military troops.

democracy: A form of government in which the power lies in the hands of the people, who can govern directly, or can be governed indirectly by representatives elected by its citizens.

denationalize: To remove from government ownership or control.

deportation: To carry away or remove from one country to another, or to a distant place.

depression: A hollow; a surface that has sunken or fallen in.

deregulation: The act of reversing controls and restrictions on prices of goods, bank interest, and the like.

desalinization plant: A facility that produces freshwater by removing the salt from saltwater.

desegregation: The act of removing restrictions on people of a particular race that keep them socially, economically, and, sometimes, physically, separate from other groups.

desertification: The process of becoming a desert as a result of climatic changes, land mismanagement, or both.

détente: The official lessening of tension between countries in conflict.

devaluation: The official lowering of the value of a country's currency in relation to the value of gold or the currencies of other countries.

developed countries: Countries which have a high standard of living and a well-developed industrial base.

development assistance: Government programs intended to finance and promote the growth of new industries.

dialect: One of a number of regional or related modes of speech regarded as descending from a common origin.

dictatorship: A form of government in which all the power is retained by an absolute leader or tyrant. There are no rights granted to the people to elect their own representatives.

dike: A artificial riverbank built up to control the flow of water.

diplomatic relations: The relationship between countries as conducted by representatives of each government.

direct election: The process of selecting a representative to the government by balloting of the voting public, in contrast to selection by an elected representative of the people.

disarmament: The reduction or depletion of the number of weapons or the size of armed forces.

dissident: A person whose political opinions differ from the majority to the point of rejection.

dogma: A principle, maxim, or tenet held as being firmly established.

domain: The area of land governed by a particular ruler or government, sometimes referring to the ultimate control of that territory.

domestic spending: Money spent by a country's government on goods used, investments, running of the government, and exports and imports.

dominion: A self-governing nation that recognizes the British monarch as chief of state.

dormant volcano: A volcano that has not exhibited any signs of activity for an extended period of time.

dowry: The sum of the property or money that a bride brings to her groom at their marriage.

draft constitution: The preliminary written plans for the new constitution of a country forming a new government.

Druze: A member of a Muslim sect based in Syria, living chiefly in the mountain regions of Lebanon.

dual nationality: The status of an individual who can claim citizenship in two or more countries.

duchy: Any territory under the rule of a duke or duchess.

due process: In law, the application of the legal process to which every citizen has a right, which cannot be denied.

durable goods: Goods or products which are expected to last and perform for several years, such as cars and washing machines.

duty: A tax imposed on imports by the customs authority of a country. Duties are generally based on the value of the goods (*ad valorem* duties), some other factors such as weight or quantity (specific duties), or a combination of value and other factors (compound duties).

dyewoods: Any wood from which dye is extracted.

dynasty: A family line of sovereigns who rule in succession, and the time during which they reign.

earned income: The money paid to an individual in wages or salary.

Eastern Orthodox: The outgrowth of the original Eastern Church of the Eastern Roman Empire, consisting of eastern Europe, western Asia, and Egypt.

EC *see* European Community

ecclesiastical: Pertaining or relating to the church.

echidna: A spiny, toothless anteater of Australia, Tasmania, and New Guinea.

ecological balance: The condition of a healthy, well-functioning ecosystem, which includes all the plants and animals in a natural community together with their environment.

ecology: The branch of science that studies organisms in relationship to other organisms and to their environment.

economic depression: A prolonged period in which there is high unemployment, low production, falling prices, and general business failure.

economically active population: That portion of the people who are employed for wages and are consumers of goods and services.

ecotourism: Broad term that encompasses nature, adventure, and ethnic tourism; responsible or wilderness-sensitive tourism; soft-path or small-scale tourism; low-impact tourism; and sustainable tourism. Scientific, educational, or academic tourism (such as biotourism, archetourism, and geotourism) are also forms of ecotourism.

elected assembly: The persons that comprise a legislative body of a government who received their positions by direct election.

electoral system: A system of choosing government officials by votes cast by qualified citizens.

electoral vote: The votes of the members of the electoral college.

electorate: The people who are qualified to vote in an election.

emancipation: The freeing of persons from any kind of bondage or slavery.

embargo: A legal restriction on commercial ships to enter a country's ports, or any legal restriction of trade.

emigration: Moving from one country or region to another for the purpose of residence.

empire: A group of territories ruled by one sovereign or supreme ruler. Also, the period of time under that rule.

enclave: A territory belonging to one nation that is surrounded by that of another nation.

encroachment: The act of intruding, trespassing, or entering on the rights or possessions of another.

endangered species: A plant or animal species whose existence as a whole is threatened with extinction.

endemic: Anything that is peculiar to and characteristic of a locality or region.

Enlightenment: An intellectual movement of the late seventeenth and eighteenth centuries in which scientific thinking gained a strong foothold and old beliefs were challenged. The idea of absolute monarchy was questioned and people were gradually given more individual rights.

enteric disease: An intestinal disease.

epidemic: As applied to disease, any disease that is temporarily prevalent among people in one place at the same time.

Episcopal: Belonging to or vested in bishops or prelates; characteristic of or pertaining to a bishop or bishops.

ethnolinguistic group: A classification of related languages based on common ethnic origin.

EU *see* European Union

European Community: A regional organization created in 1958. Its purpose is to eliminate customs duties and other trade barriers in Europe. It promotes a common external tariff against other countries, a Common Agricultural Policy (CAP), and guarantees of free movement of labor and capital. The original six members were Belgium, France, West Germany, Italy, Luxembourg, and the Netherlands. Denmark, Ireland, and the United Kingdom became members in 1973; Greece joined in 1981;

Spain and Portugal in 1986. Other nations continue to join.

European Union: The EU is an umbrella reference to the European Community (EC) and to two European integration efforts introduced by the Maastricht Treaty: Common Foreign and Security Policy (including defense) and Justice and Home Affairs (principally cooperation between police and other authorities on crime, terrorism, and immigration issues).

exports: Goods sold to foreign buyers.

external migration: The movement of people from their native country to another country, as opposed to internal migration, which is the movement of people from one area of a country to another in the same country.

faction: People with a specific set of interests or goals who form a subgroup within a larger organization.

fallout: The precipitation of particles from the atmosphere, often the result of a ground disturbance by volcanic activity or a nuclear explosion.

family planning: The use of birth control to determine the number of children a married couple will have.

Fascism: A political philosophy that holds the good of the nation as more important than the needs of the individual. Fascism also stands for a dictatorial leader and strong oppression of opposition or dissent.

federal: Pertaining to a union of states whose governments are subordinate to a central government.

federation: A union of states or other groups under the authority of a central government.

fetishism: The practice of worshipping a material object that is believed to have mysterious powers residing in it, or is the representation of a deity to which worship may be paid and from which supernatural aid is expected.

feudal estate: The property owned by a lord in medieval Europe under the feudal system.

feudal society: In medieval times, an economic and social structure in which persons could hold land given to them by a lord (nobleman) in return for service to that lord.

final jurisdiction: The final authority in the decision of a legal matter. In the United States, the Supreme Court would have final jurisdiction.

Finno-Ugric language group: A subfamily of languages spoken in northeastern Europe, including Finnish, Hungarian, Estonian, and Lapp.

fiscal year: The twelve months between the settling of financial accounts, not necessarily corresponding to a calendar year beginning on January 1.

fjord: A deep indentation of the land forming a comparatively narrow arm of the sea with more or less steep slopes or cliffs on each side.

fly: The part of a flag opposite and parallel to the one nearest the flagpole.

fodder: Food for cattle, horses, and sheep, such as hay, straw, and other kinds of vegetables.

folk religion: A religion with origins and traditions among the common people of a nation or region that is relevant to their particular life-style.

foreign exchange: Foreign currency that allows foreign countries to conduct financial transactions or settle debts with one another.

foreign policy: The course of action that one government chooses to adopt in relation to a foreign country.

Former Soviet Union: The FSU is a collective reference to republics comprising the former Soviet Union. The term, which has been used as both including and excluding the Baltic republics (Estonia, Latvia, and Lithuania), includes the other 12 republics: Russia, Ukraine, Belarus, Moldova, Armenia, Azerbaijan, Uzbekistan, Turkmenistan, Tajikistan, Kazakhstan, Kyrgizstan, and Georgia.

fossil fuels: Any mineral or mineral substance formed by the decomposition of organic matter buried beneath the earth's surface and used as a fuel.

free enterprise: The system of economics in which private business may be conducted with minimum interference by the government.

free-market economy: An economic system that relies on the market, as opposed to government planners, to set the prices for wages and products.

frigate. A medium-sized warship.

fundamentalist: A person who holds religious beliefs based on the complete acceptance of the words of the Bible or other holy scripture as the truth. For instance, a fundamentalist would believe the story of creation exactly as it is told in the Bible and would reject the idea of evolution.

game reserve: An area of land reserved for wild animals that are hunted for sport or for food.

GDP *see* gross domestic product.

genocide: Planned and systematic killing of members of a particular ethnic, religious, or cultural group.

Germanic language group: A large branch of the Indo-European family of languages including German itself, the Scandinavian languages, Dutch, Yiddish, Modern English, Modern Scottish, Afrikaans, and others. The group also includes extinct languages such as Gothic, Old High German, Old Saxon, Old English, Middle English, and the like.

glasnost: President Mikhail Gorbachev's frank revelations in the 1980s about the state of the economy and politics in the Soviet Union; his policy of openness.

global greenhouse gas emissions: Gases released into the atmosphere that contribute to the greenhouse effect, a condition in which the earth's excess heat cannot escape.

global warming: Also called the greenhouse effect. The theorized gradual warming of the earth's climate as a result of the burning of fossil fuels, the use of man-made chemicals, deforestation, etc.

GMT *see* Greenwich Mean Time.

GNP *see* gross national product.

grand duchy: A territory ruled by a nobleman, called a grand duke, who ranks just below a king.

Greek Catholic: A person who is a member of an Orthodox Eastern Church.

Greek Orthodox: The official church of Greece, a self-governing branch of the Orthodox Eastern Church.

Greenwich (Mean) Time: Mean solar time of the meridian at Greenwich, England, used as the basis for standard time throughout most of the world. The world is divided into 24 time zones, and all are related to the prime, or Greenwich mean, zone.

gross domestic product: A measure of the market value of all goods and services produced within the boundaries of a nation, regardless of asset ownership. Unlike gross national product, GDP excludes receipts from that nation's business operations in foreign countries.

gross national product: A measure of the market value of goods and services produced by the labor and property of a nation. Includes receipts from that nation's business operation in foreign countries

groundwater: Water located below the earth's surface, the source from which wells and springs draw their water.

guano: The excrement of seabirds and bats found in various areas around the world. Gathered commercially and sold as a fertilizer.

guerrilla: A member of a small radical military organization that uses unconventional tactics to take their enemies by surprise.

gymnasium: A secondary school, primarily in Europe, that prepares students for university.

hardwoods: The name given to deciduous trees, such as cherry, oak, maple, and mahogany.

harem: In a Muslim household, refers to the women (wives, concubines, and servants in ancient times) who live there and also to the area of the home they live in.

harmattan: An intensely dry, dusty wind felt along the coast of Africa between Cape Verde and Cape Lopez. It prevails at intervals during the months of December, January, and February.

heavy industry: Industries that use heavy or large machinery to produce goods, such as automobile manufacturing.

hoist: The part of a flag nearest the flagpole.

Holocaust: The mass slaughter of European civilians, the vast majority Jews, by the Nazis during World War II.

Holy Roman Empire: A kingdom consisting of a loose union of German and Italian territories that existed from around the ninth century until 1806.

home rule: The governing of a territory by the citizens who inhabit it.

homeland: A region or area set aside to be a state for a people of a particular national, cultural, or racial origin.

homogeneous: Of the same kind or nature, often used in reference to a whole.

Horn of Africa: The Horn of Africa comprises Djibouti, Eritrea, Ethiopia, Somalia, and Sudan.

housing starts: The initiation of new housing construction.

human rights activist: A person who vigorously pursues the attainment of basic rights for all people.

human rights issues: Any matters involving people's basic rights which are in question or thought to be abused.

humanist: A person who centers on human needs and values, and stresses dignity of the individual.

humanitarian aid: Money or supplies given to a persecuted group or people of a country at war, or those devastated by a natural disaster, to provide for basic human needs.

hydrocarbon: A compound of hydrogen and carbon, often occurring in organic substances or derivatives of organic substances such as coal, petroleum, natural gas, etc.

hydrocarbon emissions: Organic compounds containing only carbon and hydrogen, often occurring in petroleum, natural gas, coal, and bitumens, and which contribute to the greenhouse effect.

hydroelectric potential: The potential amount of electricity that can be produced hydroelectrically. Usually used in reference to a given area and how many hydroelectric power plants that area can sustain.

hydroelectric power plant: A factory that produces electrical power through the application of waterpower.

IBRD *see* World Bank.

illegal alien: Any foreign-born individual who has unlawfully entered another country.

immigration: The act or process of passing or entering into another country for the purpose of permanent residence.

imports: Goods purchased from foreign suppliers.

indigenous: Born or originating in a particular place or country; native to a particular region or area.

Indo-Aryan language group: The group that includes the languages of India; also called Indo-European language group.

Indo-European language family: The group that includes the languages of India and much of Europe and southwestern Asia.

industrialized nation: A nation whose economy is based on industry.

infanticide: The act of murdering a baby.

infidel: One who is without faith or belief; particularly, one who rejects the distinctive doctrines of a particular religion.

inflation: The general rise of prices, as measured by a consumer price index. Results in a fall in value of currency.

installed capacity: The maximum possible output of electric power at any given time.

insurgency: The state or condition in which one rises against lawful authority or established government; rebellion.

insurrectionist: One who participates in an unorganized revolt against an authority.

interim government: A temporary or provisional government.

interim president: One who is appointed to perform temporarily the duties of president during a transitional period in a government.

internal migration: Term used to describe the relocation of individuals from one region to another without leaving the confines of the country or of a specified area.

International Date Line: An arbitrary line at about the 180th meridian that designates where one day begins and another ends.

Islam: The religious system of Mohammed, practiced by Moslims and based on a belief in Allah as the supreme being and Mohammed as his prophet. The spelling variations, Muslim and Muhammad, are also used, primarily by Islamic people. Islam also refers to those nations in which it is the primary religion.

isthmus: A narrow strip of land bordered by water and connecting two larger bodies of land, such as two continents, a continent and a peninsula, or two parts of an island.

Judaism: The religious system of the Jews, based on the Old Testament as revealed to Moses and characterized by a belief in one God and adherence to the laws of scripture and rabbinic traditions.

Judeo-Christian: The dominant traditional religious makeup of the United States and other countries based on the worship of the Old and New Testaments of the Bible.

junta: A small military group in power of a country, especially after a coup.

khan: A sovereign, or ruler, in central Asia.

khanate: A kingdom ruled by a khan, or man of rank.

kwashiorkor: Severe malnutrition in infants and children caused by a diet high in carbohydrates and lacking in protein.

kwh: The abbreviation for kilowatt-hour.

labor force: The number of people in a population available for work, whether actually employed or not.

labor movement: A movement in the early to mid-1800s to organize workers in groups according to profession to give them certain rights as a group, including bargaining power for better wages, working conditions, and benefits.

land reforms: Steps taken to create a fair distribution of farmland, especially by governmental action.

landlocked country: A country that does not have direct access to the sea; it is completely surrounded by other countries.

least developed countries: A subgroup of the United Nations designation of "less developed countries;" these countries generally have no significant economic growth, low literacy rates, and per person gross national product of less than $500. Also known as undeveloped countries.

leeward: The direction identical to that of the wind. For example, a *leeward tide* is a tide that runs in the same direction that the wind blows.

leftist: A person with a liberal or radical political affiliation.

legislative branch: The branch of government which makes or enacts the laws.

leprosy: A disease that can effect the skin and/or the nerves and can cause ulcers of the skin, loss of feeling, or loss of fingers and toes.

less developed countries (LDC): Designated by the United Nations to include countries with low levels of output, living standards, and per person gross national product generally below $5,000.

literacy: The ability to read and write.

Maastricht Treaty: The Maastricht Treaty (named for the Dutch town in which the treaty was signed) is also known as the Treaty of European Union. The treaty creates a European Union by: (a) committing the member states of the European Economic Community to both European Monetary Union (EMU) and political union; (b) introducing a single currency (European Currency Unit, ECU); (c) establishing a European System of Central Banks (ESCB); (d) creating a European Central Bank (ECB); and (e) broadening EC integration by including both a common foreign and security policy (CFSP) and cooperation in justice and home affairs (CJHA). The treaty entered into force on November 1, 1993.

Maghreb states: The Maghreb states include the three nations of Algeria, Morocco, and Tunisia; sometimes includes Libya and Mauritania.

maize: Another name (Spanish or British) for corn or the color of ripe corn.

majority party: The party with the largest number of votes and the controlling political party in a government.

mangrove: A tree which abounds on tropical shores in both hemispheres. Characterized by its numerous roots which arch out from its trunk and descend from its branches, mangroves form thick, dense growths along the tidal muds, reaching lengths hundreds of miles long.

manioc: The cassava plant or its product. Manioc is a very important food-staple in tropical America.

maquis. Scrubby, thick underbrush found along the coast of the Mediterranean Sea.

marginal land: Land that could produce an economic profit, but is so poor that it is only used when better land is no longer available.

marine life: The life that exists in, or is formed by the sea.

maritime climate: The climate and weather conditions typical of areas bordering the sea.

maritime rights: The rights that protect navigation and shipping.

market access: Market access refers to the openness of a national market to foreign products. Market access reflects a government's willingness to permit imports to compete relatively unimpeded with similar domestically produced goods.

market economy: A form of society which runs by the law of supply and demand. Goods are produced by firms to be sold to consumers, who determine the demand for them. Price levels vary according to the demand for certain goods and how much of them is produced.

market price: The price a commodity will bring when sold on the open market. The price is determined by the amount of demand for the commodity by buyers.

Marshall Plan: Formally known as the European Recovery Program, a joint project between the United States and most Western European nations under which $12.5 billion in U.S. loans and grants was expended to aid European recovery after World War II.

Marxism *see* Marxist-Leninist principles.

Marxist-Leninist principles: The doctrines of Karl Marx, built upon by Nikolai Lenin, on which communism was founded. They predicted the fall of capitalism, due to its own internal faults and the resulting oppression of workers.

Marxist: A follower of Karl Marx, a German socialist and revolutionary leader of the late 1800s, who contributed to Marxist-Leninist principles.

massif: A central mountain-mass or the dominant part of a range of mountains.

matrilineal (descent): Descending from, or tracing descent through, the maternal, or mother's, family line.

Mayan language family: The languages of the Central American Indians, further divided into two subgroups: the Maya and the Huastek.

mean temperature: The air temperature unit measured by the National Weather Service by adding the maximum and minimum daily temperatures together and diving the sum by 2.

Mecca (Mekkah): A city in Saudi Arabia; a destination of pilgrims in the Islamic world.

Mediterranean climate: A wet-winter, dry-summer climate with a moderate annual temperature range.

mestizo: The offspring of a person of mixed blood; especially, a person of mixed Spanish and American Indian parentage.

migratory birds: Those birds whose instincts prompt them to move from one place to another at the regularly recurring changes of season.

migratory workers: Usually agricultural workers who move from place to place for employment depending on the growing and harvesting seasons of various crops.

military coup: A sudden, violent overthrow of a government by military forces.

military junta: The small military group in power in a country, especially after a coup.

military regime: Government conducted by a military force.

military takeover: The seizure of control of a government by the military forces.

militia: The group of citizens of a country who are either serving in the reserve military forces or are eligible to be called up in time of emergency.

millet: A cereal grass whose small grain is used for food in Europe and Asia.

minority party: The political group that comprises the smaller part of the large overall group it belongs to; the party that is not in control.

missionary: A person sent by authority of a church or religious organization to spread his religious faith in a community where his church has no self-supporting organization.

monarchy: Government by a sovereign, such as a king or queen.

money economy: A system or stage of economic development in which money replaces barter in the exchange of goods and services.

Mongol: One of an Asiatic race chiefly resident in Mongolia, a region north of China proper and south of Siberia.

Mongoloid: Having physical characteristics like those of the typical Mongols (Chinese, Japanese, Turks, Eskimos, etc.).

Moors: One of the Arab tribes that conquered Spain in the eighth century.

Moslem: A frequently used variation of the spelling of Muslim; a follower of Muhammad in the religion of Islam.

mosque: An Islam place of worship and the organization with which it is connected.

mouflon: A type of wild sheep characterized by curling horns.

Muhammad (or Muhammed or Mahomet): An Arabian prophet, known as the "Prophet of Allah" who founded the religion of Islam in 622, and wrote *The Koran,* the scripture of Islam. Also commonly spelled Mohammed.

mujahideen (mujahedin or mujahedeen): Rebel fighters in Islamic countries, especially those supporting the cause of Islam.

mulatto: One who is the offspring of parents one of whom is white and the other is black.

municipality: A district such as a city or town having its own incorporated government.

Muslim: A follower of the prophet Muhammad, the founder of the religion of Islam.

Muslim New Year: A Muslim holiday. Although in some countries 1 Muharram, which is the first month of the Islamic year, is observed as a holiday, in other places the new year is observed on Sha'ban, the eighth month of the year. This practice apparently stems from pagan Arab times. Shab-i-Bharat, a national holiday in Bangladesh on this day, is held by many to be the occasion when God ordains all actions in the coming year.

NAFTA (North American Free Trade Agreement): NAFTA, which entered into force in January 1994, is a free trade agreement between Canada, the United States, and Mexico. The agreement progressively eliminates almost all U.S.-Mexico tariffs over a 10–15 year period.

nationalism: National spirit or aspirations; desire for national unity, independence, or prosperity.

nationalization: To transfer the control or ownership of land or industries to the nation from private owners.

native tongue: One's natural language. The language that is indigenous to an area.

NATO *see* North Atlantic Treaty Organization

natural gas: A combustible gas formed naturally in the earth and generally obtained by boring a well. The chemical makeup of natural gas is principally methane, hydrogen, ethylene compounds, and nitrogen.

natural harbor: A protected portion of a sea or lake along the shore resulting from the natural formations of the land.

naturalize: To confer the rights and privileges of a native-born subject or citizen upon someone who lives in the country by choice.

nature preserve: An area where one or more species of plant and/or animal are protected from harm, injury, or destruction.

neutrality: The policy of not taking sides with any countries during a war or dispute among them.

Newly Independent States: The NIS is a collective reference to 12 republics of the former Soviet Union: Russia, Ukraine, Belarus (formerly Byelorussia), Moldova (formerly Moldavia), Armenia, Azerbaijan, Uzbekistan, Turkmenistan, Tajikistan, Kazakhstan, and Kirgizstan (formerly Kirghiziya), and Georgia. Following dissolution of the Soviet Union, the distinction between the NIS and the Commonwealth of Independent States (CIS) was that Georgia was not a member of the CIS. That distinction dissolved when Georgia joined the CIS in November 1993.

news censorship *see* censorship

Nonaligned Movement: The NAM is an alliance of third world states that aims to promote the political and economic interests of developing countries. NAM interests have included ending colonialism/neo-colonialism, supporting the integrity of independent countries, and seeking a new international economic order.

Nordic Council: The Nordic Council, established in 1952, is directed toward supporting cooperation among Nordic countries. Members include Denmark, Finland, Iceland, Norway, and Sweden. Headquarters are in Stockholm, Sweden.

North Atlantic Treaty Organization (NATO): A mutual defense organization. Members include Belgium, Canada, Denmark, France (which has only partial membership), Greece, Iceland, Italy, Luxembourg, Netherlands, Norway, Portugal, Spain, Turkey, United Kingdom, United States, and Germany.

nuclear power plant: A factory that produces electrical power through the application of the nuclear reaction known as nuclear fission.

nuclear reactor: A device used to control the rate of nuclear fission in uranium. Used in commercial applications, nuclear reactors can maintain temperatures high enough to generate sufficient quantities of steam which can then be used to produce electricity.

OAPEC (Organization of Arab Petroleum Exporting countries): OAPEC was created in 1968; members include: Algeria, Bahrain, Egypt, Iraq, Kuwait, Libya, Qatar, Saudi Arabia, Syria, and the United Arab Emirates. Headquarters are in Cairo, Egypt.

OAS (Organization of American States): The OAS (Spanish: Organizaciûn de los Estados Americanos,

OEA), or the Pan American Union, is a regional organization which promotes Latin American economic and social development. Members include the United States, Mexico, and most Central American, South American, and Caribbean nations.

OAS *see* Organization of American States

oasis: Originally, a fertile spot in the Libyan desert where there is a natural spring or well and vegetation; now refers to any fertile tract in the midst of a wasteland.

occupied territory: A territory that has an enemy's military forces present.

official language: The language in which the business of a country and its government is conducted.

oligarchy: A form of government in which a few people possess the power to rule as opposed to a monarchy which is ruled by one.

OPEC *see* OAPEC

open economy: An economy that imports and exports goods.

open market: Open market operations are the actions of the central bank to influence or control the money supply by buying or selling government bonds.

opposition party: A minority political party that is opposed to the party in power.

Organization of Arab Petroleum Exporting Countries *see* OAPEC

organized labor: The body of workers who belong to labor unions.

Ottoman Empire: An Turkish empire founded by Osman I in about 1603, that variously controlled large areas of land around the Mediterranean, Black, and Caspian Seas until it was dissolved in 1918.

overfishing: To deplete the quantity of fish in an area by removing more fish than can be naturally replaced.

overgrazing: Allowing animals to graze in an area to the point that the ground vegetation is damaged or destroyed.

overseas dependencies: A distant and physically separate territory that belongs to another country and is subject to its laws and government.

Pacific Rim: The Pacific Rim, referring to countries and economies bordering the Pacific Ocean.

pact: An international agreement.

Paleolithic: The early period of the Stone Age, when rough, chipped stone implements were used.

panhandle: A long narrow strip of land projecting like the handle of a frying pan.

papyrus: The paper-reed or -rush which grows on marshy river banks in the southeastern area of the Mediterranean, but more notably in the Nile valley.

paramilitary group: A supplementary organization to the military.

parasitic diseases: A group of diseases caused by parasitic organisms which feed off the host organism.

parliamentary republic: A system of government in which a president and prime minister, plus other ministers of departments, constitute the executive branch of the government and the parliament constitutes the legislative branch.

parliamentary rule: Government by a legislative body similar to that of Great Britain, which is composed of two houses—one elected and one hereditary.

parochial: Refers to matters of a church parish or something within narrow limits.

partisan politics: Rigid, unquestioning following of a specific party's or leader's goals.

patriarchal system: A social system in which the head of the family or tribe is the father or oldest male. Kinship is determined and traced through the male members of the tribe.

patrilineal (descent): Descending from, or tracing descent through, the paternal or father's line.

pellagra: A disease marked by skin, intestinal, and central nervous system disorders, caused by a diet deficient in niacin, one of the B vitamins.

per capita: Literally, per person; for each person counted.

perestroika: The reorganization of the political and economic structures of the Soviet Union by president Mikhail Gorbachev.

periodical: A publication whose issues appear at regular intervals, such as weekly, monthly, or yearly.

petrochemical: A chemical derived from petroleum or from natural gas.

pharmaceutical plants: Any plant that is used in the preparation of medicinal drugs.

plantain: The name of a common weed that has often been used for medicinal purposes, as a folk remedy and in modern medicine. *Plaintain* is also the name of a tropical plant producing a type of banana.

polar climate: Also called tundra climate. A humid, severely cold climate controlled by arctic air masses, with no warm or summer season.

political climate: The prevailing political attitude of a particular time or place.

political refugee: A person forced to flee his or her native country for political reasons.

potable water: Water that is safe for drinking.

pound sterling: The monetary unit of Great Britain, otherwise known as the pound.

prefect: An administrative official; in France, the head of a particular department.

prefecture: The territory over which a prefect has authority.

prime meridian: Zero degrees in longitude that runs through Greenwich, England, site of the Royal

Observatory. All other longitudes are measured from this point.

prime minister: The premier or chief administrative official in certain countries.

private sector: The division of an economy in which production of goods and services is privately owned.

privatization: To change from public to private control or ownership.

protectorate: A state or territory controlled by a stronger state, or the relationship of the stronger country toward the lesser one it protects.

Protestant: A member or an adherent of one of those Christian bodies which descended from the Reformation of the sixteenth century. Originally applied to those who opposed or protested the Roman Catholic Church.

Protestant Reformation: In 1529, a Christian religious movement begun in Germany to deny the universal authority of the Pope, and to establish the Bible as the only source of truth. (*Also see* Protestant)

proved reserves: The quantity of a recoverable mineral resource (such as oil or natural gas) that is still in the ground.

province: An administrative territory of a country.

provisional government: A temporary government set up during time of unrest or transition in a country.

pulses: Beans, peas, or lentils.

purge: The act of ridding a society of "undesirable" or unloyal persons by banishment or murder.

Rastafarian: A member of a Jamaican cult begun in 1930 as a semi-religious, semi-political movement.

rate of literacy: The percentage of people in a society who can read and write.

recession. A period of reduced economic activity in a country or region.

referendum: The practice of submitting legislation directly to the people for a popular vote.

reforestation: Systematically replacing forest trees lost due to fire or logging.

Reformation *see* Protestant Reformation.

refugee: One who flees to a refuge or shelter or place of safety. One who in times of persecution or political commotion flees to a foreign country for safety.

revolution: A complete change in a government or society, such as in an overthrow of the government by the people.

right-wing party: The more conservative political party.

Roman alphabet: The alphabet of the ancient Romans from which the alphabets of most modern western European languages, including English, are derived.

Roman Catholic Church: The designation of the church of which the pope or Bishop of Rome is the head, and that holds him as the successor of St.

Peter and heir of his spiritual authority, privileges, and gifts.

romance language: The group of languages derived from Latin: French, Spanish, Italian, Portuguese, and other related languages.

roundwood: Timber used as poles or in similar ways without being sawn or shaped.

runoff election: A deciding election put to the voters in case of a tie between candidates.

Russian Orthodox: The arm of the Orthodox Eastern Church that was the official church of Russia under the czars.

sack: To strip of valuables, especially after capture.

Sahelian zone: Eight countries make up this dry desert zone in Africa: Burkina Faso, Chad, Gambia, Mali, Mauritania, Niger, Senegal, and the Cape Verde Islands. *Also see* Club du Sahel.

salinization: An accumulation of soluble salts in soil. This condition is common in desert climates, where water evaporates quickly in poorly drained soil due to high temperatures.

Samaritans: A native or an inhabitant of Samaria; specifically, one of a race settled in the cities of Samaria by the king of Assyria after the removal of the Israelites from the country.

savanna: A treeless or near treeless plain of a tropical or subtropical region dominated by drought-resistant grasses.

schistosomiasis: A tropical disease that is chronic and characterized by disorders of the liver, urinary bladder, lungs, or central nervous system.

secession: The act of withdrawal, such as a state withdrawing from the Union in the Civil War in the United States.

sect: A religious denomination or group, often a dissenting one with extreme views.

segregation: The enforced separation of a racial or religious group from other groups, compelling them to live and go to school separately from the rest of society.

seismic activity: Relating to or connected with an earthquake or earthquakes in general.

self-sufficient: Able to function alone without help.

separation of power: The division of power in the government among the executive, legislative, and judicial branches and the checks and balances employed to keep them separate and independent of each other.

separatism: The policy of dissenters withdrawing from a larger political or religious group.

serfdom: In the feudal system of the Middle Ages, the condition of being attached to the land owned by a lord and being transferable to a new owner.

Seventh-day Adventist: One who believes in the second coming of Christ to establish a personal reign upon the earth.